Misconceptions About the Middle Ages

Routledge Studies in Medieval Religion and Culture

EDITED BY GEORGE FERZOCO, University of Leicester and
CAROLYN MUESSIG, University of Bristol

Misconceptions About the Middle Ages

Edited by

Stephen J. Harris and Bryon L. Grigsby

Routledge
Taylor & Francis Group

New York   London

First published 2008
by Routledge
270 Madison Ave, New York, NY 10016

Simultaneously published in the UK
by Routledge
2 Park Square, Milton Park, Abingdon, Oxon OX14 4RN

Routledge is an imprint of the Taylor & Francis Group, an informa business

Transferred to Digital Printing 2009

Typeset in Sabon by IBT Global

Library of Congress Cataloging in Publication Data
Misconceptions about the Middle Ages / edited by Stephen J. Harris and Bryon L. Grigsby.
p. cm.— (Routledge studies in medieval religion and culture ; 7)

Includes bibliographical references and index.

ISBN-13: 978-0-415-77053-8 (hardback : alk. paper)

ISBN-10: 0-415-77053-X (hardback : alk. paper) 1. Civilization, Medieval. 2. Middle Ages. 3. Civilization, Medieval—Historiography. 4. Middle Ages—Historiography. 5. Europe—History—Errors, inventions, etc. 6. Common fallacies. I. Harris, Stephen J., 1966- II. Grigsby, Bryon Lee.

CB353.M565 2007
909.07—dc22   2007030588

ISBN10: 0-415-77053-X (hbk)
ISBN10: 0-415-87113-1 (pbk)
ISBN10: 0-203-93242-0 (ebk)

ISBN13: 978-0-415-77053-8 (hbk)
ISBN13: 978-0-415-87113-6 (pbk)
ISBN13: 978-0-203-93242-1 (ebk)

Contents

Preface

This collection arises out of an exchange some years ago between Julia Bolton Holloway and R. A. Ross on Med-Rel, an electronic discussion list dedicated to the study of medieval religion. List members articulated a pressing need to address some prevalent misconceptions about the Middle Ages before a more general audience. This book contributes to answering that need. We are grateful to George Ferzoco for his guidance and encouragement and to Taylor & Francis for their helpful advice and unflagging interest in the project.

Each contribution is brief, and all contributors recommend books for further reading. I am joined by my coeditor Bryon Grigsby in saying that it has been a privilege to compile this collection. We hope we have done the contributions justice, and apologize beforehand for any errors for which, of course, we are responsible. We would like to thank Carolyn Schriber, Laura Blanchard, and Kathryn Talarico at the On-Line Reference Book of Medieval Studies (ORB) for hosting Misconceptions for so long. We owe large debts of thanks. But there are so many people to thank that we can only ask leave to be grateful to all.

This book is gratefully dedicated to our grandfathers. May they rest in peace.

—*Stephen J. Harris*

—*Bryon L. Grigsby*

  6 February 2007

Introduction[1]

Stephen J. Harris

> Things are they are / Are changed upon the blue guitar.
> —Wallace Stevens, "The Man with the Blue Guitar"

I

The Middle Ages are always changing. That is because the Middle Ages come alive for us in the books, articles, lectures, classes, and documentaries of our contemporaries. Like music played on Wallace Stevens' blue guitar, the notes themselves may not change from age to age, but the tone and emphasis and tempo do change, depending on who plays that guitar. In the Toller Lecture at the University of Manchester in 1992, Professor Roberta Frank of Yale asked her audience to consider the temper and dispositions of scholars of the Middle Ages and to "observe the swings back and forth between credulity and doubt, between creative optimism and cognitive agnosticism." She warned, "The errors in our predecessor's evocations turn out to be as varied, unexpected and revealing as our own."[2] Frank remarked that misconceptions arise in a particular time and place. We have taken her observation as the theme of this book: In describing the past to a contemporary audience, one needs to be aware of the distorting effects of one's own convictions, concerns, and ideals. In unguarded moments, one risks projecting contemporary faults or ideals onto the data and records of the past. A past said to be teeming with fools may reveal our own intellectual insecurities; a past said to be teeming with heroes, our desire for reform.[3] Thus do our own insecurities and desires become a part of academic history. As Allen J. Frantzen wrote in his groundbreaking *Desire for Origins*, "The ideas and attitudes of readers accumulate around texts; the scholarship of each generation adheres to the subject and becomes *part* of the subject that the next generation then studies."[4] Scholarship today and for the last century has borne the double burden of assessing the context of ancient books as well as the accumulated, serial prejudices of their readers. As we sift through scholarly inaccuracies and half-remembered critical goals, we come slowly to an agnostic position. In the pendulum swing of scholarship, we move from a waning credulity to a confident doubt. And as we begin to appreciate the canny, clever, and inventive minds of medieval Europe, we lose a misconception about the past that for centuries set our purported sophistication against their purported naiveté. So, we find that textbooks and introductory studies today rarely begin by deprecating medieval intellectual life; fewer of us look down our noses at the giants on whose shoulders we stand. The opposite view we are content to call a misconception. This book is dedicated to describing some of the ways that we have misconceived the Middle Ages.

These essays are possible not because we're any more intelligent than our predecessors but because of recent, major developments in medieval scholarship. The first major development is better access to medieval records. The work of cataloguers, bibliographers, and librarians over the past century has made the Middle Ages far more accessible to more scholars than ever before. As historians, archaeologists, and literary critics amass data about the medieval world, it is collated, listed, and described in increasingly detailed records. From the German *Monumenta Germaniae Historica* (*MGH*) to the English Rolls Series, national projects in Europe have provided scholars convenient access to high-quality editions and images.[5] Many manuscripts are now available freely over the Internet, as are bibliographies and scholarly articles. Wider interest in the Middle Ages has allowed publishers to issue texts that until recently were available only in rare and expensive editions.[6] And mounting interest in medieval studies has given us dissertations, articles, and books from a growing body of scholars. Wider availability of books through interlibrary loan programs, library consortiums, and electronic databases makes research far more efficient than ever before. Scholars who remember paging for hours through dozens of volumes of the *Patrologia Latina*, for example, now search the same volumes electronically in milliseconds. Days spent compiling bibliographies are reduced to minutes. And, in a development that holds great promise, projects to digitize books, such as that by Google, make available instantly books few libraries could afford to house.

Another major development in medieval scholarship was a sea change in historical method in the late nineteenth century, now a matter of academic orthodoxy.[7] Leopold von Ranke (1795–1886), a brilliant and hugely influential professor of history at the University of Berlin, had insisted on historical objectivity, on keeping one's own business out of the data culled from primary sources. But the mere act of selecting facts for one's historical narrative makes such a method extraordinarily difficult to justify; moreover, history is not the fact itself but the story or interpretation to which the fact lends itself.[8] In the 1870s and 1880s, Freidrich Nietzsche took up an argument then in vogue and claimed that an object or event can only be understood as the "succession of forces which take possession of it."[9] In its more extreme manifestations, this claim suggests that a poem, for example, has no meaning in and of itself: its meaning (that is, what ought to be understood by it) derives solely from its interpreters.[10] In other words, objects or events change their meanings depending upon who observes them. A reasonable compromise position was articulated in 1945, when R. G. Collingwood published his extraordinarily influential book, *The Idea of History*. Collingwood argued that history is comprised of historical facts as well as one's theory of history, "the two things in their mutual relations."[11] Historians like Marc Bloch later asked us to consider the condition of a historical observer, and those like Hayden White now ask us to consider the political uses of historical interpretation today.[12] There is no escaping the fact that interpretations of history are as much a part of the past as the data we so efficiently mine. For most professional medievalists, this sea change in historical method means that historical and literary inquiry requires one both to establish fact and to describe the critical program to which facts contribute. In other words, one asks, "What is the text, and what are you *doing* with that text?" For example, Paul Strohm, in his essay in this volume, describes how the story of the 1381 Peasants' Revolt in England has been a central text within a larger, twentieth-century political debate. Various facts of the revolt have been excised or selected by historians and critics to contribute to one or another side of this modern debate. Strohm's essays prompts us to consider that for some twenty-first-century critics, the contemporary context and reception of a medieval text is the primary justification for our attention to it.

Finally, a third major development is a general wariness of social and political ideals. Although not directly influenced by Marx, Hegel, Horkheimer, and the Frankfurt School, this general wariness, at least in the humanities, resembles the critique of modernity offered by their followers.[13] Hegel argued that art and culture articulate a nation's ideals; cultural antiestablishmentarianism, as well as social utopianism, thus extends to a political and social critique of art and culture.[14] The claim assumes that political and social actors take direction from a nation's history and literature. Whether they do or not, major political changes in the last century in the West, the most important of which was the full political enfranchisement of women, prompted a review of stories from the past that seem to enshrine our less appealing beliefs. Such a review operates on the assumption that an institution that relies on a misconception is as liable to fail as a court case that relies on false testimony.[15] Consequently, any narrative of history that presents the modern world as a product of social evolution, for example, has been called into doubt, since social evolution itself has been called into doubt. Critical caution justifiably extends to any absolute claim, law, or category. Professional historians and critics are no longer confident of broad historical currents, of immutable historical laws, or of the accuracy of abstract categories that easily compartmentalize human experience. The misconceptions addressed in this volume each describe some of the more tendentious abstractions that have long controlled confusing, convoluted, and complex data. If there's a lesson to be learned from our efforts, perhaps it's that sometimes one has to be satisfied with confusion. This state is akin to what poet John Keats called "negative capability," defined as "when a man is capable of being in uncertainties, mysteries, doubts, without any irritable reaching after fact and reason."[16]

Misconceptions importantly provide a catalyst for new scholarly work. New scholars of any era will justify themselves by pointing out where their predecessors erred. Countless doctoral dissertations begin with exactly such a justification. This is inevitable, given unforeseen changes in academic interests and priorities. Henry David Thoreau once wrote that we are made to put the gods of our fathers into the cupboard. After all, their shibboleths aren't always ours. Their memories aren't always ours, either. At the same time, scholars discover evidence or offer assessments that reject or revise our stories of the past, of tradition.[17] This book hopes to remind younger scholars that tradition, ironically, changes. Martin Heidegger, the great twentieth-century German philosopher, wrote correctively that tradition "makes us suppose that the necessity of going back to . . . sources is something which we need not even understand."[18] In other words, beware, since tradition does not always conserve its sources well. The essays in this volume ask us to reconsider details of that long tradition that has lately directed our vision, sustained our efforts, and governed our debates. They ask readers to examine sources and to consider the effects of contemporary thought on the imagined world of the past. And they remind readers that the Middle Ages are no singular object, and deserving of the plural.

II

The study of the Middle Ages is not only a dispassionate inquiry into events that occurred, people who lived, and art that was made during the Middle Ages; but it is also an academic discipline with its own characteristics, prejudices, and aims. Those aims do not always reflect the concerns of medieval people. We know, for example, that slavery was an essential component of medieval economic life. But up until the 1990s, there was very little written on medieval slavery—not because it wasn't important to the Middle Ages, but because it didn't seem to occupy many professional scholars.[19] Almost nobody wrote on medieval homosexuality until the late twentieth century. Very few scholars concentrated on the lives of medieval women. But we need to be careful about drawing conclusions about scholarly interests from bibliographies. Sometimes, interests are governed by available sources, and there is not much surviving evidence that concerns the daily social lives of women, as Helen Conrad O'Briain points out in her essay. Less evidence survives concerning the everyday lives of slaves. As a consequence, what the Middle Ages looked like is determined as much by surviving primary sources as by the interests of scholars. (Imagine how people in the future would reconstruct the daily life of your city or town were only a few books and artifacts to survive. Such is the humorous premise of Walter Miller's 1959 *A Canticle for Liebowitz,* in which, among other things, a shopping list and a circuit diagram come to be considered religious texts.)

It is nevertheless important to recognize that scholarship is not undertaken in a vacuum. As much as scholarship is conditioned by surviving evidence, it also sometimes answers to institutional and professional pressures. One of these pressures has been the slow fragmentation of medieval studies due in part to a restructuring of American and European universities during the last half-century. As a consequence, the Middle Ages appear to us to be fragmented, as well. An author like Augustine of Hippo (354–430) might well appear on syllabi for theology courses, history courses, and literature courses, his works subdivided accordingly, and each work speaking only to a course's governing discipline. One can easily imagine a historian mining history from the God-besotted pages of Augustine's *The City of God,* or a theologian summoning the spirit from amid the historical details of the same book. But Augustine likely would not have seen his work as capable of sustaining these subdivisions easily: to him, history was a part of theological inquiry. The events of history are one thing, but their meaning another. And historical events take their meaning in part from their extrapolation within a larger context. If the facts are extrapolated or unpacked in a theology course, they take theological meaning; in a literature course, literary meaning. Problems start to arise when we dissect a book like *The City of God* and declare its parts appropriate only to our own ends. Often, we find then that we have a dead thing on our hands whose bits no longer fit together. J. R. R. Tolkien once described the poem *Beowulf* as a tower pushed down by philologists.[20] They successfully examined the fallen stones but failed to marvel at the beauty and construction of the tower they had destroyed. The poem had come to take its revised (and impoverished!) meaning from the narrow historical and philological contexts in which it was being studied.

Ernst Robert Curtius, author in 1953 of one of the most esteemed books of literary history, wrote of the fragmentation of the modern university that he saw around him:

> The medieval Latinists, the historians of Scholasticism, and the political historians, however, have little contact with one another. The same is true of the modern philologists. They also work on the Middle Ages, but they usually remain as aloof from medieval Latin philology as they do from general literary, political, and cultural history. Thus the Middle Ages is dismembered into specialties which have no contact.[21]

For Curtius, the Middle Ages, like the tower of Tolkien's *Beowulf,* were being divided into pieces. As Curtius argued, these newfangled divisions compromised the integrity of academic study as they compromised the integrity of the objects being studied. This view is not untypical—it is a jeremiad heard from ancient Athens to contemporary centers of learning—but one sympathizes with Curtius's compelling vision of academic integrity. Some academics are fortunate enough to participate in a close circle of scholars, an *Arbeitskreis*, dedicated to a shared and specific purpose, in which goals for future research are set out beforehand. Curtius himself was trained during an era that saw the development of some of the greatest scholarly collaborations yet envisioned, including the German *MGH*, the British Rolls Series, and the French *Recueil des historiens de la France*. In pursuit of such a communal scholarly ideal, fragmentation becomes anathema. Looking to this ideal, some scholars have responded to a pervading sense of fragmentation by seeking to transcend the divisive (and fragmenting) boundaries common to the academy, as if these divisions were arbitrary and therefore culpable of deception. But Curtius' compelling vision, its occasional realization, and its concomitant ideal run up against the exigencies of professional academia in the twenty-first century. A resulting compromise is a unified multiplicity, to borrow a Neoplatonic notion, and is called *multidisciplinarity*. One must, in an image popular in medieval books, gather flowers from many fields. To continue with the metaphor, one studies the flowers for what they hold in common, but one allows that the appeal of the resulting bouquet is as much in its variety as in its integrity.

As a nod in that florid direction, this book is arranged like a medieval *florilegium*, a gathering of flowers. Its many contributors are from many disciplines, interested in a wide variety of subjects, and dedicated to the common aim of finding in sources the evidence to undermine a scholarly misconception. They are seasoned scholars as well as novices. And they are subject to the misconceptions of our own times. As such, their contributions also serve to document the unrecognized prejudices of our own age, as we translate the past into our own language and shape it to our own ends. One of those prejudices (among many) is the apparent naturalness of our fragmented academy, one which makes the *florilegium* and its variety somewhat representative of contemporary academic practice. We are conditioned perhaps by habit to ignore the capriciousness of the *florilegium* when it appears in the form of a journal or in the form of bound conference proceedings. In the bound and collected essays of a single scholar, a sort of biographical *florilegium*, we imagine its unity to proceed from a scholar's life or his cluster of interests. But the bound essay collection is an awkward thing: it hovers between our generic expectations of a journal and a monograph; it promises both variety and integrity. Its difficulties are, in a way, a microcosm of the discipline's tensions.

As a necessary compromise between multidisciplinarity and a book's governing *ordo*, this *florilegium* is organized loosely around several themes while it entertains varied interests. These themes are vague enough to escape the postmodern charge of advancing a master narrative and specific enough, we hope, so as not to be vapid. History—literary, political, institutional, and social—is commonly written now, not from a great height, but low to the ground, local, and detailed. The scholarly imagination is trained to have weights, not wings, in Francis Bacon's phrase. Nevertheless, master narratives do arise. Sometimes they are useful, reasonable, and justified. Sometimes they arise from a need to make our focused work more widely applicable. And sometimes we demand too much of slim evidence. For example, life in the Mâconnaise or in Catalonia might be asked to stand in as a synecdoche for life in all of medieval Europe. To a small degree, it could, but we need to be especially cautious in extrapolating local examples to illustrate Continental tendencies. One might argue that this *florilegium* unwittingly illustrates the loose coherence of academic medievalists today. But that claim is too large for the slim evidence this volume commands, and this book was, in the end, much more capriciously assembled.

Almost ten years ago, a discussion took place on Medieval-Religion, an electronic discussion list. Julia Bolton Holloway and R. A. Ross prompted a discussion on pedagogy, and members wrote in about students whose assessment of the Middle Ages had been built on clichés about knights, women, peasants, dragons, and so forth. Importantly, members of the list were convinced that this resulted from insufficient resources, not from incapable students. As Bryon and I picked up the gauntlet, we decided to arrange this *florilegium* according to themes likely encountered in the American high school and college classroom. (For our purposes, these are religion, war, science, the arts, and society.) Teachers and professors tend to design curricula around themes that will attract interest—and these tend to be drawn from political and social issues they see debated around them daily. The political role of women, questions of just war, poverty, education, and so forth all figure largely in programs of literature and history that, at least since the 1930s, have tried more cogently to pursue social aims.[22] Medieval literature and history are made relevant, or so one argument goes, by speaking to the social and political issues of the day. Bryon and I surveyed curricula, and then asked contributors to respond loosely to themes teachers currently find attractive. These themes seem to correspond to a changing demographic in the American academy. For example, as of 2006, more women study humanities at all levels of education in the United States than do men. This fact may or may not explain why the role of women in the Middle Ages is a popular area of study. We also considered the priorities of grant agencies and foundations, as well as redefined canons, courses, and graduate curricula at some of the major universities and colleges in the United States. These confirmed general areas of interest in teaching, which was unsurprising. Bryon and I assembled topics, grouped them into themes, and gathered contributions. The process of putting together this collection led us to think about what was occupying the minds of medievalists today. What follows are some informal observations that arose during the process of compiling and editing this volume.

III

Academics are, in part, keepers of the past, or *custos historiae,* as St Augustine called us, inheriting a long tradition and passing it on to students. Academics study the past, as well, in order to bring a record of timeless experience to bear on problems and issues in the present. This latter, more utilitarian view of scholarship sees scholarship as a mirror of princes, as it were. And because Western democracies are built upon the sovereignty of the people, educating the people has sometimes been thought equivalent to educating the sovereign. Ralph Waldo Emerson wrote that history itself is of no use unless it informs the free individual: "History no longer shall be a dull book. It shall walk incarnate in every just and wise man."[23] In battling for the populist position of counselor to the people, scholars can be tempted to inform political life through historical example. Such was the case in France in the period just before 1870.[24] Scholarship in this mode aims to recruit historical players to one view or another. Thus, the past becomes a battleground, its spoils authorizing its inheritors, its worthies monumentalizing our own aims. It promises us plinths for monuments to our own ideals. The Roman historian Tacitus hinted at history's promise: "This I regard as history's highest function, to let no worthy action be uncommemorated, and to hold out the reprobation of posterity as a terror to evil words and deeds."[25] One result of this recruiting drive has been to dress medieval people in our own fashions. We make them current by making them look like us and sound like us. Medieval women and men now appear more sophisticated, more politically aware. Their stories are no longer considered rude beginnings of the childhood of our age but complex narratives that flatter our interest in them, as they monumentalize our political and social desires.

Our narratives of the Middle Ages also reflect the variety and complexity of our own time. The variety of the objects of study is a genuine consequence of far more people studying the Middle Ages than ever before, and thus of our far more varied interests. But we also tend to engage the data of the Middle Ages less abstractly, thereby producing narratives characterized by variety and complexity. In his recent history of the fall of Rome, Peter Heather notes that historical trends have led "scholars away from synthesis and into detailed studies of particular aspects."[26] In one regard, this concentration on detail is a result of historiographical method: perhaps a return to von Ranke's assumption about objectivity, about which E. H. Carr says,

> It is this heresy which during the past hundred years has had such devastating effects on the modern historian, producing in Germany, Great Britain, and in the United States, a vast and growing mass of dry-as-dust factual histories, of minutely specialized monographs of would-be historians knowing more and more about less and less, sunk without a trace in an ocean of facts.[27]

In another regard, the events of history, in order to make sense to contemporary readers, must, in the words of Benedetto Croce, vibrate within "present needs and present situations."[28] One wonders whether an affinity for undigested detail might complement a rhetorical strategy: perhaps detailed studies appeal to contemporary readers stylistically, insofar as the illusion of variety appears authentic, and implies a supporting reality. Variety and complexity always characterize the present. So a narrative of the past that is transparent to historical complexity reads like an authentic narrative of the present. As Friedrich Hayek explained simply, "Contemporary events differ from history in that we do not know the results they will produce."[29] We live today amid a mass of possibly significant detail. Eventually, patterns will emerge. By writing history and criticism with less attention to patterns and more attention to detail, we mimic our experience of the present.

How much emphasis should we place on patterns, either in writing history or in recording the present? There lies the crux of a major debate. Do these patterns constitute historical "laws"? Karl Marx thought so. He saw history as a sort of syllogism, whose conclusion would be the revolution of the proletariat. (Marx may be the most misunderstood writer in history: every time a revolution in his name fails, Marxists complain that Marx has been misunderstood again!) All history, Marx argued, progresses inevitably and according to fixed historical laws. Marx borrowed from Giambattista Vico and Johan Herder a notion that historical events can be explained as products of economic and social systems.[30] Marxist literary critics (and New Historicists and cultural materialists, among others) argue that a work of literature is also a product of a particular economic and social system. So, understanding a work of literature means understanding the system (not necessarily the author) that ultimately created it. Literary studies thus merge into cultural studies. Historical laws, though, are to be distinguished from historical patterns and a vague sense of history's larger design. People in the Middle Ages saw history as the unfolding of God's plan. A similar assumption echoes throughout President Abraham Lincoln's second inaugural address, on 4 March 1865, and continues to inform the historical sense of many Americans.

Not all historians and critics search out historical laws or systems. Herder argued that the aim of historians was not to seek out laws among the procession of events but an *Einfülung*, a "feeling into" or empathy, which re-creates the experience of an event.[31] In other words, writing history should be an attempt to re-create what it was like to be there. Similarly, Collingwood argued that historians were to avoid extrapolating from data putative universal laws and concentrate instead on the "deliberations of past agents, thereby rendering their behaviour intelligible."[32] Nevertheless, it is historians that have made our Middle Ages for us from the raw, undigested data of history. It was Petrarch (1304–74) who gave us the phrase "dark ages."[33] He was trying to connect the readers of his own age to Greek and Roman antiquity and pushed the Middle Ages aside by scoffing at them. Once the darkness of medieval Europe became a historical commonplace, generations of historians adopted it for their own narratives. Erasmus (c.1466–1536) imputed ignorance to monks and scholastics, calling them the real barbarians. Their barbarism was confirmed by selectively illustrating examples of their bad Latinity, considered far from the pure Latin of Cicero or Caesar. During the Protestant Reformation, the denigration continued, and the entire Catholic church, not just its monks, was characterized as barbarous. It purportedly had deviated from early Christianity and filled the heads of gullible Christians with childish superstition. Enlightenment historians picked up on this charge and used it to supplement their own antireligious screeds with juicy examples of medieval religious excess. An Enlightenment antipathy to religion in general and Christianity in specific took perhaps its most influential shape in Edward Gibbon's *Decline and Fall of the Roman Empire* (1776). Gibbon argued, with astonishing erudition, that Christianity had weakened the empire by substituting its superstition for native reason. It was Gibbon who gave us the influential portrait of Constantine, the first Christian Roman Emperor, as a wily, calculating atheist who used Christianity as a ruse to further his political ambitions. Since Gibbon, dozens of other narratives have been offered to explain Rome's fall and the ensuing character of medieval Europe. But many of his prejudices continue on nonetheless.

Somewhere between details and putative historical laws, misconceptions are born. Misconceptions arise not only from too abstracted a view but also from a desire to remake the past or to appeal incautiously to institutional rewards. The institutions of the humanities may seem a crude notion to intrude on the rarified air of medievalism, but in plain fact, the American academy functions in a capitalist republic, not in a vacuum. Numerous stimuli effect the directions taken by scholars—the aims of publishers, scholarly journals, academic departments, large-scale projects, and so forth. These cannot be calculated as necessary results of social causes, since the academy is not immediately or ineluctably responsive to them, nor are administrators always responsive to alumni and parents. Institutional stimuli in the academy are often the results of ideals or long-range planning rather than collated opinion—publishers anticipating trends, editors redirecting scholarly focus, departments trying to appear *en vogue*, and so forth. Some aims of humanities departments are a century or two older and derive in part from nationalist pursuits of the nineteenth and twentieth centuries. These have been built into the constitutions of colleges, universities, and secondary schools. They govern sometimes with as much force as any other factor. We need only point to departments of French and English to see the more obvious results of nationalist divisions. (In which does one properly teach Marie de France? Alcuin? Geoffrey Gaimar? Erasmus? Samuel Beckett?) Some other aims of humanities departments are more current and develop in response to administrative trends or management practices. In my own university, the issue of "diversity" now powerfully affects pedagogy and institutional support for scholarship. These more recent trends, too, have an influence on how the Middle Ages manifest themselves in the academy.

One palpable effect of nationalist pursuits has been to denude the Middle Ages of much of its literature. Departments of English reasonably teach literature written in English; departments of German, literature written in German, and so forth. But during the Middle Ages, most literature (the category is a contested one) was written in Latin. In his history of Anglo-Latin literature, A. G. Rigg points out that Latin hardly figures in the narrative of the "development" of English literature. We are accustomed to a story in which Anglo-Saxon is smothered by Norman French, then slowly regains its own in the age of Chaucer. The low points, as it were, are the twelfth and thirteenth centuries. But, Rigg reminds us, "The high point of literary excellence in England in the Middle Ages was the twelfth and thirteenth centuries."[34] Very few students read Latin anymore. And if they do, they are subject, as we have seen, to a prejudice that classical Latin sets a standard that medieval Latin fails to meet, something Rigg calls the "classical fallacy." Rigg also notes the "fallacy of literary progress," according to which "the Latin culture of the Middle Ages is seen solely as a slow blundering journey towards the Renaissance in search of the lost gold of the ancients, proceeding fitfully by minor 'renaissances' in the Carolingian age and the twelfth century. . . ."[35]

Such fallacies have hidden hundreds of authors under a blanket of obscurity, authors who are worth reading in their own right as well as for their contribution to national, vernacular literatures. After all, why is an English monk's Latin poetry any less English than his Anglo-Saxon poetry? Since any given medieval author was more often than not bilingual, scholars and students lose much when they lose Latin. Each author, like all creatures of the medieval world, as Alan of Lille (c.1125–1203) says, "quasi liber et pictura / nobis est in speculum" ("like a book or a picture, is to us a mirror [or reflection]").[36]

It bears remembering that nationalist pursuits have also resulted in astounding advances in scholarship. The Benedictine order of Maurists set the stage in the seventeenth century. Under the direction of Luc D'Achery, and boasting the incomparable talents of Jean Mabillon, they published an extensive collection of medieval texts.[37] Their collection paralleled similar efforts, and one that still stands as one of the great achievements of scholarship. In The (Protestant) Netherlands, a country then under the control of (Catholic) Spain, the Catholic Jesuit order sought to conserve hagiographies—stories of saints. Jean Bolland organized the efforts in 1630 and launched the monumental *Acta Sanctorum*. Individual scholars were also collecting and collating sources, including André du Chesne (sources relating to Normans, in 1619), John Selden (1584–1654, various English sources, especially *Englands epinomis*, 1681), and so forth. Selden was praised for *The Historie of Tithes* (1618), in which he recommended skeptical scrutiny of the sources and offered a bibliography and index of manuscripts.[38] In the eighteenth century, French academic historians for the first time had the direct support of the government in these efforts. The French government sponsored the collection, study, and publication of sources for the history of France, resulting in the *Recueil des histoires des Gaules et de la France*. Similar collections were sponsored by their respective governments in England, Italy, Germany, and Austria. National historical and literary societies were soon founded, including the English Society of Antiquaries (1717), the Bavarian Academy of Science (1759), and so forth. By the nineteenth century, governments and universities were cooperating extensively, with the result that projects undertaken then are still unsurpassed today. These include publications of the École Nationale des Chartres in Paris, the British Camden Society, Royal Historical Society, Selden Society, and Early English Texts Society, among others. In the mould of the French *Recueil*, mentioned above, were the British Rolls Series and the astounding German *MGH*, whose contributors included Wilhelm von Humboldt, the brothers Grimm, G. H. Pertz, and Theodore Mommsen.

So despite the popular image of their ivory tower, academics and teachers are not isolated from the public sphere. As in the nineteenth century, and continuing into the twenty-first, the cooperation of government and the academy can have magnificent results. But there are risks, as well, in blurring the lines between the academy and the government, and the academy and the marketplace. And here we come to one of the issues facing twenty-first-century academics generally and medievalists specifically. In its search for larger and larger profit margins, the academy risks adopting deleterious practices and aims of business managers and public policymakers. In most management contexts, product, rather than process, is the first measure of value. A risk in courting product over process in education is that one confuses education with vocational training. In concentrating on product—on vocation—and in assessing progress in the humanities quantitatively, susceptible administrators unsurprisingly tend to value courses thought to forge demonstrable habits of mind. These habits are thus distinguished from course content and from discipline-specific methodology. Few will fail to recognize here what has become the least common denominator of pedagogy, *critical thinking*, the shibboleth of academic mission statements. It seems to mean the ability to reason and an awareness of one's own guiding principles and assumptions. One might well ask, "Why is critical thought a quality of *educated* men and women and not of *all* men and women?" As an academic high-water mark, "critical thinking" severely underestimates students and demeans (by overgeneralizing) the benefits of an education in medieval history or literature. After all, the details of medieval history and literature are superfluous to this vague if ubiquitous goal. If you can learn critical thinking in a hotel management course, why study Old English?

To take one public example, in their respective commencement addresses to the graduating classes of 2004, the heads of Harvard and Yale lauded critical thinking above all else in an undergraduate education. Harvard's president at the time, economist Lawrence H. Summers, asked students to acknowledge "the most valuable skill learned at Harvard: the ability to think deeply about problems that confront them." (One might quibble that *solving* such problems is the point.) Summers did not ask that psychologists know psychology, classicists Greek, accountants accounting, chemists chemistry, historians history, medievalists the Middle Ages, but that all equally be capable of thinking deeply, whatever that might mean. Richard H. Brodhead, Dean of Yale College and an English professor, allowed that forgetting information learned in courses is fine—in fact, expected. The desired end of a Yale education, after all, is "trained deep habits of mind that survive the specific content that was originally attached to them and can be put to different use."[39] In this false analogy of thinking-as-physical-exercise, the Middle Ages, misconceived or not, are of small matter. As long as you think, Brodhead seems to say, we're relatively unconcerned with what you think about. In the end, Brodhead implies, it doesn't matter whether you think the medieval church was corrupt or not, as long as Yale was able "to nourish and confirm your will to grow." One might note that such, too, is the will of ferns.

In all fairness to Summers and Brodhead (and with apologies to my coeditor, Provost Grigsby), academic administration sometimes requires such strategic vapidity. A sufficiently empty phrase can transcend disagreements within the university, because abstraction allows us to synthesize competing views. Faculty might not all agree on what to teach students, but we can all agree that we want to produce *intelligent* graduates. We might not be able to agree on whether or not to teach Chaucer, but we can agree that we should teach *important* authors. In the end, we can agree nominally, although we might mean entirely different things by *intelligent* and *important*. So, in an address meant to enthuse alumni and parents, one can empathize with the likely motivations of Summers and Brodhead for vague phrases and empty catchwords. The important point here is that in stressing ends, goals, and products (even if it be "critical thinking"), the machinery of the university sets the conditions by which one justifies one's academic field. Thus compelled by perpetually changing institutional settings to answer concerns about the utility of medieval studies, medievalists refashion themselves and the field to best ensure its survival. (That refashioning inspired a number of collections and conferences addressing with some urgency the future of the Middle Ages.) In literary studies, it is not uncommon for medievalists to follow the lead of Renaissance and Early-Modern studies, perhaps because Shakespeare and Milton, the gold standards of cultural capital, transcend institutional justification. All this is to say that the disciplines of medieval study are subject to the influence of administrators, publishers, departmental vision statements, social and political agendas, and the like. As a consequence, the prevailing picture of the Middle Ages given to undergraduates and to secondary-school students is a convoluted mixture of sources and qualified perspectives. And yet, the discipline itself continues to survive and to flourish. In fact, if one takes the evidence of book catalogues and graduate prospectuses, medieval studies are growing rapidly despite, or perhaps on account of, these various institutional pressures.

IV

Archimedes is reported to have said that given a place to stand (and, presumably, a fulcrum and a strong lever), he could move the world. That image is a useful one for scholars. Small movements can influence large ones. The smallest assumption can affect the course of a lifetime of scholarship. A single manuscript, for example, can change entirely our picture of the Middle Ages, as did the publication of the unique *Beowulf* manuscript in English in the 1830s. But there are small, detrimental assumptions, too, that color our approaches and conclusions of historical and literary evidence. Four of them seem particularly important. One assumption seems to be particularly American—at least according to our European colleagues. It is to assume the benefits of a defiant novelty. Our business and political leaders commonly talk about breaking the rules, thinking outside the box, changing paradigms, and so forth. A *defiant* novelty is an attractive quality in the United States: as Frits van Oostrom notes of American medievalists, Europeans see in us "an unconventional fondness for publications that advocate a point, a central thesis, that preferably flies in the face of a contested more conventional view."[40] We read in an influential 2005 assessment of medieval studies, Professor Stephen G. Nichols of Johns Hopkins University writing that medievalists, like Turks at the walls of Rhodes, have "succeeded in breaching the ramparts."[41] Nichols is playing the Turk only rhetorically, but Americans might note that we are strangely compelled by such recusancy, as we are by the scent of revolution. Martin Aurell of the Université de Poitiers wonders if a relative lack of interest in thirteenth-century France among medievalists is due to "the apparent absence of social tensions or of military upheavals."[42] Why such an interest in defiance? But we must also ask whether this interest in defiance actually yields novelty. Van Oostrom warns of an American "tendency to self-fashioning, for instance in the proliferation of self-congratulatory so-called *new* paradigms that, while they are good, are often far from new."[43] Once again, we can turn for illustration to Nichols, who reviews a book by Howard Bloch, *The Anonymous Marie de France* (Chicago, 2003). Bloch proposes, and Nichols celebrates, a *new* paradigm: "the concept of speech as identity." But is it new? There is clear awareness of language as an essential part of identity in the book of Genesis during the dispersion of tribes at Babel, in hundreds of antique and early medieval authors (such as Caesar and Tacitus and Jordanes), and in the *Historia Ecclesiastica* of Bede written in 723. Bede identifies the tribes of Britain according to their languages.

Other general assumptions that typify American medievalism today appear to underlie Nichols's review. It may be instructive to our purposes to observe them. One assumption is the ease with which he uses terms like "society" and "culture." (Readers will note that I have been equally free and easy with these terms.) For most speakers of English, "society" is only vaguely meaningful. What is it? What body of evidence do we consider when we consider medieval *society*? Is it, as the *Oxford English Dictionary* defines the term, an association or fellowship of people, "the system or mode of life adopted by individuals," the upper classes, or people "associated together by some common interest" such as a guild? In other words, is it a group of people, a set of ideas, the upper classes, or an institution? None of these uniquely limits our view, for example, of medieval Irish society. Eric Wolf tried to define "society" in an enlightening paper in 1985 and offered a useful historical overview of the term.[44] What he concludes in part is that the limits of communities we designate by capital-S Society (distinguishing, for example, between societies and nations) are not the limits understood by our European predecessors. Medieval writers used terms like *gens, natio, provincia, res publica*, and *populus* to designate collectives that we gather under the English terms "society" or "culture."[45] These English terms develop into abstractions with lives of their own. They accumulate rich bibliographies but are so abstract as to be universally applicable and therefore practically useless as research tools. They exist like the abstractions of Prudentius's *Psychomachia*, doing battle in imaginary spaces. But instead of Amor and Luxuria fighting it out, we now see Gender versus Hegemony, and Society versus Freedom. I imagine that scholars after us will play Aristotle to these Neoplatonic forms.

Nichols remarks on a book by Jeffrey Hamburger, *The Visual and the Visionary* (1998). Hamburger makes the very important point that "gender as a category of interpretation" can distort our appreciation of medieval evidence (p. 429). One reads—almost without noticing—Nichols's phrase "the status of women." If one stops to consider Nichols's phrase in light of Hamburger's point, one wonders if the term "women" has come to designate not the female sex, but a legal or political class of persons. Perhaps the influence of nineteenth- and twentieth-century legal battles in Europe and America has conditioned us to think of women as a homogenous (legal) category, distinct from the categories of class, race, nation, and family that may have been more meaningful to medieval women. Given any two medieval women, would they have seen themselves as having something female in common, something that transcended their other differences? For example, can we elide the differences between England's Queen Emma (d. 1052) and a Yorkshire milkmaid without compromising the lived experience of two medieval women? To take another example, could we elide the differences between Richard III and a Cornish stable boy in order to say something meaningful about the status of medieval men? In searching after the status of women, we also risk eliding differences between medieval experience and modern experience. Hildegard von Bingen (1098–1179) is popular in college classrooms and often serves as an example of a medieval woman and, by extension, of all women. But by abstracting so far from individual experience, we run the risk of erroneously equating a profoundly religious Rhenish adept of a Catholic rule to, for example, a British prime minister, a French-Canadian policewoman, or a twenty-year-old suburban American housewife. (If we compared Hildegard to Sister Mary Frances Clarke [d. 1887] of the Sisters of Charity of the Blessed Virgin Mary, would our views of medieval women change?) We also distort our understanding of medieval Europe when we assume that one or two or even a handful of women offer sufficient evidence for a general conclusion about the Middle Ages. Given the population of Europe in, say, 1066 AD, can a single woman reasonably stand in for millions?

The false analogy described above (that is, like Hidegard are all women throughout time) also bedevils Nichols's phrase, a "female artifact" (429), by which he presumably means an artifact made by a woman. Given that all women do not speak the same way, write the same way, carve wood the same way, how can an artifact be female? Perhaps it participates, in Plato's sense, in femaleness. The phrase "female artifact" implies that something fundamentally female is transferred magically from a woman into an artifact, some womanly essence that can later be recovered. One cannot help but to conclude the irrationality of a claim that there may be something indescribably but perceptibly female (rather than feminine) about a poem or a staircase. (Is it hypocritical to mock the German denigration of "Jewish science" but to embrace its mirror image in this "progressive" guise of female art?) Isn't a female poet of the Middle Ages just as likely to write from the perspective of a wife or sister or daughter or mother as she is to write from the perspective of a noble, or a Burgundian, or a Catholic, or a lover of Italian verse? To disencumber a poem of its multiple perspectives on behalf of isolating a female element places a great deal of faith in a mystical, universal femaleness that can travel outside of women's bodies. If one is not a committed Platonist, then such a persistent femaleness may depend instead on a materialist view of individuals that sees us produced by the invisible forces of history and society. In this view, we are not individuals, but "subject positions," empty husks filled with meaning by the institutions and languages surrounding us. In short, a simple phrase like "female artifact" requires a complicated ontological scaffolding—either explicit or implied—in order to be meaningful. To understand Nichols is to entertain his ontology, an ontology teeming with unexamined or untheorized assumptions.

Finally, Nichols's review depends upon another unexamined assumption. In its celebration of "empowerment" and "representation" (in the parliamentary sense), his review illustrates a preference for negative, as opposed to positive, liberty. He is in no way alone. The philosopher Isaiah Berlin (1909–97) famously distinguished these from one another and explained that negative liberty is conceived as a *freedom from*—from bondage, from coercion, from control, from government, and so forth. In this view, we are free as long as we are unencumbered.[46] Lord Acton wrote in his 1906 study of the development of liberty in Europe, "It is by the combined efforts of the weak, made under compulsion, to resist the reign of force and constant wrong, that, in the rapid change but slow progress of four hundred years, liberty has been preserved, and secured, and extended, and finally understood."[47]

Positive liberty is conceived in part as freedom granted to us by law. We are free *because of* the coercive power of law: free to speak as we choose, to assemble, to vote, and so forth, because the law enshrines and protects these freedoms and punishes those who would oppose them. Our freedom thus depends on our common submission to the law, to an authority. In celebrating the freedom of medieval women, among others, academics tend to value their subjects' antipathy towards authority. Someone who criticizes the church, for example, is generally considered more liberated—freer—than someone who obeys rules. Peasants who rebel are consider more democratic than those who do as they are expected. In other words, negative liberty looks to be the measure by which we tend to determine the sophistication of medieval individuals. The more they rebelled, it seems, the better they were.[48] Yet, a scholarly sympathy for rebellion and institutional antithesis is paradoxical, given the constructive force of positive liberty in the classroom, the university, scholarly communities, and Western democracies generally. Nevertheless, the valorization of negative liberty, as van Oostrom points out earlier, is a characteristic of much American critical and scholarly work.

These are only some of the assumptions that appear to characterize American medievalists today. The next generation will have its own assumptions and misconceptions. As we recognize our own fallibility, we look charitably to the generations before us to correct or qualify their misconceptions. And, as we do so, we pay close attention to the extracurricular influences that shaped their conclusions in the hopes that we might be more circumspect in mitigating our own distorting influences. In the subject area of religion, we are grateful to have the contributions of Professors Elaine Beretz, Peter Dendle, Michael Drout, Mary Dockray-Miller, Frans van Liere, Vincent DiMarco, Ethan Felsen, and Michael Frasetto. Each responds to misconceptions that took shape largely during the Protestant Reformation. As in any fierce debate, one side comes to characterize the other unfairly. And the debate between Protestant and Catholic was nothing if not fierce. Since Protestant Europe defined itself in part by setting itself against Catholic Europe, Protestant accounts of medieval Christianity were especially vitriolic. These have given rise to many misconceptions of medieval religious life. Some contributors in this section respond to general misconceptions. Dendle points out that the Middle Ages were far more than an "age of faith." Drout adds that, even among those whom we count as faithful Christians, few were as orthodox and submissive as Protestant propagandists would have them. Beretz shows that the notion of papal infallibility, which fuels antagonistic views of medieval Christians as especially submissive, was a doctrine unknown to the Middle Ages. Neither was the church a seedbed of corruption, as van Liere demonstrates, or a mindless enemy of Islam and Judaism, as Frassetto explains. Some contributors respond to specific misconceptions that have served as vivid examples of the purported dangers of medieval Christianity and, by extension, of Catholicism. Dockray-Miller describes how not all medieval nuns were virgins and that marriage was not denied female religious in Anglo-Saxon England. In doing so, she complicates a prevailing positivistic narrative. DiMarco takes on one of the great chestnuts of medieval misconceptions, Pope Joan. He describes the origins of the myth that has served for so long to mock the papacy.

War is our second subject area. Medieval warfare has long been considered brutal and its warriors unschooled. Perhaps, for that reason, there have been very few studies of medieval warfare outside of hobbyists and enthusiasts. Another reason may be that military science is rarely taught outside of professional military schools. Thus, there are no institutional motives for pursuing a purely historical study of medieval warfare. Also, warfare in general is often eclipsed either by the Crusades or by its romantic portraits in courtly literature. But as we focus on the experiences of medieval men and women, the face of battle has become an area of renewed interest. So have the varieties of medieval fighting forces, from private to regional to royal armies. James Patterson describes the wide variety of medieval warriors, attempting to dissuade readers from thinking the mounted knight central to medieval warfare. He offers, as do many of our contributors, an extensive bibliography. Turning to more general concerns, Jessalyn Bird describes how the Crusades were not an expedient solution for ridding one's estates of dissolute second sons. She reviews some of the major misconceptions that have clouded our appreciation of the complex causes of medieval crusading. One of our contributors withdrew his essay at the last minute, so we are left without a discussion of misconceptions of the power of the state. We recommend that those interested in this topic consult Rosenwein and Little, as well as Otto Gierke, *Political Theories of the Middle Ages*, F.W. Maitland (trans.), (1900) Bristol: Thoemmes, 1996.

Perhaps nowhere are the Middle Ages thought so backwards as in the realm of science, our third area of interest. Our contributors in this area show how medieval people were not as vacant and credulous as is often portrayed. In fact, given the knowledge they were able to accumulate, their responses to disease and health were both rational and often effective. Besides offering purely historical interest, medieval medical texts also offer clues to new treatments and medications. The fact is that some of these cures worked; it is incumbent on us to discover why. More generally, medieval medicine offered medieval people an image and rationale of the inner workings of their bodies. The body was a microcosm of the world, and medieval medicine prescribed a balanced disposition, a good diet, and a holistic approach to health that may yet be of use to modern physicians. Van Arsdall offers a historical overview of how medieval medicine has been portrayed, especially during the last two hundred years. Grigsby reviews the relation between morality and health in the Middle Ages. He observes that based on a theory of humors, medieval physicians supposed that people were predisposed to certain sins. If we secularize this assertion, we arrive at the unsurprising claim that people are predisposed to certain unhealthy behaviors. Continuing the line that medieval people were not credulous fools, Peter Dendle offers his second contribution, describing how the Middle Ages were not a time of uncontrolled superstition. He makes the very sane observation that superstitions are of all time and not characteristic of any one age. (We cross our fingers that this is true!) As a corollary to this claim, Richard Raiswell next describes some humanist attacks on medieval universities that resulted in a misconception of medieval scholars as inane, arguing endlessly about angels and pinheads. Louise Bishop describes the myth of the flat earth—that medieval people believed the world was shaped like a pancake. And Ronald Ganze explores the many ways that some medieval individuals conceived of selfhood. Ganze puts a crimp in the canard that selfhood wasn't invented until the Renaissance.

Our fourth area of interest is the arts. In the culinary arts, Christopher Roman and Jean-François Kostha-Théfaine discuss medieval food, which is usually portrayed as a bucket of hogs' swill or the dog's breakfast. Readers of both these essays may find some of the recipes to be surprisingly complex. These recipes testify to a sophisticated medieval palate. The recipes are also useful for establishing the extent of the spice trade. The culinary arts offer an extremely interesting body of evidence for the intersection of commerce, agriculture, animal husbandry, theories of humors and health, composition of flavors, and the rituals of eating. From the culinary arts, we turn to drama. Carolyn Coulson-Grigsby discusses several misconceptions that have arisen over the years concerning medieval drama. Perhaps the most abiding is that medieval drama developed from liturgical processions. Marijane Osborne turns to the languages of medieval England and describes some differences between Old English and Shakespeare's English. Her essay also describes the basics of inflected languages, which we hope will be useful in the classroom. This is followed by another essay dedicated directly to classroom issues: C. David Benson on Chaucer. A great deal is lost when students read Chaucer in a modern English version and ignore the Middle English. Benson offers some thoughts on what is lost and encourages teachers to return to the rich Middle English verse. Finally, Michael George tackles the perception that no one in the Middle Ages laughed. He offers some very funny examples from medieval drama and literature to show that medieval people knew how to enjoy a good guffaw.

Our fifth area of interest is society, by which we shamelessly mean all those things we couldn't put into the other categories. Paul Strohm challenges the reign of the Peasants' Revolt of 1381 as the vivid example of class struggle in the Middle Ages. He describes the composition of the rioters and concludes that whatever might have happened, the uprising was not executed by peasants. Dinah Hazell gives us some clearer idea of who peasants were. She takes on the Romantic view of peasants that we find in the poems of Wordsworth, for example, and confounds a view of peasants secure in their feudal tenure.

Richard Godden counters the misconception that medieval people had no sense of history. He describes a number of models of historical thinking extant during the period. Ironically, Anita Obermeier next illustrates how we moderns have collapsed Renaissance and medieval history and reviews the misconception that the Middle Ages were lit by witches aflame! She offers a historical overview of witches and witch burning. Just as George addressed the apparent lack of laughter in the Middle Ages, so does Sophie Oosterwijk address the apparent lack of children. We are accustomed to seeing paintings of medieval children in which they look like tiny adults. Ooserwijk explains why and lays the misconception to rest. Helen Conrad-O'Briain addresses the misconception that women during the Middle Ages could neither read nor write. She offers us the salutary caution that we need to be alert to the many facets of female literacy. Finally, Linda Keyser unlocks the secrets of the female chastity belt. For those to whom the chastity belt is familiar medieval chattel, we apologize for having to reveal that it is an invention of a much later age.

Bryon and I are extremely grateful to the contributors for their cheerful participation in this project. We trust that readers will find the result to be informative, amusing, and interesting. And we hope in the end to have pressed the point that one cannot appeal to sources uncontextualized by the tenor and aims of their interpreters. Nevertheless, going back to the sources is a first and necessary step. Medieval studies will always need men and women competent in languages, paleography, codicology, archaeology, and other disciplines that concentrate on the things themselves. Editions and translations are our fondest *desiderata*. Fuller descriptions of the medieval landscape, of towns and cities, and of daily life are also required. And we have need of people to synthesize this data, that is, to interpret it. There are degrees of interpretation, and we have need both of people who stay close to the ground and of people who take larger views. And to keep us alert, we need critics to ask how our studies are being put to use. Bryon and I agreed that those uses, not history itself, are well conceived or misconceived. And it is this sense of *misconception* that Bryon and I have pursued. We have asked contributors to examine academic narratives that undergird grander theories of culture, society, politics, religion, genre, and so on. We asked after narratives that have sufficiently abused the medieval evidence. Our criteria for inclusion were sufficient evidence of that abuse, contrary or contradictory primary evidence, and the relevance of the topic to observed interests in medieval studies. We are very pleased with the results. Our thanks go out to the contributors, who gave generously of their time and effort.

Stephen Harris

Feast of St. Colette

Amherst, MA

SUGGESTIONS FOR FURTHER READING

Bibliographies

These are the first step in any research program. The worth of a good bibliography cannot be overestimated. Rely first and foremost on your librarian, teacher, or professor—someone who knows her or his way around the sources. Each discipline has its preferred sources for up-to-date bibliographies. For example, in Anglo-Saxon studies, the *Old English Newsletter* publishes an annual bibliography of all pertinent, recent publications, as does *Anglo-Saxon England*. *Toronto Medieval Bibliographies* has produced several important research tools, one of which is listed below. D. S. Brewer has a series entitled *Annotated Bibliographies of Old and Middle English Literature*. The *On-Line Reference Book of Medieval Studies*, listed following, includes Professor James Marchand's "What Every Medievalist Should Know," a terrific annotated bibliography for undergraduates organized by topic. What follows are useful for getting you started in literary and historical research.

Raoul C. van Caenegem, *Guide to the Sources of Medieval History*, New York: North-Holland, 1978.
———. *Introduction aux Sources de l'Histoire Médiévale*, L. Jocqué (ed.), Turnhout, Belgium: Brepols, 1997.
R. H. C. Davis, *Medieval European History, 395–1500: A Select Bibliography*, London: Routledge & Kegan Paul, 1963.
James Harner, *Literary Research Guide: An Annotated Listing of Reference Sources in English Literary Studies*, New York: Modern Language Association of America, 2002.
International Medieval Bibliography, CD-Rom, Turnhout, Belgium: Brepols, 1995. Now online with subscription.
R. E. Kaske, *Medieval Christian Literary Imagery: A Guide to Interpretation*, Toronto: University of Toronto, 1988.
Lexikon des Mittlealters, München: Artemis, 1980–1999. Available online with subscription from Brepols Publishers, Turnhout, Belgium.
Modern Language Association International Bibliography, Ipswich, MA: EBESCO, 1963.
Katherine Talarico (ed.), *The On-Line Reference Book for Medieval Studies*, 2007. Available at http://www.the-orb.net/. Follow links for "Reference," then "WEMSK"; also a good source for studies and primary sources online.
The Year's Work in English Studies, London: John Murray, 1919.

Primary Sources

There are thousands of collections and series of primary sources. Often, a standard history of your period will include many such sources in its bibliography or in its list of abbreviations. Again, consult a librarian, teacher, or professor. Research guides such as that by van Caenegem (preceding) will direct you to various primary sources (e.g., for Great Britain, see pp. 306–12). Collections of primary sources are listed in *Repertorium Fontium Historiae Medii Aevi, I: Series Collectionum*, Rome, 1962; and its continuation, *Additamenta, 1: Series Collectionum Continuata et Aucta (1962–1972)*, Rome, 1977. What follows are some sources to get your feet wet.

Cetedoc Library of Christian Latin Texts, Turnhout, Belgium: Brepols, 1991. Electronic resource includes *CCSL*, following. Now *The Library of Latin Texts*, available online with subscription.

Corpus Christianorum Series Latina (= *CCSL*), Turnhout, Belgium: Brepols, 1954–.

David C. Douglas (ed.), *English Historical Documents*, 10 vols., London: Routledge, 1996. The first five volumes concern the Middle Ages.

Early English Text Society, Oxford: Oxford University, 1864–.

George Philip Krapp and Elliott van Kirk Dobbie, *The Anglo-Saxon Poetic Records*, 6 vols., New York: Columbia University, 1931–1942.

Patrologia Cursus Completus . . . Series Latina (= *PL*), 221 vols., Jean-Paul Migne (ed.), Paris: Migne, 1844–1902.

Patrologia Cursus Completus . . . Series Graeca (= *PG*), 81 vols., Jean-Paul Migne (ed.), Paris: Migne, 1856–1867.

Recueil des Historiens des Gaules et de la France, 13 vols., Paris, 1738–1786. Continued as *Recueil des Historiens de la France*, Paris, 1899–1992.

Rerum Britannicorum Medii Aevi Scriptores (Rolls Series), 253 vols., London, 1858–96.

Russell A. Peck (ed.), *Consortium for the Teaching of the Middle Ages*, 2007. Texts available at http://www.teamsmedieval.org/texts/index.html.

Sharpe, *A Handlist of the Latin Writers of Great Britain and Ireland before 1550*, Turnhout, Belgium: Brepols, 2001. Supplemented by *Additions and Corrections (1997–2001)*.

John Edwin Wells (ed.), *A Manual of the Writings in Middle English, 1050–1500*, 10 vols., New Haven: Connecticut Academy of Arts and Sciences, 1919–1951.

Some Important Monographs and Collections

Consult your teacher or professor for a more thorough bibliography. WEMSK offers good guidance, as well. What follows are a few good, trustworthy sources.

Ernst Robert Curtius, *European Literature and the Latin Middle Ages*, Willard R. Trask (trans., 1952), Princeton, NJ: Princeton University, 1992.

New Catholic Encyclopedia, 15 vols., 2nd ed., Detroit, MI: Gale, 2003.

Catholic Encyclopedia, 16 vols., New York: Appleton, 1907–14. Now online, 2007. Available at http://www.newadvent.org/cathen/index.html.

Gustav Ehrismann, *Geschichte der deutschen Literatur bis zum Ausgang des Mittelalters*, 4 vols., München: Beck, 1932.

Johan Huizinga, *The Autumn of the Middle Ages*, Rodney J. Payton and Ulrich Mammitzsch (trans.), Chicago: University of Chicago, 1996.

E. F. Jacob, *The Fifteenth Century, 1399–1485*, Oxford: Oxford University, 1961.

David Lyle Jeffrey (ed.), *A Dictionary of Biblical Tradition in English Literature*, Grand Rapids, MI: Eerdman's, 1992.

M. L. W. Laistner, *Thoughts and Letters in Western Europe, AD 500–900*, Ithaca, NY: Cornell University, 1957.

Jacques Le Goff et al. (eds.), *Dictionnaire Raisonné de l'Occident médiévale*, Paris: Fayard, 1999.

C. S. Lewis, *The Allegory of Love: A Study in Medieval Tradition*, London: Oxford University, 1938.

May McKisack, *The Fourteenth Century, 1307–1399*, Oxford: Oxford University, 1959.

The New Cambridge Medieval History, 8 vols., Cambridge: Cambridge University, 1995–2005.

A. L. Poole, *Domesday Book to Magna Carta, 1087–1216*, 2nd ed., Oxford: Oxford University, 1955.

Maurice Powicke, *The Thirteenth Century, 1216–1307*, 2nd ed., Oxford: Oxford University, 1962.

Pierre Riché, *Education and Culture in the Barbarian West: From the Sixth through the Eighth Century*, John J. Contreni (trans.), Columbia, SC: University of South Carolina, 1978.

Beryl Smalley, *The Study of the Bible in the Middle Ages*, Notre Dame, IN: University of Notre Dame, 1964.

R. W. Southern, *The Making of the Middle Ages*, New Haven, CT: Yale University, 1953.

Joseph R. Strayer (ed.), *Dictionary of the Middle Ages*, 13 vols., New York: Scribner, 1982–2004.

Frank Stenton, *Anglo-Saxon England*, Oxford: Oxford University, 1943.

NOTES

1. The views of this Introduction are entirely my own, and do not necessarily represent the views of the contributors. My thanks go to Michael Drout, Tom Hall, and Robert Sullivan for their comments.
2. Roberta Frank, "The Search for the Anglo-Saxon Oral Poet," in *Textual and Material Culture in Anglo-Saxon England: Thomas Northcote Toller and the Toller Memorial Lectures*, Donald Scragg (ed.), Cambridge: D. S. Brewer, 2003, pp. 137–160, p. 140. See for his similar assessment of historiographical swings, as well as for a good overview of historiography in general, E. H. Carr, *What Is History?* New York: Penguin, 1961.
3. These categories are described by James Simpson in his assessment of some of the effects of periodization on medieval scholarship: *The Oxford English Literary History, 1350–1547: Reform and Cultural Revolution*, Oxford: Oxford University, 2002.
4. Allen J. Frantzen, *Desire for Origins: New Language, Old English, and Teaching the Tradition*, New Brunswick, NJ: Rutgers University, 1990, p. 125. This is a model study of critical historiography concerning the Middle Ages. (Bryon and I are extremely grateful to Allen for his guidance and generosity over the years.) Frantzen's claim is part of a response to empiricism that dates back to the early twentieth century. Sir George Clark, for example, wrote in 1907 that historians of his generation "consider that knowledge of the past has come down through one or more human minds, has been 'processed' by them, and therefore cannot consist of elemental and impersonal atoms which nothing can alter"; cited in Carr, *History*, pp. 7–8.
5. A good description and bibliography of these national projects is offered by R. C. van Caenegem, *Kurze Quellenkunde des westeuropäischen Mittlealters*, Göttingen, Germany: Vendenhoeck & Ruprecht, 1962, pp. 165–201.

6. This was the aim of the Early English Text Society, which transformed medieval literary study in the nineteenth century. See David Matthews, *The Making of Middle English, 1765–1910*, University of Minnesota, 1999, chapter 6.

7. R. G. Collingwood, *The Idea of History* (1946), Oxford: Oxford University, 1994. See also Carr, *History*; Raoul C. van Caenegem, *Introduction aux sources de l'histoire médiévale*, L. Jocqué (ed.), Turnhout, Belgium: Brepols, 1997, pp. 219–76; and Bryce Lyon, *The Origins of the Middle Ages*, New York: W. W. Norton, 1972. Van Caenegem offers compendious further reading on the historiography of the Middle Ages, pp. 219–20, n. 1.

8. See Carr, *History*, p. 19.

9. Gilles Deleuze, *Nietzsche and Philosophy*, Hugh Tomlinson (trans.), New York: Columbia University Press, 1983, p. 3. See also G. P. Gooch, *History and Historians in the Nineteenth Century*, 2nd ed., London: Longmans, 1913.

10. Much the same claim was made in 1935 by the English philosopher F. H. Bradley in his *The Presuppositions of Critical History*, Chicago: Quadrangle, 1968. Collingwood calls this work "the Copernican revolution in the theory of historical knowledge," *Idea of History*, p. 240. Carr reasonably objects, "If the historian necessarily looks at his period of history through the eyes of his own time, and studies the problems of the past as a key to those of the present, will he not fall into a purely pragmatic view of the facts, and maintain that the criterion of a right interpretation is its suitability to some present purpose?" (p. 27).

11. Cited in Carr, *History*, p. 21.

12. Marc Bloch, *The Historian's Craft*, New York: Vintage, 1953; and Hayden White, *The Content of the Form*, Baltimore: Johns Hopkins, 1987.

13. For a peerless description, see Leszek Kolakowski, *Main Currents of Marxism*, P. S. Falla (trans.), New York: Norton, 2005. Many of these critiques were combined by Herbert Marcuse, who became an academic celebrity in the United States during the 1960s. Kolakowski writes that "the main point about Marcuse's writing is not that he professes to be a Marxist despite clear evidence to the contrary, but that he seeks to provide a philosophical basis for a tendency already present in our civilization, which aims at destroying that civilization from within for the sake of an apocalypse of the New World Happiness of which, in the nature of things, no description can be given" (p. 1119). The 1950s and 1960s also saw the rise of the New Left in Britain and the US, who in France were known as *gauchistes*, generally "groups who emphasize their opposition to all forms of authority" (p. 1178). See below for a discussion of this notion of negative liberty. For a historical background of the Frankfurt school, especially "the combination of radical beliefs and a bourgeois standard of living," see Martin Jay, *The Dialectical Imagination: A History of the Frankfurt School and the Institute of Social Research, 1923–1950*, Berkeley: University of California, 1973 (quote at p. 36).

14. See David Ingram, *Critical Theory and Philosophy*, New York: Paragon, 1990, p. 13. Max Weber (1864–1920) argued that most people are unaware of the ideology they serve and operate under a false consciousness. It is the business of sociologists to point out that modern culture is "a sphere of covert manipulation, unconsciously programming individuals with uniform and invariant habits of thought" (p. 51).

15. But it is important to note that misconceptions are not the same as fictions. Fictions, as French philosopher Henri Bergson pointed out in 1933, are fundamental to the human condition. See Henri Bergson, *Les Deux Sources de la moral et de la religion*, Paris, 1933, cited in Curtius, following. We are all storytellers. But as reasonable people, we must distinguish as carefully as we can between facts and their effects, and fiction and its effects.

16. A letter of John Keats to his brothers, 21 December 1817; *The Complete Poetical Works and Letters of John Keats*, Boston: Houghton Mifflin, 1899, p. 277.

17. James Simpson distinguishes these as two basic categories of historical transition: "One kind of historical transition aims to destroy and efface the immediate past, while another recognizes historicity. I call the first the revolutionary model, and the second the reformist model," p. 35.

18. In Allen Frantzen, "By the Numbers: Anglo-Saxon Scholarship at the Century's End," in *A Companion to Anglo-Saxon Literature*, Phillip Pulsiano and Elaine Treharne (eds.), Oxford: Blackwell, 2001, pp. 472–95, at p. 472.

19. See Allen Frantzen, "The Work of Work: Servitude, Slavery, and Labor in Medieval England," in Frantzen and Douglas Moffat (eds.), *The Work of Work: Servitude, Slavery, and Labor in Medieval England*, Glasgow: Cruithne Press, 1994, pp. 1–15, p. 5.

20. J. R. R. Tolkien, "*Beowulf*: The Monsters and the Critics," in *An Anthology of Beowulf Criticism*, Lewis Nicholson (ed.), Notre Dame, IN: University of Notre Dame, 1980, pp. 51–103, at pp. 54–5. See, for commentary, Michael Drout, *Beowulf and the Critics*, Tempe, AZ: Arizona Center for Medieval and Renaissance Studies, 2002.

21. Ernst Robert Curtius, *European Literature and the Latin Middle Ages*, Willard R. Trask (trans.), London: Routledge, 1953, p. 13.

22. I rely for much of my understanding of the institutional history of literary study in Britain on Chris Baldick, *The Social Mission of English Criticism*, Oxford: Clarendon Press, 1983.

23. Ralph Waldo Emerson, *Essays by Ralph Waldo Emerson*, New York: Harper & Row, 1926, p. 28.

24. Van Caenegem, *Introduction*, p. 261: "Les divers groupes politiques découvraient certaines institutions ou catégories médiévales qui leur semblaient particulièrement intéressantes." He recommends S. Mellon, *The Political Uses of History: A Study of Historians in the French Restoration*, Stanford, CA: Stanford University, 1958.

25. In Mortimer J. Adler, "History," *The Great Ideas: A Synopticon of Great Books of the Western World*, 2 vols., Chicago: William Benton, 1952, 2:713. See also Bede, *Historia Ecclesiastica gentis Anglorum*, Bertram Colgrave and R. A. B. Mynors (eds.), Oxford: Clarendon, 1969, p. 2: "Siue enim historia de bonus bona referat, ad imitandum bonum auditor sollicitus instigatur." The sentiment is known as the *vera lex historiae*; see Roger Ray, "Bede's *Vera lex historiae*," *Speculum* 55.1, 1980, 1–21. The sentiment is proverbial. Stanley Fish advised academics to shy from public affairs, warning that when a scholar recasts his or her work in the vocabulary of public affairs, he or she risks destroying the discipline of which academic vocabulary is constitutive. See his *Professional Correctness: Literary Studies and Political Change*, Oxford: Clarendon, 1995, p. 85.

26. Peter Heather, *The Fall of the Roman Empire: A New History of Rome and the Barbarians*, Oxford University Press, 2006, p. xiii.

27. Carr, *History*, p. 15.

28. In Carr, *History*, p. 21, n. 1.

29. F. A. Hayek, *The Road to Serfdom*, Chicago: University of Chicago, 1944, p. 1.

30. With specific reference to the Middle Ages, see Lyon, *Origins*, pp. 48–54.

31. See Patrick Gardener, "History of the Philosophy of History," *The Oxford Companion to Philosophy*, Ted Honderich (ed.), Oxford: Oxford University Press, 1995, pp. 360–4, p. 362. An intriguing development in this area of

historiography is by Michael Bentley, "Past and 'Presence': Revisiting Historical Ontology," *History and Theory* 45, 2006, 349–61.

32. Gardener, "History," p. 363. Note that Collingwood says *intelligible*, not rational. It is not always the case that people act rationally in their own best interests. Barbara Tuchman record dozens of famous instances when foolishness, or folly, seems to have motivated events; see her *The March of Folly: From Troy to Vietnam*, London: Abacus, 1985.

33. Lyon, *Origins*, p. 17. What follows in this paragraph owes a great deal to Lyon's useful overview of historiography. I am also indebted to van Caenegem, *Introduction*, pp. 219–76. For an illustrative study of German historiography during the Renaissance, see Frank L. Borchardt, *German Antiquity in Renaissance Myth*, Baltimore: Johns Hopkins University, 1971; and illustrative of English historiography, Samuel Kliger, *The Goths in England: A Study in Seventeenth and Eighteenth Century Thought*, Cambridge, MA: Harvard University, 1952.

34. A. G. Rigg, *A History of Anglo-Latin Literature, 1066–1422*, Cambridge: Cambridge University, 1992. See also Whitney F. Bolton, *A History of Anglo-Latin Literature, 597–1066*, Princeton, NJ: Princeton University, 1967; F. J. E. Raby, *A History of Christian-Latin Poetry from the Beginnings to the Close of the Middle Ages*, Oxford: Clarendon, 1927; Raby, *A History of Secular Latin Poetry in the Middle Ages*, Oxford: Clarendon, 1934; and Max Manitius, *Geschichte der lateinischen Literatur des Mittelalters*, 3 vols., München: Beck, 1923–59.

35. Rigg, *Anglo-Latin Literature*, p. 4.

36. Text in *Patrologia Latina*, J.-P. Migne (ed.), 210:579. Conveniently collected with more medieval Latin verse and translated into German by Paul Klopsch, *Lateinische Lyrik des Mittelalters*, Stuttgart: Reclam, 1985, pp. 302–3.

37. Van Caenegem, *Introduction*, p. 229. What follows in this paragraph is an abridgment of van Caenegem.

38. Paul Christianson, "Selden, John (1584–1654)," in *Oxford Dictionary of National Biography*, Oxford University, 2004. For a history of nineteenth-century British medievalists, see Michael Lapidge (ed.), *Interpreters of Early Medieval Britain*, Oxford: Oxford University, 2002.

39. Both are from authorized Web sites of Harvard and Yale. The first is taken from Alvin Powell of the *Harvard News* (6/8/04), "Summers advises a reasoned life in Baccalaureate"; the second, an address of 23 May 2004, is recorded at Yale's Office of Public Affairs. Yale's systemic deviation from the expressed aims of its college mission statement and the prized virtues of American federalism is famously taken to task by William F. Buckley, Jr., *God and Man at Yale: The Superstitions of "Academic Freedom,"* Chicago: Henry Regoery, 1951.

40. Frits van Oostrom, "Spatial Struggles: Medieval Studies between Nationalism and Globalization," *Journal of English and Germanic Philology* 105, 2006, 5–24, at 8.

41. Stephen G. Nichols, "Writing the New Middle Ages, *PMLA* 120.2, 2005, 422–41, at 422. See by comparison *The State of Medieval Studies*, a volume of the *Journal of English and Germanic Philology* 105, 2006; Roger Dahood (ed.), *The Future of the Middle Ages and the Renaissance*, Turnhout: Brepols, 1998; Lester K. Little and Barbara Rosenwein (eds.), *Debating the Middle Ages*, Oxford: Blackwell, 1998; and Matthews, *Making of Middle English*. Little and Rosenwein collect some of the more influential recent essays in the history of the Middle Ages and provide excellent introductions and bibliographies. Overviews of medieval subject areas such as the body and soul, feudalism, heresy, Islam, the individual, nature, nobility, sexuality, and symbolism

are given in the very useful *Dictionnaire Raisonné de l'occident médievale,* Jacques Le Goff and Jean-Claude Schmitt (eds.), Paris: Fayard, 1999.

42. Martin Aurell, "Medieval Studies in France at the Threshold: 2000," *JEGP* 105, 2006, 156–69, at 160.

43. Van Oostrom, "Spatial Struggles," p. 8.

44. Eric Wolf, "Inventing Society," *American Ethnologist* 15:4, 1988, 752–61. See also Anthony Smith, *The Ethnic Origins of Nations,* Oxford: Blackwell, 1986; Reinhard Wenskus, *Stammesbildung und Verfassung: Das Werden der frühmittelalterlichen Gentes,* Köln, Germany: Böhlau, 1961; Patrick Geary, *Before France and Germany,* Oxford: Oxford University, 1988; and Geary, *The Myth of Nations: The Medieval Origins of Europe,* Princeton, NJ: Princeton University, 2002. For a model study, see Walter Pohl, *Die Germanen,* München: Oldenbourg, 2000.

45. Van Oostrom, "Spatial Struggles," p. 9, regrets that English and American scholars read so little of the remarkable scholarship available in other languages. One need only peruse the bibliographies of *The Year's Work in English Studies,* or similar bibliographies, to note a paucity, if not utter absence, of works in German, French, Spanish, or Italian.

46. Isaiah Berlin, *Four Essays on Liberty,* London: Oxford University, 1969; see also Charles Taylor, *Philosophy and the Human Sciences: Philosophical Papers 2,* Cambridge University, 1985, p. 213; and *Isaiah Berlin: A Celebration,* Edna and Avishai Margalit (eds.), Chicago: University of Chicago, 1991, p. 82.

47. In Carr, *History,* p. 115.

48. Nichols writes approvingly that nuns who broke with the expectations of their religious houses, or houses that broke with monastic tradition, were "female religious institutions at their best," p. 429. This judgment flies in the face of medieval expectations that religious houses that were regulated in their behavior (literally, that followed *regulae,* or rules) were religious institutions at their best. See, for example, Dom David Knowles, *The Monastic Order in England: A History of Its Development from the Times of St Dunstan to the Fourth Lateran Council, 943–1216,* Cambridge: Cambridge University, 1949, p. 4: a monastic community "has no function in the life of the Church save to provide an ordered way of life based on the teaching of the gospel, according to which its inmates may serve God and sanctify their souls apart from the life of the world."

I
The Church

1 Was the Medieval Church Corrupt?[1]

Frans van Liere

In the popular imagination, the medieval church was populated by fat monks given to luxurious living, sinister popes who sought to control a superstitious laity by keeping them ignorant of the true tenets of Christianity, and a corrupted clergy who enriched themselves by exacting tithes from impoverished peasants and extorting indulgence money from misguided believers. The medieval church is often depicted as an authoritarian institution in which dissent or criticism was quickly squelched by the powerful arm of the Holy Inquisition, which burned innocent people at the stake for criticizing the wayward lives of the clergy or for the simple act of reading the Bible. All this may seem a caricature, but it is a pervasive one. Consider, for example, a description of the medieval church from William Manchester's *A World Lit Only by Fire*: "[T]he Church became the wealthiest landowner on the Continent, and the life of every European, from baptism through matrimony to burial, was governed by popes, cardinals, prelates, monsignors, archbishops, bishops, and village priests." While, according to Manchester, "reliable reports of misconduct by priests, nuns, and prelates, much of it squalid, were rising," the medieval Church still "found its greatest strength in total resistance to change."[2]

The notion that the medieval church was corrupt is, of course, a gross generalization, and for this very reason evidence can always be found to support it. But generalizations of this type resist historical assessment and tell us very little about historical reality. To come to a more accurate and honest assessment of the medieval church, we have to ask ourselves, firstly, who, or what, was the "Church"? Was it the papacy, the clergy, or the laity? Were the actions of Innocent IV, one of the most worldly popes of the thirteenth century, somehow more representative of the "medieval church" than those of Bernard of Clairvaux, the great twelfth-century monastic reformer? And secondly, what exactly do we mean by "medieval"? The Middle Ages span one thousand years of Church history. The power and influence that early medieval popes had over the church, for instance, differed greatly from that of later medieval popes. To represent "the medieval church" as a corrupt institution is to lump one thousand years of church history together without due regard for historical development.

More serious investigation of the thousand years that comprise the Middle Ages reveals that between 500 and 1500, Christianity established itself firmly in European culture and displayed a great vitality and creativity, diversification of religious ideals, creative experimentation in the realm of political power and theory, and a resurgence of lay piety. The popular image of stagnation, of a "thousand years of uncertainty,"[3] is misplaced. In fact, Christianity experienced a transformation that makes it almost impossible to speak of "the medieval church" as if it were a unified entity. This diversity of the medieval church is not only diachronic but also synchronic. There was a rich variety of religious experiences, depending on the differences between social classes and estates, between clergy and laity, between the various monastic orders, and between monks and mendicants. The purpose of the present chapter is not to demonstrate whether or not the medieval church was corrupt (for there is no doubt that in many ways it was) but to argue that the medieval church defies easy generalization, and that "corruption" is not a constructive concept when interpreting medieval church history or medieval religion.

The notion of a corrupt medieval church has it roots in the Protestant historiographical tradition of the sixteenth and seventeenth centuries, represented by works such as the *Magdeburg Centuries* of Matthias Flacius Illyricus and the *Book of Martyrs* by John Foxe.[4] These polemical histories posited a corrupted Church of Rome as an antithesis to the uncorrupted New Testament Church, and they credited Luther's Reformation with bringing back the church to its original uncorrupted state. For Flacius Illyricus and Fox, the true church, the church of the martyrs, proved its veracity by being persecuted. They saw in the adversaries of the popes and in most medieval heresies manifestations of this true church, a proto-Protestant movement, which eventually culminated in Luther's Reformation. In doing so, they created a false dichotomy in the Middle Ages between the corrupted, "official" ecclesiastical hierarchy of the Church of Rome and the true believers, who were persecuted by the Church of Rome, just as the early Christians were persecuted by the Roman Empire. As we will see next, this historical interpretation was problematic at best, and it was very much determined by the situation in which Protestants found themselves in the fifteenth and sixteenth centuries. Their interpretation of the early church was highly idealized and that of the medieval church was heavily anachronistic. While the historical context has changed and very few people still subscribe to the theological model underlying the works of these Protestant historiographers, the influence of this type of historiography persists in popular imagination.

One example of how Foxe's anachronistic interpretation of the history of the medieval church led him to dubious interpretations of medieval church history is his description of the crusade against the Cathars, or Albigensians, which lasted from 1209 to 1229. Foxe listed this episode as an example of one of the many persecutions of "people of the reformed religion"[5] by a corrupted papacy. By the beginning of the thirteenth century, the Cathar church had become a widespread popular movement in southern France, where its popularity was often fueled by resentment against the northern clergy and nobility. The austere asceticism of the Cathar preachers persuaded many that they represented the "true" church, and the bishop of Toulouse, who presided over a bishopric too large to be governed effectively, proved unable to stem the spread of this heresy. In 1209, after some Cathars murdered a papal legate, the Pope called for a crusade, and the king of France took this opportunity to subjugate the rebellious south. This Crusade amounted to cultural genocide, sanctioned by the church, and the struggle against the Albigensians would eventually lead to the establishment of the medieval Inquisition. It was by no means the medieval church's finest hour. But Foxe's characterization of the Cathars as followers of the "reformed religion" is quite misleading. Cathar belief combined a stark asceticism for its leaders with moral libertinism for its followers, and held to a dualism reminiscent of early Christian Gnosticism. To equate these doctrines with the Protestant movement of Luther and the later reformers seems questionable at best.[6]

Protestant polemicists used the medieval Inquisition to give the "corrupted" medieval church a distinctly sinister character. Even today, the Inquisition still evokes an image of horror and relentless persecution. Nineteenth-century studies by Protestant scholars such as Henry Charles Lea, while based on substantial archival research, perpetuated this almost mythical image of the medieval Inquisition.[7] But this image of the medieval Inquisition actually owes more to the situation in the Roman and Spanish Inquisitions of the sixteenth and seventeenth centuries than to the Middle Ages. The perception of the Spanish Inquisition, undoubtedly influenced by the infamous "black legend," belongs to early-modern, not medieval, history. One should point out that the Spanish Inquisition, established in 1480 as an independent organization responsible only to the Spanish crown, was quite different from its medieval predecessors. The medieval Inquisition was an initiative of Innocent III (1198–1215), who sought to remedy some of the legal conundrums that the persecution of heresy presented for the medieval ecclesiastical courts. Unlike modern courts, medieval courts did not have the power of prosecution; crimes and misdemeanors could only be brought into court by presentment, that is, if someone demanded reparation for a past crime. Obviously, this did not work very well for tracing and correcting heresy, which had become a matter of concern for the church in the thirteenth century. In 1215, the Fourth Lateran Council referred heresy to episcopal courts and admonished the bishops to hold visitations (called "inquisitions," or inquests) to elicit testimonies from parishioners, to see if any of the flock had strayed from Catholic doctrine. The medieval Inquisition was thus mainly an information-gathering hearing, in which, however, witnesses could become the accused. Those persisting in doctrinal error after correction were handed over to secular authorities for further punishment. Some procedures of the medieval Inquisition were decidedly unfair from our modern perspective (not to mention that torture was seen as a legitimate way to elicit confessions, which was an accepted notion in medieval secular courts as well). The rights of the accused, for instance, were not always clearly spelled out, nor was it clear whether the person interrogated was a witness or a suspect, and the court was sometimes intentionally vague about the character of the accusation, which made it almost impossible to defend oneself. These measures were intended to prevent heretics from intentionally concealing their beliefs; heretics usually did not feel bound to speak the truth and denied the validity of oath taking, so they had to be "trapped" into confessing to their heresy.[8] Aiding the bishop in his task were papal judge delegates, who were often mendicants (Franciscans or Dominicans). In special cases, these "inquisitors" were given a certain measure of autonomy and were made responsible only to the Pope. There was never a permanently established "Inquisition" in the Middle Ages; there were only inquisitors.[9] The image of the medieval Inquisition as a sinister organization is an unfortunate anachronism.

That the historiographical model of the Protestant polemicists cannot withstand critical historical analysis also becomes clear when examining, for instance, the residence of the popes in Avignon (1305–78), which is often used as an example of the degeneration of the medieval papacy and the corruption of the medieval church. The Avignon papacy probably owes its bad name to Petrarch (1304–74), who called Avignon the "Babylon of the West." This theme was picked up by Luther, who called the Avignon period the "Babylonian captivity of the papacy."[10] Umberto Eco's novel *The Name of the Rose* popularized the notion that papal corruption and luxury reached it apex in this period. In the fourteenth century, however, the fact that the popes had departed from Rome and taken up residence elsewhere was not really seen as a problem. In fact, medieval popes rarely resided in Rome. The idea of Rome as the inalienable turf of the representative of Saint Peter is of more recent date, and, as is often the case, later ideals may have been projected onto a nonexistent medieval reality. Medieval canon lawyers were clear on the matter: "Where the Pope is, there is Rome."[11] Was the Avignon papacy corrupt? In some ways, yes. The problems the papacy faced in this period were manifold, and not all of them were adequately addressed. It is true, for instance, that the Avignon popes were inclined to nepotism, but one might see this as an attempt of the popes to build a reliable *curia* in a period when the increased political prestige of the papacy led to undesirable party struggles between French and Italian cardinals. The Avignon papacy had persistent financial troubles, which the popes tried to meet by creating novel means of taxation. This gave them a bad name, but it did not mean that the popes were living in luxury.[12]

The myth of the luxury of the papal court in Avignon probably resulted from the persistent and ongoing controversy between the popes and the Franciscan order on the subject of the poverty of Christ, an outgrowth of the failed attempt by John XXII (1316–34) to reform the Franciscan order's finances in 1323. For the Franciscans to maintain a state of absolute poverty, which they said was necessary to follow Christ and lead a life of evangelical perfection, their property was officially owned by the Holy See. But in 1323, John XXII returned the ownership of these goods to the order, with the argument that absolute poverty was not essential to the life of evangelical perfection, since Christ had had ownership over temporal goods while he lived on earth. In the long run, the discussion that ensued was to have widespread ramifications for political discussions about the secular power of the papacy. Some Franciscans saw the Pope's position as an attack on one of the founding principles of their order. They started a diatribe against the Pope, in which the accusation of luxury was a persistent theme. Not surprisingly, this theme was eagerly picked up later by Protestant polemicists for their own ideological reasons. But modern students of the papacy should be careful not to take this polemical literature at face value.[13]

The Avignon popes were generally able popes, most of whom were dedicated to the reform and abolition of clerical abuses. John XXII was intent on reforming church administration and sanitizing church finances, which were in a disastrous state after the rule of his predecessor, Clement V. His successor, Benedict XI (1334–42), was a stern ascetic, dedicated to ending nepotism, corruption, and malpractice among the clergy. He reduced the papal bureaucracy and the distribution of benefices and tried to ensure that benefices were only given to clergy of good repute. He greatly reduced the number of clergy residing in Avignon. The beneficial effect of most of these measures was, however, undone by the largesse of his spendthrift successor, Clement VI (1342–52). One of the unwanted effects of the reform policy of the Avignon popes was, however, an ever-increasing centralization and bureaucratization of church leadership. This, in turn, gave cardinals an opportunity to use their position to gain favors for friends and relations, which made them susceptible to bribery. Still, even one of the harshest critics of the papal court in the late fourteenth century, Nicholas de Clamanges, admitted that the corruption at the papal court was nothing compared to the corruption in some of the secular courts of the time, like those of France and Burgundy.[14]

Another instance that has often been cited to show the corruption of the medieval church is the Western Schism (1378–1417). Although this was only a brief interlude in the long period that the Middle Ages span, and although it was certainly not the first time there had been two (or even more) popes in Western Christendom, this episode certainly did damage the notion of papal monarchy, the idea that the bishop of Rome ruled in monarchical fashion over the secular and spiritual affairs of a unified Christendom. This papal monarchy had started in the eleventh century, with popes such as Leo IX (1049–54) and Gregory VII (1073–85). Upon the death of Gregory XI (1370–78), who had brought back the papacy from Avignon to Rome, the cardinals were divided into Italian and French factions. Under pressure from riotous crowds in Rome, Urban VI was elected while many French cardinals remained in Avignon. The Italian Urban VI, not exactly a tactful personality, insulted and threatened the French cardinals, who eventually decided that the election had been made under pressure and was not valid. They elected another Pope, Clement VII, who took up residency Avignon. While earlier schisms had often been caused by conflicts about who could elect a Pope, the cardinals or the emperor, never before had there been a choice between two legitimately elected pontiffs, who had equal claim to be the one head of a unified Christendom.

While this schism did much damage to the reputation of the church and the papacy (most of Europe's countries now divided their allegiance along political lines), it was also the direct cause of the growth of conciliarism, the notion that not the Pope but all bishops in council together are qualified to make canonical decisions. The resulting general councils, of Pisa (1409–11), Constance (1414–17) and Basel (1431–39), would fundamentally alter the way people thought about ecclesiastical authority and church government. In this way, the theory of conciliarism had a profound impact on the later Protestant Reformation, with its idea of the "priesthood of all believers." But to see the schismatic popes as representatives of the "medieval Church" and the conciliarist movement as a "proto-Reformation" is a historical fallacy. Both are equally representative of the "medieval" Church.[15]

All this is not to deny the reality of clerical abuses during the later Middle Ages. One issue justly addressed by the Protestant reformers was the traffic in indulgences. An indulgence is "the remission of the temporal penalty due to forgiven sin, in virtue of the merits of Christ and the saints."[16] The granting of indulgences, a practice that became generally accepted with the first Crusade and grew considerably during the later Middle Ages, had fallen victim to commercial exploitation; professional pardoners sold indulgences on a large scale. The practice of Luther's adversary Tetzel went far beyond the legal and doctrinal limits the official church had set, even though it was encouraged by the financial policy of Renaissance popes like Julius II and Leo X, whose patronage of the arts left them in dire want of cash. The commercial trafficking in indulgences was eventually prohibited by Pius V in 1567. The late medieval malversations with ecclesiastical benefices (the monetary stipend connected with church offices) might be considered another such abuse. In the fourteenth century, when the papal administration grew explosively and the papacy did not collect enough revenues to pay for this growth, local revenues were increasingly used to fund clerics at higher levels of papal administration. For example, while a cleric might receive an income from his position as Bishop of Armagh in Ireland, in practice he could be employed as administrator at the papal court in Avignon. This practice made it lucrative for clerics to accumulate ecclesiastical functions and collect revenues, while their offices did not require them to be present or to minister to the souls in their domain. The result was a misuse of ecclesiastical funds and an increasing absenteeism of the clergy, as Luther was certainly not the first to point out.

But Luther's main point of difference with the church of his time was theological, not practical. He not only objected to the commercial exploitation of indulgences, but he also denied the role of the Pope as the treasurer of the merits of Christ and the saints. The main question was not how to abolish clerical abuses, but rather, "How does Man partake in God's salvation?" Many of the abuses Luther fulminated against were abolished some fifty years later by the Catholic Church at the Council of Trent (1545–63), but this did not reconcile the Protestant and Catholic churches. Luther's Reformation was more than just the righting of a number of abuses and corruption; it brought a new type of theology and spirituality, which, however, in its emphasis on the centrality of Christ's passion and its insistence on the primacy of biblical doctrine, did have roots in the medieval church.[17]

Luther and his contemporaries were not the first to bring up the theme of "reform." In medieval monastic and theological sources, corruption and the wealth and luxury of monastic orders was almost a *topos*, and it is probably this literature that gave us the image of the worldly monk. One should keep in mind that these texts may not give a historically accurate representation of the state of church affairs in their own time; they are colored by what Giles Constable calls the "rhetoric of reform."[18] The call for reform in Christianity is as old as the New Testament itself (Romans 12.2). Many polemical monastic treatises depicted their opponents' lives in the blackest possible terms, as filled with luxury, worldliness, and corruption, in order to establish a *raison d'être* for their renovation of the old monastic ideal. This hardly reflects a realistic representation of the state of affairs in the church; it is, rather, a call to internalize religion and to convert. This call to reform, a constant reapplication of old Christian ideals to new situations, is in fact typical of the spirit of medieval Christianity, rather than a dissenting voice within it.

How, then, can we generalize about the history of the medieval church? Instead of a model that juxtaposes a "corrupt" church with a "true" church, I would propose a model that is dynamic, in that it takes the historical development of the medieval church seriously, and that is inclusive, in that it defines the church as including clergy and laity, leaders and dissenters, men and women. This model would allow for the ambivalence of historical evidence, rather than apply black-and-white models of interpretation. Was the medieval church corrupt? No doubt there was corruption in the medieval church, as there is wherever humans come into the temptation to abuse power for their own gain. The medieval church was not the only such place, and the abuse of religion to extort money is by no means unique to the Middle Ages. But the overall impression of vitality and diversity that characterized the medieval church does not justify the characterization of the medieval church as a corrupt body. To call the abuses that occurred during the Middle Ages "typical of the medieval church," while depicting its critics and reformers as "ahead of their time," is a historical fallacy. To better understand the medieval church, we must reclaim church history from the polemical tradition of sixteenth-century Protestant historiography, without, of course, falling into the triumphalist view of their Catholic opponents. We need to interpret the medieval church on its own terms. The medieval church was a place where corruption went hand in hand with reform, and where good and bad were mixed together, as they were (and are) in the church throughout all ages.

SUGGESTIONS FOR FURTHER READING

Arnold Angenendt, *Geschichte der Religiosität im Mittelalter,* Darmstadt: Wissenschaftliche Buchgesellschaft, 1997.

Marshall W. Baldwin, *The Medieval Church* (The Development of Western Civilization), Ithaca: Cornell University, 1953.

Geoffrey Barraclough, *The Medieval Papacy* (History of European Civilization Library), New York: Harcourt Brace and World, 1968.

Rosalind B. Brooke and Christopher N.L. Brooke, *Popular Religion in the Middle Ages: Western Europe, 1000–1300,* London: Thames and Hudson, 1984.

Giles Constable, *The Reformation of the Twelfth Century,* Cambridge: Cambridge University, 1996.

Gerhardt B. Ladner, *The Idea of Reform: Its Impact on Christian Thought and Action in the Age of the Fathers,* Cambridge: Harvard University, 1959.

Bernard McGinn, John Meyendorff, and Jean Leclercq (eds.), *Christian Spirituality* (World Spirituality: An Encyclopedic History of the Religious Quest, 16–17), New York: Crossroad, 1996–97.

Guillaume Mollat, *The Popes at Avignon 1305–1378,* trans. Janet Love, London: Nelson, 1963.

Francis Oakley, *The Western Church in the Later Middle Ages,* Ithaca and London: Cornell University, 1979.

Edward Peters, *Inquisition,* Berkeley and Los Angeles: University of California Press, 1989.

Richard Southern, *Western Society and the Church in the Middle Ages* (The Penguin History of the Church, 2), Harmondsworth, UK: Penguin, 1970.

NOTES

1. I wish to thank my wife, Katherine Elliot van Liere, for her constructive feedback on this chapter and her thorough revision of the English text.
2. William Manchester, *A World Lit Only by Fire: The Medieval Mind and the Renaissance,* Boston and Toronto: Little, Brown, 1992, pp. 11, 20, and 25.
3. Kenneth S. Latourette, *A History of the Expansion of Christianity, vol. 2: The Thousand Years of Uncertainty, A.D. 500–A.D. 1500,* London: Harper, 1938.
4. Various editions: Matthias Flacius Illyricus and others, *Ecclesiastica Historia . . . per Aliquot Studiosos et Pios Uiros in Urbe Magdeburgina Conscripta,* Basel: I. Opinorum, 1560–1574; and John Foxe, *Actes and Monuments of Matters most Special and Memorable,* London: John Day, 1583. The latter is still in print, in an abridged form: *Fox's Book of Martyrs,* ed. William B. Forbush, Grand Rapids: Zondervan, 1967.
5. Forbush, *Fox's Book of Martyrs,* p. 45.

6. A good historical analysis is given by Jonathan Sumption, *The Albigensian Crusade*, London and Boston: Faber, 1978.

7. Henry Charles Lea, *A History of the Inquisition of the Middle Ages*, New York: Harper and Bros., 1888.

8. For a good description of inquisitorial proceedings, read Bernard Gui, *Manuel de l'inquisiteur*, Guillaume Mollat (ed. and trans.), Paris: Les Belles Lettres, 1964. This same Bernard Gui figured prominently as a character in Umberto Eco's novel *The Name of the Rose*, Orlando: Harcourt Brace, 1983.

9. For an excellent introduction to the medieval inquisition, see Edward Peters, *Inquisition*, Berkeley and Los Angeles: University of California, 1989.

10. *Petrarch's Book without a Name: A Translation of the Liber Sine Nomine*, Norman Zacour (trans.), Toronto: Pontifical Institute for Medieval Studies, 1973; and Martin Luther, *Three Treatises*, Charles M. Jacobs (trans.), Philadelphia: Muhlenberg, 1947.

11. See Michele Maccarone, "Ubi papa, ibi Roma," in Hubert Mordek (ed.), *Aus Kirche und Reich. Studien zu Theologie, Politik und Recht im Mittelalter: Festschrift für Friedrich Kempf zu seinem fünfundsiebzigsten Geburtstag und fünfzigjährigen Doktorjubiläum*, Sigmaringen: Thorbecke, 1983, pp. 371–82.

12. Guillaume Mollat, "Jean XII, fut-il un avare?" *Revue d'histoire ecclesiastique* 5, 1904, 522–34, and 6, 1905, 34–45.

13. For a good, brief introduction to the topic, see Malcolm David Lambert, "The Franciscan Crisis under John XXII," *Franciscan Studies* 32, 1972, 123–43.

14. Ezio Ornato, *Jean Muret et ses amis Nicolas de Clamanges et Jean de Montreuil*, Geneva and Paris: Droz, 1969, p. 58. Clamanges wrote a devastating criticism of the Avignon papal court and *plaidoyer* for a more conciliar church around 1400: *Le Traité de la ruine de l'eglise de Nicolas de Clamanges*, Alfred Coville (trans.), Paris: Droz, 1936, pp. 111–56.

15. For a good historical overview, see Francis Oakley, *The Western Church in the Later Middle Ages*, Ithaca, NY, and London: Cornell University, 1979.

16. "Indulgences," in F. L. Cross and E. A. Livingstone, *Oxford Dictionary of the Christian Church*, Oxford: Oxford University, 1974, p. 700. See also Nikolaus Paulus, *Geschichte des Ablasses im Mittelalter. Vom Ursprunge bis zur Mitte des 14. Jahrhunderts*, Paderborn: Schoeningh, 1922–3; and Robert W. Shaffern, *The Penitents' Treasury: Indulgences in Latin Christendom, 1175–1375*, Scranton, PA: University of Scranton, 2007.

17. On the Reformation in its medieval context, see Heiko A. Oberman, *The Dawn of the Reformation: Essays in Late Medieval and Early Reformation Thought*, Edinburgh: T&T Clark, 1986. See also Oberman, *Luther, Mensch zwischen Gott und Teufel*, Berlin: Severin und Siedler, 1982.

18. Giles Constable, *The Reformation of the Twelfth Century*, Cambridge: Cambridge University, 1996, p. 125.

2   Papal Infallibility

Elaine M. Beretz

The doctrine of papal infallibility, that most emphatic claim of the Pope's authority, divides Christianity. It separates Roman Catholics from Protestants of all sorts and from adherents to Eastern Orthodoxy. Perhaps more importantly, it pits Catholic against Catholic. Whenever we introduce the papacy into a course about the Middle Ages, we risk drawing on this factionalism. Consciously or unconsciously, we might interject our personal preconceptions about papal power, or communicate those in the texts we consult.

This chapter will not rehearse all the controversies about papal infallibility and certainly will not participate in them. Its very selective bibliography does not begin to represent the vast and extremely contentious literature on the subject. The purpose of this chapter is much more modest: to pinpoint some of the common misconceptions about infallibility that obscure historical developments within the papal office and thus result in a misleading view of papal power as medieval people would have defined or experienced it.

MISCONCEPTION 1: THE POPE HIMSELF AND HIS EVERY DECREE IS INFALLIBLE

The first official definition of papal infallibility, made at Vatican Council I (1869–70), came very late in the history of Catholicism. It reads as follows:

> When the Roman Pontiff speaks *ex cathedra*, that is, when he performs the duty of pastor and teacher of all Christians, in accordance with his supreme apostolic authority, he defines doctrine concerning faith and morals that the Universal Church ought to hold. Through the divine assistance promised to him in blessed Peter, he possesses in abundance that infallibility with which the Divine Redeemer wished his church to be furnished for defining doctrine concerning faith and morals. And so, therefore, such definitions of the Roman Pontiff

are irreformable in and of themselves, not from the consent of the Church.[1]

This decree synthesized a long tradition of defining papal power. At the same time, each of its assertions masked ancient tensions within the institution and still spark heated debate.[2]

For all the lofty posturing of those formulating it, the doctrine of infallibility is actually a very limited power. Since it resides in the papal office, not in the individual holding it, the Pope's own theological views and his personal insights remain fallible. Even the strongest expressions of infallibility do not claim that the Pope himself is all-knowing or unable to err. Further, infallibility does not apply to each and every papal pronouncement. The only infallible doctrines are "irreformable"; that is, the Pope's successors cannot change them and the doctrines themselves cannot alter previous teaching. Only two doctrines to date, both Marian, have met those criteria: the Immaculate Conception (1854, and thus predating Vatican I) and the Assumption (1950).

The doctrine of infallibility assumes an importance in Catholic ecclesiology that far outweighs its limited administrative applicability. The ecclesiology in general, as its specific expression in infallibility, embodies Neoplatonic philosophy. According to that vision, the church as Christ founded it is a Platonic ideal: residing with God in heaven, perfect from all eternity, and unchanging. The Ideal Church, therefore, participates in the lack of error characteristic of all heavenly things. By contrast, the church on earth, rooted in time and the imperfect world, changes and is capable of error. Nonetheless, the earthly church distantly reflects its prototype in the Ideal Church. The agency of its divine founder and the means of grace he established allow the earthly church to participate—partially and imperfectly—in heavenly inerrancy. The papal office, as one mediator between the heavenly and the earthly church, in that way acquires a measure, limited as it is, of divine infallibility.

Protestant scholars have long disparaged the idea of papal infallibility by pointing to the corruption of the medieval church and the personal failings of the popes. Some Catholic scholars have responded by locating the roots of papal infallibility in Christ's earthly mission, all too often equating the Ideal Church with the bureaucratic structures of the earthly church. Both positions focus on the dogmatic aspects of infallibility: on the Ideal Church and the way the divine is revealed through it. In the process, both tend to ignore historical development within the papal office.

By contrast, historians focus on human interpretation of the ideal in a particular time and place.[3] Historians seek to understand the policies and actions of the popes as contemporaneous political and social circumstances shaped them. Those circumstances often have thwarted attempts to translate theories of papal power into disciplinary and doctrinal practice.[4] Historians also focus on the ways in which the popes shaped the world around them. This involves tracing the development of a centralized administration and the evolution of canon law as two means of implementing papal policy. But canon law and an effective bureaucracy evolved only after the late eleventh century. Even then, the popes asserted themselves very slowly and unevenly among the other power structures in medieval society.

MISCONCEPTION 2: INFALLIBILITY IS THE SAME AS PRIMACY

Over the past century, the doctrine of papal infallibility has become intertwined with claims to papal primacy. But the two are distinct in important ways. Infallibility concerns the Pope's pivotal relationship to the Ideal Church; primacy describes his place in the hierarchical structure of the earthly church. The theoretical foundation of primacy rests in the tradition that the apostle Peter established the papacy and that all the popes inherited the authority Christ granted to this "prince of the apostles" (Matthew 16:18–9). From an early period, the popes used this and other biblical passages to claim supreme governing authority in the universal church. Initially, they did so to counter competing claims by other apostolic sees, especially those in the Greek-speaking part of the old Roman Empire. Papal claims to primacy were a key factor in the split, not yet healed, between Roman Catholicism and Eastern Orthodoxy.

The concept of papal primacy distills an idealized dynamics of power within a hierarchical institution. Teamed with the notion of papal infallibility, primacy is often misunderstood as the expression of an earthly monarchy under an absolute, even deified, ruler. When projected back into the Middle Ages, it feeds the stereotype of the church as a monolithic monster exercising control over the minds and pocketbooks of everyone in Europe. The articles by Profs. Bird and van Liere in this collection concisely redress this stereotype.

The reality was quite different. Throughout the Middle Ages, the papacy was often weak and unstable, prey to political pressures in Italy and marginal to the rest of Europe. Even more significantly, every assertion of papal power met an equal and opposite response from within the church itself. The strongest (although, by no means, the only) resistance has come from bishops and from ecclesiastical councils.

MISCONCEPTION 3: INFALLIBILITY IS THE POLICY OF AN ABSOLUTE MONARCHY

Episcopal resistance to a papal monarchy derives from the belief that each bishop owes his office directly to God. In this view, church authority is the collective responsibility of bishops. The Pope, as Bishop of Rome, is merely a "first among equals." The feudal lordship of most European bishops during the Middle Ages strongly reinforced this belief. Episcopalism, as Kenneth Pennington has termed it, is every bit as old a claim as papal primacy.[5] Both draw on canon law—often on the same laws—to support their positions. A strong, independent episcopacy has never fit neatly, if at all, into a papalist blueprint.

Conciliarism shares an ancient heritage, and many basic tenets, with episcopalism. But ecclesiastical councils challenge papalism much more explicitly than do bishops. The theory of conciliarism, in fact, evolved during the thirteenth and fourteenth centuries as a hedge against the expanding papal administration. In its strictest construction, conciliarism argues that ecclesiastical councils constitute the highest authority in the church. According to this view, councils are superior to the Pope and able to override his directives. The Great Schism (1378–1417) gave the movement a historical urgency. The movement achieved its epitome in the Council of Constance (1414–8), which resolved the schism, and in the Council of Basel (1431–49), which dealt with the ensuing crisis. The basic arguments of conciliarism, as they were articulated then, still emerge forcefully during periods of crisis in the Catholic Church, especially when the decrees of ecclesiastical councils are at odds with papal pronouncements.

Not surprisingly, episcopalism and conciliarism fuel the most consistent Catholic opposition to the doctrine of infallibility. Many of the bishops assembled at Vatican I objected to defining papal infallibility at all. Drawing on medieval conciliar theory, they argued that the church as a whole needed to ratify papal decisions before they became "doctrines concerning faith and morals that the Universal Church ought to hold." The final phrase of the council's definition—that infallible doctrines are "irreformable in and of themselves, not from the consent of the Church"—sought to silence that protest. The attempt failed. Efforts since Vatican I to refine the doctrine, to implement it as institutional policy, or to analyze possible precedents in church history have only generated more controversy.

Modern tensions within Catholicism continue those that shaped the medieval church. Factions advocating a monarchic structure are repeatedly at odds with those seeking a more inclusive model of authority. The long history of these tensions acts as a corrective to theoretical posturing, from whatever quarter, that equates papal infallibility with totalitarianism. Social conditions and political events have defined the papacy, as much as the papacy has shaped the world around it. Sharply opposing notions of ecclesiastical authority have continually circumscribed the papal office, as have the many obstacles to translating theological verity into earthly policy. Each Pope perpetuates the tradition of Peter and is charged with mediating between the Ideal Church and the earthly. But every Pope remains a human being, who (as all other Christians) is "at one and the same time righteous and a sinner [*simul justus et peccator*]."[6]

However lofty the theory of papal authority, it has always had to accommodate a humbling reality.

SUGGESTIONS FOR FURTHER READING

Short Treatments

Thumbnail sketches: "Church, Theology of," "Ecclesiology," and "Infallibility" in *New Catholic Encyclopedia*, New York: McGraw-Hill, 1967; "Conciliar Theory" and "Papacy, Origins and Developments of," in J. R. Strayer et al. (eds.), *Dictionary of the Middle Ages*, New York: Scribner, 1982–9; "Infallibility" and "Primacy, Papal," in R. P. McBrien (ed.), *The HarperCollins Encyclopedia of Catholicism*, San Francisco: HarperCollins, 1995.

Short essays (from various perspectives): W. Ullmann, *The Relevance of Medieval Ecclesiastical History: An Inaugural Lecture*, Cambridge: Cambridge University, 1966; L. Hertling, *Communio: Church and Papacy in Early Christianity*, J. Wicks (trans.), Chicago: Loyola University, 1972; R. P. McBrien, *Catholicism: Study Edition,* San Francisco: HarperCollins, 1981; T. F. X. Noble, "Morbidity and Vitality in the History of the Early Medieval Papacy," *Catholic Historical Review* 81, 1995, 505–40; F. A. Sullivan, "The Meaning of Conciliar Dogmas," in D. Kendall and S. T. Davis (eds.), *The Convergence of Theology: A Festschrift Honoring Gerard O'Collins, S.J.*, New York: Paulist, 2001, pp. 73–86.

For further bibliography: A. Dulles and P. Granfield (eds.), *The Church: A Bibliography*, Wilmington, DE: Michael Glazier, 1985.

Küng and Tierney

Indispensable for exploring this issue in more depth: H. Küng, *Infallible? An Inquiry*, E. Quinn (trans.), New York: Doubleday, 1971; B. Tierney, *Origins of Papal Infallibility, 1150–1350: A Study on the Concepts of Infallibility, Sovereignty, and Tradition in the Middle Ages*, Leiden, Netherlands: Brill, 1972.

Reviews of these books demonstrate how the issues of modern Catholicism often shape discussion of the medieval church. Among the more detailed reviews:

Of Tierney: esp. A. M. Stickler, in *Catholic Historical Review* 60, 1974, 427–41; J. J. Ryan in *Journal of Ecumenical Studies* 13, 1976, 37–50; Tierney's exchange with D. L. D'Avray in *Catholic Historical Review* 66, 1980, 417–21, and 700–1; and ibid., 67, 1981, 60–4; Tierney's exchange with J. L. Heft in *Journal of Ecumenical Studies* 19, 1982, 744–80, and 787–93; and ibid., 20, 1983, 111–7.

Of Küng: esp. H. Haag's preface (ix–xx) and new materials (201–76) in the second edition of Küng's book: *Infallible? An Unresolved Enquiry*, New York: Continuum, 1994. Also: J. F. Costanzo, *The Historical Credibility of Hans*

Küng: An Inquiry and Commentary, North Quincy, MA: Christopher, 1979; *The Küng Dialogue: A Documentation on the Efforts of the Congregation for the Doctrine of the Faith and of the Conference of German Bishops to Achieve an Appropriate Clarification of the Controversial Views of Dr. Hans Küng (Tübingen),* Washington, DC: U.S. Catholic Conference, 1980; P. Chirico, "Infallibility: Rapprochement between Küng and the Official Church?" *Theological Studies* 42, 1981, 529–60.

Infallibility—Selected Topics

General: the essays in *Journal of Ecumenical Studies* 8, 1971, 751–877; U. Horst, *Unfehlbarkeit und Geschichte: Studien zur Unfehlbarkeitsdiskussion von Melchior Cano bis zum I vatikanischen Konzil,* Mainz, Germany: Matthias Grünewald, 1982.

Medieval ideas: E. W. Kemp, *Canonization and Authority in the Western Church,* Oxford: Oxford University, 1948; T. M. Izbicki, "Infallibility and the Erring Pope: Guido Terreni and Johannes de Turrecremata," in K. Pennington and R. Somerville (eds.), *Law, Church, and Society: Essays in Honor of Stephen Kuttner,* Philadelphia: University of Pennsylvania, 1977, pp. 97–111; L. Meulenberg, "Une Question toujours ouverte: Grégoire VII et l'infaillibilité du Pape," in H. Mordek (ed.), *Aus Kirche und Reich: Studien zur Theologie, Politik, und Recht im Mittelalter,* Sigmaringen, Germany: J. Thorbecke, 1983, pp. 159–71.

Protestant and Orthodox Challenges, Ecumenical Discussion

Survey: J. F. Puglisi (ed.), *Petrine Ministry and the Unity of the Church,* Collegeville, MN: Liturgical, 1999; W. Fleischmann-Bisten (ed.), *Papstamt—Pro und Con: geschichtliche Entwicklungen und ökumenische Perspektiven,* Göttingen, Germany: Vandenhoeck & Ruprecht, 2001; W. Kasper (ed.), *The Petrine Ministry: Catholics and Orthodox in Dialogue,* New York: Newman, 2006.

More focused studies: W. R. Farmer and R. Kereszty, *Peter and Paul in the Church of Rome: The Ecumenical Potential of a Forgotten Perspective,* New York: Paulist, 1990; A. Nichols, *Rome and the Eastern Churches: A Study in Schism,* Edinburgh: T & T Clark, 1992; J. Baycroft, "An Emerging Ecumenical Consensus on Papal Primacy?" *Journal of Ecumenical Studies,* 35, 1998, 36–69.

Vatican Council I

Sources: *Acta et decreta sacrosancta oecumenici concili vaticani in quatuor prioribus sessionibus,* Rome: P. Lazzarini, 1872.

Survey: R. McClory, *Power and the Papacy: The People and Politics behind the Doctrine of Infallibility,* Ligouri, MO: Triumph, 1997.

More detailed studies: J. Hennesey, *The First Council of the Vatican: The American Experience*, New York: Herder & Herder, 1963; A. Hasler, *How the Pope Became Infallible: Pius IX and the Politics of Persuasion*, P. Heinegg (trans.), New York: Doubleday, 1981; M. O'Gara, *Triumph in Defeat: Infallibility, Vatican I, and the French Minority Bishops*, Washington, DC: Catholic University, 1988; K. Schatz, *Vaticanum I, 1869–70, Vol. III: Unfehlbarkeitsdiskussion und Rezeption*, Paderborn, Germany: Schöningh, 1992; J. R. Page, *What Will Dr. Newman Do? John Henry Newman and Papal Infallibility 1865–75*, Collegeville, MN: Liturgical, 1994; A. Houtepen, "Modernity and the Crisis of Spirituality in the Nineteenth Century: The Case of Papal Infallibility," in J. Frishman, W. Otten, and G. Rouwhorst (eds.), *Religious Identity and the Problem of Historical Foundation: The Foundational Character of Authoritative Sources in the History of Christianity and Judaism*, Leiden, Netherlands: Brill, 2004, pp. 95–113; R. F. Costigan, *The Consensus of the Church and Papal Infallibility: A Study of the Background of Vatican I*, Washington, DC: Catholic University, 2006.

Histories of the Papacy

Medieval surveys: G. Barraclough, *The Medieval Papacy*, New York: W.W. Norton, 1979; W. Ullmann, *A Short History of the Papacy in the Middle Ages*, 2nd ed., London: Routledge, 2003.

Sources: B. Tierney, *The Crisis of Church and State, 1050–1300*, Englewood Cliffs, NJ: Prentice Hall, 1980; C. Ryan (ed.), *The Religious Roles of the Papacy: Ideals and Realities, 1150–1300*, Toronto: Pontifical Institute of Medieval Studies, 1989.

Recent general surveys (from various perspectives): J. M. Miller, *The Shepherd and the Rock: Origins, Development and Mission of the Papacy*, Huntington, IN: Our Sunday Visitor, 1995; W. J. La Due, *The Chair of Saint Peter: A History of the Papacy*, Maryknoll, NY: Orbis, 1999; P. Collins, *Upon This Rock: The Popes in Their Changing Role*, New York: Crossroad, 2000; E. Duffy, *Saints and Sinners: A History of the Popes*, second edition, New Haven, CT: Yale University, 2002; M. Collins, *The Fisherman's Net: The Influence of the Papacy on History*, revised edition, Mahwah, NJ: HiddenSpring, 2005.

Ecclesiology

Survey: "Church," in K. Rahner, et al. (eds.), *Sacramentum Mundi: An Encyclopedia of Theology*, New York: Herder & Herder, 1968, Vol. 1, pp. 313–37.

Sources: T. P. Halton (ed.), *The Church*, Wilmington, DE: Michael Glazier, 1985; A. Flannery (ed.), *Vatican II, Vol. 1: The Conciliar and Post-Conciliar Documents*, new rev. ed., Northport, NY: Costello, 1996.

More focused studies: S. J. Grabowski, *The Church: An Introduction to the Theology of St. Augustine*, St. Louis, MO: Herder, 1957, esp. pp. 3–227; Y. M.-J. Congar, *L'Écclesiologie au moyen âge de saint Grégoire le Grand à la désunion entre Byzance et Rome*, Paris: Éditions de Cerf, 1968; S. Ozment, *The Age of Reform, 1250–1550: An Intellectual and Religious History of Late Medieval and Reformation Europe*, New Haven: Yale University, 1980, esp. pp.135–81.

Papal Primacy

Survey: K. Schatz, *Papal Primacy: From Its Origins to the Present*, Collegeville, MN: Liturgical, 1996.

More focused studies: K. F. Morrison, *Tradition and Authority in the Western Church, 300–1140*, Princeton, NJ: Princeton University, 1969; F. Dvornik, *Byzantium and the Roman Primacy*, revised edition, New York: Fordham University, 1979; T. M. Izbicki, "Papalist Reaction to the Council of Constance: Juan de Torquemada to the Present," *Church History* 55, 1986, 7–20; the essays in *Communio: International Catholic Review*, Winter 1998, 576–629; S. K. Ray, *Upon This Rock: St. Peter and the Primacy of Rome in Scripture and the Early Church*, San Francisco: Ignatius, 1999; R. Pesch, *Die biblischen Grundlagen des Primat*, Freiburg, Germany: Herder, 2001.

Episcopalism

Survey: W. Henn, *The Honor of My Brothers: A Short History of the Relation between the Pope and the Bishops*, New York: Crossroad, 2000.

Ancient and medieval manifestations: J. Benzinger, *Invectiva in Romam: Romkritik im Mittelalter vom 9. bis zum 12. Jahrhundert*, Lübeck, Germany: Matthiesen, 1968; G. Dix, *Jurisdiction in the Early Church: Episcopal and Papal*, London: Church Literature Association, 1975; K. Pennington, *Popes and Bishops: The Papal Monarchy in the Twelfth and Thirteenth Centuries*, Philadelphia: University of Pennsylvania, 1984; A. Cunningham (ed.), *The Bishop in the Church: Patristic Texts on the Role of the Episkopos*, Wilmington, DE: Michael Glazier, 1985.

Conciliarism

Places to start: B. Tierney, *Foundations of the Conciliar Theory: The Contribution of the Medieval Canonists from Gratian to the Great Schism*, Cambridge: Cambridge University, 1955; and F. Oakley, *Council over Pope? Towards a Provisional Ecclesiology*, New York: Herder & Herder, 1969. These two books have shaped most subsequent scholarship on this question. Oakley's new study extends his analysis into the modern period: *The Conciliarist Tradition: Constitutionalism in the Catholic Church, 1300–1870*, Oxford: Oxford University, 2003.

For later works: Tierney's preface to *Foundations of the Conciliar Theory*, enlarged new edition, Leiden, Netherlands: Brill, 1998, pp. ix–xxix; and the bibliographical essays: A. Black, "What Was Conciliarism? Conciliar Theory in Historical Perspective," in B. Tierney and P. Linehan (eds.), *Authority and Power: Studies in Medieval Law and Government Presented to Walter Ullmann on his Seventieth Birthday*, Cambridge; Cambridge University, 1980, pp. 213–35; C. J. Nederman, "Conciliarism and Constitutionalism: Jean Gerson and Medieval Political Thought," *History of European Ideas* 12, 1990, 189–209; F. Oakley, "Verius Est Licet Difficilius: Tierney's *Foundations of the Conciliar Theory* after Forty Years," in G. Christianson and T. M. Izbicki (eds.), *Nicholas of Cusa on Christ and the Church: Essays in Memory of Chandler McCuskey Brooks for the American Cusanus Society*, Leiden, Netherlands: Brill, 1996, pp. 15–34; C. Fasolt, "Voluntarism and Conciliarism in the Work of Francis Oakley," *History of Political Thought* 22, 2001, 41–52.

NOTES

1. "Pastor Aeternus," Vatican Council I, 18 July 1870, translated by the author from *Acta et decreta sacrosancta oecumenici concili vaticani in quatuor prioribus sessionibus*, Rome, 1872, p. 172.
2. Vatican II did little to resolve this. See esp. "Lumen gentium," Vatican II, 21 November 1964, #18–19 and #25, in A. Flannery (ed.), *Vatican II, Vol. 1: The Conciliar and Post-Conciliar Documents*, new rev. ed., Northport, NY: Costello, 1996, pp. 369–70 and 379–81.
3. On the imperative, and the perils, of taking an historical approach to the issue: most recently, P. Collins, *Upon this Rock: The Popes in Their Changing Role*, New York, Crossroad, 2000, pp. vii–x. Hans Küng and Brian Tierney, publishing nearly contemporary books about papal infallibility, triggered ongoing debates that center largely on this tension between theology and history. See my "Suggestions for Further Reading," section II.
4. This is to take a position midway between those of Geoffrey Barraclough and Walter Ullmann, whose short histories of the medieval papacy are standard in the field. Barraclough sought to divorce the events of papal history entirely from abstract policies and motivations; that is, he saw the papacy simply as a product of historical forces: *The Medieval Papacy*, New York: W. W. Norton, esp. pp. 7–10. By contrast, Ullmann considered the ideals of papal power as the primary force shaping the office: *A Short History of the Papacy in the Middle Ages*, second edition, London: Routledge, 2003, esp. pp. 1–3.
5. K. Pennington, *Pope and Bishops: The Papal Monarchy in the Twelfth and Thirteenth Centuries*, Philadelphia: University of Pennsylvania, 1984, esp. pp. 41–74 and 192–3.
6. R. Kress, "Simul Justus et Peccator: Ecclesiastical and Ecumenical Perspectives," *Horizons* 11, 1984, 255–75. This idea also shaped Eamon Duffy's historical survey of the papacy, and gave the book its title: *Saints and Sinners: A History of the Popes*, second edition, New Haven, CT: Yale University, 2002.

3 "The Age of Faith"
Everyone in the Middle Ages Believed in God

Peter Dendle

Ever since the European Renaissance, which largely defined itself by deni-grating the European Middle Ages, the medieval era has been stigmatized as one of closed-minded credulity—a period of unquestioned superstitions, entrenched religiosity, and a childlike acceptance of received doctrines. His-tory does indeed provide us with examples of societies whose members were intensely religious, and whose communal life was integrally related to its church teachings and spiritual beliefs (some examples that come to mind include the Qumran community who left the Dead Sea scrolls, and the Puri-tans of early America), but it would be a gross caricature to paint the entire sweep of the European Middle Ages with such broad strokes. Some people were more fervent than others, of course, but life for the vast majority of people in the thousand-year span of the Middle Ages was not demonstrably more of a spiritual enterprise than it is today.

To be sure, the written records of the Middle Ages generally insist on the existence, the omnipotence, and the benevolence of a Creator deity. This very insistence, however, should give pause for thought: the truly unques-tioned premises within a belief system (what Ludwig Wittgenstein called the "bedrock") necessarily remain unspoken. The person who walks around holding up his hand, and who insists to friends and family that "this is my hand," does not win the community's approval for assenting to a true proposition—rather, the person's sanity is questioned for doubting it in the first place. The articulation of a position is only meaningful in the face of doubt or potential dissent. Seen in this light, the repeated assertions of God's existence, justice, and goodness imply a society deeply anxious about those issues in some way or other. The flags and ribbons that went up across the United States following September 11, 2001—with the accompanying rhetoric of strength and unity—were clear signs of a society badly shaken.

Our impression of a predominantly religious society is skewed by several factors, most obviously by the fact that the majority of our extant documents were generated within the ecclesiastical community. Throughout much of the Middle Ages, the church fulfilled a large number of legal, medical, administrative, and cultural functions that today are mostly secular. Having children, organizing a festival or putting on a play, traveling, planning land use, recording business transactions, resolving disputes with neighbors, preparing a will—all of these were greatly facilitated within, if not completely dominated by, the infrastructure of the church, and would thus necessarily leave a documentary record implying a religious perspective. This does not mean, however, that these were primarily spiritual activities for the participants in every case, any more than using modern currency that reads "In God We Trust" implies every participant's personal belief in God.

The literate Christian community of the European Middle Ages was, throughout its long history, continuously exposed to incompatible belief systems and forced to ponder the grounds of adjudication among them. Early medieval thinkers refined their beliefs as the result of missionary activity among pagans, as Christianity spread gradually through the various tribal regions and encountered the diverse paganisms and nature cults of pre-Christian Europe. Some pockets of paganism resisted conversion almost through the entirety of the medieval period (the Lithuanians, for instance, were not permanently converted until 1386). Jewish communities also subsisted throughout Europe in various places, and their recurrent persecution is testimony to the threat their beliefs evidently presented.

Most of Europe, however, had converted to Christianity by the tenth or eleventh century. Christianity itself had generally developed in organic response to local religions, resulting in hybridized belief structures. Forms of Christian worship were not the same in town and country, and were not the same in one region as in another. (Virtually all medieval forms of Christian belief and worship, in any event, would be largely alien to modern Christians, Catholic and Protestant alike.) No sooner was this hybrid Christian worldview more or less thoroughly assimilated among the peasantry, however, than the Catholic Church found itself defending its beliefs on another front. Beginning at the end of the eleventh century, the Crusades forced Europeans to begin systematically confronting two competing intellectual systems: first, a powerful rival monotheism (Islam), and second, classical pagan philosophy (especially that of Aristotle, whose works began to be translated into Latin and disseminated widely in the twelfth century). Through the twelfth and thirteenth centuries, both Judeo-Arabic theology and the newly translated systems of classical Greek philosophy became increasingly important, packaged in formal logical methods far more advanced than the argumentative tools available to Latin Christianity of the time. These confrontations remind us that medieval Christians could never rest blithely or unthinkingly entrenched in their worldview as a matter of course but were forced to continuously reassert beliefs in the face of sometimes powerful, and always threatening, alternatives.

At the other end of the spectrum from these competing monotheisms might be placed atheism. Atheism has never been a popular position to maintain publicly—even in classical Athens, it was one of the charges that ushered Socrates toward the death penalty—and we should not expect to find many sources seriously contesting the religious hypothesis as a whole in the pre-Enlightenment period. What we do find, however, is a continuously sustained dialogue within the church, from Augustine's introspective *Confessions* and Anselm's celebrated argument against "the fool" who "hath said in his heart there is no God" (Psalms 14.1, 53.1), to Peter Abelard's *Dialogue between a Philosopher, a Jew, and a Christian*. These may often strike us as disingenuously transparent attempts to undermine doubt through a literary *fait accompli*—to have the cards artificially stacked in their favor from the outset, as it were. But as a whole they display an ongoing interest in and anxiety over the certainty of one set of religious beliefs against another. They show that clashes in worldview were near the front of many thinkers' minds, in a variety of ways, during every century of the Middle Ages.

Even within this dialogue of competing forms of worship, however, voices of more profound dissent, skepticism, and even atheism do trickle to the surface on occasion. John Arnold has recently collected a number of these in his *Belief and Unbelief in Medieval Europe*. From Alpert of Metz in the eleventh century to Thomas Tailour (in England) and Hermann of Ryswick (in Germany) in the fifteenth century, serious questions can be found regarding the immortality of the soul.[1] In the thirteenth century, for instance, Thomas of Cantimpré relates a dialogue in which one man tells another, "We are shamelessly fooled by the bad clerics who say that the soul can live separately after the destruction of the body," to which the other agrees. Diego of Barrionuevo declares rather paradoxically, "I swear to God that this hell and paradise is nothing more than a way of frightening us, like people saying to children, 'the bogeyman will get you.'" There are interpretive problems with our sources for these sorts of passages, of course: some occur as *exempla* (moral vignettes used to illustrate sermons in various ways); others come up during the course of inquisitorial interrogation. When an early thirteenth-century prior of Holy Trinity, Aldgate, writes that "there are many people who do not believe that God exists," was this a fact he observed, or was this simply a rhetorical stance (perhaps loosely based on the "fool" of the Psalms)—a foil from which to articulate his own position? There is room for debate, but what remains clear is that belief in God and in the teachings of the church were ongoing topics of active questioning and engagement.

Every age is an age of "faith" in something or other—every culture relies on a matrix of mutually supporting premises that form the silent foundation for other, more publicly disputed claims—but for the literate community, belief in the existence, nature, and goodness of God was by no means such an unspoken, implicit premise underlying medieval thought. It was not the "bedrock" (to return to Wittgenstein's metaphor) but a vibrant, swirling eddy within the current itself.

And what of the majority of the general population—the countless illiterate villagers and peasants whose knowledge of religion essentially started and ended at the local pulpit? Did they all just unthinkingly believe in God?

What it is to "believe in God" means different things to different people. For some, it is a powerful empirical proposition about the world and the entities in it, a vital and pervasive fact that colors virtually every aspect of thought and behavior. For others, it is a distant and mutely acknowledged idea passively inherited from family and community, inviting assent for lack of any more compelling alternative but not otherwise commanding great urgency. There is nothing to suggest that this spectrum was any less true for the general populations of the Middle Ages, as a whole, than it is for our societies of the twenty-first century.

SUGGESTIONS FOR FURTHER READING

Peter Abelard, *A Dialogue of a Philosopher with a Jew and a Christian*, Pierre Payer (trans.), Toronto: Pontifical Institute of Medieval Studies, 1979. One medieval thinker's approach to a dialogue among religions, providing a contemporary point of reference. An interpretive essay on religious toleration in Abelard's *Dialogue* by Constant Mews appears in Laursen and Nederman (eds.) (following).

John H. Arnold, *Belief and Unbelief in Medieval Europe*, London: Hodder Arnold, 2005. Investigates the multivalent nature of belief as it functioned in formal religion, popular devotion, and the everyday life of medieval Europeans. Arnold provides a nuanced reading of popular religion, as it appears (necessarily) through the lens of official accounts disseminated by the church.

Will Durant, *The Age of Faith*, New York: Simon and Schuster, 1950. Provides a workable discussion on medieval devotion ("apparently there were village atheists then as now") and problematizes simplistic overviews of medieval spirituality with obscure contemporary quotations from medieval authors who are curiously dissonant from the mainstream religious sensibilities of the Middle Ages. See esp. pp. 732 and forward.

Michael Goodich, *Other Middle Ages: Witnesses at the Margins of Medieval Society*, Philadelphia: University of Pennsylvania Press, 1998. A collection of primary texts in translation, along with commentary, representing nonmainstream voices from the High Middle Ages (Jews, heretics, sexual nonconformists, etc.).

Bernard Hamilton, *Religion in the Medieval West*, London: Edward Arnold, 1986. A broad, accessible overview of religion in the Western Middle Ages, both public and private. See esp. pp. 189 and forward for belief and skepticism.

John C. Laursen and Cary J. Nederman (eds.), *Beyond the Persecuting Society: Religious Toleration before the Enlightenment*, Philadelphia: University of Pennsylvania, 1998. Includes four essays on the medieval roots of modern religious toleration, providing useful overviews as well as focusing on Abelard, John of Salisbury, and the Jewish scholar Ha-Me'iri.

Jay Newman, *Foundations of Religious Tolerance*, Toronto: University of Toronto, 1982. A clear and succinct introduction to the social and philosophical problems inherent in a range of positions on religious belief (relativism, absolutism, etc.).

Jill Raitt (ed.), *Christian Spirituality: High Middle Ages and Reformation*, New York: Crossroad, 1987. Collection of essays on various aspects of religious expression, including individual treatment of the spirituality of the different medieval religious orders, as well as a helpful survey on late medieval devotional expression by Richard Kieckhefer.

James Thrower, *Western Atheism: A Short History*, Amherst, NY: Prometheus, 2000. Provides a skeletal overview of secular versus religious thinking throughout the history of Western civilization. Such a study can help to qualify the belief that secularism is a modern invention in any straightforward sense.

NOTE

1. All examples in this paragraph are from Arnold, pp. 225–30.

4 Everyone Was an Orthodox, Educated Roman Catholic

Michael D. C. Drout

The Middle Ages in Western Europe were in large measure an "Age of Faith" (to quote the famous Time Life book title). Roman Catholic Christianity was the established state religion, great cathedrals towered over major cities, and monasteries and churches were the leading cultural institutions of the time. But it is wrong to deduce from this cultural dominance the idea that all the individuals in any given medieval culture were equally pious and equally orthodox.[1]

As an example of the attitude I am talking about, let me quote T. H. White's *The Once and Future King*, a work of fiction but one that has done much to shape popular perceptions of the later Middle Ages, and one whose author knew a great deal about medieval history and culture.

> The villagers went to church in the chapel of the castle. They wore their best clothes and trooped up the street with their most respectable gait on Sundays, looking with vague and dignified looks in all directions, as if reluctant to disclose their destination, and on week-days they came to Mass and vespers in their ordinary clothes, walking much more cheerfully. Everyone went to church in those days, and liked it. (pp. 40–41)

But *did* everyone go to church and like it? If this were the case, we might wonder why, for example, William Langland spends so much time in *Piers Plowman* inveighing against people who skip church. The figure of Sloth, for instance, says:

> If this were my dying day, I still couldn't be bothered to keep awake. I don't even know the Paternoster perfectly, not as a priest should really sing it. I know plenty of ballads about Robin Hood and Randolph Earl of Chester, but I don't know a verse about our Lord or our Lady ....

> I have made hundreds of vows, and forgotten them the next morning. I have never yet managed to do the penance the priest has given me, or felt sorry for my sins. And when I'm saying my Rosary, my heart is miles

away from the words, except when I say them in a fit of temper. I spend every day, holydays and all, gossiping idly at the pub—sometimes even in church—and I never give a thought to the Passion of Christ . . . .

> I don't keep account of vigils or fast-days—they just seem to slip by. And in Lent, I am lying in bed with my mistress in my arms til long after Mass and Matins are over, then I go to the Friary for a late Mass. And once I get to the "Ite, Missa est," I've had enough! Why, unless illness drives me to it, I sometimes go a whole year without making a confession, and then I do it by guesswork (p. 73).[2]

Now, let us grant Langland his satire. He is exaggerating the figure of Sloth by imputing to him *all* of the possible versions of this sin. Nevertheless it is hard to imagine that Langland is making things up out of whole cloth. Clearly there were people who acted in this way, skipping church, avoiding confession and prayers and otherwise not participating in Christian worship. This does not mean that Christianity was not the dominant ideology of the time, but it does suggest that not everyone espoused that ideology as vigorously as others (and we are setting aside here the special case of heretics, who actively opposed certain tenets of the Roman Catholic Church).

Furthermore, even among those who had no particular quarrel with Roman Catholic Christianity—those who went to church and liked it—there seems to have been a fairly wide range of knowledge about and acceptance of various elements of Roman Catholic dogma. A few examples from the later Middle Ages in England suffice to illustrate my point. These texts are part of the famous English Mystery Plays or Corpus Christi Plays, which were put on by wealthy towns throughout England on Corpus Christi day. The Mystery Plays attempted to show the complete Christian history of the world, from the Creation to the Last Judgment. Because we know that these plays were performed for every person in the city, the plays can give us some idea of what level of theological sophistication had been attained by the "man in the street"—at least in the eyes of the monks or priests who wrote the plays.

Our first example is "Joseph's Trouble about Mary," sponsored by the Pewterers and Founders, which begins with poor old Joseph lamenting the fact that his young, virgin wife is pregnant.[3] Were he not so old, Joseph would seem to protest too much. But in the context of the play (which is a dramatization and expansion of its biblical source in Matthew 1.18–25, augmented with material from the Apocrypha), Joseph's lament fulfills a function far more important than the mere comedy engendered by his vociferous and repeated protestations to the effect that "I did not have sexual relations with that woman." First, Mary's virginity is affirmed and reaffirmed by Joseph, by Mary herself, and by the angel who arrives to tell Joseph whose child Mary actually carries. This affirmation is obviously important as part of

Christian doctrine. But more significant for the purposes of our argument, the overdone lament of Joseph serves very clearly and powerfully to answer that perpetual, impudent Sunday-school question: How do we know that Joseph didn't just have sex with Mary?

The answer is dramatized in the play: Joseph is willing to go into exile (lines 66–67) in order to avoid having to accuse Mary of adultery. If he had any belief at all that the child might be his (that is, if he had engaged in intercourse with Mary), the plot of the play would make no sense. Joseph's reaction when Mary says that the child is "God's and yours" (line 104), "With me fleshly was thou never filed, and I forsake it here forthy" (lines 106–7), again emphasizes Mary's virginity. The testimony of the Maiden that Mary has only been visited by an angel but by no other man then serves to clear her of the charge of adultery.

Here Joseph serves as the skeptical voice of an impudent audience:

> Then see I well your meaning is
> The angel has made her with child.
> Nay, some man in angel's likeness
> With somekin gaud has her beguiled
> And that trow I (lines 134–138).

Joseph's continued harsh questioning of Mary—"But who is the father? Tell me his name?" (line 176), "Who had thy maidenhead Mary? Has thou aught mind" (line 206)—changes Joseph's tone from that of a skeptical, apparently legitimately aggrieved husband to that of a cruel interrogator. In effect, all the audience's difficult questions about the virginity of Mary (traditionally one of the sticking points of Christian ideology) are not only answered by the play but are shown to be cruel and impious. If the audience originally feels sorry for Joseph and sees the situation from his point of view, the playwright's manipulations of the scene causes them, by the end of the play, to see themselves, along with Joseph, as having been abusive. The playwright has preempted the very questions likely to be raised by an audience about Mary's virginity.

This strategy of preemption (and comedy) is even more obvious in "The Resurrection" play, sponsored by the Carpenters. Although the main plot of the play is obviously the Resurrection itself, there is an extensive subplot involving the soldiers who are commanded to guard the tomb so that no one can steal the body of Jesus. The soldiers act well-prepared to follow Pilate's orders. When they are sent to guard the tomb, the first soldier says:

> Lordings, we say you for certain,
> We shall keep him with mights and main.
> There shall no traitor with no train
> Steal him us fro (lines 175–80).

The second soldier threatens violence against anyone who would try to remove the body of Jesus from the tomb. This is all obviously a setup for what occurs after the Resurrection: the soldiers need somehow to explain the empty tomb to Pilate. The comedy arises from their attempts to come up with an explanation (eventually they decide to tell Pilate the truth) and their struggle to understand the Resurrection and the natural phenomena surrounding it. When Annas says:

> Now, Sir Pilate, since that is so
> That he is risen dead us fro,
> Command your knights to say, where they go,
> That he was ta'en
> With twenty thousand men and mo,
> And them near slain;
> And thereto, of our treasury
> Give to them a word forthy (lines 407–14).

We see that in fact the point of the play has been not only to dramatize the Resurrection, but also to preempt the impudent question: How do we know that the disciples didn't just take Jesus' body out of the tomb? Of course the Biblical account itself, with the emphasis on the size of the stone in front of the tomb, also provides such a preemptive answer, but in the York play this preemption is additionally dramatized, becoming the focus of the entire second half of the play and the source of all its comedy. We must ask why a playwright would bother to provide an answer to a question if he thought no one would ever bother to ask it. It seems more reasonable to conjecture that the playwright would have in fact known that questions about the empty tomb, like questions about the virginity of Mary, are endemic to Christian doctrine. Only the question of the Trinity might be more vexed. The use of comedy and preemption to avoid difficult questions are standard rhetorical tactics. That we see these employed in the York Mystery Plays strongly suggests that the playwrights thought that questions about Mary's virginity and about the empty tomb were worth preempting.

Both "The Resurrection" and "Joseph's Trouble About Mary" make a significant effort to answer questions that no fully orthodox Roman Catholic, the kind of person postulated as living in the Age of Faith, would have ever needed to ask. They are exactly the sorts of questions that children ask in Sunday school, but the audience of the Mystery Plays was not limited to children. Nor would the discussion of Joseph's trouble and his concern to prove that he had not had sex with Mary really need to be the focus of a play that was aimed at children. It seems much more likely that the plays focused on the troubling questions of Christian doctrine not because the audience was filled with heretics, or even skeptics, but because, then as now, some people had difficulty believing the more difficult aspects of Christian theology (the virgin birth, the Resurrection). It is also worth noting that the plays are not simply expanded and dramatized to illustrate difficult points of doctrine: the kind of comedic preemption that I have discussed above is completely absent from the Harrowing of Hell, although the Harrowing is far less central to Christian doctrine in the Middle Ages than is the virginity of Mary or the resurrection of Christ.

The weight of the evidence, then, suggests that even in an audience of believers there were those who doubted the literal truth of some points of Christian doctrine, that members of the church knew this, and that rather than launching a search for heretics, they felt that their best hope of combating this particular skepticism was to mock and preempt it. Such simple evidence as I have discussed above should help to clear up the misconception that in the Middle Ages everyone believed uncritically in Roman Catholic dogma. In fact, under the aegis of a generally Christian and Catholic worldview, there was probably a great diversity of belief and practice. It is important for us to recognize this diversity and not merely to assume that everyone in the Middle Ages was aware of all the fine points (or even believed in some of the more coarse points) of medieval Christian theology.

SUGGESTIONS FOR FURTHER READING

Richard Beadle and Pamela M. King (eds.), York Mystery Plays: *A Selection in Modern Spelling*, Oxford: Oxford University, 1984.
David Bevington, *Medieval Drama*, Boston: Houghton Mifflin, 1975.
Owen Chadwick, *A History of Christianity*, New York: St. Martin's, 1995.
David Knowles, *The Middle Ages*, New York: Paulist, 1983.
William Langland, *Piers the Ploughman*, J. F. Goodridge (ed.), New York: Penguin, 1966.
Robert P. Miller, "Chaucer's Pardoner, the Scriptural Eunuch, and the Pardoner's Tale," *Speculum* 30, 1955, 180–9.
The New Catholic Encyclopedia, New York: McGraw Hill, 1967.
D. W. Robertson, Jr., *A Preface to Chaucer: Studies in Medieval Perspectives*, Princeton, NJ: Princeton University, 1962.
T. H. White, *The Once and Future King*, New York: G. P. Putnam's Sons, 1939 (1987 edition).

NOTES

1. I do not want to create a straw man here, but the idea that medieval authors (and by extension, their audiences) were exceptionally orthodox and knew the subtle details of theology was first promulgated by the great critic D. W. Robertson. While Robertson himself was nuanced about the level of theological sophistication (and belief) in the general, secular population, many of his followers were not. Robertson's opus is *A Preface to Chaucer*, and well worth reading. For an overly "Robertsonian" approach that commits the errors I am criticizing, see Robert P. Miller, "Chaucer's Pardoner, the Scriptural Eunuch, and the Pardoner's Tale," *Speculum*, 30, 1955, 180–9.

2. Langland's B Text is cited here from the Penguin translation by J. F. Goodridge. The differences between the A, B, and C Texts and the actual specifics of the Middle English are not relevant to my discussion.
3. For the purposes of this essay, it is sufficient to use Richard Beadle and Pamela M. King, *York Mystery Plays: A Selection in Modern Spelling.*

5   The Myth of the Virgin Nun

Mary Dockray-Miller

In the secular culture of the twenty-first century, the word "nun" brings to mind a cloistered woman in prayer, a strict elementary-school teacher (perhaps wielding a ruler), or an old woman (like Mother Theresa) engaged in charitable work. All of these women, in current popular perception, are virgins.

We tend to assume that virginity—the state of never having had sexual intercourse—has been a prerequisite throughout history for nuns. Movies, television, and popular literature typically depict nuns without sexual desire or activity—when a nun does have sexual desires, the story attracts our attention, for a nun who is not a virgin seems like an anomaly. (Maria in *The Sound of Music* is a classic example, since the other nuns in her convent are presented as completely virginal, no matter their age, while the story focuses on her transformation from novice nun to wife of the captain.)

In much of medieval Europe, however, many nuns, especially those in positions of power in the church hierarchy, were not virgins—indeed, they had been married and had given birth. In Anglo-Saxon England specifically, it is more common than not to find a royal widowed mother ruling a religious house as its abbess. While other medieval examples abound, a focus on Anglo-Saxon England most neatly disproves the myth of the medieval virgin nun.

The Anglo-Saxon period is usually dated from 597 (the date of the arrival of Augustine in Kent on his conversion mission from Rome) to 1066 (the date of the Norman Conquest). Enormous cultural changes occurred during these 469 years, of course, many of them driven by the conversion of the various tribes to Christianity. The evidence from the early part of the period, most of it from the first half of the seventh century, provides a number of examples of widowed mothers who were also abbesses.

These abbesses did not rule what we would call "convents," religious houses for women. In the early Anglo-Saxon period, religious women lived in "double monasteries" that housed both women and men. Interestingly enough, these houses were always ruled by women—abbots governed monasteries, the houses for men only. The seventh century double monasteries were important institutions in all the Anglo-Saxon kingdoms (especially in

Kent, Northumbria, East Anglia, and Mercia); their abbesses were always members of the royal family who could then act as connections between the church and the state. The double monasteries served as regional centers of government, as hospitals, schools, libraries, and as powerful church institutions. The double monastery of Whitby, ruled by the abbess Hild in the mid-seventh century, is a good example: Hild hosted the Synod of Whitby in 664, a meeting at which the heads of the English church decided to follow the practices of the Roman rather than the Celtic Church. Historians generally agree that Hild was a widow as well as an abbess, although Bede does not explicitly call her a widow in his *Ecclesiastical History* of 731, the most important primary source for the period.

One of Hild's successors fits more clearly the pattern of a widowed royal mother who becomes the abbess of a double monastery. Hild was followed by a joint mother-daughter abbacy of Eanflæd and her daughter Ælfflæd. These women were both royal (Eanflæd was the daughter of Edwin, King of Northumbria, and Æthelburh, princess of Kent; she married Oswiu, King of Northumbria, with whom she had Ælfflæd). Eanflæd—obviously not a virgin—served as coabbess from the death of Hild to her own death in about 690.

Further south, more nonvirgin nuns populated a religious landscape full of double monasteries ruled by royal widows. Two houses (for which we have a relatively large amount of documentary evidence) will have to suffice as examples. Minster-in-Sheppey and Minster-in-Thanet, both Kentish double monasteries, were powerful and important institutions during the seventh century. Sheppey was founded by a royal widow, Seaxburh, who was an East Anglian princess, a Kentish queen, and the mother of a number of kings and queens. Seaxburh was succeeded as abbess of Sheppey by her daughter Eormenhild, who was also a widowed queen with children. Sheppey's abbesses were therefore most obviously not secluded virgins.

Similarly, the founder and first abbess of Minster-in-Thanet was a queen and mother. Æbbe, sometimes referred to by the Latinate Domne Eafe, was a Kentish princess who married Merewalh, King of the Magonsæton, and had four children. Her daughter Mildrith followed her as abbess at Thanet.

This propensity for abbesses to be socially prominent and (at some point) sexually active continues into the tenth century, the period of the Benedictine Reform. After the Viking invasions and destruction of the ninth century, the Anglo-Saxon church regrouped and reformed under the leadership of such prominent ecclesiastics as Sts. Dunstan and Æthelwold. That reform did not exclude nonvirgins; widows and other women with histories of sexual activity held places of prominence in the late tenth-century religious houses. The double monasteries of the early period were not duplicated, and the houses of the Benedictine Reform conform more closely to our modern conceptions of a convent—a religious house for women only. One of the more prominent of these convents was Wilton Abbey, and from Wilton comes the most obvious example of a powerful and important medieval nun who was not a virgin—indeed, who was at the time of her abbacy the discarded concubine or wife of the reigning king. Abbess Wulfthryth of Wilton, who was renowned for her sanctity and strong governance of the abbey, was either the concubine or first wife of King Edgar (who ruled from 957–75). Their daughter Edith lived at the abbey with Wulfthryth from about 960–84. Wulfthryth outlived her daughter, who died at the age of 23 and was sanctified and revered at Wilton. Wulfthryth's uncontested control of a powerful and important religious house testifies to the acceptability of a discarded sexual partner as an abbess.

Virgin nuns certainly existed—and were celebrated—throughout the medieval period. This short discussion has indicated, however, that many of the nuns of Anglo-Saxon England were not cloistered virgins but active, socially prominent and powerful women who had been sexually active and borne children before their assumption of their abbacies. Double monasteries and convents throughout continental Europe were similarly occupied and governed by royal widows with children. We need to discard the myth of the cloistered, silent medieval nun and qualify that image with one of an older, active, powerful woman who had political interests, financial resources, and grown children to protect and promote.

SUGGESTIONS FOR FURTHER READING

Clarissa Atkinson, *The Oldest Vocation: Christian Motherhood in the Middle Ages*, Ithaca, NY: Cornell University, 1991.

John Blair, *The Church in Anglo-Saxon Society*, Oxford University, 2005.

Bertram Colgrave and R. A. B. Mynors (eds.), *Bede's Ecclesiastical History of the English People*, Oxford: Clarendon, 1969.

Mary Dockray-Miller, *Motherhood and Mothering in Anglo-Saxon England*, New York: St. Martin's, 2000.

Sean Gilsdorf (trans.), *Queenship and Sanctity: The* Lives *of Mathilda and the* Epitaph *of Adelheid*, Washington, DC: Catholic University of America, 2004.

Stephanie Hollis, *Anglo-Saxon Women and the Church*, Woodbridge: Boydell, 1992.

Clare A. Lees and Gillian R. Overing, *Double Agents: Women and Clerical Culture in Anglo-Saxon England*, Philadelphia: University of Pennsylvania, 2001.

Susan Ridyard, *The Royal Saints of Anglo-Saxon England*, Cambridge: Cambridge University, 1988.

Barbara Yorke, *Nunneries and the Anglo-Saxon Royal Houses*, London: Continuum, 2003.

6 The Medieval Popess

Vincent DiMarco

This unhistorical fable, widely reported without refutation from the mid-thirteenth century to well into the Renaissance, continues both to captivate the imaginations and satisfy the longings of contemporary antiestablishment conspiracy theorists, unreconstructed critics of Roman Catholicism, and determined feminists eager to restore to women a voice and power that the male writing of history and the church in particular have denied them. This essay concentrates on the legend as it evolved in the Middle Ages, with only brief discussion of modern analyses and interpretations, a more comprehensive list of which is appended.

The story was first reported about 1260 by the Dominican Jean de Mailly in his *Chronica Universalis Mettensis,* where in an entry under 1099 is noted, as a query to be investigated, the report of a female disguised as a man who rose, by dint of character and talents, to the positions of curial secretary, cardinal, then Pope.[1] One day, however, while mounting a horse she gave birth to a child, which swift Roman justice decreed punishable by death: she was tied to a horse, dragged, and stoned by the populace for half a league; at the place where she died an inscription was placed: *Petre, Pater Patrum, Papisse Prodito Partum* ("O Peter, Father of Fathers, Betray the Childbearing of the Woman Pope").

Jean's account was taken over and embroidered by a fellow Dominican, Etienne de Bourbon, in *De Diversis Materiis Praedicabilibus* (ca. 1261).[2] To him, the affair, which he dates "around 1100," constitutes an occurrence "of wonderful audacity or rather insanity," which demonstrates "how such rash presumptuousness leads to so vile an end." Curiously, a variant that Etienne introduces into the inscription, *Parce* ('Forbear") for *Petre*, seems nonsensically to reverse its meaning and that of the moralization he gives to the alleged incident, as well as to suggest that the basis of the memorial inscription was probably an ancient inscription only partially legible or abbreviated by its initial letters. Rosemary and Darroll Pardoe (pp. 44–6) note that *P.P.P.* often stands for *Pecunia Propria Posuit* ("He placed it with his own money") and that *Pater Patrum* was a recognized Mithraic title centuries before the birth of the Popess legend. Likewise, the various accounts of a statue of the Popess and her child (e.g., John Burchard, 1486; Martin

Luther, ca. 1510; Robert Bellarmine, 1577)[3] probably refer to one or more preexisting images from the classical period, perhaps that of Juno suckling Heracles.

That the story's potential as exemplum was soon exploited by what Boureau calls the "Dominican network" is readily apparent from Jacopo da Voragine's *Chronica Januensis* (*Chronicle of Genoa*, written in 1292 when Jacopo was archbishop of the city), Part 9, Chapter 8,[4] where, although introducing the poignant detail that at the onset of labor pains the Popess entered "into a little house on the street there; died there in the pains of childbirth, and was buried there," Jacopo makes clear the antifeminist *sentence:* "Woman . . . begins to act with presumption and audacity, but fails to take into consideration the end of the action and what accompanies it; she thinks she has already done great things; if she can begin something grand, she is no longer able . . . to pursue with sagacity what has been begun, and this is because of a lack of discernment" (Boureau, trans. Cochrane, p. 122).

By Jacopo's time the date of 1099–1100 of the Popess's alleged reign had been abandoned, doubtless under the weight of the incontrovertible fact of Paschal II's consecration just two weeks after the death of Urban II at the end of July, 1099. R. and D. Pardoe, however, plausibly suggest that the date specified in the founding narrative by Jean de Mailly (who "delays" Paschal's elevation to the papal throne until 1206) was prompted by the existence during the pontificates of Urban and Paschal of the antipopes Clement III (1080–1100), Theodoric (1100–02), Albert (1102), and Sylvester IV (1105–11). But the 1099 date of Paschal's coronation may figure in yet another way in the development of the legend, in the two "pierced chairs" supposedly employed to allow for a manual verification of the papal claimant's testicles, as we shall see.

The eleventh-century date was soon superseded by a much earlier attestation. The *Chronica Minor* of an anonymous Franciscan of Erfurt, about 1265, includes as an early interpolation the story of the *pseudopapa,* "whose name and year are unknown," but is inserted in the text between notices of Pope Formosus (891–6) and Pope Boniface VI (896).[5] But what came to be the "traditional" dating was established in a late thirteenth-century interpolation in one of the two revisions (1268, 1277) of the widely copied *Chronica de Romanis Pontificibus et Imperatoribus* of the Dominican papal chaplain Martinus Polonus (Martin of Troppau). Here, "John Anglicus" (Boureau: perhaps an error for *Angelicus,* playing off the familiar phrase *angelicus papa?*), was a young woman from Mainz, taken as an adolescent by her lover to study in Athens, and disguised as a man; from there she went to Rome, taught with distinction, and was elected Pope at the death of Leo IV in 855 (notwithstanding the fact that Benedict III succeeded Leo to rule 855–8). She ruled for two years, seven months and four days, until, having been made pregnant by her lover, she gave birth and died during a procession from St. Peter's to the Lateran, between the Colosseum and the church of St. Clement's. "And since the lord pope always makes a detour from this route, many people believe that this is done out of abhorrence of the event."[6] Persistent attempts (most recently, that of Rinaldi and Vicini) to cite earlier texts that mention the Popess, such as the *Liber pontificalis* (ending with notice of Nicholas I, 858–67), the *Historiographi* of the Benedictine Marianus Scotus (d. 1086), the *Chronographia* of Sigebert of Glembours (ending in the year 1112), Gotfried of Viterbo's *Pantheon* (ca. 1185), and Gervase of Tilbury's *Otia imperialia* (1211) are all vitiated by the fact that these allusions are late interpolations drawn from the Martinus tradition. Indeed, no uncritical reliance on the strength of "oral tradition" can stand against the utter lack of documentary evidence of the alleged Popess over a four-hundred-year period. Stanford (32–4 and passim), an ardent believer in the Popess's historicity, draws curious strength from the fact of these late interpolations: in his view, they belie the "time-honored retort of the Catholic church" to the story, that is, that it was a Reformation forgery. But this is to ignore or distort the existence of scores, if not hundreds, of known pre-Reformation allusions; to read Catholic rebuttals to Protestant attempts to scandalize the church back into a pre-Reformation *Weltanschauung*; and to confuse the medieval church's lack of interest—for whatever reasons—in formally pronouncing against the story (which was often turned by clergy to homiletic ends, as we have seen) with a massive, and massively unsuccessful, attempt to cover up.

What factors may have shaped the legend, which is the product, after all, of medieval churchmen? Almost 150 years ago, Döllinger noted the rapid spread of the story from the end of the thirteenth century, that is, at the time of the pontificate of Boniface VIII (1294–1303), who was often at odds with the mendicant orders. More recently, Boureau has masterfully traced the tension between the papacy and the orders from 1254–60, and has brought attention to the tumult over the abdication of the aged and unsuited Celestine V, called by many the "angelic Pope," and the subsequent election of Boniface, who was widely criticized as an illegitimately installed "pseudopope." The analogy with the Popess is intriguing, especially as we remember that the story in Martinus's chronicle concludes on a question of applied canon law, in declaring her reign invalid, since she was ineligible, even if elected legally: She is not placed on the list of the holy pontiffs "by reason of the nonconformity that the female sex involves in this matter." The Pardoes (56 ff.) cite a 1054 letter of Pope Leo IX to Michael Cerularius, patriarch of Constantinople, in which the pontiff, inveighing against the practice of promoting eunuchs to important ecclesiastical positions, alludes to the Eastern Church having "once raised a woman to the seat of its pontiff"; the *Chronicon Salernitanum* (ca. 980) relates that during the time of Charlemagne (742–814), the niece of the patriarch of Constantinople, disguised as a eunuch, was chosen as bishop over all and reigned for almost a year and a half before an evil spirit exposed the scandal. A betrayal by the devil, we note, figures in a number of the Popess narrations, for example,

Chronica Minor and *Flores Temporum*. Perhaps the memory of a eunuch allegedly rising to the Patriarchate supplied an analogy with a woman Pope or a mistress of a Pope assuming the Chair of St. Peter, or with a dissolute pope himself being satirically "identified" as female.

Two aspects of the legend during the Middle Ages deserve a moment's attention: the supposed detour made by popes along the coronation route from the Vatican to the Lateran, allegedly to shun the street where the Popess gave birth; and the reputed manual verification of the papal claimant's testicles. As regards the former, it appears that from the mid-twelfth century the route of the papal procession did in fact change its course near the Church of San Clemente, away from a narrow street (now the Via dei Querceti), in favor of what is now the Via Labicana, to reach the Colosseum. This was, as D'Onofrio (212–40) makes clear, almost certainly the result of the increased number of people in the procession; during a time when the papacy was solidifying its power and the last vestiges of the earlier Roman carnival/parodic spirit of the old Cornomannia festival were being rooted out, it was early interpreted as a deliberate detour, as we have seen. Boureau (90) reports the rumor that the narrow Via dei Querceti created a bottleneck that hastened the Popess's labor; at any rate, the street came to be called the *vicus papisse*, and a chapel there with a fresco of the Virgin and Child came to be seen as a shrine to the Popess and her child.

The alleged manual examination of the papal claimant's genitalia, performed by a junior deacon through a opening in the papal chair, aimed, of course, to guard against the election of another woman Pope. It was first reported by the Benedictine Geoffrey de Courlon and the Dominican Robert d'Uzès in the mid-1290s, then not again until the late fourteenth century in the continuation of the chronicle of Johannes of Viktring, and in 1379 by Adam of Usk, whose impossible "eyewitness" account is perhaps to be explained by the Welsh cleric's bitter disappointment in returning home without having received the preferment from Rome he sought.[7] By 1406, the humanist Jacopo d'Angelo, apparently more successful in *his* quest for papal preferment, denies in his report of the coronation of Gregory XII that such a rite existed, and accounts for the false belief along largely correct lines by explaining the meaning and function of various chairs in the coronation ritual: one chair at the Lateran, called the *sedes stercoraria*, on which the Pope sits to remind him "that he rises out of clay and dung," that is, that he is subject to the failings of our human nature; and two porphyry seats in the Chapel of San Sylvester (which, because they are pierced, Jacopo says, "the common people tell the senseless fable that someone touches him as he sits to prove that he is indeed a man"). Seated in the latter, the Pope receives, respectively, the papal staff and keys (i.e., the power to govern, granted by Christ to Peter) and a red belt hung with twelve precious stones (invoking the Old Testament priesthood).[8] The two porphyry chairs had first been noted in the investiture of Paschal II in 1099, as found in the *Liber Pontificalis*. The legend of the rite of verification gained some currency in the fifteenth century, sometimes linked to the story of the Popess, sometimes without explicit reference to her. But by 1474, when the humanist Platina (Bartolomeo Sacchi of Piádena) finished his *Vitae pontificum*, a continuation of the *Liber pontificalis*, the legend had become confused and debased: Platina relates the story of the Popess as something told by obscure and untrustworthy authors whom many people nonetheless believe. He then gives the most grudging acceptance—"I will not deny it," he says—to the alleged reason for the change in the route of the procession, but "collapses" the various chairs into one: the chair is pierced, he concludes, so the Pope will know he is subjected to nature and must defecate![9] In fact, the "stercory chair" was eliminated from the rite of investiture in 1560, while the two pierced chairs were last used in the accession of Leo IX in 1513. One was taken from the Vatican by Napoleon after the Treaty of Tolentino and is now in the Louvre; the other is still in the Vatican Museum, where Stanford, writing in 1998 and still confusing the pierced chair with the *sedes stercoraria*, surreptitiously sat on it and declared it to be definitely not a commode!

SUGGESTIONS FOR FURTHER READING

The imaginary character I have referred to here as "the Popess" is either unnamed in early sources or called Johannes (hence Johanna/Joan, though Boccaccio, who calls her Johanna in the title of the section devoted to her in the *De Mulieribus claris* [1375; G. Guarino (trans.), 1963, ch. XCIX], refers to her as perhaps named Giliberta in the actual text). To Wycliffe, her name is Anna; to Adam of Usk and John Hus, Agnes. As Johannes, she is sometimes identified as Pope John VIII.

The most complete and comprehensive list of sources regarding the Popess is that of Alain Boureau, *La Papessa Jeanne*, Paris, 1988; Lydia G. Cochrane (trans.), *The Myth of Pope Joan*, Chicago and London: University of Chicago, 2001. This is and will remain the definitive treatment of the subject; citations and bibliography in this chapter owe a heavy debt to Boureau's masterly analysis. Earlier collections of notices include, most notably, Friederich Spanheim, *Disquisitio historica de Papa foemina inter Leonem IV et Benedictum III*, Leiden, 1691, consulted in its French adaptation, *Histoire de la papesse Jeanne*, 2 vols., Paris, 1720; Johann Joseph Ignaz von Döllinger, *Die Papst-Fabeln des Mittelalters*, Munich, 1963; Alfred Plummer (trans.), *Fables Respecting the Popes of the Middle Ages*, London, Oxford, and Cambridge: Rivingtons, 1871; and, to be used with caution, Emmanouël D. Rhoidēs, *Pope Joan, the Female Pope: A Historical Study*, Charles H. Collette (trans.), London: Redway, 1886; originally published in Greek, 1879.

The story's unhistoricity was early recognized by J. Aventinus; Onofrio Panvinio, Revision of Platina, *Vitae pontificum,*Venice, 1563; with many subsequent editions; Robert Bellarmine, *Disputationes de controversiis christianae fidei*, 1.3.24, Ingolstadt, 1586; and the Protestant David Blondel, *Familier esclaircissement de la question, si une femme a esté assise au siège papal de Rome* . . ., Amsterdam, 1647. Later works include Döllinger, *Fables Respecting the Popes of the Middle Ages*; Herbert Thurston, *Pope Joan*, London: Catholic Truth Society, 1917; Boureau, *The Myth of Pope Joan*, and that same author's entry "Joan," in *The Papacy: An Encyclopedia*, Philippe Levillain (gen. ed.), New York and London: Routledge, 2002, 2:829–30; Cesare D'Onofrio, *La Papessa Giovanna*, Rome, 1979; and Rosemary and Darroll Pardoe, *The Female Pope*, Wellingborough, Northamptonshire, UK: Aquarian, 1988. This last item along with Boureau's study constitute the two most important works on the subject. More sympathetic and credulous studies include Emmanouël Rhoidēs, *Pope Joan, the Female Pope*; Henri Perrodo-Le Moyne, *Un Pape nommè Jeanne*, Angiers: Coopèrative Angevine, 1972; Elizabeth Gould Davis, *The First Sex*, New York: Putnam, 1971, pp. 267–70; Joan Morris, *Pope John VIII, an English Woman, Alias Pope Joan*, London, 1985; Mariangela Rinaldi and Mariangela Vicini, *Buon Appetito, Your Holiness* (1998), Adam Victor, New York: Macmillan, 2000, pp. 57–68 (including a number of aphrodisiac recipes dedicated to her!); and Peter Stanford, *The Legend of Pope Joan*, New York: Henry Holt, 1998. Treatments in drama and fiction include Elkanah Settle, *The Female Prelate: Being the History of the Life and Death of Pope Joan*, 1680; Renée Dunan, *Pope Joan*, H. Graeme (trans.), London: Hutchinson, 1930; Richard Ince, *When Joan Was Pope*, London: Partridge, 1931; Clement Wood, *The Woman Who Was Pope: A Biography of Pope Joan, 853–855 A.D.*, New York: Faro, 1931; George Borodin, *The Book of Johanna*, London: Staples, 1947; Emmanouël Rhoidēs, *Pope Joan, A Romantic Biography* (1866), Lawrence Durrell (trans.), London: Verschoyle, 1971; and Donna Woolford Cross, *Pope Joan: A Novel*, New York: Crown, 1996. I have not seen E. M. Van der Helder, *Pope Joan in Legend and Drama: A Case Study in German Medieval Drama*, Armidale, 1987. For the Popess in religious polemic, Renaissance to twentieth century, see especially R. and D. Pardoe, *The Female Pope*, pp. 64–71 and their bibliography, p. 102; for the Popess card in the Tarot deck, see Boureau, pp. 165–71, and Pardoe, pp. 93–5.

NOTES

1. Jean de Mailly, *Chronica universalis mettensis*, in *Monumenta Germaniae Historica, Scriptores*, 24: 514.
2. Etienne de Bourbon (Stephanus de Borbone), *Tractatus de diversis materiis praedicabilibus*, Paris, MS. BN Lat. 15970, fol. 574r.
3. Johann Burchard, *Diarium*, Louis Thusane (ed.), Paris, 1883, 1:233; for Luther's report, see Eugène Müntz, "La légende de la Papessa Jeanne," *La Bibliofilia* 1900, pt. 2, p. 333; Robert Bellarmine, *Opera omnia*, ed. 1872, 1:474–5.

4. *Iacopo de Voragine e la sua Cronaca di Genova dalle Origini al* MCCXCVII, Giovanni Monleone (ed.), Rome, 1941, 2:4.
5. *Chronica minor*, Oswald Holder-Egger (ed.), in *Monumenta Germaniae Historica, Scriptores*, 24:181, 212.
6. *Chronica de Romanis pontificibus et imperatoribus*, in *Monumenta Germaniae Historica, Scriptores*, 22:428.
7. Geoffroy de Courlon, *Chronique de l'Abbate de Saint-Pierre-le-Vif de Sens*, G. Julliot (ed.), Sens, 1876, pp. 296–9; Robert de Uzès, *Le Livre de visions*, Jeanne Bignami Odier (ed.), *Archivum fratrum praedicatorum* 25, 1955, 274; Johannes, Abbot of Viktring, *Liber certarum historiarum, Monumenta Germaniae Historica, Scriptores Rerum Germanicarum*, 1:106–7; Adam of Usk, *Chronicon Adae de Usk 1377–1404*, E. M. Thompson (ed. and trans.), London, 1876, pp. 88, 215.
8. Jacopo d'Angelo of Sarperia, Letter to Emmanuel Chrysoloras, appendix to *Leonardi Dathi . . .Epistolae XXXIII*, L. Mehus (ed.), Florence, 1743.
9. *Vitae pontificum*, ed. Giacinto Gaida (ed.), *Rerum Italicarum Scriptores*, Bologna, 1932, 1:151–2.

7 Medieval Monks
Funnier Than You Thought

Liam Ethan Felsen

In "An Austere Age Without Laughter," Michael George examines the mistaken idea that medieval people lacked a sense of humor by tracing a theoretical view of laughter as it existed in the Middle Ages. In this chapter, I focus not on the general theory of medieval laughter but on one particular figure: the medieval monk. It is a popular misconception among students that medieval monks are stereotypically bald (tonsured) old men, huddled over a candle in a scriptorium, laboriously copying manuscripts, never speaking, and never laughing. This is, however, not the case, as the surviving literature can attest. Humor existed not only in the vernacular tradition but also in the writings of the very monks who argued against laughter.

When focusing on the medieval monk, an examination of the place of laughter in the Middle Ages rightly begins with the various rules for monks, in particular Benedict's Rule.[1] There is something of an urban legend that seems to indicate a definite sense of humor within the rule itself. According to the legend, the passage reads:

> If any pilgrim monk come from distant parts—if he wish as a guest to dwell in the monastery, and will be content with the customs which he finds in the place and do not perchance by his lavishness disturb the monastery, but is simply content with what he finds: he shall be received for as long a time as he desires. If, indeed, he find fault with anything, or expose it, reasonably, and with the humility of charity: the Abbott shall discuss it prudently, lest perchance God had sent him for this very thing. But if he have been found lavish or vicious in the time of his sojourn as guest—not only ought he not to be joined to the body of the monastery, but also it shall be said to him, honestly, that he must depart; lest, by sympathy with him, others also become contaminated.[2]

This passage, however funny it might seem, is found only in a gloss of the Rule, not in the Rule itself. But by closely examining certain key passages from the Rule, it is possible to see that medieval monks were allowed to laugh, albeit quietly and without excess.[3] Chapter 4.53 of the Rule instructs monks "not to speak useless words and such as provoke laughter" and also "not to love much or boisterous laughter."[4] Chapter 6.8 says that "coarse jests, and idle words or speech provoking laughter, we condemn everywhere to eternal exclusion; and for such speech we do not permit the disciple to open his lips."[5] And Chapter 7 of the Rule describes the degrees of humility towards which a proper monk should strive:

> The tenth degree of humility is, when a monk is not easily moved and quick for laughter, for it is written: "The fool exalteth his voice in laughter" (Ecclesiasticus 21.23). (7.59)

> The eleventh degree of humility is, that, when a monk speaketh, he speak gently and without laughter, humbly and with gravity, with few and sensible words, and that he be not loud of voice, as it is written: "The wise man is known by the fewness of his words." (7.60–1)[6]

Taken together, these strictures give a definite impression of the level of seriousness with which medieval monks were expected to conduct themselves. Nonetheless, as E. R. Curtius shows, the rule "tacitly permitted moderated laughter" (p. 421) as long as the monks refrained from *risum multum et excussum* (much or boisterous laughter) or *scurrilitates* (coarse jests). Curtius also points to later authors who, following upon the looseness of the rule, also examine the "question to what extent clerics might jest": Sulpicius Severus, Hugh of St. Victor, John of Salisbury, Peter Cantor, and Walter of Chatillon. These authors suggest that monks were allowed a modicum of laughter, as long as the rest of the time they remained as serious as possible (p. 421).

Rules other than St. Benedict's suggest the same, that "it is only immoderate or excessive laughter which must be condemned, and not laughter *per se*" (Resnick 94). The sixth century *Regula Pauli et Stephani* advises that laughter beyond its proper bounds leads to argument and opens up the soul to the devil.[7] Donatus's *Regula ad virgines* forbids monks to tell stories or laugh only while at work or in choir (although it is not specifically forbidden anywhere else).[8] Isidore of Seville's *Regula monachorum* prescribes a penance of only three days for a monk who laughs during choir.[9] And St. Columban's *Regula coenobialis* prescribes a special fast for anyone who laughs unpardonably during a psalm service (Resnick 94–5).[10] All of these various rules seem to restrict only the *risum multum et excussum* that Benedict describes; Smaragdus, in a commentary on Benedict's Rule, describes how laughter is not completely forbidden unless it leads to lightmindedness (*levitas*).[11] While secular authors often disregarded these strictures, Resnick suggests that the monks who wrote those strictures stood by them:

> While it may have been incumbent upon the worthy knight to laugh in the face of danger, the monk saw his spiritual dangers as all too real and found no cause to laugh. The penitent in particular would not

accept that laughter and compunction could co-exist in the same mind or heart. The former, then, had to be rooted out in order to develop the latter. The desire to imitate the virtues of Christ and the saints as well led monastic authors to caution that laughter ought to be avoided—if not always, then at least very often. (Resnick 100)

If this were true, however, the monastic literature that has survived should include only texts that exhibit a modicum of laughter, not texts which contain *risum multum et excussum*. This is, however, not the case.

Medieval monks often engaged in writing a popular, vulgar brand of religious dialogue such as that of the *Joca monachorum* and the *Altercatio Hadriani augusti et Epictetus philosophi*. These texts are typically sets of questions and answers, varying in number, that deal with the more colorful, trivial aspects of biblical lore. Examples of the types of questions these texts ask are paradoxes ("Who was born and did not die?"—Adam); famous firsts ("Who was the first priest?"—Melchisedech); short, quirky definitions ("What is sleep?"—"The image of death"); and riddles ("What is that which, if you remove the head, it rises up even taller?"—"Go to bed and there you will discover the answer").[12] These texts intermingled and spread widely. They were copied, rearranged, and excerpted until they could be found not only in such texts as the *Joca monachorum* and the *Altercatio Hadriani augusti et Epictetus philosophi*, but also the *Collectanaea pseudo-Bedae*, the *Disputatio Adriani augusti et Epicteti philosophi*, Alcuin's *Disputatio regalis et nobillisimi iuvenis Pippini cum Albino scholastico*, the *Prebiarum de multorium exemplaribus*, the Old English *Solomon and Saturn* and *Adrian and Ritheus*, and the Middle English *Questiones bytwene the Maister of Oxenford and his Clerk*. All of these texts display a vulgarization of religious subjects, treating them as popular trivia, meant more for fun and humour than for any overtly didactic, serious purpose.

Mild parodies such as the *Cena Cypriani*, while not necessarily the ribald *fabliaux* of Chaucer's "Miller's Tale," nevertheless also stretch the limits of what would be considered *risum multum et excussum*. The *Cena Cypriani*, completely rewritten four times (twice into verse), and likewise reworked nearly every time it was copied, shows "a greater creativity on the part of scribes than might be supposed and reveals in addition a remarkable enthusiasm on the part of the average cleric, not only for literary creativity, but for humor and frivolity" (Bayless 14). The *Cena Cypriani* describes a fictional feast attended by a large number of Old and New Testament figures; the feast is described by using a mix of scriptural passages and allusions, in which these characters reenact their traditional roles in new, humorous ways. For example, upon arriving at the feast, celebrating the wedding of Theos, son of Abatheos, it was perfectly normal for Sampson to offer *mandibulam asini* (the jawbone of an ass) and for Judas to bring *argentum* (silver). When Abatheos suggests that those in attendance exercise in order to build up a good appetite, Noah *arcam edificavit* (built an ark) and Moses *legem dedit* (gave the law). And finally, when everyone was sitting, Jesus *benedixit* (blessed) those in attendance while Pilate *manus abluit* (washed his hands). The *Cena Cypriani* is a powerful example of the way that monks often disregarded their own strictures. While it is only mildly satirical, the *Cena* was one of the most widely circulated texts of the early Middle Ages, surviving in fifty-four different manuscripts (Bayless 10). Clearly, the monks enjoyed both the reading and writing of this type of mildly humorous text.

There are other texts that go far beyond the *Cena Cypriani* in the scope of their ribald humor. In drinkers' masses and hymns, riotous parodies of liturgical texts, "condemnation is much like commendation" (Bayless 93). These kinds of drinkers' texts are centered around the tavern, in which Jesus has been supplanted by Bacchus, the god of wine. In the drinkers' mass *Confitemini dolio*, the writer clearly parodies the liturgy far beyond the bounds of what Benedict would have considered acceptable. In this example, the author has corrupted the Lord's Prayer:

> *Pater Bacche qui es in schyphis, sanctificetur bonum vinum. Adveniat damnum tuum. Fiat tempestas tua sicut in schypho sic etiam in taberna. Potum nostrum da hobis hodie. Et dimitte nobis pocula nostra, sicut et nos dimittimus compotatoribus nostris. Et sic nos inducas inebrietatem, sed ne libera nos a vino.*

> (Father Bacchus who art in cups, hallowed be good wine. Thy ruination come. Thy turmoil be done in the cup as it is in the tavern. Give us this day our daily drink. And send forth our cups to us as we send forth to our fellow drinkers. And lead us not into drunkenness, but do not deliver us from wine.) (Bayless 349, 352–3.)[13]

The parody is amplified further in a similar drinkers' Mass, the *Missa potatorum*, which, instead of "do not deliver us from wine," reads *sed libera nos a vomitu* (but deliver us from vomit; Bayless 340, 344).[14]

Other texts go even further past the bounds of *risum multum et excussum*. *Quondam fuit factus festus* is a particularly graphic example, in which a solitary, sober monk describes the "descent into inebriation" of his brethren:

Abbas vomit et Prioris;	(The abbot vomited and the prior;
Vomis cadit super floris;	The vomit fell on the floor [sic];
Ego pauper steti foris,	I, a poor man, stood outside,
Et non sum laetitia.	and I was not happy.) (Bayless 96–7)[15]

The next morning (according to a separate version of the poem), the degradation continues:

Abbas mingit suum stratum,	(The abbot wets his bed,
Prior merdans ad cellatum,	The prior craps his cell,
Cocus vomit in ollatum	The cook vomits in the pot
De turpis material.	A nasty substance.) (Bayless 97–8)[16]

Similar to this is the now (in)famous line, *Meum est propositum in taberna mori* (It is my intention to die in the tavern), originally found in what is now termed "The Archpoet's Confession,"[17] but these days more likely to be seen on college students' t-shirts than anywhere else. Far from being a serious condemnation of drinking, poems such as this one seem more to celebrate it, for "if drinking transformed a man into a fool, the comic value was even greater if the fool was a cleric: drinking had the thrill of being improper, and the degradation was greater when drunkenness brought down the supposedly dignified man of God" (Bayless 96). Excessively describing the gross details in order to create *risum multum et excussum*, medieval monks often participated in disregarding the strictures they were meant to follow.

While Benedict's Rule does restrict the amount and type of laughter that monks were allowed to enjoy, the surviving literature shows us that humor was much more prevalent among the clergy than the Rule would suggest. Medieval monks were much more than old, boring, and bald—they engaged in exercises of trivia, riddles, and paradox. They wrote humorous parodies that reworked the scriptural passages with which they were so familiar. And going far beyond the bounds of what the Rule would term *risum multum et excussum*, they wrote drinkers' masses and hymns that seem to commend rather than condemn the very vices that they were supposed to avoid. It is a clear misconception to conceive of medieval monks as stereotypically boring, poring over manuscripts in the half-light of the scriptorium. They were vibrant, intellectual, humorous people, no different than we are today.

SUGGESTIONS FOR FURTHER READING

Martha Bayless, *Parody in the Middle Ages*, Ann Arbor: University of Michigan, 1996.
Martha Bayless and Michael Lapidge (eds.), *Collectanea pseudo-Bedae*, Dublin: School of Celtic Studies, Dublin Institute for Advanced Studies, 1998, pp. 13–24.
J. Cross and T. Hill (eds.), *The Old English Prose Solomon and Saturn and Adrian and Ritheus*, McMaster Old English Studies and Texts 1, Toronto: University of Toronto, 1982.
E. R. Curtius, *European Literature and the Latin Middle Ages*, Willard R. Trask (trans.), Princeton: Princeton University, 1990.
L. W. Daly and Walther Suchier, *Altercatio Hadriani augusti et Epicteti philosophi*, Illinois Studies in Language and Literature 24 (nos. 1–2), Urbana: University of Illinois, 1939.
Timothy Fry (ed.), *The Rule of St. Benedict: In Latin and English with Notes*, Collegeville MN: Liturgical, 1981.

Paul Lehmann, *Die Parodie im Mittelalter*, Munich, 1922.

I. M. Resnick, "'Risus Monascticus': Laughter and Medieval Monastic Culture," *Revue Benedictine* 97, 1987, 90–100.

Walter Suchier, *Das mittellateinische Gesprach Adrian und Epictitus mebst verwandten Texten (Joca monachorum)*, Tubingen, 1955.

J. S. P. Tatlock, "Medieval Laughter," *Speculum* 21, 1946, 289–94.

Thomas Wright, *The Latin Poems Commonly Attributed to Walter Mapes*, London, 1841.

NOTES

1. While a wider focus would begin with passages from the Old and New Testaments, and perhaps with more classical and patristic authors (in particular John Chrysostom, bishop of Constantinople), it seems much more proper to begin a discussion of medieval monks with the very handbook that governed their existence. See Timothy Fry (ed.), *The Rule of St. Benedict: In Latin and English with Notes*, Collegeville MN: Liturgical, 1981.

2. "St. Benedict's Monastic Rule," in *Library of Original Sources*, Oliver J. Thatcher (ed.), New York: University Research Extension, 1907, p. 160.

3. The following translations of the rule are from the translation by Timothy Fry (1981).

4. Fry, pp. 184–5, 4.53, "Verba vana aut risui apta non loqui, risum multum aut excussum non amare."

5. Fry, pp. 190–1, 6.8, "Scurrilitates vero vel verba otiosa et risum moventia aeterna clausura in omnibus locis damnamus et ad talia eloquia discipulum aperire os non permittimus."

6. Fry, pp. 200–1, 7.59–61, "Decimus humilitatis gradus est si non sit facilis ac promptus in risu, quia scriptum est: Stultus in risu exaltat vocem suam. [60] Undecimus humilitatis gradus est si, cum loquitur monachus, leniter et sine risu, humiliter cum gravitate vel pauca verba et rationabilia loquatur, et non sit clamosus in voce, [61] sicut scriptum est: Sapiens verbis innotescit paucis."

7. *Regula Pauli et Stephani*, J. M. Villanova (ed.), Montserrat, 1959.

8. Donatus, *Regula ad virgines* XVII, *Patrlogia Latina* 87.

9. Isidore of Seville, *Regula monachorum* 17.1, *Patrologia Latina* 83.

10. In *Medieval Handbook of Penance*, J. T. McNeill and H. M. Gamer (eds. and trans.), New York: Columbia University, 1938.

11. See Smaragdus, *Commentaria in regulam Sancti Benedicti* VII, *Patrologia Latina* 103.

12. The answer to this last riddle is "pillow."

13. Martha Bayless has edited this text for the first time, although parts of it are reproduced in Antony Marks, "The Parody of Liturgical and Biblical Texts in Germany in the Sixteenth and Seventeenth Centuries," PhD diss., University of Cambridge, 1970, pp. 320–2.

14. Bayless has edited this version of the text for the first time.

15. From London, British Library, Harley MS 913, originally printed in Thomas Wright and James Orchard Halliwell, *Reliquiae Antiquae*, 2 vols., London: William Pickering, 1841–43; reprinted New York: AMS, 1966, 1:141.

16. Originally printed in W. Wattenbach, "Das Fest des Abts von Gloucester," *Anzeiger fur Kunde der deutschen Vorzeit* 28, 1881, cols. 121–8.

17. There are a great number of parodies of the "Archpoet's Confession"; see Lehmann, pp. 164–7.

8 Medieval Attitudes Toward Muslims and Jews

Michael Frassetto

The calling of the First Crusade by Pope Urban II in 1095 illustrates for many the fundamental attitude that medieval Christians held toward the members of the other Abrahamic faiths, Judaism and Islam. Indeed, the Crusades dramatically reveal the adversarial relationship that character-ized much of Western Christendom's relationship with Muslims and Jews. Clearly, the Crusades were aimed at rescuing the Holy Lands from what Westerners thought were pagans and infidels. The image of Muslims as idol-aters and heretics was increasingly developed in medieval Europe from this time forward, as was the image of Muhammad (570–632) as a drunken and lascivious blasphemer. The first and later crusades also contributed toward violence against the Jews, most notably the pogroms of Mainz, Cologne, and Speyer in 1096. The image of the Jew also suffered as a stereotypical portrait of a greedy, lustful, and diabolical Jew began to emerge after the year 1000. Indeed, a persecuting mentality emerged in European society beginning in the eleventh century, as the stereotypes of Muslims and Jews demonstrate;[1] at the same time, however, a more open and tolerant view of Muslims and Jews developed alongside the negative stereotypes.

Ecclesiastics in most of Western Christian Europe, unlike those in the Byzantine Empire, paid little attention to Islam and Muhammad before the eleventh century, the era Richard Southern called the "age of ignorance."[2] But as European self-confidence reappeared and as the boundaries of Europe expanded, leaders of church and state became increasingly engaged with defining Muslims and their faith. Already at the beginning of the eleventh century, Christian authors portrayed Muslims as enemies of the faith, min-ions of Antichrist set on the destruction of all Christendom.[3]

In the generations to come, an even harsher and more scandalous per-ception of Muslims and Islam would emerge, and this view is perhaps best revealed in the *Chanson de Roland*, which appeared in written form around 1100. The *Chanson* depicts Muslims as pagans and idolaters who worship the false gods Apollyon, Tervagant, and Mahomet. Muslims are described as deceitful, treacherous, cowardly, and in error. They destroy their idols when they lose a battle and are willing to sacrifice their children for personal gain. Later *chansons* identified Muslims in similar fashion and made them even crueler and cowardly as well as worshippers of Satan. The stereotype of the Muslim "other" is reinforced by the crusaders and crusade literature, despite the close proximity to and presumed greater knowledge of Islam of the crusaders in the Holy Lands. The leaders of the two crusading orders informed Pope Innocent IV that Muslims worshipped their "God Mahometh." In one of the chronicles of the First Crusade, Muslims are portrayed as barbarians and persecutors of Christians, who worship Muhammad and other gods and make "diabolical sounds." According to the *Gesta Tancredi*, the Muslims worshipped a silver idol of "Mahummet" that was encrusted with gems and gold and was seated on a throne, which the crusaders found in a mosque in Jerusalem.[4] And in yet another account of the first crusaders, a Muslim leader is shown drinking the blood of a martyred Christian.

Muhammad himself was the focus of much attention by Christian scholars in Europe, and the portrait of the prophet was almost uniformly unflattering, to say the least.[5] Consigned to the level of hell with heretics and schismatics by Dante (*Inferno* 28:31–3), Muhammad was described by Christian writers as the Beast of the Apocalypse or a false prophet and a heretic who was taught by a Nestorian Christian and then perverted that teaching. His revelations were designed to satisfy his personal desires for money and power, and he used them as an excuse for war and plunder. Muhammad was also portrayed as using his revelations to satisfy his sexual urges, including his desire for the divorced wife of a close follower. Medieval writers noted not only his heresy and lasciviousness but identified him as a criminal who secretly killed neighbors he envied. According to medieval beliefs, Muhammad's life of criminal behavior, perversion of the faith, deception of the Arabs, and lasciviousness ended in an equally monstrous way. In some accounts, Muhammad was trampled by pigs; in others, he proclaimed that he would rise from the dead but after three days his body was eaten by dogs. His life and death, in the Western understanding, was the opposite of that modeled by the true Christian saint.

Ironically, some of the most scandalous literature owed a debt to Islamic traditions, although much perverted. Indeed, this suggests a familiarity with Islam that is not readily apparent in the polemical traditions already outlined. Moreover, a very different perspective of Islam emerged alongside the polemical tradition. Peter the Venerable, most notably, strove to gain a better understanding of Islam by sponsoring a translation of the Qur'an, even if only to be better equipped to convert the Muslims to Christianity.[6] Crusaders living in the Holy Lands developed good relations with their Muslim subjects, and many of the most ardent foes of Islam recognized that Muslims were monotheists who worshipped neither Muhammad nor idols. Guibert of Nogent (ca. 1060–ca. 1125) recognized that Muhammad was a prophet, and Humbert of Romans argued against the belief in the West that Muslims worshipped the prophet. Moreover, real and fictional Muslims were treated well by Western writers. Saladin (1137/38–93) emerged as a great chivalric hero in medieval romances, was recognized as an honorable opponent by crusaders, and placed in limbo with other worthy pagans by Dante. In Wolfram von Eschenbach's version of the Grail legend from the first half of the thirteenth century, Percival's half brother is a Muslim who appears as literate and noble, and Wolfram himself seems to have held that the virtuous pagan will be saved by God. In *Le Morte Darthur* in the fifteenth century and in earlier Arthurian romances, the Saracen Palomides is regarded as a great and virtuous knight.[7] He is eloquent, humble, strong, and possesses all the virtues of a Christian knight.

Finally, medieval literature and philosophy also owe a great debt to Islamic culture.[8] It has been suggested that Dante's great work was influenced by Islamic traditions, and many scholars have noted the influence of Arabic verse on the development of medieval poetry. Beginning in the twelfth century, Christian philosophy and theology were profoundly influenced by the translations and commentaries of the great Muslim thinkers Avicenna and Averroes.[9] Although the medieval West cultivated a highly negative image of Muslims and Islam, it also enjoyed benefits from Islamic civilization and developed an image that was much closer to the truth.

While Christian attitudes toward Muslims evolved during the Middle Ages, Christian Europe created an equally baseless and hostile image of the Jews. Once again, the turning point in this development seems to have been the eleventh century, which may well have contributed to the massacres of 1096.[10] In fact, in the early part of the century forced conversion and massacres of Jews took place in Aquitaine. Behind the violence stood an image of the Jew as the diabolical enemy of the Christian faith, an image that became increasingly developed over the next few centuries. Medieval writers believed that the Jews, like the Muslims, sought the destruction of Christendom, and many believed that Muslims and Jews conspired to bring about Christendom's demise. Both Ademar of Chabannes and Rodulfus Glaber wrote that the Jews of the West secretly corresponded with al-Hakim, the Egyptian leader who tried to destroy the Holy Sepulcher.[11] Jews were deemed minions of Antichrist, whom they follow thinking him the Messiah, and of Satan. Indeed, it was from the devil that the Jews learned magic and sorcery, which they used against Christians, to damage crops and to invoke demons. They were also accused during the Black Death of poisoning wells and causing epidemics.

At the heart of the negative image of the Jews was the belief that they were responsible for killing Christ, either out of ignorance of who he was or because they knew who he was and refused the truth. The Jews were accused of killing Christ and rejecting the teachings of his church, in part, because they allegedly failed to understand their own scriptures. Moreover, because they killed Christ himself, the Jews were accused of a wide range of crimes against Christians and the church. They were believed to desecrate the cross and other Christian symbols, most notably the eucharistic host. The belief that Jews were magicians and enemies of Christ merged with the notion that they desecrated the Host. It was alleged that they used the Host in their secret, diabolical practices, and it was also believed that the Jews again crucified Christ by mutilating the Host. It was also widely held that they ritually murdered Christian boys. Indeed, one of the most famous legends involved the murder of the fourteen-year-old St. William of Norwich in 1144, which was chronicled by Thomas of Monmouth.[12] The ritual murder of William and of others came about because of an alleged Jewish hatred of humanity and a desire to reenact the crime of deicide. In the thirteenth century, the blood libel emerged, which held that the Jews killed Christians and used their blood in Passover ceremonies. The notion that they were subhuman also developed. Jews were depicted in animal forms, with horns and tails, crooked noses, and were thought to give off a foul odor. They were also perceived as lascivious and greedy.[13]

The Jews were subjected not only to this negative stereotype but faced repeated attacks and were expelled from England, France, and Spain. Their medieval history, however, was not one of unending persecution and hostility. In the early Middle Ages, until roughly the year 1000, the Jews enjoyed relative peace and prosperity. In fact, Agobard of Lyons criticized the Carolingian emperor Louis the Pious for showing excessive favoritism to the Jews. Moreover, the church and the clergy were guided by the principle enunciated by St. Augustine of Hippo, who argued that the Jews should not be harmed because they stand as witness to the truth of Christianity.[14] This teaching greatly tempered relations with the Jews and influenced some of the most important medieval thinkers from Pope Gregory I to Bernard of Clairvaux.[15] Papal policy, too, was shaped by the doctrine of witness, and most popes enjoyed good relations and routinely protected the Jews of Italy. In the eleventh and twelfth centuries, as the anti-Semitic stereotype emerged, Christian scholars and theologians were in frequent contact with learned Jewish men. The works of the great scholar Rashi (Rebbi Shelomoh ben Yitshaq, 1042–1105) were known to many Christian scholars and exegetes. The Victorines of Paris, most notably Andrew of Saint Victor, studied the Hebrew Scriptures more closely as a result of the influence of Rashi and shaped their commentaries according to some of his ideas.[16] Several twelfth-century theologians wrote dialogues or disputations between Jews and Christians. Gilbert Crispin and Peter Abelard wrote such treatises that treated the Jews and their beliefs with a degree of sympathy and toleration that stand in stark contrast with a developing anti-Semitic view.[17] Clearly, contacts between Christian and Jewish scholars occurred and led to greater understanding of and sympathy toward the Jews and their religion. In the thirteenth century, too, Jewish thinkers shaped the works of Christian writers, and Christians gained a better understanding of the Talmud and of contemporary, rather than biblical, Judaism. Finally, the Calabrian abbot and prophet, Joachim of Fiore, developed an eschatological vision that maintained that God would save Gentiles and Jews and that Jews and Christians would join together to form one flock at the end of time.[18] Joachim's vision, like much of his thought, would influence various Christian thinkers throughout the thirteenth and fourteenth centuries.[19]

Although the relations between Christians and Jews were often portrayed stereotypically, the full picture of relations between the faiths is more complicated. Clearly, the prevailing view in the medieval West of Muslims and Jews, which is one of the legacies of the Middle Ages to the modern world, was overwhelmingly negative and hostile. A persecuting mentality, as R. I. Moore noted, formed during the Middle Ages, which contributed to a Christian sense of Jewish (and Muslim) otherness. Muslims and Jews were thought to be the enemies of all Christians and to seek the destruction of Christendom. The negative image of the Muslim and Jew as other, however, existed alongside a positive one. Some medieval writers understood, if only in a limited way, Islam and Judaism and represented the followers of these faiths in a more realistic, if sometimes idealized, fashion. Not only did some medieval scholars and ecclesiastics have a more accurate perception of the rival faiths, but they also learned from them and applied this learning to poetry, philosophy, and other disciplines. Medieval Christian views of Islam and Judaism, therefore, were a complex blend of animosity and respect, of stereotypes and understanding.

SUGGESTIONS FOR FURTHER READING

David R. Blanks and Michael Frassetto, *Western Views of Islam in Medieval and Early Modern Europe: Perception of Other*, New York: Palgrave Macmillan, 1999.

Robert Chazan, *Medieval Stereotypes and Modern Antisemitism*, Berkeley: University of California, 1997.

Jeremy Cohen, *Living Letters of the Law: Ideas of the Jew in Medieval Christianity*, Berkeley: University of California, 1999.

Norman Daniel, *Islam and the West: The Making of an Image*, Oxford: Oneworld, 1993.

Richard Fletcher, *The Cross and the Crescent: Christianity and Islam from Muhammad to the Reformation*, New York: Viking, 2003.

Dominique Iogna-Prat, *Order and Exclusion: Cluny and Christendom Face Heresy, Judaism, and Islam (1000–1150)*, Graham Robert Edwards (trans.), Ithaca, NY: Cornell University, 2002.

Gavin Langmuir, *History, Religion, and Antisemtism*, Berkeley: University of California, 1990.

Robert E. Lerner, *The Feast of Saint Abraham: Medieval Millenarians and the Jews*, Philadelphia: University of Pennsylvania, 2001.

Bernard Lewis, *Islam and the West*, New York: Oxford University, 1993.

María Rose Menocal, *The Arabic Role in Medieval Literary History: A Forgotten Heritage*, Philadelphia: University of Pennsylvania, 2003.

R. I. Moore, *The Formation of a Persecuting Society: Power and Deviance in Western Europe, 950–1250*, Oxford: Basil Blackwell, 1987.

Léon Poliakov, *The History of Anti-Semitism: From the Time of Christ to the Court Jews*, Richard Howard (trans.), London: Elk Books, 1965.

Richard Southern, *Western Views of Islam in the Middle Ages*, Cambridge, MA: Harvard University, 1962.

John Victor Tolan, *Saracens: Islam in the Medieval European Imagination*, New York: Columbia University, 2002.
Joshua Trachtenberg, *The Devil and the Jews: The Medieval Conception of the Jew and its Relation to Modern Anti-Semitism*, Philadelphia: Jewish Publication Society, 1983.

NOTES

1. R. I. Moore, *The Formation of a Persecuting Society: Power and Deviance in Western Europe, 950–1250*, Oxford: Basil Blackwell, 1987, pp. 27–44.
2. R. W. Southern, *Western Views of Islam in the Middle Ages*, Cambridge, MA: Harvard University, 1962, pp. 1–27.
3. Michael Frassetto, "The Image of the Saracen as Heretic in the Sermons of Ademar of Chabannes," in David R. Blanks and Michael Frassetto (eds.), *Western Views of Islam in Medieval and Early Modern Europe: Perception of Other*, New York: Palgrave Macmillan, 1999, pp. 83–96.
4. Raoul de Caen, *Gesta Tancredi* c. 129, in *Recueil des Historiens des Croisades: Historiens Occidentaux*, Paris: Imprimerie Royale, 1841–1906.
5. Useful surveys of the negative portrait among medieval Christian writers can be found in Norman Daniel, *Islam and the West: The Making of an Image*, Oxford: Oneworld, 1993, pp. 100–30; and John Victor Tolan, *Saracens: Islam in the Medieval European Imagination*, New York: Columbia University, 2002, pp. 135–69.
6. On the ideas of Peter the Venerable, see Dominique Iogna-Prat, *Ordonner et exclure: Cluny et la société chrétienne face à l'hérésie, au Judaïsme et à l'Islam, 1000–1150*, Paris: Aubier, 1998, esp. pp. 324–59.
7. Nina Dulin-Mallory, "'Seven Trewe Bataylis for Jesus Sake': The Long-Suffering Saracen Palomides," in Blanks and Frassetto, *Western Views of Islam*, pp. 165–72.
8. María Rose Menocal, *The Arabic Role in Medieval Literary History: A Forgotten Heritage*, Philadelphia: University of Pennsylvania, 2003.
9. David Knowles, *The Evolution of Medieval Thought*, New York: Vintage Books, 1962, pp. 193–205.
10. Robert Chazan, *European Jewry and the First Crusade*, Berkeley and Los Angeles: University of California, 1987.
11. Michael Frassetto, "Heretics and Jews in the Writings of Ademar of Chabannes," *Church History* 71, 2002, 1–15.
12. Gavin Langmuir, "Thomas of Monmouth: Detector of Ritual Murder," in Gavin Langmuir, *Toward a Definition of Antisemitism*, Berkeley and Los Angeles: University of California, pp. 209–36.
13. The classic study of this development is Joshua Trachtenberg, *The Devil and the Jews: The Medieval Conception of the Jew and Its Relation to Modern Anti-Semitism*, Philadelphia: Jewish Publication Society, 1983.
14. Jeremy Cohen, *Living Letters of the Law: Ideas of the Jew in Medieval Christianity*, Berkeley and Los Angeles: University of California, 1999, pp. 19–65.
15. Cohen, *Living Letters of the Law*, pp. 67–270.
16. Beryl Smalley, *The Study of the Bible in the Middle Ages*, Notre Dame, IN: University of Notre Dame, 1964, pp. 149–95.
17. For discussion of the attitudes of 12th-century theologians, see Constant Mews, "Abelard and Heloise on Jews and *Hebraica Veritas*," and Alex Novikoff, "Reason and Natural Law in the Disputational Writings of Peter Alfonsi, Peter Abelard, and Yehuda Halevi" in Michael Frassetto (ed.), *Christian Attitudes*

toward the Jews in the Middle Ages: A Casebook, New York: Routledge, forthcoming.

18. Robert E. Lerner, *The Feast of Saint Abraham: Medieval Millenarians and the Jews*, Philadelphia: University of Pennsylvania, 2001, pp. 5–37.

19. Lerner, *The Feast of Saint Abraham*, pp. 54–117.

II
War

9 The Crusades
Eschatological Lemmings, Younger Sons, Papal Hegemony, and Colonialism

Jessalynn Bird

The Crusades encompass so many factors that attempts to treat them simplistically have generated the most common misconceptions about them, including the Crusades as colonialism, the "younger-son" or "loot" theory, the "eschatological-lemming" theory, the "papal-hegemony" theory, the "abuse" theory, and the "elite" Crusade. Images adopted as intellectual mascots of sorts by proponents of these and other theories enter the popular discourse and dominate public assumptions concerning the Crusades. They include ergotism-riddled peasants quaking in fear of the millennium and following geese to Jerusalem, hermit preachers rousing mobs to assault the Jews in Northern Europe before proceeding eastwards, the cannibalism of the starving Tafurs, crusaders' horses wading through the stagnant blood of slaughtered Muslims, and King Richard parleying with Saladin.

Historians from the Near East and non-European countries have often seen the Crusades as the first emergence of a cyclical European colonialism that would lead to Columbus, the British Empire, and the partitioning of the globe following World War Two. Adherents of this "colonialist" theory characterize the Crusades in the Baltic as a nascent *Drang nach Osten*, the *Reconquista* in Spain, and the crusade against the Albigensians in the Midi as wars of expansion window-dressed with religion. A populace thirsty for indulgences was dragooned into service and new sources of money from the church requisitioned to serve the territorial ambitions of kings and petty princes. Similarly, the "younger-son" theory originated from the assumption that humans are ultimately motivated by economic reasons, in this case the increasing scarcity of land, which led families to save themselves from financial ruin by making the eldest son the sole heir. Eager to rid themselves of their younger sons, they sent them on Crusade in the hope that they would carve out inheritances for themselves in the East. This theory was dealt an effective coup de grâce by Giles Constable and Jonathan Riley-Smith through their studies of the financial sacrifices many families made to send members on Crusade who were, as often as not, heads of the family or elder sons.[1]

The "eschatological-lemming" theory found its most poetical expression in the works of Alphandéry and Cohn,[2] the result of a cross-pollination between what could be dubbed the "common man," "Marxist," or "Protestant" theory and the concept that popular enthusiasm of the Chicken Little "the-sky-is-falling-down" variety was the true origin of the Crusades. These historians rejected the notion that the "true" Crusade was the creation of pope Urban II and a breed of church-tamed noblemen and instead credited its origins to the more unpredictable catalyst of group enthusiasm, which was later supplanted by the institutionalization of the Crusade, its domination by pragmatic kings and noblemen, and the systematic diversion of devotional fervor into acceptable channels. Its most important contribution was to ask, What defines the Crusade, the attitudes of those leading it, or those who go on it?—a question most recently revisited by Christopher Tyerman (with an entirely different conclusion).[3] The "elite" theory, on the other hand, argues that individual choice or popular enthusiasm played little role in the pragmatic success of the Crusades. For strategic victory, a viable military expedition was essential, and Crusades that did not win the patronage of kings or powerful magnates soon evaporated. Proponents of this school focus on the financing, equipage, and mustering of the Crusade's military force, which leads them to conclude that kin-groups and feudal ties of loyalty were the predominant factors in the recruiting of the military men essential for the actual Crusade campaign, while Crusade preaching and popular enthusiasm merely served as a means of funneling alms into the hands of the fighting elite and the mercenaries they hired.

The antithesis to the "lemming" or "layman" theory is the "papal-hegemony" theory, which in its positive form defines the Crusade as a holy war called by the Pope, who proffers the indulgence and privileges without which a true Crusade cannot come into being. A Crusade is *de facto* defined by the Pope; any "crusade" that takes place without the Pope's approbation, such as that of Frederick II in 1229, or the Fourth Crusade once it diverted toward Constantinople, is no Crusade at all. This definition easily gives rise to the "abuse" theory, in which a Crusade promulgated by the Pope for the "pure" motive of liberating the Holy Land is twisted by other parties into a vehicle for their own ambition, including the seizure of land and the combating of political enemies (a charge that could easily be leveled against some popes). A negative variation, which could be labeled the "papal-hegemony" theory, sees the Crusade as a mere prop for papal ambition, an excuse for instituting systematic taxation of the church, and for increasing the Roman pontiffs' ability to meddle in secular affairs in the name of saving the Holy Land. Unfortunately, these theories tend to credit the papacy with the ability to control a coherent crusading movement, assuming it possessed tools of communication and bureaucracy akin to those of the Ministry of Peace in Orwell's *1984*. In reality, medieval popes constantly fought to secure their own political existence and were dependant upon poor and irregular sources of information and faulty lines of communication. Once a Crusade bull left the papal camera, it was a constant and often doomed struggle to ensure that an individual pope's vision of a particular crusade prevailed.

All these theories have been presented in an artificially pure form. Few of the historians cited here and in the bibliography would point to the dominance of one factor alone in the makeup of a Crusade. However, popular misconceptions often latch onto one of these factors, resulting in distorted portrayals of the Crusades. Alternatively, the image of the Crusade is often completely recast and invoked to justify multifarious religious, social, and political campaigns, most recently by both sides in the "war on terrorism." The best hope of understanding the Crusades is to understand the medieval mentality, which was foreign to our own in its lack of neat compartmentalization. Those who went on the Crusades managed to combine without dissonance a dogged dedication to both the Holy Land and the Christian religion with a nagging dread about the possibility of broiling in hell rather than basking in heaven; financial sacrifice and the devotion of the pilgrim with the hardened acumen of an experienced warrior concerned with procuring his next meal from the alien towns and villages through which he passed; the strategic plotting essential for the successful recovery of Jerusalem and the Holy Land with the hope of returning home; and, to the modern mind carefully inculcated in tolerance, an often shocking disregard for persons of other cultures and religions. Just as individuals were capable of balancing varying motivations, so the crusading movement itself was not dictated by any one party but was a true discourse in which the idea and image of the Crusade was constantly recast and recreated in a dialogue between various groups in their quest for differing goals. This approach far better explains the full gamut of movements labeled Crusades, including those headed for the Holy Land, those directed against "pagans," heretics, and political enemies, and the multifarious Crusades of the later Middle Ages.

SUGGESTIONS FOR FURTHER READING

Good single-volume treatments of the Crusades include Norman Housley, *Contesting the Crusades*, Oxford, 2006; Hans Eberhard Mayer, *The Crusades*, John Gillingham, Oxford, 1972; Thomas F. Madden, *The New Concise History of the Crusades*, updated edition, Lanham, MD, 2005; Jean Richard, *The Crusades, c.1071–c.1291*, Cambridge, 1999; Jonathan Riley-Smith, *The Crusades: A History*, 2nd rev. ed., New Haven/London, 2005; Jonathan Riley-Smith, *The Oxford Illustrated History of the Crusades*, Oxford, 1995; Christopher Tyerman, *The Invention of the Crusades*, Toronto/London, 1998; and Christopher Tyerman, *Fighting for Christendom: Holy War and the Crusades*, Oxford, 2004.

Although treatments of Crusades against pagans in the Baltic, the Moors in Spain, heretics in the south of France, and political enemies can be found in the single-volume works listed above, those further interested can turn to Eric Christiansen, *The Northern Crusades*, London, 1997; Norman Housley,

The Italian Crusades, Oxford, 1982; Norman Housley, *The Later Crusades from Lyon to Alcazar, 1274–1580*, Oxford, 1992; Walter L. Wakefield, *Heresy, Crusade and Inquisition in Southern France, 1100–1250*, Berkeley, CA, 1974; Jonathan Sumption, *The Albigensian Crusade*, London, 1978; Michael Costen, *The Cathars and the Albigensian Crusade*, Manchester, UK, 1997; and Beverly Mayne Kienzle, *Cistercians, Heresy, and Crusade in Occitania, 1145–1229*, Rochester, NY, 2001.

Some notable collections of sources on the Crusades include *The Crusades: A Documentary Survey*, James A. Brundage (ed.), Milwaukee, WI, 1962; *The Crusades: Idea and Reality, 1095–1274*, Jonathan and Louise Riley-Smith (eds.), London, 1974; Edward Peters (ed.), *The First Crusade: The Chronicle of Fulcher of Chartres and other Source Materials*, 2nd rev. ed., Philadelphia, 1998; *Christian Society and the Crusades, 1198–1229*, Edward Peters (ed.), Philadelphia, 1971; *Documents on the Later Crusades, 1274–1580*, Norman Housley (ed.), London, 1996; *The Crusades: A Reader*, Emilie Amt and S. J. Allen (eds.), Peterborough, ON, 2003; Francesco Gabrieli (ed. and trans.), *Arab Historians of the Crusades*, E. J. Costello (trans.), New York, 1969; *Crusades: Islamic Perspectives*, Carole Hillenbrand (ed.), New York, 2000.

Regarding the historiography of the Crusades, for excellent treatments of the colonialist and other theories, see James A. Brundage, *The Crusades: Motives and Achievements*, Lexington, MA, 1964; Jonathan Riley-Smith, *The First Crusaders, 1095–1131*, Cambridge, 1997; Christopher Tyerman, *Invention*; and Tyerman, *Fighting for Christendom*, preceding. For a strong statement of the papal position, see Jonathan Riley-Smith, *What Were the Crusades?* London, 1977 (revised in subsequent works); for the "lemming" theory, see P. Alphandéry and A. Dupront, *La Chrétienté et l'idée de croisade*, 2 vols., Paris, 1954–9; and Norman Cohn, *The Pursuit of the Millennium*, Oxford, 1970. For excellent recent work on the contributory role of popular enthusiasm, see Gary Dickson, "The Advent of the *Pastores* (1251)," *Revue Belge de philologie et d'histoire* 66.2, 1988, 249–67; Gary Dickson, "Stephen of Cloyes, Philip Augustus, and the Children's Crusade of 1212," in *Journeys Toward God: Pilgrimage and Crusade*, B. N. Sargent-Baur (ed.), Kalamazoo, MI, 1992, pp. 83–105; and Gary Dickson, "The Flagellants and the Crusades," *Journal of Medieval History* 15, 1989, 227–67. On the role of kings, families, and feudal society, see John France, "Patronage and the Appeal of the First Crusade," in *The First Crusade: Origins and Impact*, Jonathan Phillips (ed.), Manchester, 1997, pp. 5–20; Simon Lloyd, *English Society and the Crusade, 1216–1307*, Oxford, 1988; Jonathan Riley-Smith, *The First Crusaders*, Cambridge, 1997; and Christopher Tyerman, *England and the Crusades, 1095–1588*, Chicago, 1988. Classic formulations of the "papal-hegemony" theory can be found in Henry Charles Lea, *A History of Auricular Confession and Indulgences in the Latin Church*, 3 vols., Volume III: Indulgences, Philadelphia, 1896; and Walter E. Lunt (ed.), *Papal Revenues in the Middle Ages*, 2 vols., New York, 1934; or Lunt, *Financial*

Relations of the Papacy with England to 1327, Cambridge, MA, 1939. For a particularly blatant modern rendition, see R. B. Ekelund et al., *Sacred Trust: The Medieval Church as an Economic Firm*, Oxford, 1996.

Key monographs on the pilgrimage movement closely associated with the Crusades include Jonathan Sumption, *Pilgrimage: An Image of Medieval Religion*, London, 1975, reprinted as *The Age of Pilgrimage: The Medieval Journey to God,* Mahwah, NJ, 2005; and Diane Webb, *Pilgrims and Pilgrimage in the Medieval West,* London/New York, 1999. For fundamental works on the theory of holy war and the concepts of knighthood in service of the church and knightly piety, see Karl Erdmann, *The Origin of the Idea of the Crusade*, Marshall W. Baldwin and Walter Goffart (trans.), Princeton, 1977; and Marcus Bull, *Knightly Piety and the Lay Response to the First Crusade*, Oxford, 1993. For the Peace of God and Truce of God, see H. E. J. Cowdrey, "The Peace and Truce of God in the Eleventh Century," in *Past and Present* 46, 1970; and more recently, Thomas Head and Richard Landes (eds.), *The Peace of God: Social Violence and Religious Response in France around the Year 1000*, Ithaca/London, 1992. For material on indulgences in English, see the works listed on pilgrimage preceding, Bernhard Poschmann, *Penance and the Anointing of the Sick*, T. Courtney (trans. and rev.), Freiburg/London, 1964; and the classic, albeit biased, Henry Charles Lea, *A History of Auricular Confessions and Indulgences in the Latin Church*, 3 vols., *Volume III: Indulgences*, Philadelphia, 1986. For the legal and spiritual privileges granted to crusaders, see James A. Brundage, *Medieval Canon Law and the Crusader*, Madison, 1966. For the preaching of the Crusades, see Christoph T. Maier, *Preaching the Crusades: Mendicant Friars and the Cross in the Thirteenth Century*, Cambridge, 1994; Christoph Maier, *Crusade Propaganda and Ideology: Model Sermons for the Preaching of the Cross,* Cambridge, 2000; and Penny J. Cole, *The Preaching of the Crusades to the Holy Land, 1095–1270*, Cambridge, MA, 1991. For valuable treatments of critics of the Crusades, see Elizabeth Siberry, *Criticism of Crusading*, Oxford, 1985; and Palmer A. Throop, *Criticism of the Crusade: A Study of Public Opinion and Crusade Propaganda,* Amsterdam, 1940 (reprint, Philadelphia, 1975).

NOTES

1. Giles Constable, "The Financing of the Crusades in the Twelfth Century," in *Outremer: Studies in the History of the Crusading Kingdom of Jerusalem Presented to Joshua Prawer*, Jerusalem, 1982, pp. 64–88; Jonathan Riley-Smith, *The First Crusaders, 1095–1131*, Cambridge, 1997.
2. P. Alphandéry and A. Dupront, *La Chrétienté et l'idée de croisade*, 2 vols., Paris, 1954–9; Norman Cohn, *The Pursuit of the Millennium*, Oxford, 1970.
3. Christopher J. Tyerman, "Were There Any Crusades in the Twelfth Century?" *The English Historical Review* 110, 1995, 553–77.

10 The Myth of the Mounted Knight

James G. Patterson

Perhaps no image of the Middle Ages has greater iconic power than that of the mounted knight. Covered from head to foot in burnished steel, the warrior on horseback is the very embodiment of the so-called age of chivalry. Yet contained in this potent image are a number of misconceptions about the nature of medieval warfare. These errors include the impression that from roughly 500 to 1500, armor was an unalterable constant. In reality, protective metal evolved as much during the period as modern aircraft have changed since Kittyhawk. Another fallacy is that knights constituted the majority of the medieval army. The truth is that most armies in the Middle Ages were predominantly made up of infantry, and the knights themselves often fought on foot. Even among the mounted element, true knights were in the minority. A related misconception is that the charge of heavily armored cavalry was irresistible to any force not similarly constituted. In fact, when foot soldiers held their ground—something that occurred far more often than is traditionally realized—they usually triumphed over their mounted counterparts unless the latter were supported by infantry, and possibly archers of their own.[1]

Tradition tells us that Charles Martel's epic victory over the Saracens at Poitiers (Tours) in 732 effectively saved the Christian West from Islamic domination. Whether or not this battle played the pivotal role so often ascribed to it is open to debate. What is more certain is that the triumph of the Frankish host reveals much about the early development of medieval warfare. Recent work by Victor Davis Hanson demonstrates that we have been laboring under a number of misconceptions about the true nature of the army of Charles "the Hammer." The relevance of this research should not be underestimated, for the mounted Frankish warrior is traditionally seen as the progenitor of the medieval knight and the necessity of maintaining him the very basis of feudalism itself. Simply put, Merovingian cavalry utilizing the technological advantage provided by the recent arrival of the stirrup in the West (which allowed the kinetic energy generated by the charging horse and man to be focused on the point of a twelve-foot lance) were able to deliver a charge that was irresistible to those, like the invading Moors, who were not similarly equipped.

The problem posed by Poitiers for this traditional interpretation is the fact that the Franks fought on foot, not on horseback. Wave after wave of *Muslim* cavalry crashed against the Frankish phalanx and were broken. Indeed, superior armor, both chain mail and scale, and discipline were central in Martel's victory. The supposed dawn of the mounted knight must be postponed.[2]

When then can we effectively date the battlefield dominance of the mounted knight? In reality, the answer is never. This is not to say that European chivalry did not come to play a central role in medieval warfare; it certainly did. Armored horsemen could indeed be devastating when encountering untrained levies of feudal infantry, who often fled at their appearance, or when pursuing defeated footmen who had been broken by combined attacks of arms (archers and infantry as well as horse). Moreover, knights served as officers in armies comprised of sizable foot elements. Yet throughout the Middle Ages, unsupported cavalry suffered severely when confronted by disciplined infantry.

This fact, in turn, begs the question: Why? The answer is remarkably simple. Horses, no matter how well-trained, will not charge headlong into an unmoving block of men, especially when this monolith is bristling with sharpened steel. In fact, if the infantry holds its ground, no collision occurs. Cavalry inevitably pulls up short of impact and the riders hack at the mass of men in front of them from the saddle. The mounted rider's superiority in elevation and reach are more than compensated by the foot soldier's density in numbers and ability to thrust up at the exposed stomachs and limbs of the mounts. This fact is confirmed in example after example, even after the stirrup was firmly established in the West by about the year 1000.[3]

William the Conqueror's victory at Hastings in 1066 transformed England. This transitional battle pitted the English King Harold Godwinson's Anglo-Saxons against William's mixed army of Normans and assorted adventurers and mercenaries drawn from across Europe. Although Hastings is sometimes viewed as a triumph of horse over foot, in fact William's victory was the result of a well-integrated assault by a combined force of arms comprising missile (archers), infantry, and shock (cavalry) elements. Yet despite its inferiority in numbers and technology, the English shield wall (both armies were similarly protected with coats of chain mail and conical open-faced helmets) held out at Hastings for most of a very long day against repeated attacks by William the Bastard's Normans.[4]

The 200-year period between 1100 and 1300 is still perceived as the true epic of the mounted knight as the undisputed master of the battlefield. This interpretation also bears qualification. For both in the East, where Europeans were waging the Crusades, and at home, most military activity of the time focused on the siege of cities and castles.[5] In fact, until the advent of effective artillery (ca. 1420), the tremendous advantage offered by defensive fortifications served to dramatically curtail the willingness of combatants to gamble all in open battle. The weaker, or more cautious, side simply retired behind stone walls until disease, shortage of food, or impatience drove off the attacker or conquered the besieged. Throughout the Middle Ages, the great risks involved made decisive open field battle the exception rather than the rule.

During the course of the fourteenth century, disciplined infantry repeatedly demonstrated its superiority over armored cavalry. At Courtrai (1302), the well-armed and highly trained civic militias of the Flemish cities administered a crushing defeat to the chivalry of France. Fighting on foot with bow and, more importantly, pike (a long, metal-tipped lance), the burghers of Ghent and Bruges killed over a thousand of the supposedly invincible mounted French knights.[6] A short time later, the English aristocracy learned the cruel price of class-based military arrogance at the hands of the Scots. At the decisive battle of Bannockburn in 1314, King Robert the Bruce's schiltrons, hedgehogs of well-trained pikemen drawn from the ranks of Scotland's commoners, administered the greatest defeat English chivalry suffered in the Middle Ages. Some thirty-four English lords and hundreds of knights (all of whom rode into combat) fell, while nearly one hundred others were captured. This pivotal event insured the survival of Scotland as an independent nation.[7] Further east, Swiss halberdiers (a halberd is a variation of the pike) destroyed an imperial army consisting primarily of mounted men at arms at Morgarten (1315).

Unlike the French, the English learned from their defeats early in the fourteenth century and radically altered the way in which they waged war. The knights of England gave up their horses, or, more accurately, got off them prior to battle. Of greater import, the English (influenced by the Welsh) dramatically modified one of mankind's oldest weapons, the bow and arrow. Six-foot "longbows" in the hands of commoners came for a time to dominate the battlefields of Europe. The centrality of infantry during the fourteenth century as well as the decisive advantage offered by combined forces of arms is strikingly illustrated by a series of English victories over the French during the Hundred Years War. At Crécy (1346), a vastly outnumbered English army comprised of archers and dismounted men at arms repelled some fifteen cavalry charges mounted by the cream of French chivalry, inflicting thousands of casualties in the process. Ten years later at Poitiers, French knights themselves fought on foot, but the English archers again proved the determining factor. Similarly at Agincourt (1415), Henry V's small English army of 5,000 longbowmen and 1,000 dismounted men at arms faced a French feudal host of 25,000. Despite their overwhelming superiority in numbers, the French (again fighting on foot) failed to modify their tactics and lost some 1,600 lords and knights as well as uncounted thousands of lesser soldiers.[8] By the end of the first quarter of the sixteenth century, gunpowder insured that the centuries-long process in which elite European warriors had encased themselves in armor would reverse itself.

A final question remains: if the mounted knight was never the omnipotent force that has been depicted, what are the origins of the myth? Here the answer must by necessity involve some conjecture. But in all likelihood, it has its basis in class. The literature and art on which we base our popular perceptions of the Middle Ages were sponsored by the only elements in society with the means to support it—the nobility and clergy. When combined with the fact that these groups monopolized political power and religious authority, it is hardly surprising that we are left with a skewed view of the knight's predominant role in combat. Moreover, the primary justification of the entire feudal system, at least initially, was the maintenance of heavily armored, mounted warriors. This, in turn, explains why the most enduring image left us from the cultural flowering of the High Middle Ages is the physical manifestation of its (pre)dominant classes' *raison d'être*. By the fourteenth century, when lowborn archers and pikemen had established their tactical superiority over the noble horsemen, realistic depictions of the nature of warfare would have been psychologically devastating to the seigniorial class.

SUGGESTIONS FOR FURTHER READING

Jim Bradley, *The Routledge Companion to Medieval Warfare*, London: Routledge, 2004.

Kelly DeVries, *A Cumulative Bibliography of Medieval Military History and Technology*, Leiden, Netherlands: Brill, 2005.

———. *Infantry Warfare in the Early Fourteenth Century*, Woodbridge, UK: Boydell, 1996.

David Eggenberger, *An Encyclopedia of Battles: Accounts of Over 1,560 Battles from 1479 BC to the Present*, New York: Dover, 1967.

Victor David Hanson, *Carnage and Culture: Landmark Battles in the Rise of Western Power*, New York: Doubleday, 2001.

John Keegan, *The Face of Battle*, New York: Dorset, 1976.

———. *A History of Warfare*, New York: Alfred A. Knopf, 1993.

Maurice Keen (ed.), *Medieval Warfare: A History*, New York: Oxford University, 1999.

Geoffrey Parker (ed.), *Cambridge Illustrated History of Warfare*, Cambridge University, 1995.

Terence Wise, *Medieval Warfare*, New York: Hastings House, 1976.

NOTES

1. This article is heavily influenced by Victor David Hanson's *Carnage and Culture: Landmark Battles in the Rise of Western Power*, New York: Doubleday, 2001, particularly chapter 5, pp. 135–69.
2. Hanson, *Carnage and Culture.*
3. For the unwillingness of horses to attack an unmoving wall of infantry, see John Keegan, *The Face of Battle*, New York: Dorset Press, 1976, pp. 94–7, 153–9; John Keegan, *A History of Warfare*, New York: Alfred A. Knopf, 1993, p. 297; Hanson, *Carnage*, pp. 135–7; and John Gillingham, "An Age of Expansion, c. 1020–1204" in Maurice Keen (ed.), *Medieval Warfare: A History*, New York: Oxford University, 1999, 76–8.

4. Gillingham, "Age of Expansion," particularly pp. 70–3 and 76–8.
5. Gillingham, "Age of Expansion," pp. 78–81.
6. For Courtrai, see Clifford J. Rogers, "The Age of the Hundred Years War," in *Medieval Warfare: A History*, pp. 136–42.
7. For Bannockburn, see Andrew Ayton, "Arms, Armour, and Horses" in *Medieval Warfare: A History*, pp. 202–3; Rogers, "Age," p. 142.
8. For the three major English victories in the Hundred Years War, see Terence Wise, *Medieval Warfare*, New York: Hastings House, 1976, pp. 110–20, and Keegan, *Face of Battle*, chapter 2.

III
Science

11 The Myth of the Flat Earth

Louise M. Bishop

Many medieval texts present a spherical earth as well as a spherical cosmos; these contradict a notion many first hear in elementary school: medieval people believed the earth was flat. Even people who should know better, such as the historian and former Librarian of Congress Daniel Boorstin, trot out the story of Columbus proving the earth was round as proof of a medieval belief in a flat earth (see his *The Discoverers*, New York, 1983). Instead of proving a medieval belief in a flat earth, accounts like Boorstin's prove the astonishing persistence of what medievalist Jeffrey Burton Russell wryly refers to as the Flat Error. Russell has taken it upon himself not only to track in detail medieval conceptions of a spherical earth but also to suggest the Flat Error's genesis in the eighteenth and nineteenth centuries and to account for its persistence. Russell's brief book, *Inventing the Flat Earth: Columbus and Modern Historians* (Praeger, 1991), provides a comprehensive and detailed account of medieval ideas about the cosmos. The following essay uses points along the complete trail Russell marks, from the Greeks to the twentieth century, along with some Web-based images of the spherical earth and cosmos and evidence from a fifteenth-century manuscript held by Oxford University, to convince the reader that medieval people thought of and represented their earth as a sphere.

Virtually every thinker and writer of the thousand-year medieval period affirmed the spherical shape of the earth. St. Augustine (354–430) claimed moral, not scientific, meaning for the Bible. Since the shape of the earth makes no moral difference to human salvation, its proof rightly belongs, according to Augustine, in the hands of Greek philosophers, and Augustine counseled trust in their opinions.[1] Every major Greek philosopher declared the earth a sphere: Pythagoras, Parmenides, Plato, Aristotle, Euclid, Archimedes, virtually every philosopher who predates the Common Era. As for the Common Era, marked by Christian theology and philosophy, innumerable Greek and Latin church fathers asserted a spherical earth: Sts. Ambrose (ca. 340–397), Gregory of Nyssa (d. ca. 386), Origen (185–ca. 254), John Chrysostom (ca. 347–407), and John Damascene (677–?), to name only a few. The Venerable Bede (673–735) makes especially clear that the earth is not simply round but a globe like a ball, thus removing any doubt caused by the fact that Latin "orbis" means both "round" and "circular."[2] Later influential theologians, such as Thomas Aquinas (1225–74), Hildegard of Bingen (1098–1179), and Oxford's Robert Grosseteste (1175–1253), all attested to the earth's spherical nature.[3]

Visual evidence is as broad and striking as literary evidence that affirms a ball-like earth. According to Ptolemy of Alexandria (90–168), the planetary and stellar spheres, the complex motions of which included "epicycles" and "deferents," circle a stationary spherical earth. His theory, which uses Aristotle's sphere-based cosmology, was current in the West from the twelfth through the fifteenth centuries. Two-dimensional representations can only approximate three-dimensional objects, and manuscript illustrations of the medieval cosmos, showing labeled concentric rings—the best representation possible—accompany descriptions of the cosmos' spherical nature. John de Sacrobosco's work *De sphaera (On the Spheres)* was the main astronomy textbook in universities in the West from the thirteenth through the mid-sixteenth centuries. One of its manuscript pages is available on the Web courtesy of the New York Public Library.[4] Medieval cosmological calculating instruments such as the astrolabe, a series of calibrated circular metal bands that plots planetary motion as well as figures time, indicate the widespread understanding of the earth as orb.[5] Consider too the work of Geoffrey Chaucer, whose *Treatise on the Astrolabe,* written to "little Louis" his son, illustrates the sophistication of medieval cosmological thinking and its proper audience.

Like literary representations of a spherical earth found in the writings of the church fathers, few, if any, of these visual representations are divorced from the divine. In one example, God the cosmic architect oversees his spherical earth.[6] The kingly orb, symbol of the king's earthly dominion as opposed to God's heavenly one, also testifies to a medieval understanding of the earth as sphere.[7] But even humble, everyday manuscripts repeat the supposition of a round earth. An undecorated handbook-sized collection of medical texts copied in the fifteenth century, held by the Bodleian Library at Oxford University and known by the designation "Bodley 591," explains that "Earth is but a little round ball in the middle of the circle of heaven right as the yolk is in the middle of the egg." In its explanation of eclipses, this same text suggests using an apple for the earth in order to understand the shadow it casts on the moon. Medieval maps figured the earth's spherical nature in ways similar to those used in modern maps: they project a three-dimensional land mass onto a two-dimensional surface with an understanding, like our own, that a flat surface is not the same as a round one.

In light of the overwhelming visual and literary evidence of a medieval understanding of a spherical earth, how did the Flat Error get started? Russell names two medieval flat-earthers: Lactantius (265–345) and Cosmas Indicopleustes (ca. 540), who were, he points out in the third chapter of *Inventing the Flat Earth*, essentially unknown in the Middle Ages, and certainly less influential than the major church fathers or Sacrobosco's university textbook on spheres. While medieval philosophers and teachers ignored Lactantius—perhaps because the church had declared his works heretical (he was too literal-minded)—his work was revived by Renaissance humanists because, according to Russell, they admired his Latin style. Subsequently, Lactantius got another boost in name recognition when, in 1543, Nicholas Copernicus (1473–1543) used Lactantius as a whipping boy for mistaken cosmology generally. Copernicus subtly likens Lactantius's erroneous views to contemporary opinion that rejected his own (Copernicus) heliocentric universe. While Copernicus never presented Lactantius's view as the majority opinion (quite the opposite, in fact), nineteenth-century scientists, bent on demonizing religion's role in the history of science and needing to cast medieval science in a negative light, portrayed Lactantius's work as central and influential.

The uses made of the obscure Greek Cosmas Indicopleustes reflect a similar history. Cosmas insisted on a literal interpretation of Biblical metaphors, such as the tabernacle's squareness, to argue the literal flatness or squareness of the earth. Cosmas was clearly a minority of one—only three Greek manuscripts of his work survive, according to Russell (34)—and his views were condemned in the ninth century by the Patriarch of Constantinople. Most interestingly, Cosmas's work was translated *into Latin* for the first time in 1706; it was never translated into Latin during the Middle Ages. His works reached the West only at the beginning of the eighteenth century, after the scientific revolution was in full swing. Once Cosmas's work was translated into English at the tail end of the nineteenth century (1897) as proof of medieval wrongheadedness, the die had been cast to make both his and Lactantius's condemned minority opinions the "official" positions of the medieval church.

Admittedly, then, two medieval philosophers—both of them remote, censured, and virtually unknown in the Middle Ages—propounded a flat earth. It is also true that, like the imprecision of the word "orb" indicating either a circle or a sphere, another word, "antipodes," leads to some confusion. Literally speaking, "antipodes" means those whose feet touch the ground opposite yours. The concept of the "antipodes," however, took on another meaning: a possible land mass different from the known land mass of Europe, Asia, and northern Africa. Regarding the antipodes as a land mass, some claimed it to be in the southern hemisphere; others saw the antipodes as a land mass opposite the known land mass, but in the known land mass's own northern hemisphere. The existence of the antipodes, either as land mass or people, was debated by medieval philosophers. There was also debate about the size of the earth sphere's circumference: Ptolemy said 180,000 stades, or 93 million feet; Erastothenes, 252,000 stades, or about 130 million feet, remarkably close to modern calculations.[8] But despite these calculations, both of which were known in the Middle Ages, and the surprising accuracy of Erastothenes, estimates of the distance to the antipodes were quite varied because no one quite knew where they were or even whether they existed.

Nor was there an accurate calculation of the known land mass's size. Yet the existence and location of, and distance to, the antipodes, as well as the size of the known land mass, were of great importance to someone looking to sail to the opposite side of the known world, for whose potential financial backers the smallest distance and most direct route were crucial. That was, of course, the situation for Columbus. Resistance to his plan came not from the idea that the world was flat but from his potential financiers' concerns that the voyage was too long to succeed and that something antipodal might be in the way—which, in the event, turned out to be true.[9]

In the last two chapters of his book, Russell eloquently and convincingly outlines the way "science" as conceived in the eighteenth and nineteenth centuries needed, for all kinds of social reasons, to demonize the Middle Ages (they had learned the technique from Petrarch, inventor of the term "Dark Ages"). The conviction that medieval people believed in a flat earth supports an ideology of scientific progress necessarily achieved at the expense of wrongheaded religion. Many medievalists have unmasked the ways such positivist thinking continues to inflect our understanding of the far-from-unified Middle Ages; they have also critiqued the Romantic sensibility that encourages a rosy-hued assessment of medieval culture. Whatever balancing act a medievalist must perform, no one should use an utter falsity to make a historical point. Russell is surely right that it is high time for modern people to reject the false notion of medieval people's belief in a flat earth.

SUGGESTIONS FOR FURTHER READING

Besides the Web sources already noted, a number of printed books provide good evidence for the medieval idea of a spherical earth. If you are looking for primary sources, you can consult the astronomical textbook of the medieval university in The *Sphere of Sacrobosco and Its Commentators*, edited and translated by the founder of modern medieval scientific studies, Lynn Thorndike (Chicago, 1949). William Caxton's 1490 version of the thirteenth-century *Mirror of the World*, edited by Oliver H. Prior in 1913 and reprinted in 1966 for the Early English Text Society (no. 110), assumes a spherical earth: you can read about the earth being shaped like an apple on page 52. To read about the real challenges Columbus faced on his voyage, among which the fear of a flat earth is entirely absent, read *The Diario of Christopher Columbus's First Voyage to America 1492–1493, Abstracted by Fray Bartolome de las Casas*, Oliver Dunn and James E. Kelley, Jr. (eds. and trans.), Norman, OK, 1989.

For a brief but precise refutation of the Flat Error, see Francis S. Betten, "Knowledge of the Sphericity of the Earth During the Earlier Middle Ages," *Catholic Historical Review* 3, 1923, 74–90, and Charles W. Jones, "The Flat Earth," *Thought* 9, 1934, 296–307. On medieval sciences more generally, read Edward Grant's *The Foundations of Modern Science in the Middle*

Ages: Their Religious, Institutional, and Intellectual Contexts, Cambridge History of Science, Cambridge University, 1996. Grant is one of the most important historians of science working today, and his command of medieval materials, as well as his interpretation of their use, should eliminate any remaining advocates of the Flat Error. Likewise, the first five essays in the collection edited by David Lindberg and Ronald Numbers, *God and Nature: Historical Essays on the Encounter between Christianity and Science*, University of California, 1986, flesh out the picture of the relationship between science and the church in the Middle Ages. Lindberg, who wrote the foreword to Russell's *Inventing the Flat Earth*, has also edited and translated the work of Roger Bacon, the thirteenth-century English philosopher (and believer in a spherical earth), whom some have considered an anomalous medieval thinker. Certainly when it came to the spherical earth, Bacon was in the majority.

For an explanation of the theories behind medieval mapmaking and of the different kinds of medieval maps, see Evelyn Edson's *Mapping Time and Space: How Medieval Mapmakers Viewed Their World*, British Library Studies in Map History 1, London, 1997. Edson explains that the popular name for the "T-O" map does not derive from "orbis terrarum." Instead, the tripartite division in this ancient form of map only accidentally resembles the Latin letter "T," while its circular outside border resembles the letter "O." Finally, for the best selection of illustrations, see Edward Grant's *Planets, Stars, and Orbs: The Medieval Cosmos, 1200–1687*, Cambridge, 1994, an expensive but illustrated history likely available in many local libraries.

NOTES

1. Russell, p. 88, note 61, refers to the relevant passages in *De Genesi ad litteram (The Literal Meaning of Genesis)*, John Hammond Taylor (ed. and trans.), 2 vols., New York, 1982, 1:42–3, 58–60.
2. Bede, *De Rerum Natura*, chapter 46: again, see Russell, p. 87, note 55.
3. Russell refers to Aquinas's *Summa theologiae* and *De Coelo et mundo*, Hildegard's *Scivias* 1:3, and Robert Grosseteste's *De Sphaera* as all denoting a spherical earth (p. 86, note 50).
4. Available at http://seeing.nypl.org/2t.html.
5. See a medieval astrolabe available at either http://www.thebritishmuseum. ac.uk/compass/ixbin/goto?id=OBJ606 (a British Museum site) or http://www. astrolabes.org/.
6. See http://iws.ccccd.edu/Andrade/WorldLitl2332/Psalter.html.
7. See one image of a king holding a map of the earth, the position of which demonstrates two-dimensional representation of a three-dimensional object, at http://www.henry-davis.com/MAPS/EMwebpages/EM1.html.
8. Edson, *Mapping Time and Space*, provides these calculations on p. 4.
9. In his book's first chapter, pp. 6–11, Russell provides the narrative of Columbus's navigational knowledge, drawn from Columbus's own books and diaries, as well as an account of Columbus's appeals for funding.

12 The Medieval Sense of Self

Ronald J. Ganze

To refute the misconception that there was no sense of self before the
Early Modern period is a task that can only be partially accomplished in a
chapter as brief as this one. This is in large part because there is not really
a single misconception—rather, there are a number of separate misconceptions based on very different definitions of what constitutes a self. To deny
the medieval period a sense of self in the Cartesian sense, for example, is
quite different from denying it a sense of self in the manner of Stephen
Greenblatt's *Renaissance Self-Fashioning*; and though Greenblatt tacitly
relies on a Marxist-derived understanding of the self—or perhaps I should
say "subject"—in society, his account still differs in some respects from
the Marxist-derived account of subjectivity we find in Louis Althusser,
which has been so influential in conceptualizing subjectivity in its postmodern sense.

On the other end of the equation, there is no *single* medieval sense of
self with which to refute these misconceptions; the Augustinian concept of
self, which is commonly used as representative of the period, is only one
of many, and even that concept can hardly be called singular, given the
evolution of Augustine's ideas from an early work like the *Soliloquia* and a
late work like *De civitate dei* (*The City of God*), as well as the differences
between the Bishop of Hippo's writings aimed at his flock and those aimed
at his fellow philosophers and theologians. Yet the Augustinian concept
of self, as well as the metaphysics that underpin it, remained influential
throughout the medieval period, so I will rely upon Augustine (354–430)
to a greater extent than other medieval writers in establishing the medieval
sense of self. In addition, since it is to Augustinian metaphysics that Descartes turns in establishing his new method of philosophy—turning deci-
sively away from what he saw as the erroneous and entrenched methods of
Scholasticism—Augustine provides a vital link between the medieval and
early modern periods.[1]

Before delving into Augustine, however, I think it is first useful to examine the arguments against a medieval sense of self—the misconception itself.
In modern scholarship, this notion finds its strongest adherents among
scholars of the early-modern period and in large part can be traced back

to the nineteenth-century historian Jacob Burckhardt, whose definition of medieval "man" casts its long shadow over more than a few contemporary studies of the Renaissance:

> In the Middle Ages, both sides of human consciousness—that which was turned within as well as that which was turned without—lay dreaming and half aware beneath a common veil. The veil was woven of faith, illusion, and childish prepossession, through which the world and history were seen clad in strange hues. *Man was conscious of himself only as a member of a race, people, party, family, or corporation—only through some general category.*[2]

Burckhardt's view of the Middle Ages remains surprisingly pervasive, despite his Hegelianism and his Romantic-infused humanism, methods even his successors acknowledge as being somewhat outmoded.[3] His teleological view of history and somewhat Romantic espousal of individualism are altered to suit the philosophical landscape in which contemporary early modernist scholars are writing, with the concept of the individual generally abandoned altogether in favor of the more *au courant* notion of subjectivity, as we shall see shortly. The dividing line between medieval and Renaissance, however, all too often remains firmly in place, along with a generally unacknowledged argument that the understanding of self progresses from one age to the next.

We find this division between medieval and Renaissance in the writings of scholars working under the rubric of the New Historicism. Granted, the focus on the individual we find in Burckhardt has all but vanished, as the New Historicism has called the entire notion of the individual agent into question, but what we do find is a commonplace assertion that the subjects of the early modern period are more complex than those of the Middle Ages, as they are being constructed by a greater number of ideological discourses than their medieval counterparts. The result is that the New Historicism, at least as practiced by many early modernists, has retained the notion of the monolithic Middle Ages we see in Burckhardt's description; in the parlance of the New Historicism (and their British counterparts, the Cultural Materialists), medieval people were offered a very limited number of "subject-positions" to occupy. The subjectivity of their Early Modern counterparts is characterized then by a greater complexity as well as by a greater tension.

The most influential New Historicist work to deal with the issue of the medieval versus the early modern self remains Stephen Greenblatt's *Renaissance Self-Fashioning*, in which the claim is made that "in sixteenth-century England there were both selves and a key sense that they could be fashioned."[4] Greenblatt clarifies this somewhat odd statement by admitting that there have always been selves, but on goes on to argue that

> there is in the early modern period a change in the intellectual, social, psychological, and aesthetic structures that govern the generations of

identities. This change is difficult to characterize in our usual ways because it is not only complex but resolutely dialectical. If we say that there is a new stress on the executive power of the will, we must say that there is the most sustained and relentless assault upon the will; if we say that there is a new social mobility, we must say that there is a new assertion of power by both family and state to determine all movement within society; if we say that there is a heightened awareness of the existence of alternative modes of social, theological, and psychological organization, we must say that there is a new dedication to the imposition of control upon those modes and ultimately to the destruction of alternatives.[5]

At first glance, the self presented by Greenblatt appears caught between the new individuality argued for by Burckhardt and the sort of social construction common to Marxist-derived theories of subjectivity. However, this self is not the self that Greenblatt is arguing for, though it is the understanding of self being presented in the early modern texts he is examining. Men like Sir Thomas More (1478–1535) believed themselves to be exercising agency in the fashioning of a self, but Greenblatt contests that belief:

In all my texts and documents, there were, so far as I could tell, no moments of pure, unfettered subjectivity; indeed, the human subject itself began to seem remarkably unfree, the ideological product of the relations of power in a particular society. Whenever I focused sharply upon a moment of apparently autonomous self-fashioning, I found not an epiphany of identity freely chosen but a cultural artifact. If there remained traces of free choice, the choice was among the possibilities whose range was strictly delineated by the social and ideological system in force.[6]

Greenblatt's subject is, of course, not original to him; at its core, it is essentially the same model of subjectivity posted by the French Marxist philosopher Louis Althusser in "Ideology and Ideological State Apparatuses."[7] But it is with Greenblatt's formulation of subjectivity that most critics addressing the issue of the medieval self are engaged.

Greenblatt's argument for the inability of medieval Christians to engage in self-fashioning rests largely on a fragment from Augustine's Sermon 169:

Such self consciousness had been widespread among the elite in the classical world, but Christianity brought a growing suspicion of man's power to shape identity: "Hands off yourself," Augustine declared. "Try to build up yourself, and you build a ruin." This view was not the only one available in succeeding centuries, but it was influential, and a powerful alternative began to be fully articulated only in the early modern period.[8]

Greenblatt's "evidence" is a prime example of selective quoting from the Augustinian corpus. A single quotation from a single sermon is scant evidence on which to base an assessment of twelve hundred years of human history. Furthermore, the differences between sermons—written in a didactic register for a general audience—and his more exploratory, philosophical texts are not taken into account. Finally, the fact that Sermon 169 exhorts one to be dissatisfied with one's self and to always be walking on the pilgrimage of life, which is also conceptualized here as a pilgrimage to the self, is left unmentioned. In both the "elite" and "nonelite" registers, then, Augustine is concerned with both self-fashioning and self-knowledge.

These arguments indicate, I think, what we actually mean when we deny the medieval period a sense of self. What we are denying the period isn't necessarily its own unique sense of self; we are instead denying it our sense of self, whether it is Burckhardt denying the period a nineteenth-century sense of self or the New Historicism denying it a late-twentieth-century sense of self. Simply put, we are looking to find our own sense of self reflected back at us from the texts we study, and when we don't find this, we conclude that the period lacked a sense of self.

But this is erroneous, of course, and for two reasons. The first is that there was a concept of self in the Middle Ages; philosophically, there has *always* been some concept of self, even if it has not always been formulated as such. When Plato discusses the soul in *Phaedo*, he makes the argument that the "core of each person's existence is an immaterial soul, which by nature is immortal."[9] For Aristotle, the soul is both the principle of life and, in the case of the intellectual soul (as Aristotle divides soul into three categories: the vegetative soul, the sensitive soul, and the intellectual soul), the source of human reason. Both philosophers *are* discussing the self; they are simply doing so within a different framework from the one in which the modern reader is used to working.[10] With Augustine, our touchstone in the medieval period, we find fully developed concepts of soul, memory, will, mind, reason, and being, each of which provides us with a piece of the puzzle which is the Augustinian self. One of Augustine's earliest works, the *Soliloquia*, contains an interior dialogue between Augustine and his Reason, as the interlocutors attempt to gain a better understanding of God and of the soul. The interior nature of Augustine's project in the *Soliloquia* cannot be stressed enough; for some writers, Augustine represents the birth of the inner self in philosophy. Here, I will limit myself to making the claim that central to Augustinian thought is the notion that such answers can be found within and that it is only the individual's journey towards the self and towards God that can bring him closer to these answers.

It is Augustine's concept of memory, particularly as it relates to the construction of narrative, that best lends itself to an analysis of the Augustinian self. Memory is ostensibly the subject of the *Confessions*, which, as an autobiography, provides us with an account of the self and the elusive nature of self-knowledge that speaks clearly to the modern reader in search of a

106 Ronald J. Ganze

medieval sense of self. This is not to say that studying the Augustinian self presents no problems for the modern reader. Augustine can appear inconsistent at times, particularly when dealing with the questions of predestination, free will, works, and grace—all important to conceptualizing the degree of agency enjoyed by self. This inconsistency stems in part from the fact that Augustine began his career refuting the Manichees and ended it refuting the Pelagians. As a result, his earlier writings are more likely to argue on the side of free will and works, whereas the later writings are more likely to argue on the side of predestination and grace.[11] Selective quoting, then, can be made to yield a number of answers on the question of the self in Augustine. But careful consideration of the entire corpus reveals a conception of the self that is as rich and as complex as any from the early modern period on.

There are also aspects of Augustine's understanding of the nature of the afterlife that may lead readers to question the conception of self he posits. In *The City of God*, for example, the transcendent soul is seen as having little or no individuality, as the perfected will each of us will enjoy is seen as singular: "Erit ergo illius ciuitatis et una in omnibus et inseperabilis in singulus uoluntas libera" ("In the Heavenly City, then, there will be freedom of will: one freedom for all, and indivisible in each").[12] And in Book Ten of *Confessions*, Augustine seems to advocate an abrogation of self even in this plane of existence: "Tu refulges et places et amaris et desideraris, ut erubescam de me et abiciam me atque eligam te et nec tibi nec mihi placeam nisi de te" ("It is you whom I love and desire, so that I am ashamed of myself and cast myself aside and choose you instead, and please neither you nor myself except in you").[13]

As modern readers, we see in these passages a rejection of the sort of individualism it is often argued was born in the early-modern period, but that assessment is only partially correct. What Augustine is referring to in these passages and in others written in the same vein is the true nature of the self, at least as he conceptualizes it within a Christian framework heavily influenced by Platonism. But this true self, *Confessions* Ten makes clear, exists only with God, whose eternal vantage point is the only one from which the entirety of the self can be comprehended. The self that we can gain knowledge of on this plane of existence is one which is reconstructed from memory, as is clear from specific passages of *Confessions*:

> Ibi mihi et ipse occurro meque recolo, quid, quando et ubi egerim quoque modo, cum agerem, affectus fuerim. ibi sunt omnia quae sive experta a me sive credita memini. ex eadem copia etiam similitudines rerum vel expertarum vel ex eis quas expertus sum creditarum alias atque alias, et ipse contexo praeteritis atque ex his etiam futuras actiones et eventa et spes, et haec omnia rursus quasi praesentia meditor.

> (In it I meet myself as well. I remember myself and what I have done, when and where I did it, and the state of my mind at the time. In my

memory, too, are all the events that I remember, whether they are things that have happened to me or things that I have heard about from others. From the same source I can picture to myself all kinds of different images based either upon my own experience or upon what I find credible because it tallies with my own experience. I can fit them into the general picture of the past; from them I can make a surmise of actions and events and hopes for the future; and I can contemplate them all over again as if they were actually present.)[14]

Augustine's description of the actions and workings of memory allows us to locate in *Confessions* a project of self-understanding that appears to entail a certain degree of self-fashioning. As Augustine searches through his memory for himself, he deliberately chooses from what he finds there those incidents that best reveal the working of God's providence within his life—those incidents that help him construct the narrative that ends in the "minor" *telos* of his conversion to orthodox Christianity and the "major" *telos* that will be his reunion with God in eternity. That Augustine weaves this narrative through the lens of the greater narrative of Creation as found in the Bible—constructing his life, in part, according to the methods of typology—is not an argument against finding a modern sense of self in his writings; on the contrary, this aspect of *Confessions* brings the self found there even closer to that being argued for by Greenblatt, as Augustine's act of self-fashioning involves "submission to an absolute power or authority situated at least partially outside the self," and this is an authority that Augustine experiences as an "inward necessity."[15]

Some would argue that Augustine's use of typological construction in *Confessions* precludes a conception of selfhood in the modern sense, but to refute this argument, it is helpful to consider the similarities between medieval and modern biography and autobiography. It is true that most medieval saints' lives, for example, are highly constructed narratives, striving either for *imitatio Christi* (the imitation of Christ) or to incorporate events recorded in earlier saints' lives that became conventional over time. Saints' lives are extreme examples of this practice, but most if not all of the texts generally cited in support of a sense of self in the Middle Ages are to some degree constructing and reconstructing events within established conventions, with biographical texts in particular drawing heavily on saints' lives. Yet for all the individuality that is lost in medieval biography as a result of this practice, we are not left with a self wholly constructed by convention, as demonstrated by the unique events of Augustine's *Confessions*—a text written to portray specific events in the life of its individual author. All autobiography is teleological and attempts to explain how the self that writes came to be over time. In many respects, Augustine's use of convention is no different from a modern-day American telling a rags-to-riches tale and drawing on the conventions of the Horatio Alger story. Convention is a tool for communication; it is not necessarily an impediment to individual expression. As for Greenblatt's concept of self-fashioning, I hope I have demonstrated that there is little difference between the constructed, teleological narrative of *Confessions*, which presents a life "interpreted" in light of Augustine's conversion to orthodox Christianity, and the constructed, teleological narratives characteristic of the modern political autobiography, in which events are chosen and imbued with retroactive importance in relation to their relevance to the subject's taking up of political office. Both are attempts to fashion a self for public consumption, regardless of their differing metaphysical content.

The impact of Augustine's views on selfhood on later writers is easily found. In the *Soliloquia*, as I noted earlier, Augustine introduces the concept of the inner journey towards knowledge of the self and of God. We find this advice heeded, I believe, in the translation of the *Soliloquia* undertaken by King Alfred (ca. 849–899), the ninth-century Anglo-Saxon king whose project it was to translate from Latin into English "those books most necessary for all men to know." Alfred's translation of the *Soliloquia* takes certain liberties with its source material. To begin, the king engages in the common Anglo-Saxon practice of "cultural translation," bringing a work written in late antiquity into an Anglo-Saxon cultural register. But perhaps more important for our purposes here, Alfred's translation reveals a gradual infusion of the Augustinian "I" of the original with the Alfredian "I" of the translation. In other words, there are points in the text in which it can be argued that the "I" speaking with its faculty of reason is more Alfred than Augustine.

One example of this conflation can be found in the passage where Reason asks Augustine to what extent he would know his friend, Alypius. Augustine's version reads

> R[atio]. quid? illum familiarem tuum, quem te adhuc ignorare dixisti, sensu vis nosse an intellectu?
>
> A[ugustinus]. sensu quidem quod in eo novi, si tamen sensu aliquid noscitur, et vile est et satis est. illam vero partem, qua mihi amicus est, id est ipsum animum, intellectu adsequi cupio.
>
> (*Reason:* What about that friend of yours, whom you say you still do not know, do you wish to know him by sense or by intellect?
>
> *Augustine:* What I know of him by sense, if indeed anything can be known by sense, is worthless, and I have had enough of it. But that part of him that makes him my friend, that is to say his soul, I want to grasp by the intellect.)[16]

The Augustinian emphasis on interiority is clear here; the knowledge he seeks of his friend Alypius is knowledge of Alypius's own interiority, knowledge that it is of course impossible to obtain, at least in the material world.

Alfred retains this emphasis on interior knowledge but adds to it a concern that is both individually his own as well as a concern that is indicative of the nature of Anglo-Saxon society:

> Þa cwæð heo: h(w)æðer woldest þu ðonne þinne cniht þe wet er æmbe sprecon cun(n)an, þe mid ðam utram gewitum, þe mið þam inran?

> Þa cwæð ic: ic hine can nu swa ic hine of ðam uttram gewitum cunnan mæge. Ac ic wilnode þæt ic cuðe hys ingeþanc of minum ingeþance. *Ðonne wiste ic hwilce treowða he hæfde wið me.*

> (Then he said: By which would you rather then know your disciple whom we were speaking about before, with the outer senses, or with the inner?

> Then said I: I know him now as I may know him with the outer senses. But I would that I knew his thoughts with my thoughts. *Then I would know what troth he has with me.*)[17]

The Old English word *treowða* ("troth") captures the core of what Alfred is adding to Augustine's conception of the self, as well as voicing what seems to be the concern of a lord toward his thegns, not necessarily a concern unique to Anglo-Saxon society but certainly central to it.

Perhaps even more striking is Alfred's addition to Book II of Augustine's *Soliloquia* of a passage that explains metaphorically how each individual finds his or her own path to Truth; though that Truth remains singular, the journey towards it is conceptualized as highly individualized. This is in part authorized by Augustine's original text, in which Reason, speaking of the path to Divine Truth, tells Augustine, "Sed non ad eam una uia per uenitur. quippe pro sua quisque sanitate ac firmitate comprehendit illud singulare ac uerissimum bonum" ("But there is not just one way to her. Indeed, each one seizes that unique and truest good, according to his or her own strength").[18] Though this statement is not compatible with later Augustinian theology, it is definitely what he meant when he wrote it, as his entry in his *Retractions* makes clear:

> Item quod dixi "ad sapientiae coniunctionem non una uia perueniri," non bene sonat, quasi alia uia praeter Christum qui dixit: "ego sum uia" [John 14:6]. uitanda ergo erat haec offensio aurium religiosarum quamuis alia sit illa uniuersalis uia, aliae autem uiae, de quibus et in Psalmo canimus: "uias tuas, Domine, notas fac mihi, et semitas tuas doce me" [Psalms 24:4].

> (Likewise, this statement of mine does not sound well: "There is more than one way of attaining union with wisdom," as if there were another

way besides Christ who said: "I am the way." I should, therefore, have avoided this offense to pious ears; even though there is that one universal way, yet there are other ways about which also we sing in the Psalm: "O Lord, make known to me Thy ways and teach me Thy paths.")[19]

For his part, Alfred takes this notion that each individual has his or her own path to wisdom and expands upon it more than he does any other point made by Augustine in his *Soliloquia*:

Geðenc nu hweðer awiht mani mann cynges ham sece þer ðær he ðonne on tune byd, oððe hys gemot, oððe hys fird, oððe hweðer ðe ðince þæt hi æalle on anne weig þeder cumen. Ic wene þeah ðæt hi cumen on swiðe manige wegas: sume cumað swiðe feorran, and habbað swiðe læ(n)gne weig and swiðe yfelne and swiðe earfoðferne; sume habbað swiðe langne and swiðe rihtne and swiðe godne. Sume habbað swiðe scortne, and þeah wone and nearone and fuulne; sume habbað scordne and smeðne and rihtne; and þeah cumað æalle to anum hlaforde, sume æð, sume uneð. naðer ne hi þeder gelice eaðe cumað, ne hi þer gelice eaðe ne beoð. Sume beoð on maran are and on maran eðnesse þonne sume, sume on læssan, sume ful neah buton, buton þæt an þæt he lufað. swa hit bið æac be þam wisdome: ælc þara þe hys wilnað and þe hys geornful byt, he hym mæg cuman to and on hys hyrede wunian and be lybbam, þeah hi hym sume nær sian, sume fyer. swa swa ælces cynges hama beoð sume on bure, sume on healle, sume on odene, sume on carcerne, and lybbað þeah æalle be anes hlafordes are, swa swa æalle men lybbað under anre sunnan and beo hyre leothte geseoð þæt þæt hy geseoð. Sume swiðe scearpe and swiðe swotele lociað. Sume unæaðe awiht geseoð. Sume beoð stæreblinde and nyttiað þeah þare sunnan. Ac swa swa þeos gesewe sunne ures lichaman æagan onleoht, swa onliht se wisdom ures modes æagan, þæt ys, ure angyt; and swa swa þæs lichaman æagan halren beoð, swa hy mare gefoð þæs leohtes þære sunnan, swa hyt byð æac be þæs modes æagan, þæt is, andgit. Swa swa þæt halre byð, swa hyt mare geseon mæg þære æccan sunnan, þæt is, wysdom.

(Think now whether at all many men seek there the king's home when he is in town, or at his assembly, or with his army, or whether you think that they all come hither by one path. I believe, however, that they come on very many paths: some from very far away, and have a very long road and great misery and difficulty; some have paths which are very long and very straight and very good. Some have very short ways, and yet dark and narrow and foul; some have ways which are short and smooth and straight; and yet all come to one lord, some easily, some uneasily. Neither do they come thither with like ease, nor are they there likewise at ease. Some are in more honor and in more ease than others, some in less, some just about without, except that one which he loves. So it is also concerning wisdom; each of them who wills it and is eager for it, it may come to him and dwell in his household and live by him, although some are nearer him, some farther. So is the home of each king, some in cottages, some in halls, some on the threshing-floor, some in prison, and all live there by the favor of one lord, just as all men live under one sun and by her light see what they see. Some look very sharply and very clearly. Some see with unease. Some are stark blind yet use the sun. But just as the visible sun lights the eyes of our body, so wisdom lights the eyes of our mind, that is, our reason; and just as the eyes of the body are more whole as they receive more of the light of the sun, so it is also concerning the eyes of the mind, that is, reason. Just as what is healthier, as it may see more that eternal sun, that is, wisdom.)[20]

The sheer length of the addition is enough to attract the attention of a reader familiar with Augustine's original work. Alfred has obviously taken great care not only in making the analogy but in drawing it out and providing very specific cultural details. As in Augustine, the *sanitate ac firmitate* ("health and strength") of the individual are of primary importance to his or her ability to come to wisdom and are the primary determinants of the individual's proximity to Divine Truth. Yet this addition of a social dimension to Augustine's discussion of the individual paths to Divine Truth focuses the reader's attention on the fact of the socially divergent paths each of us takes while we are on pilgrimage in the material world. It also emphasizes the fact that throughout the *Soliloquies*, Alfred is not afraid to come to his own understanding of various points of theology, a trait that distinguishes our next medieval writer, Peter Abelard (1079–1142).

A twelfth-century scholastic philosopher and theologian, Abelard is best known to posterity for his autobiographical work, the *Historia calamitatum*, and for a series of letters exchanged with Héloise, a former student with whom he had an affair. Abelard's *Historia calamitatum* is often compared to and contrasted with Augustine's *Confessions*, and like that earlier text provides us with an example of self-fashioning, self-understanding, and interiority. Like most medieval writers, Abelard interprets the events of his life through the events in the lives of other Christians. In particular, the persecution of Saint Jerome (347–420) is used as a means of understanding Abelard's own persecution, both for Abelard himself and for us as readers. But the *Historia* also provides the reader with a forceful assertion of individuality, often in the form of Abelard's somewhat arrogant stance against authority. Abelard frequently asserts the superiority of his own personal understanding of theology, as when he tells of his "victory" in a debate with the bishop of Châlons or champions his own writing and understanding over that approved by the church. He does, of course, rely on select authorities himself, for example, when he asserts the authority of the

Venerable Bede (ca. 673–735), an Anglo-Saxon monk and theologian, over that of Hilduin, the bishop of Paris, on the question of whether Dionysius the Areopagite had been bishop of Corinth. But what we see stressed in Abelard's text are his actions as a careful and considerate reader who makes personal choices about the validity of the arguments in question, revealing the work of an intellect constantly reflecting upon its own activity. He is not, as some would characterize writers of the Middle Ages, blindly adhering to authority but testing the conclusions of that authority using his own faculties of logic and reason.

Abelard also provides an example of the sort of textual inwardness said to have been born with Hamlet.[21] When Abelard is brought before the Council of Soissons to answer charges of heresy stemming from his teachings on the Trinity, he is asked "to profess his faith before [the Council] . . . so that it may be duly approved and corrected."[22] Abelard is prepared to answer in his own words, to explain his own understanding of his faith. Instead, he is forced to recite the Athanasian Creed "as any boy could do," which he does tearfully, replacing a sophisticated and personal response with the words prescribed for nontheologians. His recitation of the creed, then, indicates the sort of gap between his inner thoughts and his spoken words—between his "true" self and the self he presents to the council. From the point of view of the social constructionists, this incident would be read as indicative of the church's desire to stifle individual expression in an attempt to retain its monopoly on religious truth. Yet when reading this incident from that point of view, it is equally clear that the voice of resistance—Abelard's—cannot be totally silenced. We are, after all, reading Abelard's version of the events nearly a millennia later.

There are, of course, many other examples of self-fashioning, interiority, subjectivity, and many of the other criteria used by modern readers in searching for a medieval sense of self. In addition to the works I have examined in this essay, there are a number of other biographical and autobiographical works to which one can turn: Boethius (ca. 480–ca. 526), Bede, and Gregory of Tours (ca. 539–594) are prime examples from the early Middle Ages, and Guibert of Nogent (d. 1124), Margery Kempe (ca.1373–ca.1438), Julian of Norwich (1342–ca.1416), and Christina of Markyate (ca.1096–ca.1145) round out a survey of the later period. In literature, the Anglo-Saxon elegies, with their emphasis on exile and alienation, reveal speakers who emerge as individual voices, despite their use of poetic convention. The voice of Geoffrey Chaucer (ca.1343–1400) is easily detected in his poetry, particularly the early dream visions, and Dante's *Vita Nuova* is an exercise in rereading the author's personal past not unlike Augustine's and Abelard's. Chrétien de Troyes' (ca.1140–ca.1200) *Yvain*, with its depiction of the protagonist's madness, provides but one fictional representation of selfhood in medieval literature, and a level of psychological awareness that might at first surprise the modern reader.

Some of these medieval texts communicate selves for which modern readers find great affinity, as the emergence of collections like *Augustine and Postmodernism* attest.[23] Others present selves that may seem strange or incompatible with our own sense of what it means to be a self, but there is one commonality that they all share, a starting point, perhaps, for embarking on a new scholarly project in the areas of both selfhood and medieval studies. Each of the examples I have examined, as well as the additional examples I have mentioned in passing, present the self—or the self's world— as *narrative*. The narrative self would appear to answer the concerns of social constructionists, as few would argue that an individual can create his or her own narrative from whole cloth; the narrative self is always "composed" in conjunction with others. The narrative self also serves to counter objections raised by those who would deny a sense of self to any period. The growing dialogue between cognitive psychology, neurology, and phenomenology—particularly hermeneutical phenomenology—indicates that the narrative self is part of the very structure of the human brain and thus cannot be said to have been "born" in any particular era but is rather one of the many products of human evolution.[24]

But regardless whether one wishes to pursue such a line of inquiry into the medieval self, I think that this essay has made it clear that there are more than enough examples of rich, robust selves from the Middle Ages to permanently put this misconception to rest. All that remains for readers to do is to explore some of these works and discover for themselves the multiple and complex senses of self contained therein.

SUGGESTIONS FOR FURTHER READING

Primary Sources

Alfred the Great: Asser's Life of King Alfred *and other Contemporary Sources*, Simon Keynes and Michael Lapidge (trans.), New York: Penguin, 1983.

Augustine, *Soliloquies: Augustine's Inner Dialogue*, John E. Rotelle (ed.) and Kim Paffenroth (trans.), Brooklyn: New City, 2000.

Boethius, *The Consolation of Philosophy*, Richard Green (trans.), New York: Macmillan, 1962.

Chrétien de Troyes, *The Knight with the Lion, or, Yvain*, Willian W. Kilber (ed. and trans.), New York: Garland, 1985.

Dante Alighieri, *La Vita Nuova*, Barbara Reynolds (trans.), New York: Penguin, 1969.

Einhard and Notker the Stammerer, *Two Lives of Charlemagne*, Lewis Thorpe (trans.), New York: Penguin, 1969.

Guibert of Nogent, *A Monk's Confession: The Memoirs of Guibert of Nogent*, Paul J. Archambault (trans.), University Park, PA: Pennsylvania State University, 1996.

Jocelin of Brakelond, *Chronicle of the Abbey of Bury St Edmunds*, Diana Greenway and Jane Sayers (trans.), Oxford: Oxford University, 1989.

Margery Kempe, *The Book of Margery Kempe*, Barry Windeatt (trans.), New York: Penguin, 1985.

Francesco Petrarch, *Petrarch's Secretum* (ed. and trans.), Davy A. Carozza and H. James Shey, New York: Peter Lang, 1989.

C. H. Talbot (ed. and trans.), *The Life of Christina of Markyate: A Twelfth Century Recluse*, Toronto: University of Toronto, 1998.

Carolinne White (ed. and trans.), *Early Christian Lives*, New York: Penguin, 1998.

Secondary Sources

David Aers, "A Whisper in the Ear of Early Modernists; or, Reflections of Literary Critics Writing the 'History of the Subject,' " *Culture and History, 1350–1600: Essays on English Communities, Identities, and Writings*, David Aers (ed.), London: Harvester Wheatsheaf, 1992, pp. 177–202.

Phillip Cary, *Augustine's Invention of the Inner Self: The Legacy of a Christian Platonist*, Oxford: Oxford University, 2000.

M. T. Clanchy, *Abelard: A Medieval Life*, Oxford: Blackwell, 1997.

Aaron Gurevitch, *The Origins of European Individualism*, Oxford: Blackwell, 1995.

Antonina Harbus, *The Life of the Mind in Old English Poetry*, Amsterdam: Rodopi, 2002.

Colin Morris, *The Discovery of the Individual, 1050–1200*, New York: Harper & Row, 1972.

Charles M. Radding, *A World Made by Men: Cognition and Society, 400–1200*, Chapel Hill: University of North Carolina, 1985.

Jerry Root, *"Space to Speke": The Confessional Subject in Medieval Literature*, New York: Peter Lang, 1997.

Jerome Seigel, *The Idea of the Self: Thought and Experience in Western Europe Since the Seventeenth Century*, Cambridge: Cambridge University, 2005.

David Gary Shaw, *Necessary Conjunctions: The Social Self in Medieval England*, New York; Palgrave, 2005.

Brian Stock, *Augustine the Reader: Meditation, Self-Knowledge, and the Ethics of Interpretation*, Cambridge, MA: Harvard University, 1996.

Charles Taylor, *Sources of the Self: The Making of Modern Identity*, Cambridge, MA: Harvard University, 1989.

Dan Zahavi (ed.), *Hidden Resources*, Charlottesville, NC: Imprint Academic, 2004.

———. *Subjectivity and Selfhood: Investigating the First-Person Perspective*, Cambridge, MA: MIT, 2006.

Michel Zink, *The Invention of Literary Subjectivity*, David Sices (trans.), Baltimore: Johns Hopkins University, 1999.

NOTES

1. For a thorough analysis of the connections between Augustinian and Cartesian thought, see Stephen Menn, *Descartes and Augustine*, Cambridge: Cambridge University, 1998; Gareth B. Matthews, *Thought's Ego in Augustine and Descartes*, Ithaca: Cornell University, 1992; Gareth B. Matthews, "Augustine and Descartes on Minds and Bodies," in *The Augustinian Tradition*, Gareth B. Matthews (ed.), Berkeley: University of California, 1999, pp. 222–32; Gareth B. Matthews, "Knowledge and Illumination," in *The Cambridge Companion*

to Augustine, Eleonore Stump and Norman Kretzmann (eds.), Cambridge: Cambridge University, 2000, pp. 171–85; and Charles Taylor, *Sources of the Self*, Cambridge, MA: Harvard University, 1989, particularly Chapters 7 and 8, on Augustine and Descartes, respectively.

2. Jacob Burckhardt, *The Civilization of the Renaissance in Italy*, S. G. C. Middlemore (trans.), London: Penguin, 1990, p. 98. Emphasis mine.

3. See particularly William Kerrigan and Gordon Braden, *The Idea of the Renaissance*, Baltimore: Johns Hopkins University, 1989. Pages 11–13 in particular examine Burckhardt's reliance on Hegel.

4. Stephen Greenblatt, *Renaissance Self-Fashioning*, Chicago: University of Chicago, 1980, p.1.

5. Greenblatt, *Renaissance Self-Fashioning*, pp. 1–2.

6. Greenblatt, *Renaissance Self-Fashioning*, p. 256.

7. Louis Althusser, "Ideology and Ideological State Apparatuses," in *Lenin and Philosophy and Other Essays*, Ben Brewster (ed. and trans.), New York: Monthly Review, 1971.

8. Greenblatt, *Renaissance Self-Fashioning*, p. 2. It is important to note that Greenblatt has not consulted the primary source, the text of Sermon 169, but instead takes this quote from Peter Brown's *Religion and Society in the Age of Saint Augustine*, London: Faber and Faber, 1972. Had he consulted the actual sermon, he might have found passages that directly refute his argument.

9. Jerrold Seigel, *The Idea of the Self: Thought and Experience in Western Europe Since the Seventeenth Century*, Cambridge: Cambridge University, 2005, p. 46.

10. See *From Soul to Self*, M. James C. Crabbe (ed.), New York: Routledge, 1999, for a thorough discussion of the continuity between classical, medieval, and modern accounts of what we now term "the self." For the classical period, Richard Sorabji's "Soul and Self in Ancient Philosophy," on pages 8–32 of this collection, is particularly useful.

11. Though it is common to divide Augustine's theological output in this manner, generally citing the pre-*Confessions* work *Ad Simplicianum de diversis quaestionibus* as the point at which Augustine rereads the Pauline epistles and moves toward a theology characterized by a focus on predestination and grace, a recent work, Carol Harrison's *Rethinking Augustine's Early Theology: An Argument for Continuity*, Oxford University, 2006, may cause this division to be reconsidered.

12. *De Civitate Dei* 22.30.74–5, in *Corpus Christianorum Series Latina*, Vols. 47 and 48, Bernard Dombart and Alphonse Kalb (eds.), Turnhout, Belgium: Brepols, 1955. All Latin quotations are taken from this edition. English translations are taken from *The City of God against the Pagans*, R. W. Dyson (ed. and trans.), Cambridge: Cambridge University, 1998. This passage appears on p. 1180 of Dyson's translation.

13. *Confessions* 10.2.(2), in *Confessions*, Vol. 1, J. J. O'Donnell (ed.), Oxford: Oxford University, 1992. All Latin quotations are taken from this edition. English translations are taken from *Confessions*, R. S. Pine-Coffin (trans.), New York: Dorset Press, 1961. This passage appears on p. 207 of Pine-Coffin's translation.

14. *Confessions* 10.8.(14); Pine-Coffin, pp. 215–16.

15. Greenblatt, *Renaissance Self-Fashioning*, p. 9.

16. *Soliloquia* 1.3.(8), in *Corpus Scriptorum Ecclesiasticorum Latinorum*, Vol. 89, Wolfgangus Hormann (ed.), Wien: Hoelder-Pichler-Tempsky, 1986. All Latin quotations are taken from this edition. English translations are taken from *Soliloquies: Augustine's Inner Dialogue*, John E. Rotelle, O.S.A. (ed.),

and Kim Paffenroth (trans.), Brooklyn: New City, 2000, unless otherwise indicated.

17. My italics. *King Alfred's Version of St. Augustine's Soliloquies*, Thomas A. Carnicelli (ed.), Cambridge, MA: Harvard University, 1969, p. 59, lines 10–4. Translations are my own. I have consulted Hargrove's 1904 translation for a few of the more difficult constructions and have followed his practice of placing Alfred's additions to Augustine in italic font.

18. Augustine, *Soliloquia*, 1.13.(23).

19. *Retractationes*, 1.4.31–6, in *Corpus Christianorum Series Latina*, vol. 57, Almut Mutzenbecher (ed.), Turnhout, Belgium: Brepols, 1984. All Latin quotations are taken from this edition. English translations are taken from *The Retractations*, Sister Mary Inez Bogan (trans.), Washington, DC: Catholic University of America, 1968, unless otherwise indicated.

20. Alfred, *Soliloquies*, p. 77, line 5 to p. 78, line 8.

21. For a discussion of the "birth of inwardness" on the Renaissance stage, see Katherine Eisaman Maus, *Inwardness and Theater in the English Renaissance*, Chicago: University of Chicago, 1995. A similar argument, couched in the terms of poststructuralism (and thus without the inwardness), can be found in Catherine Belsey, *The Subject of Tragedy: Identity and Difference in Renaissance Drama*, London: Methuen, 1985.

22. Peter Abelard, *Historia calamitatum*, in *The Letters of Abelard and Heloise*, Betty Radice (ed. and trans.), London: Penguin, 1974, p. 84.

23. *Augustine and Postmodernism: Confessions and Circumfession*, John D. Caputo and Michael J. Scanlon (eds.), Bloomington: Indiana University, 2005. The book was born from a 2001 conference at Villanova University that sought to put postmodern thought into conversation with Augustine, primarily through the use of Jacques Derrida's work "Circumfession," a journal he kept during the illness and death of his mother. The conference itself is indicative of a larger trend within Augustinian studies, and that is the conceptualization of Augustine as "anticipating" the arguments of postmodernism, particularly in areas related to language and to the self.

24. For an introduction, see *The Self in Neuroscience and Psychiatry*, Tito Kircher and Anthony David (eds.), Cambridge: Cambridge University, 2003. Some of the essays in this volume craft analogies between philosophy and neuroscience; Dan Zahavi (pp. 56–75) makes a compelling argument for reading the neurological concept of the core self through phenomenology and the narrative self through hermeneutics, utilizing the work of Husserl (among others) and Ricoeur, respectively. Other essays advocate a complementary approach to the question of the self, arguing that the points of view represented by philosophy (a first-person point of view), psychiatry (a second-person point of view), and neuroscience (a third-person point of view) each come at the question from different but equally important perspectives, and each contributes a valuable piece to the puzzle.

13 The Middle Ages Were a Superstitious Time

Peter Dendle

The Middle Ages are commonly portrayed as deeply superstitious. A popular Web site devoted to life in the Middle Ages is typical in its sweeping dismissal of the state of medieval knowledge: "Medieval superstitions held sway over science, but traveling merchants and returning crusaders told of cultures in Asia, the Middle East and Africa that had advanced learning of the earth and the human body. . . . Schools and universities were forming across Western Europe that would help medieval society evolve from the Dark Ages on its way to a Renaissance of art and learning."[1] Finding examples of this sort is as easy as grabbing most any popular history of religion, science, or technology (and many academic ones, too). The story in the back of many people's minds probably goes something like this: having lost the advances in learning slowly built up over the classical period, and not yet privy to the wonderful breakthroughs in science, art, and philosophy that manifestly characterize the Renaissance, the Middle Ages are unhappily trapped in a backward and barbarous time in which arbitrary local customs, old wives' tales, and corrupt vestiges of classical thinking inform the thoughts and behaviors of peasants and scholars alike.

Such a story, however, implies a misunderstanding not only of the Middle Ages but also of the classical world, the Renaissance, and even of our modern world. It neglects two important considerations: 1) that educated medieval thinkers themselves lamented the state of popular ignorance and superstition, making it unfair for us to characterize the entire age as uniformly superstitious; and 2) that our own age is not much different: the majority of people even in the modern, developed world continue to believe in entities, causalities, and practices long disproved by the scientific community. Characterizing the Middle Ages in particular as superstitious thus loses its force when we admit that no culture, time, or civilization—our own included—has not been equally superstitious.

If we wish to catalogue the superstitions of the Middle Ages, we would undeniably have a vast body of material from which to choose. The last Monday in April, the first Monday in January, and the first in August were among the unlucky "Egyptian" days, and a person daring to have his or her blood let or to eat goose meat on these days would, according to some sources, die shortly thereafter. Against diarrhea, one early medieval medical compilation recommends inscribing a lengthy phrase of gibberish mixing Hebrew, Greek, Latin, and something resembling Irish ("Ranmigan adonai eltheos mur O ineffabile Omiginan . . .") on a parchment strip and wearing it around the neck. Other items worn as amulets include hair, wax, barley (this for insertion in the ear), and a fox's tooth wrapped in a fawn's skin. Springs, brooks, rivers, and wells were thought to be inhabited by sprites or spirits; crossroads were places of special magic and danger. People were sometimes believed to turn into wolves during a full moon, which Gervase of Tilbury (ca. 1140–1220) noted was quite common in England and France. Untold energies were directed into warding off the "evil eye" throughout the Mediterranean. Miracle healings at saints' tombs were a daily occurrence, if saints' lives and miracle registries are taken at face value. Gathering such evidence from the premodern societies of medieval Europe—covering hundreds of language and dialect regions over the course of a thousand years—one can easily generate an amusing list of quaint beliefs and absurd practices.

We must be careful, though, to define "superstition" meaningfully: academic historians and psychologists find it most useful to approach "superstition" as a belief or practice that is irrational as defined against the state of knowledge of that particular society, not as defined against our own current state of knowledge or against some abstract standard of Pure Truth. Thus, Ben Franklin was not superstitious for practicing bloodletting, since that was the consensus of medical authorities in his time; it becomes superstitious, however, to continue in that practice after medical learning has moved on. Doctors who prescribed thalidomide to pregnant women in the 1960s unknowingly caused thousands of birth defects: they were mistaken, but it hardly seems fitting to label them "superstitious." It is unproductive to brand an individual or a society with the term "superstitious" in any pejorative sense, for simply operating within the boundaries of human knowledge for their own time and place. A more constructive approach—one that doesn't amount to simply patting ourselves on the back for having progressed scientifically beyond what they believed 500 or 1,000 years ago—is to explore what was or wasn't considered a superstition in the Middle Ages. Only by understanding the framework of their rationality can we have a context for identifying their irrationalities.

"Superstition" is thus not always a meaningful category for one time period to impose on another. More frequently, and more interestingly, it is a category imposed by one sector of society on another sector of that same society to belittle and demean it—and this has been true for all historical periods. Throughout Western civilization, the untutored populace has always been kept at arm's length by an educated elite: scholars and scribes in ancient Greece and Rome, clergy and schoolmen in the Middle Ages, scientists and humanist scholars in the early-modern period, the academic and scientific community in the modern world. In his *Character Sketches*, the

Greek philosopher Theophrastus derided what he perceived to be superstitions of fourth-century BCE Athens, such as avoiding graves and consulting auguries (e.g., dream interpreters or bird-omen readers). Cicero mocked the popular belief that it is a bad omen when statues sweat or when two yoked animals defecate at the same time (*On Divination*). For many of these early thinkers, such as Plato (in *The Republic*) and Plutarch (in *On Superstition*), critiques against "superstition" (Greek *deisidaimonia*, Latin *superstitio*) usually amount to a critique against overzealous extremes of religious enthusiasm and its consequences. Thus, Plato writes that preachers and diviners who charge for their ability to read auguries or to influence the course of events will be excluded wholesale from his ideal republic. It is unhealthy, he believes, to dupe the public in that way. Modern scholars can debate exactly how earlier generations of intellectuals decided what was sound science or religion and what was merely superstition—it differed over time for different areas—but this should remind us that if superstition is nothing new in Western civilization, neither is critical enquiry and skepticism.

Like the classical scholars before them and Renaissance scholars after them, intellectuals of the Middle Ages continuously drew attention to the unsubstantiated beliefs and irrational practices of "most people." Agobard of Lyon, in the ninth century, wrote vigorously about how ignorant the general populace was for believing that some sorcerers can, through magic or ritual, influence the weather. The celebrated Anglo-Saxon abbot Ælfric of Eynsham (ca. 950–ca. 1010) lamented at length that the uneducated continued to believe in a wide range of pagan superstitions. We can gain some idea of what sorts of rites he may have had in mind through Burchard of Worms (d. 1025), the provocative list known as the *Indiculus superstitionum* ("Handlist of Superstitions"), and other sources. Thinkers such as Gregory of Tours (ca. 539–594), Rudolph Glaber (ca. 980–1045), and Geoffrey Chaucer (ca. 1343–1400) complained of contemporary charlatans who peddled animal bones as saints' relics and thereby took advantage of the gullible masses. Glaber snidely commented on the "ignorant people" of the mountain regions, noting that the "vulgar crowd . . . amongst the rustic population" too easily gave credence to false relics.[2]

Even as Ælfric of Eynsham decried popular attachment to various folk practices, he was equally desirous of assuring his contemporaries that Christian miracles were alive and well. Like Gregory the Great (ca. 540–604) and Haymo of Auxerre (fl. 840–865) before him, Ælfric apologizes in a sermon (*On the Ascension of God*) for the apparent lack of miracles performed in his own day. He notes that physical miracles were indeed performed back in the time of Christ because they were necessary then, but now that the truth of the Gospel has taken root so effectively and spread so widely, miracles are no longer required as much. In fact, he goes on to state that miracles are now (in his own day) just as frequent, but they are "spiritual" rather than "physical" ones. This sort of explanation—even if it does sound like special pleading—is certainly plausible even in a modern worldview and so does not imply that those in the Middle Ages lived in a perceptual world too radically different from ours.

The Capitulary of Charles the Bald for 872 reprimands those who believe that, in their dreams, they are whisked off by the pagan goddess Diana to attend nighttime covens. In fact, what is frequently legislated against in early medieval law is not the practice of certain sorceries but the belief that such sorceries are possible in the first place: thus a Carolingian statute warns that anyone who believes someone to be a witch, and who burns her for it, will him- or herself suffer the death penalty. This is a far cry from the six-teenth and seventeenth centuries, when secular and ecclesiastical authorities not only failed to check widespread popular belief in witches but actively fueled the hysteria further. Medieval societies did not by any means accept superstitions wholesale or unthinkingly, then: they struggled continually to distinguish between valid beliefs and nonsense.

Even if we still wish to preserve our privileged vantage point from the twenty-first century, however—even if we wish to compare the entirety of the Middle Ages to ourselves and say, "Yes, that's all well and good, but objectively speaking, medieval people all believed, peasants and intellectuals alike, in a lot of funny, absurd things"—it is still unclear that we have the high ground. It is not a given that, even from an absolute standpoint, people in the Middle Ages entertained more superstitions in their day-to-day lives than, for instance, twenty-first century Americans do. Upon closer inspec-tion, we are a deeply superstitious people ourselves. Many modern profes-sions and recreations are rife with internal cultures of lore that amount to "magical" rather than rational thinking: over 70% of college basket-ball players believe they must bounce the ball a set number of times before shooting the free throw, and over 30% wear a lucky item of clothing; gam-blers engage in all manner of fetishistic supplications to achieve the desired throw of the dice or draw of the cards (crapshooters, for instance, talk to the dice, rub them, or snap their fingers when throwing); air pilots in World War II and Vietnam conducted a wide range of preflight rituals (such as tapping on the lid of the parachute box) and often carried some personal charm or talisman considered good luck. American soldiers occupying Baghdad in Operation Iraqi Freedom insisted to a CNN reporter that eating M&Ms on top of a tank turret is very bad luck, as is touching a tank barrel after it's been realigned.

Superstitious thinking, by any reasonable definition of the term, affects all levels of contemporary society in all walks of life and is notoriously dif-ficult to reduce to demographics such as age, gender, profession, income, or level of education. Modern televangelists, self-affirmation mongers, get-rich-quick merchants, and infomercial product hawkers thrive in a consumer culture fueled by gullibility. Gallup polls regularly show that surprisingly large numbers of Americans believe in ghosts, ESP, clairvoyance, alien visi-tations and/or abductions, channeling, and past lives. Many followers of neo-pagan Wicca and fundamentalist Christians—though opposed to each other in so many other ways—alike willingly give intellectual assent to the reality of witches, Ouija boards, and spell casting. Even science and industry are not free from occasional recourse to the patently "magical" as opposed to the scientifically calculated: folklorists readily recognize magical numbers in antibiotics that come in three- and seven-day cycles or leases contracted for 99 years. Quite possibly, more people believe in astrology today than did in the early Middle Ages.

The Renaissance did, of course, usher in a host of unprecedented advances in astronomy, mathematics, medicine, and a wide range of other sciences and arts. However, it also saw the rise of wide-scale witch burnings, the high point of the Inquisition, and other institutions that are more commonly, and unfairly, associated with the Middle Ages in the popular imagination. In the early seventeenth century, the physician Thomas Browne wrote a treatise on the popular superstitions still rampant in his day and attempted to uncover their social and psychological causes (the *Pseudodoxia epidemica,* or *Enquiries into Very Many Received Tenets, and Commonly Presumed Truths,* 1646). What is clear, in any event, is that there is no unequivocal, linear rise in "knowledge" and decrease in "superstition" along the path of Western civilization but that different kinds of irrational beliefs thrive in different times.

There are often deep-seated psychological motives for beliefs that are, on the face of things, irrational: for instance, the perpetuation and enactment of ritual lore can give people a psychological sense of comfort and group identity and link them with their heritage, and can relieve anxiety by providing a sense of control over circumstances that are in fact beyond all control. This facet of human behavior does not show any signs of having arisen in any one historical time or place, nor does it show signs of abating or being eventually supplanted by reason or science. There is little sense in singling out the Middle Ages, then, as a time of especially pronounced or absurd superstition.

SUGGESTIONS FOR FURTHER READING

Michael Bailey, *Magic and Superstition in Europe: A Concise History from Antiquity to the Present,* Lanham, MD: Rowman & Littlefield, 2007. Traces the shifting conceptualizations of magic and superstition over the course of the European Middle Ages, in the context of the ever-shifting backdrop of European rationality itself.

J. H. G. Grattan and Charles Singer, *Anglo-Saxon Magic and Medicine,* London: Oxford University, 1952. Grattan and Singer's edition of the fascinating Anglo-Saxon charm and recipe collection known as the *Lacnunga* Book, while not the most recent, is still the most accessible for many. It also reproduces a number of illustrations from the manuscript and provides facing-page English translation. See Anne van Arsdall's chapter in this volume.

Karen L. Jolly, *Popular Religion in Late Saxon England: Elf Charms in Context*, Chapel Hill, NC: University of North Carolina, 1996. Karen Jolly's study of Anglo-Saxon popular charms (such as those in the *Lacnunga* Book, mentioned in the Grattan and Singer reference preceding) is an exemplary instance of current trends of scholarship, which situate seemingly irrational beliefs in their broader social and religious context.

Richard Kieckhefer, *Magic in the Middle Ages*, Cambridge: Cambridge University, 1989. An overview of many of the broad intellectual trends of magic in its various medieval guises (e.g., necromancy, astrology, alchemy) that commonly strike the modern observer as superstitious. Kieckhefer provides a cohesive and eminently readable, single-volume narrative of the development of these important threads of medieval intellectual thought from the classical period through the Renaissance.

Carl Lindahl, John McNamara, and John Lindow (eds.), *Medieval Folklore: A Guide to Myths, Legends, Tales, Beliefs, and Customs*, Oxford: Oxford University, 2002. Provides a solid starting point in a single encyclopedic volume cataloguing a variety of folk customs (such as weaving and burial practices) and beliefs (such as mermaids, giants, and dream visions).

Dale B. Martin, *Inventing Superstition: From the Hippocratics to the Christians*, Cambridge, MA, and London: Harvard University, 2004. Examines the evolving notion of "superstition" itself, from the early Greeks through the early centuries of the Christian era. Some of the preceding examples come from this work, which analyzes their contemporary significance and context with greater nuance and detail than are possible here.

Venetia Newall, *The Encyclopedia of Witchcraft and Magic*, New York: Dial, 1974. Demonstrates broadly the evolution of magical beliefs (and in fact a wide range of folkloric beliefs, from "Abracadabra" to "Zombie") from ancient and medieval times to the present, supported richly with photos and illustrations.

Iona Opie and Moira Tatem (eds.), *A Dictionary of Superstitions*, Oxford and New York: Oxford University, 1989. The model of the *Oxford English Dictionary*—a dictionary along historical principles—is applied to folklore, resulting in succinct entries containing historical citations for many hundreds of subjects (from adulterers curing warts to unlucky yews).

Gordon Stein (ed.), *The Encyclopedia of the Paranormal*, Amherst, NY: Prometheus Books, 1996. A humbling catalogue of contemporary beliefs—such as spoon bending, therapeutic touch, and spontaneous human combustion—that should give us some pause before we accuse other times and places of being superstitious.

Stuart A. Vyse, *Believing in Magic: The Psychology of Superstition*, New York: Oxford University, 1997. Vyse's book is an invaluable and approachable meditation on how superstitious patterns of thought and practices can thrive even in an educated society and even among intelligent, rational, and educated individuals, supported with current research in psychology. It provides psychological explanations of the origins, contexts, and uses of "magical thinking" in contemporary society.

NOTES

1. "Life During the Middle Ages," available at http://www.medieval-life.net/life_main.htm.
2. From "False Relics and Imposters," in Mary-Ann Stouck (ed.), *Medieval Saints: A Reader*, Peterborough, ON: Broadview, 1999, pp. 395–7 (quoting a translation by John France).

14 The Age Before Reason

Richard Raiswell

In the opening decades of the sixteenth century, the great Dutch humanist Desiderius Erasmus launched a scathing attack on the university masters of his day. Masters, he complained, were arrogant and egotistical, far more interested in puffing up their own reputations by debating the most irrelevant theoretical subtleties than in contributing any knowledge of practical value to humanity. In particular, he noted, masters devoted far too much effort trying to work out such things as the length of time the Christ-fetus spent in Mary's womb. Even more ridiculous, perhaps, were the speculative questions masters asked about the extent of God's omnipotence. For instance, could God hate his son? More absurdly: could God have taken the form of a woman, a devil, a donkey, a gourd, or even a piece of flint? And if he could have taken the form of a gourd, could this holy vegetable have preached sermons, performed miracles, and redeemed humanity on the cross? To Erasmus, this state of affairs was an insult to simple Christian piety and an affront to basic common sense.[1]

This damning critique of the late-medieval university system is often epitomized in the image of medieval scholars debating the number of angels that can dance on the head of a pin. But like so many of the conceits in this book, this image has nothing to do with the Middle Ages. Indeed, these dancing angels can be traced back only as far as the early nineteenth century when Isaac D'Israeli, father of the famous British Prime Minister Benjamin Disraeli, satirized Thomas Aquinas's treatment of the issue of the corporeality of angels, adding that he might as well have asked: "How many angels can dance on the point of a very fine needle, without jostling one another."[2]

But this portrait of the Middle Ages as the very antithesis of the age of reason—a period devoid of intellectual progress, characterized by scholars who delighted in obscurantism and who devoted their energies towards speculative and unverifiable ends, perversely ignoring the "objective truths" of the natural world around them—completely misses the point. In the first place, every intellectual system is concerned with uncovering the "truth." But second, that the medieval version of this quest for truth rested upon premises modern scholars would dismiss, and that they considered different types of data to constitute facts, does not mean that their intellectual system was fundamentally flawed—scholars who critique the people and ideas of the past according to the ideals of the present risk lapsing into the worst form of historical condescension. Indeed, it is important to remember that there is no intrinsically "correct" way to study the world and its inhabitants. There is no Platonic form of *science* towards which scholars through the ages groped blindly; there is no bearded protoscientist handing down the ten commandments of dispassionate analysis from some lofty mountaintop. Instead, the way a society understands the world is a product of the questions it asks, and these questions are themselves a reflection of the society's values, concerns, and aspirations. That the questions with which medieval intellectuals were concerned, the premises upon which they built their edifices, and their conceptions of what constituted proof were different from those of modern scientists does not mean that medieval scholars were somehow "wrong"; rather, it means simply that they inhabited a different culture from ours. The explanations they accepted may seem strange, but they made sense within the context of their conception of the universe. In order to understand the way medieval scholars thought, then, it is vital to cast aside these Renaissance and Enlightenment slanders and to ask two fundamental questions: to what ends did medieval scholars seek knowledge, and how did they know what they thought they knew? Once their intellectual aims are placed in context in this way, it becomes clear that medieval intellectuals were not only rational; they were *hyper*rational—to them, logic was more than just a means of constructing an argument; it was the single most important tool for the investigation of the natural world and the discovery of what they construed to be new knowledge.

Modern science is essentially concerned with investigating the natural world in order to manipulate it in such a way as to produce specific desirable effects. This is precisely what medieval scholars were *not* concerned with doing. To them, this was the sort of thing that a blacksmith or an artisan did. While a blacksmith might be able to smelt a lump of iron, in no real sense could he be said to know anything about iron in general. He might know something about the properties of a particular chunk of iron or about Bucephalus, the specific horse he was about to shoe, but these observations could not be extrapolated into general laws about *iron* or *horses*. This is because Bucephalus and the iron in question, like all things in the world, are subject to change: over time, the iron will rust, and Bucephalus will get old. If these things are constantly changing, then, how can anyone use observations about them to formulate conclusions that are always going to be true? At best, knowledge derived from such shaky intellectual foundations could be treated only as opinion, for it was as sound as a house built upon sand. Instead, medieval scholars were primarily concerned with uncovering truths that were always true. To them, this was what constituted real knowledge; after all, we only truly know something if what we know is always true. Accordingly, they tended not to begin their quest with the things of visible things of the world; rather, they applied their talents to unlocking the fundamental *eternal* truths of the universe, truths that were always true regardless of time or place. As a result, the medieval search for truth was always inextricably intertwined with knowledge of the one thing immune to change—God.

Concerned, then, with ultimate reality, it was inevitable that the intellectual system that emerged through the course of the Middle Ages would tend to place a premium on deductive reasoning.[3] That being said, though, medieval scholars began their search for the truth inductively, extrapolating from a single empirical observation: there were things to observe. To them, this simple fact immediately implied that there must have been a creator. As St. Augustine stated at the beginning of the fifth century, the heavens and earth cry out that they were made—and made by something other than themselves.[4] The existence of a creator, then, was a necessary conclusion derived from a simple observation. Of course, the existence of a creator was also obvious to medieval scholars from the Bible. To them, the Bible was no ordinary text, for its authors had been inspired directly by the Holy Spirit. This meant that nothing in Scripture rested upon human conjecture; instead, everything described on the Sacred Page was true in a real and absolute sense. Moreover, the text must be completely without contradiction; after all, truth cannot be contradicted by truth. In the second half of the sixth century, Cassiodorus summed up the nature of the Scriptures this way: "Everywhere in them the truth holds sway; everywhere the divine excellence beams forth; everywhere matters of use to humanity are related."[5] Because the Bible is a font of truth like no other, it was natural for medieval scholars to accept the data and analyses it provided as the starting point for their investigation of creation. Unlike René Descartes in the seventeenth century, medieval intellectuals did not have to waste time seeking out the first fact about which there can be no doubt; the Bible already supplied them with lots of these. The job of scholars, then, was to fit the observable evidence of the natural world into the framework of fundamental truth provided by Scripture.

To provide just one example of this dynamic, the Bible explained the problem of cultural diversity. After the Flood, Genesis makes clear, the world was repopulated by the progeny of Noah's three sons and their wives, each of whom became the founder of one of the nations of the three regions of the earth. According to the ordinary gloss of the Bible, Sem and his children received Asia, the best and most affluent part of the world; Cham received Africa, while Europe was given to Japheth.[6] But, Genesis continues, shortly after the waters of the Flood subsided, humanity again became proud and haughty, constructing an enormous tower at Babel that reached up to heaven itself. As a punishment for this arrogance, God destroyed the tower and then confounded the universal language that all of humanity had spoken up to this point.[7] To the medieval mind, then, the *fact* that there was a variety of languages spoken across the breadth of the world could easily be assimilated into the framework of history provided by the biblical account. Indeed, when Europeans traveled overland across Asia at the height of the Mongol Peace in the late thirteenth and early fourteenth centuries, they tended to seek out the visible remains of the events described in the Bible. And, of course, they found them—the apparent ruins of the Tower of Babel near Baghdad were noted by many travelers as they made their way to India and China (or "Cathay").[8] Seeing may be believing but believing also ensures that there is plenty to see.[9]

But if the observable facts of the world could be assimilated, so too could much of the learning of the ancient world. While the issue of the extent to which pagan learning could be appropriated to the Christian agenda was a hotly debated subject in the first four centuries of the church, Augustine's treatment of the works of the Platonists came to serve as a model. To Augustine, the Platonists had come as close to discovering some of the truths of the faith from exclusively rational principles as was possible for human reason acting alone; indeed, it was the thought of the Platonists that had brought him to the pinnacle of conversion.[10] Thus, when the Christian Augustine came to try to understand the truths he accepted through faith, he did so through the lens of the Platonists. In this sense, his theology amounts to a Christianized Platonism.

But the Middle Ages also inherited a succession of classical texts that contained some decidedly odd things. The great first-century encyclopedist, Pliny the Elder, for instance, described some of the most distant lands of the world as inhabited by a succession of strange and curious beings in his *Natural History*. The sciopodes, for instance, were a group of people who had only a single massive foot. Despite this, they were able to run exceptionally fast, and, in particularly hot weather, they were able to shade themselves in its great shadow.[11] Likewise, there were the astomi. They had no mouth and subsisted only on the odor of flowers and roots.[12] Perhaps the most popular of these monstrous peoples were the blemmyae. They had no head; instead, their eyes and mouth were in their chest.[13] When Augustine came to discuss these creatures, he had to admit that they were strange and perhaps exaggerated, but it was clear to him that God had created many wondrous things in the world. This was plain from Scripture itself: "Come see the works of the Lord, the wonders which he placed on the earth."[14] But more than this, there was nothing in Scripture to suggest that these creatures did not exist. In fact, the omnipotence of God suggested precisely the opposite; it suggested that were he so inclined, God could readily create creatures that seemed to defy the ordinary course of nature. In this sense, the omnipotence of God left space for the assimilation of all manner of oddities and curiosities. The danger in this conception of the universe lies not in being too credulous; it lies in not being credulous enough.

While the omnipotence of God implied that the world was a wonder-filled place, the Bible did act as a spur for the study of the natural world. This was partly because the sense of the text itself was frequently far from clear. Indeed, this seemed deliberate, for as the psalmist helpfully pointed out, "I will open my mouth in a parable: I will utter dark sayings of old."[15] Moreover, the text was full of obscure images and contained allusions to all sorts of flora and fauna that were alien to Europeans. In order to penetrate to the core of the text and unlock its essential truths, then, it was important to have an extensive knowledge of the nature and properties of the things of the visible universe.[16]

This is the rationale behind the medieval encyclopedia tradition, as well as that of the more limited bestiaries and lapidaries. These works were compendia of data about all manner of celestial and terrestrial phenomena, compiled to help scholars understand the images of the Sacred Page. However, in compiling these works, scholars tended not to make new observations; rather, they borrowed heavily from the works of the ancients. Not only were works like Pliny's *Natural History* full of observations about the things of the world; they were all the more attractive because they had stood the test of time. As Cassiodorus pointed out, "It will be more efficacious not to sip at the cup of audacious novelty, but to drink deeply from the fount of the ancients."[17] Consequently, scholars borrowed and pilfered specific data from the ancients, freely appropriating this material to their quest.

But facts about the natural world, regardless of where they came from, helped medieval scholars understand fundamental truths about the universe in another sense as well. In the same way that a building can be construed as an expression of the will of the architect who designed it, creation is a visible expression of the benevolence and omnipotence of God. Indeed, Aquinas went so far as to argue that the whole of creation and everything in it could be perceived as a series of statements by God about himself. In the same way that a person cannot communicate a complicated idea by means of a single word, the perfect goodness of God cannot adequately be communicated through a single created thing. Accordingly, in the same way that a human speaker uses a number of words to make an argument, so God created a rich variety of things in order to communicate his perfection more completely.[18] The natural world, then, is like a book, its individual components like its words. It was vital, then, for the medieval scholar to read, understand, and interpret the message of this other sacred text. This point was underscored by Romans 1.20: "For the invisible things of him from the creation of the world are clearly seen, being understood by the things that are made, even his eternal power and Godhead."

This tradition of reading the book of nature is epitomized by St. Ambrose in the fourth century in his allegorical interpretations of the creatures of the world. To Ambrose, the fact that God created dogs in such a way that they bark to protect their master, for instance, communicates to humanity that people should shout to protect their true master, Christ. Similarly, the industry and foresight of the ant suggests that people should not use their free will simply to gratify their senses but rather use prudence to provide for their later needs.[19] Though many of the interpretations offered by Ambrose and his successors seem decidedly far-fetched and sometimes downright contrived, such readings persisted because they conformed to the rule of faith. In *On Christian Doctrine*, Augustine argued that an interpretation of a figure or allusion that was not contrary to the principles of the faith had some validity. To him, a scholar who finds an eternal truth but who misses the author's intention is like a traveler who has strayed from the road but still reached the destination. In other words, the particular details of the created world mattered less than the higher truths they were thought to convey.

The effect of this mode of reasoning is important, for it means that all particular facts about the world tend to be subsumed into the worldview furnished by the Sacred Page. The result is a logical circle: the premises determine how things are construed, and then the perception of the things themselves underscores the apparent truth of the original premises. In this context, conclusions that cannot readily be assimilated into this circle tend to be discounted. This is quite apparent in the reception of the Aristotelian corpus in the early thirteenth century. While Aristotle would go on to become the favorite philosopher of most medieval scholastics, this was by no means inevitable when his teachings became known in full, for he made a number of arguments that were wholly at odds with the most basic elements of the faith. Chief amongst these was the notion that the world must be eternal. To Aristotle, this was an inevitable conclusion derived from the eminently sensible proposition that nothing can create nothing. Of course, this argument was wholly repugnant to medieval scholars, for it flatly contradicted Genesis. After a series of failed attempts to ban the works of Aristotle, by the end of the thirteenth century, scholars generally pointed to Aristotle's argument about the eternity of the world as proof of the deficiency of human reason unassisted by faith—a deficiency that was a result of the expulsion of Adam and Eve from the Garden of Eden.

It was not just much of the data provided by the ancients that was appropriated by medieval scholars; they also adopted and adapted the educational curriculum of the late antique world and harnessed it to their intellectual agenda. As Cassiodorus pointed out, the understanding of scared literature is greatly enhanced if the reader approaches the page with a sound knowledge of the rules of grammar, rhetoric, dialectic (i.e., formal logic), arithmetic, geometry, astronomy, and music (i.e., musical theory). Indeed, he went so far as to imply that the books of the Bible were crafted by authors who were well aware of these secular arts, for "one finds this knowledge diffused everywhere in sacred literature, as it were in the origin of universal and perfect wisdom." [20] These disciplines were known as the seven liberal arts and they came to form the backbone of the medieval educational system. They were known as *liberal* arts because they integral to the education of a free (i.e., *liber*) man in the late republican period in Rome.

Medieval scholars divided the liberal arts into two groups. The *quadrivium* (i.e., *four roads*) was concerned with the production of knowledge and comprised arithmetic, geometry, astronomy, and music; by contrast, the *trivium* (i.e., *three roads*) was concerned with the techniques of expression and was made up of grammar, rhetoric, and dialectic. While the monastic schools of the early Middle Ages had stressed the importance of grammar and rhetoric, as the intellectual agenda passed to the cathedral schools in the eleventh century, there was a renewed interest in dialectic. The popularity of logic owes much to the work of the early twelfth-century Breton teacher Peter Abelard and his influential *Yes and No*.[21] In this work, Abelard laid out more than 150 questions that dealt with the nature and mysteries of the faith. But rather than answer each question himself, what Abelard did was to supply his readers with a series of pertinent passages lifted from Scripture and the writings of the church fathers that seemed mutually contradictory. Of course, coming from such veritable sources, the disagreement between these passages could not be real, for truth cannot contradict truth—the fault must lie with the reader rather than the sources themselves. It was the job of the reader of *Yes and No*, then, to use the tools of formal logic to harmonize the apparent discrepancies between the authorities. In this way, by asking difficult questions about the sense and context of the passages, by introducing logical distinctions and qualifications between them, Abelard argued, weaker minds would learn how to seek the truth. As he pointed out, "through doubting we come to questioning and through questions, we perceive the truth."[22] In Abelard's hands, then, logic becomes more than just a mode of expression; it is a tool of research and investigation. However, it was a tool of investigation that again rested not upon observation of the natural world, but upon analysis of accepted written truths.

The critical approach Abelard helped develop proved exceptionally influential for the scholars of the later Middle Ages. In the middle years of the twelfth century, Peter the Lombard, probably one of Abelard's former students,[23] used it as the basis for his *Four Books of Sentences*—a work that became the fundamental textbook in theology for the balance of the Middle Ages.[24] At about the same time, an Italian monk named Gratian used the same method to construct his massive manual of church law known as *The Decretum*.[25] In the same way that the *Sentences* set forth apparently contradictory truths from the fundamental sources for theology, Gratian's *Decretum* was a collection of authoritative contradictory legal texts dealing with issues in church law. And again, like the *Sentences*, Gratian then showed how there could be no disagreement between the texts he presented. It was this application of logic that gave the text its revealing subtitle, *The Concordance of Discordant Canons*—the agreement of disagreeing points of law. Increasingly, then, from the middle of the twelfth century forth, medieval scholars were formally schooled in the art of reconciling the apparently irreconcilable. In practice, this meant that there was little they could not accommodate at some level into their worldview.

Of course, in the hands of obtuse scholars this approach could lead to an appalling manipulation of the spirit of texts, causing many to lament that authorities had noses of wax such was the ease with which their intentions could be twisted. However, in the hands of a master like Thomas Aquinas, it represented a powerful and effective method of investigating the nature of God and the things of creation. In Aquinas, the scholastic method diagnostic of the medieval university was perfected, epitomized in his greatest masterpiece, the *Summa Theologica*. This was a comprehensive manual of all theology that rested upon the application of the dialectical method to authorities in order to deduce or explain his conclusions. The work is structured as a series of questions, each of which is subdivided into a number of thematically related articles. Each article is structured in precisely the same way: Aquinas begins by laying out a number of authorities both for and against the proposition under examination. He then proposes his solution, before dealing with the apparent disagreement of his authorities. While this was an especially effective and rigorous way of presenting his argument, to Aquinas, as for Abelard, it was also an effective method of research—of deducing new knowledge which must necessarily be true given the veracity of the original premises. This method, then, allowed him and his scholastic successors in the universities of the later Middle Ages to advance the investigation of God and the things beyond the natural world with a new confidence and certainty. It is quite likely D'Israeli's quip about dancing angels was based upon the fact that Aquinas asked "whether several angels can be in the same place at the same time." But to Aquinas, this was not a matter of speculation: through the application of logic to the correct premises, it was perfectly clear that it was impossible to have two angels in the same place.[26]

Furnished, then, with an array of propositions construed as universally true, scholastic logic served as a launching pad for scholars to deduce all sorts of subtleties—precisely the kind of things that Erasmus complained so bitterly about. But what Erasmus failed to appreciate was that the scholastic method was more than just a particularly effective way to present an argument. It was an active method of deductive research by which new truths could be grasped. Precisely because they knew the premises whence their argument had to proceed, and they understood the framework into which the facts they adduced had to fit, medieval scholastics thought they could probe the fundamental mysteries of the universe without leaving the confines of their room. It was all an exercise in deductive logic—albeit construed from a different starting point and towards a different goal.

SUGGESTIONS FOR FURTHER READING

Primary Sources

Peter Abelard, *Sic et Non*, in *Patrologiae Cursus Completus: Series Latina*, vol. 178, J. P. Migne (ed.), Paris, 1844–64.
Ambrose, *Hexameron, Paradise, and Cain and Abel*, John J. Savage (trans.), New York: Fathers of the Church, 1961.

Thomas Aquinas, *Summa Contra Gentiles*, Vernon J. Bourke (trans.), Notre Dame University, 1989.
——. *Summa Theologica*, Fathers of the English Dominican Province (trans.), London, 1922.
Augustine, *Confessions*, R. S. Pine-Coffin (trans.), Harmondsworth, UK: Penguin, 1961.
——. *City of God*, Henry Bettenson (trans.), Harmondsworth, UK: Penguin, 1984.
——. *On Christian Doctrine*, D. W. Robertson (trans.), New York: Liberal Arts, 1958.
Cassiodorus, *An Introduction to Divine and Human Readings*, Leslie Webber Jones (trans.), New York: Octagon Books, 1966.
Erasmus, *Praise of Folly*, B. Radice (trans.; 1971), Harmondsworth, UK: Penguin, 1993.
Gesta Romanorum: Or Entertaining Moral Stories, C. Swan and W. Hooper (trans. and eds.), London: Constable, 1959.
Glossa ordinaria, in *Patrologiae Cursus Completus: Series Latina*, vol. 113, J. P. Migne (ed.), Paris, 1844–64.
Pliny the Elder, *Natural History*, H. Rackham, W. H. S. Jones and D. E. Eichholz (trans. and eds.), 10 vols., London: Heinemann, 1979.
Alexander Pope, *Memoirs of the Extraordinary Life, Works, and Discoveries of Martinus Scriblerus*, Dublin, 1741.
Edward Topsell, *The historie of foure-footed beastes*, London, 1607.
Henry Yule (ed.), *Cathay and the Way Thither, Being a Collection of Medieval Notices of China*, vol. 2, *Odoric of Pordenone*, London: Hakluyt Society, 1913.

Secondary Sources

John W. Baldwin, *The Scholastic Culture of the Middle Ages, 1000–1300* (1971), Prospect Heights: Waveland, 1997.
L. J. Daston, and K. Park, *Wonders and the Order of Nature, 1150–1750*, New York: Zone Books, 1998.
Isaac D'Israeli, "Quodlibets, or Scholastic Disquisitions," in *Curiosities of Literature and the Literary Character Illustrated, with Curiosities of American Literature by Rufus W. Griswold*, New York, 1875.
Robin Lane Fox, *The Unauthorized Version: Truth and Fiction in the Bible*, London: Viking Penguin, 1991.
Amos Funkenstein, *Theology and the Scientific Imagination from the Middle Ages to the Seventeenth Century*, Princeton, NJ: Princeton University, 1986.
E. Gilson, *Reason and Revelation in the Middle Ages*, New York: Scribner, 1938.
Simon Hornblower and Antony Spawforth (eds.), *Oxford Classical Dictionary*, 3rd ed., Oxford University, 1996.
David Knowles, *The Evolution of Medieval Thought*, New York: Vintage Books, 1962.
C. S. Lewis, *The Discarded Image: An Introduction to Medieval and Renaissance Literature* (1964), Cambridge: Canto, 1994.
David Luscombe, *The School of Peter Abelard: The Influence of Abelard's Thought in the Early Scholastic Period*, Cambridge University, 1969.
Samir Okasha, *Philosophy of Science: A Very Short Introduction*, Oxford University, 2002.
Beryl Smalley, *The Study of the Bible in the Middle Ages*, Notre Dame University, 1964.

Rudolf Wittkower, "Marvels of the East: A Study in the History of Monsters," *Journal of the Warburg and Courtauld Institutes* 5, 1942, 159–97.

NOTES

1. Erasmus, *Praise of Folly*, B. Radice (trans.), Harmondsworth, UK, 1971, pp. 85–9.
2. Isaac D'Israeli, "Quodlibets, or Scholastic Disquisitions," in *Curiosities of Literature and the Literary Character Illustrated, with Curiosities of American Literature by Rufus W. Griswold*, New York, 1875, p. 18. D'Israeli introduces this question by stating that the "reader desirous of being merry with Aquinas's angels may find them in Martinus Scriblerus, in Ch. VII." However, the image of angels dancing on the head of either a needle or a pin cannot be found there. See Alexander Pope, *Memoirs of the Extraordinary Life, Works, and Discoveries of Martinus Scriblerus*, Dublin, 1741, pp. 49–64, but esp. pp. 62–3.
3. Deduction and induction are contrary processes of reasoning. Deduction begins with accepted premises (or laws) and moves to more complicated conclusions through the application of logic. Induction, on the other hand, formulates general laws on the basis of an accumulation of particular facts. Of these, deduction is actually the more secure form of reasoning, for if the premises are true, then the conclusions cannot be anything other than true as well. Induction is less secure because the conclusion is not a necessary conclusion from the observations—that the first five eggs in a box are rotten does not necessarily mean that the sixth will be. For an excellent discussion of deduction and induction, see Samir Okasha, *Philosophy of Science: A Very Short Introduction*, Oxford, 2002, pp. 18–39.
4. Augustine, *Confessions*, R. S. Pine-Coffin (trans.), Harmondsworth, UK, 1961, p. 256. The first two of Aquinas's proofs for the existence of God also find God to be a necessary conclusion based upon observation of the natural world. The first hinges upon the fact that visible things are constantly in motion; the second rests upon the observation that there must be a cause for the effects that are apparent in the world. See Aquinas, *Summa Theologica*, Pt. 1, q.2, a.3.
5. Cassiodorus, *An Introduction to Divine and Human Readings*, Leslie Webber Jones (trans.), New York, 1966, I:16.1, p. 112.
6. *Glossa Ordinaria*, J. P. Migne (ed.), *Patrologia Latina* 113:113B. Cf. Genesis 10.
7. Genesis 11.
8. See, for instance, the account of the early fourteenth-century friar Odoric of Pordenone in *Cathay and the Way Thither, Being a Collection of Medieval Notices of China*, vol. 2, *Odoric of Pordenone*, Henry Yule (ed.), London, 1913, p. 282.
9. Robin Lane Fox, *The Unauthorized Version: Truth and Fiction in the Bible*, London, 1991, p. 212. Fox makes this comment in the context of a discussion of nineteenth-century biblical archaeology. His observation seems equally apt for medieval travel narratives.
10. Augustine, *City of God*, Henry Bettenson (trans.), Harmondsworth, UK, 1984, p. 311, VIII.9.
11. Pliny the Elder, *Natural History*, H. Rackham (ed. and trans.), London, 1979, VII.2.
12. Pliny, *Natural History*, VII.2.
13. Pliny, *Natural History*, V.8. Ultimately, the pedigree of these monstrous races of the east reaches back to the accounts of Ctesias of Cnidus and Megasthenes. Ctesias wrote about India after his extended period at the court of Artaxerxes

II of Persia in the fifth century BC; Megasthenes was an ambassador to the court of Chandragupta in northern India in the period immediately after the conquests of Alexander the Great (ca. 302–291 BC). The works of both of these authors were known only through Roman extracts in the Latin Middle Ages. See *Oxford Classical Dictionary*, 3rd ed., s.v. "Megasthenes" and "Ctesias."

14. Vulgate Psalms 46.9. The sense of Authorized Version is slightly different. Cf. Psalms 105.5.

15. Psalms 78.2.

16. This notion was central to the strategy for biblical interpretation laid down by St. Augustine in his *On Christian Doctrine*. See Augustine, *On Christian Doctrine*, II.16.24.

17. Cassiodorus, *Introduction*, p. 69.

18. Thomas Aquinas, *Summa contra Gentiles*, III.97.

19. Ambrose, *Hexameron*, in *Hexameron, Paradise, and Cain and Abel*, John J. Savage (trans.), New York, 1961, pp. 236–7. This tradition of reading the things of creation tropologically runs through the bestiaries of the Middle Ages. See, for instance, the beautiful bestiary held by Aberdeen University Library (MS 24) and that has now been digitized and is available at http://www.clues.abdn.ac.uk:8080/bestiary_old/firstpag.html. The medieval bestiary tradition continued well into the seventeenth century. For a very late example of this trend, see Edward Topsell, *The Historie of Foure-Footed Beastes*, London, 1607. Of course, it was inevitable that the monstrous races of the east would eventually be subject to the same treatment. See, for instance, *Gesta Romanorum: Or Entertaining Moral Stories*, C. Swan and W. Hooper (trans. and ed.), London, 1959, CLXXV.

20. Cassiodorus, *Introduction*, p. 127, I.27.1.

21. The text is more often known by its Latin title, *Sic et Non*.

22. Abelard, *Sic et Non*, J. P. Migne (ed.), *Patrologia Latina* 178: 1349B.

23. For Peter Lombard's debt to Abelard, see David Luscombe, *The School of Peter Abelard*, Cambridge, 1969, pp. 260–73.

24. Despite its importance for the development of the scholastic method, Abelard's work was condemned. Though the Lombard appropriated much of Abelard's material as well as his method, the *Sentences* was not condemned likely because the Lombard always took great care to set forth the church's position on most matters; in contrast, Abelard saw himself as writing something more akin to a textbook and so left his readers to find their own solutions to the questions he raised. In this sense, Abelard's work seemed to raise doubts, while that of the Lombard underscored the orthodoxies of the faith.

25. The date of the *Decretum* is not entirely clear, but given that it contains material from the Second Lateran Council (1139), it must have been completed at some point after that.

26. See Aquinas, *Summa Theologica*, Pt. 1, q. 52, a. 1–3.

15 Rehabilitating Medieval Medicine

Anne Van Arsdall

Although relevant manuscript material abounds, medieval medicine has been relatively neglected compared to scholarly studies of medieval literature. The main reason for this neglect can be traced to a negative bias set in place by a very few nineteenth- and early-twentieth-century scholars who bothered to write on the topic and laid the groundwork for what has followed.

Writing about science and medicine in a study titled *Chaucer and the Medieval Sciences*, Walter Clyde Curry summed up in one statement what might be termed a prevalent negative medievalism, dismissing pretty much out of hand the medieval medical system and its texts. Referring to medieval medical practices, Curry said, "That Chaucer should have been impressed to the point of taking seriously—at least for artistic purposes—these monstrosities of error, now seems almost unbelievable. Yet such appears to be the case."[1] Curry echoed an earlier assessment by Charles Singer, author of *Anglo-Saxon Magic and Medicine,* who said, "Surveying the mass of folly and credulity that makes up Anglo-Saxon leechdoms, it may be asked, is there any rational element here? The answer is, of course, very little."[2] Singer based many of his biases on Oswald Cockayne, the first person to present the three major Anglo-Saxon medical texts to the modern world. What happened afterward in Anglo-Saxon studies seems to have spilled into much of the reception of medieval medicine generally.

Cockayne edited and translated three medical texts written in Old English, each one of them a technical work and all written before the year 1000. In 1864, he published his translations as *Leechdoms, Wortcunning and Starcraft of Early England,* hardly a title connoting serious medicine.[3] One is an Old English version of a very famous and widely used collection of medicinal remedies known as the "Herbarium of Pseudo-Apuleius." It dates to fifth-century southern Europe, and the Anglo-Saxon translation, which Cockayne edited and translated, is now called the *Old English Herbarium.* Another is a medical manual written by or for a physician in Anglo-Saxon England containing original advice and instructions and material appropriated from a wide variety of largely Continental sources. Cockayne named this the *Leechbook of Bald* (Bald is the physician's name). The third major work Cockayne titled *Lacnunga,* or cures. Of the three, this last work contains the largest number of what the modern world considers nonrational elements, marking it as a repository for folklore and superstition. Actually, superstitions, charms, prayers, and the like make up only a small amount of the material, yet it is *this* work that has received the most attention and is often held up as typical of medieval medical writings and practices. In fact, *Lacnunga* until very recently was the only Anglo-Saxon medical work to be translated from Cockayne's rather arcane style into more modern prose.

Cockayne was a teacher of classics and mathematics at King's College School in London and an avocational Anglo-Saxonist. When he issued the Anglo-Saxon texts in translation, his prefaces to them contained a number of errors that have been widely repeated. For example, he said that the *Herbarium* would have been of little or no use to Anglo-Saxon England because the plants in it were Mediterranean (this in spite of the fact that four manuscripts exist of this one work).[4] Cockayne also claimed that many medieval medical texts were "mindlessly copied" by scribes who did not understand them. This unsupported allegation can still be found verbatim in scholarly studies.

In addition, like Sharon Turner, who wrote a history of the Anglo-Saxons at the turn of the nineteenth century,[5] Cockayne regarded the Germanic (including the Anglo-Saxon) peoples as being in the infancy of their development and therefore in awe of and less intellectually able than the Greeks and Romans. This bias permeates his assessments of Anglo-Saxon and early-medieval medicine.

To compound the biases, Cockayne preferred a quaint and deliberately antiquated translation style, which made the medical remedies read like literary curiosities. For example, one remedy from Cockayne's translation of the *Herbarium* reads, "For stirring of the inwards, take this same wort, work it to a salve, and lay it to the sore of the inwards." Nonliterary specialists may not readily recognize that a wort is a plant, not a growth on the toe, and that inwards are intestines. Another quirk of Cockayne's was to translate everything dealing with women's health into Latin, though it was in Anglo-Saxon in the original.[6]

With the publication of Cockayne's *Leechdoms,* the erroneous interpretations Cockayne offered in his prefaces and notes became linked to many other early medical texts. They were changed from serious medical reference books into misunderstood literary or folklore references. Renewed interest in these early English medical texts surfaced again in the early twentieth century; but with it, and unfortunately, the works of Charles Singer and his pupil Wilifrid Bonser became standards for studies in this field.

Taking some of their findings from Cockayne, others from their own imagination, Singer and then Bonser concentrated on the *Lacnunga* and its superstitious content. Much like the German folklorists of the nineteenth century, they looked at the medieval medical texts only as sources for pre-Christian Germanic charms and superstition, pointing out, without any type of proof, where certain terms or uses originated, and suggesting the kinds of fanciful etymologies popular in the nineteenth century.

Singer, like Cockayne, thought medieval medicine was the "last stage of a process that has left no legitimate successor, a final pathological disintegration of the great system of Greek medical thought."[7] So with Cockayne, Singer, and Bonser, the groundwork was laid for how medieval medicine would be studied. The serious medical content in the texts was assumed to be largely preposterous and unworthy of study, and the other, the charms and incantations, became the focus of interest. With the exception of the writings of a few specialists, this is the image of medieval medicine that is generally encountered—one history of medicine even titled the medieval period a Thousand Years of Darkness, and called the sick room a torture chamber.[8] (Surgery, an emergency procedure then, *was* a torture until 1846, when anesthesia was first put to use in operations.)

The groundwork laid beginning in the 1860s has proven to be solid. Negative pronouncements about Anglo-Saxon and medieval medicine abound in the literature. For example, in a 1995 article titled "The Anglo-Saxon Physician," Stanley Rubin characterized the Anglo-Saxon physician as follows:

> His difficulties were many and the vast majority of his treatments never far from useless, or, at best, of transient benefit. However before the *laece* is dismissed as essentially ineffective, uncritical and intellectually inflexible, it should be remembered that modern placebos are very often merely replacing ancient incantations and faith healing.[9]

To borrow Rubin's own terms, uncritical and intellectually inflexible are the medieval misconceptions being addressed here. Scholars and popular writers too often stereotype the medical practice of the medieval period and simply transmit erroneous notions introduced more than 150 years ago by Cockayne and amplified by Singer and others. Rubin, for example, gives almost no sources for his negative assertions. Nor does Singer or Cockayne. Too often, these very negative comments about medieval medicine go unchallenged.

Indirectly subversive is the widespread use of the term "leech" for a medieval physician. The modern world has lost any sense that "leech" once meant healer, and to the modern mind, "leech" connotes the small blood-sucking creature that was used in the eighteenth and nineteenth centuries for bloodletting, which was still a regular part of everyone's health regimen as late as the 1920s. "Leech" does not connote a medical practitioner today or in Cockayne's time, or if it does, it's the bloodletting stereotype from the movie "The Madness of King George." Analogous terms are "leechdoms," meaning remedies for health, or "leechcraft," the art of healing. Such words perpetuate the image of healers who are a bit mystified by medicine and practice it unskillfully using remedies they never question, without any diagnostic or other skills.

That this system of medicine was based on use of medicinal plants is commonly accepted today to be proof that it could not work. Yet challenges to this assumption too are being made in clinical trials of medicinal herbal remedies. There is even now a complimentary and alternative section of the National Institutes of Health in the United States, which studies herbal and other nontraditional medical treatment.[10] It should be noted that herbal medicine has always been part of treatment in mainstream Western European medicine and that scientific tests of the plants are also being done and published.

Rubin mentions two other aspects of medieval medicine—ancient incantations and faith healing—to underscore its folly. This too is a distortion begun in the nineteenth century and simply repeated. We—accepting the rational mindset of modern medicine—immediately assume that use of what we consider to be the nonrational in any part of medicine brands the healer as some kind of a quack. However, Joseph Payne suggested back in 1910 that ours is the first system of medicine that *excludes* a spiritual aspect, and he asserted that Western medicine is therefore outside the norm. A contemporary of Singer, Payne's more balanced views have unfortunately been largely ignored.[11]

Because we think nonrational elements have no place in what we categorize as scientific texts, it does not mean the medieval world must share our view and should have somehow sanitized its medical texts for our evaluation. Even now, in the twenty-first century, practicing herbalists collect medicinal plants ritually, in the firm belief that this affects how they work. It's part of a thousand-year-old system of collecting and administering medicinal plants.

What Cockayne and Singer branded "monstrosities of error" were in fact writings documenting parts of a system of healing prevalent from Greece through the Renaissance. It appears to have been quite similar to the way modern herbal medicine is practiced and largely based on use of medicinal plants. Loren MacKinney was one of the first to call for a reassessment of received biases toward medieval medicine, and his call has been answered by scholars including M. L. Cameron, M. A. D'Aronco, Monica Green, Gundolf Keil, Michael McVaugh, John Riddle, Nancy Siraisi, Jerry Stannard, and Linda Voigts (see "Suggestions for Further Reading"), among others.

Monasteries were centers for healing in the early Middle Ages, and the scribes and physicians not only preserved the medical literature of earlier times by copying and transmitting it; they also annotated the remedies with their own findings. Rather than "mindlessly copying" what was in front of them, the users combined, split apart, used, and altered texts depending on local conditions and needs. Not medical textbooks, not manuals of how to practice medicine or make diagnoses, the early medieval texts appear to have been *aides mémoires* for medics who had learned their craft by apprenticeship.

As to claims that most of the plants would not have been available outside the Mediterranean world, evidence in fact shows that nonnative medicinal plants were grown in monastery gardens and subsequently some became naturalized to other regions. There was, of course, trade for many items, including medicines. So a pan-European stock of medical supplies was available from very early times. This means that all the texts would have been useful no matter where they were copied or used.

To counter misconceptions about medieval medicine, it is important—unlike in Curry, Cockayne, and a host of others—to acknowledge that medieval people accepted the system of medicine and the healers with whom they lived just as we do our own. At the time, the healers might have been monks, nuns, laymen with a knack for using medicinal plants, or in the later Middle Ages, a university physician and his apothecary.

It is equally important to question every negative assertion encountered concerning the topic of medieval medicine. And finally, medieval medical texts should be read critically to encourage us to understand how medicine was actually practiced and to learn how what we consider nonrational elements figured into it. The medieval world did not split apart science and religion: hospitals included religious rites, and patients expected such dual treatment.

If we look at the system of medieval medicine more objectively, it can lead to a much better understanding of the time, its culture, and its literature. This system was integrated into medieval life. Negative stereotypes such as those described here lead only to dead ends and false assumptions and to negative medievalisms.

SUGGESTIONS FOR FURTHER READING

M. L. Cameron, "Anglo-Saxon Medicine and Magic," in *Anglo-Saxon England* 17 (1988): 191–215.

Sheila Campbell, Bert Hall, and David Klausner (eds.), *Health, Disease and Healing in Medieval Culture*, New York: St. Martin's, 1992.

M. A. D'Aronco and M. L. Cameron, *The Old English Illustrated Pharmacopoeia*, Copenhagen: Rosenkilde and Bagger, 1998.

Faye Getz, *Medicine in the English Middle Ages*, Princeton, NJ: Princeton University, 1998.

Monica Green, *The Trotula: A Medieval Compendium of Women's Medicine*, Philadelphia: University of Pennsylvania, 2001.

Bart Holland (ed.), *Prospecting for Drugs in Ancient and Medieval European Texts: A Scientific Approach*, Amsterdam: Harwood Academic, 1996.

Peregrine Horden and Emilie Savage-Smith (eds.), "Social History of Medicine: The Year 1000, Medical Practice at the End of the First Millennium," *The Journal of the Society for the Social History of Medicine* 13.2, 2000.

Gundolf Keil, *Fachprosa-Studien: Beiträge zur mittelalterliche Wissenschafts und Geistesgeschichte*, Berlin: E. Schmidt, 1982.

Gundolf Keil and Paul Schnitzer (eds.), *Das Lorscher Arzneibuch und die frühmittelalterliche Medizin*, Lorsch, Germany: Verlag Laurissa, 1991.

Loren MacKinney, *Early Medieval Medicine*, Baltimore: Johns Hopkins, 1937.

M. R. McVaugh, *Medicine Before the Plague: Practitioners and Their Patients in the Crown of Aragon, 1285–1345*, Cambridge: Cambridge University, 1993.

Joseph F. Payne, "English Medicine in the Anglo-Saxon Times," *The Fitz-Patrick Lectures for 1903*, London: Clarendon, 1904.

John Riddle, *Contraception and Abortion from the Ancient World to the Renaissance*, Cambridge, MA: Harvard University, 1992.

——. "Theory and Practice in Medieval Medicine," *Viator* 5, 1974, 157–84.

Margaret Schleissner, *Manuscript Sources of Medieval Medicine*, New York: Garland, 1995.

Nancy Siraisi, *Medieval and Early Renaissance Medicine*, Chicago: University of Chicago, 1990.

Jerry Stannard, *Herbs and Herbalism in the Middle Ages and Renaisssance*, London: Ashgate Variorum, 1999a.

——. *Pristina Medicamenta: Ancient and Medieval Medical Botany*, London: Ashgate Variorum, 1999b.

Anne Van Arsdall, *Medieval Herbal Remedies: The Old English Herbarium and Anglo-Saxon Medicine*, New York: Routledge, 2002.

Linda E. Voigts, "Anglo-Saxon Plant Remedies and the Anglo-Saxons," *Isis* 70, 1979, 250–68.

Linda E. Voigts and M. R. McVaugh, *A Latin Technical Phlebotomy and Its Middle English Translation*, Philadelphia: American Philosophical Society, 1984.

Read with a Very Critical Eye

Wilifrid Bonser, *The Medical Background of the Anglo-Saxons*, London: The Wellcome Historical Medical Library, 1963.

Oswald Cockayne, *Leechdoms, Wortcunning and Starcraft of Early England* (1864), London: Kraus Reprint, 1965.

J. H. G. Grattan and Charles Singer, *Anglo-Saxon Magic and Medicine*, London: Oxford University, 1952.

NOTES

1. Walter Clyde Curry, *Chaucer and the Medieval Sciences*, New York: Barnes and Noble, 1960, p. xi.
2. J. H. G. Grattan and Charles Singer, *Anglo-Saxon Magic and Medicine*, London: Oxford University, 1952, p. 92.
3. Oswald Cockayne, *Leechdoms, Wortcunning and Starcraft of Early England*, 3 vols. (1864), London: Kraus Reprint, 1965.
4. Linda Voigts refuted the assertion that the work had little value to its time in her article "Anglo-Saxon Plant Remedies and the Anglo-Saxons," *Isis* 70, 1979, 250–68.
5. Sharon Turner, *The History of the Anglo-Saxons: Comprising the History of England from the Earliest Period to the Norman Conquest*, 3 vols. (1799–1805), London: Longman, Hurst, Rees, Orme, and Brown, 1823.
6. For more on Cockayne, see Anne Van Arsdall, *Medieval Herbal Remedies: The Old English Herbarium and Anglo-Saxon Medicine*, New York: Routledge, 2002, Chapter 1.
7. Grattan and Singer, *Anglo-Saxon Magic*, p. 94.
8. S. G. B. Stubbs and E. W. Bligh, *Sixty Centuries of Health and Physik*, London: Sampson, Low, 1931.

9. Stanley Rubin, "The Anglo-Saxon Physician," in *Medieval Life*, 1995, 6–11, at 11.

10. See Bart Holland (ed.), *Prospecting for Drugs in Ancient and Medieval European Texts: A Scientific Approach*, Amsterdam: Harwood Academic, 1996.

11. See in particular Peregrine Horden and Emilie Savage-Smith (eds.), "Social History of Medicine: The Year 1000, Medical Practice at the End of the First Millennium," *The Journal of the Society for the Social History of Medicine* 13.2, 2000. See "Further Reading" for Payne citation.

16 Medical Misconceptions

Bryon Grigsby

The two greatest misconceptions about medicine arise primarily from our modern attempts at interpreting the medical system of the Middle Ages. The first misconception is to see medicine in the Middle Ages as an unsophisticated system. Early scholars of medieval medicine found medieval doctors' theories ridiculous when compared to modern ones. Charles Singer, for example, found medieval medicine demonstrative of "the wilting mind of the Dark Ages."[1] Singer also believed that medieval medicine, specifically the Anglo-Saxon herbals, "lacked any rational element which might mark the beginnings of scientific advance."[2] But recently, historians like M. L. Cameron, in *Anglo-Saxon Medicine*, and John Riddle, in *Contraception and Abortion from the Ancient World to the Renaissance*, attempt to validate medieval medicine in light of modern medicine. By analyzing common herbals, both Cameron and Riddle have found a few recipes that have therapeutic merit.

While Cameron and Riddle are both correct in seeing some validity in medieval medicine, they also commit the other misconception of interpreting the medicine of the Middle Ages: they approach medieval medicine from a positivistic framework. In other words, they attempt to see medieval medicine as a precursor or primitive form of twentieth-century medicine. In order to do this effectively, critics construct a narrative by which the discoveries of the future are foreseen in the documentation of the past. This constructed narrative feeds a type of superficial comparitivism, to borrow Peregrine Horden's term, in which modern people attempt to see their reflection in the writings of the authors of the Middle Ages.[3] While this method has significant benefits for creating interest in the Middle Ages and even pedagogical worth for undergraduate students attempting to grapple with an alien time period and culture, it does little for the scholar who is attempting to understand the complex medical and social structures of the Middle Ages. However, rather than approach the medieval medical community from a positivistic framework in which the medieval doctor is a primitive reflection of our modern doctor, some historians have adopted a social constructionist viewpoint in which they attempt to evaluate the medieval medical community as part of a larger social system.[4]

Medieval medicine is neither a precursor to our modern medicine nor a simplistic, primitive system. Rather, it is an extremely learned theory that makes sense when one considers the information doctors of the period had to rely on. To do medieval medicine justice, it is necessary to reconstruct the development of this system in relation to health and illness. One must first realize that there are few similarities between medieval and modern medicine, especially in regard to the framework through which each approaches illness. I will limit this discussion to academic medicine, as opposed to folklore medicine, because the records of academic medicine are more accessible through the publications of and translations by numerous medieval doctors and surgeons, whereas folklore medicine tends to be transmitted orally.

During the medieval period, the body reflected one's state of health, and medieval doctors relied on the body as text. Today, the body as text is rarely used as the sole witness to the health of an individual. Instead, health is evaluated by medical tests.[5] There is an obvious benefit to this: in most cases, when the body does act as a text, the disease has often progressed very far, making it more difficult to cure. However, medieval doctors had little concept of germs as the medium of disease and the cause of illness. Thus, they approached illness through a markedly different framework than do modern doctors. While the body was known to degenerate with age, medieval doctors believed that a healthy body required a state of harmony or balance. An unhealthy body represented an imbalance, usually identified through a change or sign on the outside of the body, either on the skin or from an excreted fluid, such as urine. Thus the body becomes the symbolic text that a doctor needed to interpret in order first to diagnosis and then to cure. In many ways, we can see a parallel in the interpretation of a blood test wherein a modern doctor receives a series of numbers and from them produces a diagnosis and treatment for an identified illness. For medieval doctors, the body, not the test, was the sign that needed interpretation.

Lacking any concept of viruses or bacteria as causes of illness, medieval doctors were left to reason that certain behaviors led to illness. There were three types of possible illnesses: those caused by the body's natural degeneration, those to which the body was predisposed, and those caused by immoderate living. We have a similar system in that we believe that people who smoke, eat red meat, or sunbathe are more prone to cancer and heart disease. We connect these diseases to either a predisposition, such as a hereditary line for breast cancer or heart disease, or to immoderate lifestyle, such as actions that lead to lung disease or liver cancer. While both medieval and modern medicine have a similar emphasis on the lifestyle causes of illness, medieval medicine's difference lies in its idea that certain sins could cause certain illnesses. This relation between particular sins and illnesses develops from authoritative Greco-Roman medicine and is influenced and modified by Christian thought.

These medieval notions of disease and morality are not simply metaphors; instead, they were considered literal truths. But only by understanding the authoritative medical tradition through which doctors learned that immorality caused illness can we begin to see the social construction of disease in a variety of discourses. If, for example, one believes that a certain form of moral transgression causes illness, then the only way to alleviate illness is to correct moral failings. In this sense, literature plays an essential role in the health of the community: literature helps to inform people about the consequences of immorality in the hope that people will relinquish sin and thereby help to abate epidemic diseases that threaten to destroy society. Consequently, we find a significant amount of moral literature during the time of the bubonic plague, a disease thought to be caused by the communal sin of pride.

The connection between morality and illness is not a medieval creation but part of the heritage of Greco-Roman medicine. Galen unified two competing theories, the empiricists and the dogmatists, into one philosophy, which became the foundation of medieval medicine. The empiricists believed in experience as the greatest teacher of medical learning.[6] The dogmatists, on the other hand, "granted logical arguments a place in medical thought."[7] This latter sect believed that all medical knowledge could be gained not through clinical experience but through authoritative medical writers. The dogmatists relied on a learned tradition and propounded a notion of a microcosm and macrocosm.[8] The microcosm consisted of the four bodily humours: blood, phlegm, black bile, and yellow bile. Each of the four humours reflected the elements of the macrocosm: air, water, earth, and fire, respectively. The humours also had temperature and moisture properties. Blood was hot and wet, phlegm was cold and wet, black bile was cold and dry, and yellow bile was hot and dry. According to this theory, when a person became sick, one of the four humours was out of balance. To balance the humours, one needed to take a prescription, usually made from some combination of plants or animals. Doctors categorized all plants and animals by their temperature and moisture. Thus, if a patient's illness was caused by an imbalance of phlegm, which is cold and wet, he or she needed to counteract that humour with its opposite, yellow bile. Therefore, he or she would need to take a prescription made from plants and animals that were hot and dry. According to this system, humans are inherently connected to the natural elements because these elements, not germs, influence health.

Galen believed that authoritative learning was important but must not be accepted blindly; "rather, [medical authorities] are authorities in as far as they are proved right" through clinical experience.[9] Essentially, Galen saw medicine as a cumulative process in which one studied medical authorities and appended or altered the authoritative corpus through clinical experience. Consequently, the humoural system became the lens through which doctors until the nineteenth century viewed disease.

Galen's emphasis on immoderation as a cause of illness appealed especially to early Christians. Oswei Temkin notes, "By A.D. 350 [Galen's] acceptance as the leading authority was clearly established, and from about that time his position was secured in Alexandria, once more the center of medical learning."[10] Greco-Roman medicine's emphasis that illness was a consequence of immoderation fit nicely into a Christian framework. Consequently, Greco-Roman medicine was not rejected by Christian thinkers but was Christianized. In the Old and New Testaments, disease is often a punishment for individuals who transgress God's law; consequently, Christ becomes the physician who can cure both spiritual and physical diseases.[11] While Christ was thought to be the perfect physician, his followers also gain acclaim as healers and curers. David Lyle Jeffrey recognizes, "The apostle Luke, one of the four evangelists and author also of the Acts of the Apostles, is referred to by Paul as 'the beloved physician' (Col. 4:14)."[12] The image of Christ as the perfect doctor finds a permanent place in Christian thought with the writings of Saint Ambrose (339–97 AD) Saint Augustine (354–430 AD), and Boethuis (480–524 AD).

A third misconception about medieval medicine concerns ascribing the belief to medieval people that all illness was connected to moral failings. In fact, some illnesses were believed to occur naturally or as a result of old age. The cautions that Darrel W. Amundsen makes concerning modern interpretations of medieval beliefs is worthwhile to quote at length:

> Another commonplace encountered in modern assessments of the early Middle Ages is the assertion that early medieval people saw sin as the cause of most sickness. Here there is room for much confusion because the relationship of sin with sickness can appear at three different levels. First, sin was certainly regarded by early medieval authors as the cause of sickness in the sense that without sin there would have been no material evil. This, although not expressed, was an underlying assumption of the sources. Second, one's own general sinfulness was often given as the cause of one's own sickness. Third, sickness, it was thought, might result from a specific sin. This last statement is very seldom encountered except in denunciations of and warnings to entire communities, and then the emphasis was often on general moral laxity, which makes it nearly indistinguishable from the second category. We should also note that it is one thing to maintain that a person is sick as a punishment for a specific sin to which he or she is obstinately and tenaciously clinging, but it is quite another matter to attribute one's own sickness to one's general sinfulness and see the sickness as part of God's punitive and refining process.[13]

While dysentery or gum disease certainly would have unclear moral connections, leprosy and bubonic plague are two diseases that clearly fit Amundsen's categories. Amundsen rightly recognizes this when he writes,

"Sin was commonly regarded as the immediate cause of plague, or at least the catalyst behind God's sending the plague. This was collective sin. Individual sin was seldom seen as the cause of sickness, whether mental illness or physical ailments. One notable exception was leprosy, which was associated with a variety of sins, but especially with lust and pride."[14]

While Amundsen correctly identifies that leprosy and bubonic plague were associated with individual and collective sins, respectively, a detailed study of the variety of sins associated with leprosy demonstrates that leprosy was not connected with lust as much as it was connected to a variety of sins, including envy, wrath, and simony.

In many ways, we still retain some of the medieval connection between illness and morality, a connection that influences literature as well as society. The clearest literary example of both the influence of medicine on literature and the connection between morality and illness appears in our own adjectives: sanguine, choleric, phlegmatic, and melancholy. At one time, these adjectives referred both to the emotional and moral state of the individual as well as to his or her physical constitution. More importantly, these adjectives are used throughout the literature of the Middle Ages, but few critics have examined them in a literal way. For example, in the Middle English lyric "Thirty Dayes Hath November," the author sums up the moral and physical associations:

Fleumaticus:
Sluggy and slowe, in spetinge muiche,
Cold and moist, my natur is suche;
Dull of wit, and fat, of contenaunce strange,
Fleumatike, this complecion may not change.

Sanguineus:
Deliberal I am, loving and gladde,
Laghinge and playing, full seld I am sad;
Singing, full fair of colour, bold to fight,
Hote and moist, beninge, sanguine I hight.

Colericus:
I am sad and soleynge with heviness in thoght;
I covet right muiche, leve will I noght;
Fraudulent and suttill, full cold and dry,
Yollowe of colour, colorike am I.

Malencolicus:
Envius, dissevabill, my skin is roghe;
Outrage in exspence, hardy inoghe,
Suttill and sklender, hote and dry,
Of colour pale, my nam is malencoly.[15]

Each one of these ailments corresponds to an emotional state—an emotional state that could lend itself to sin. The assumptions that underlie this poem are that the phlegmatic is prone to the sin of idleness, the sanguine is prone to the sins of lust and overindulgence, the choleric is prone to the sins of covetousness, and the melancholic is prone to the sins of deceit and envy. When a medieval author used these adjectives to describe literary characters, the medieval reader would have easily connected the adjective to its equivalent sin. Not only were humours connected to sins, but so were certain diseases, such as leprosy and bubonic plague. Around each of these diseases lies a complex discourse that infuses the medical, theological, and literary disciplines, a discourse that we misconceive at our own peril.[16]

SUGGESTIONS FOR FURTHER READING

Primary Sources

William Bullein, *A Dialogue against the Feuer Pestilence*, Mark W. Bullen and A. H. Auden (eds), London: Early English Text Society, 1888.

Ibn Butlan, *The Medieval Health Handbook Tacuinum Sanitatis*, Luisa Cogliati Arano (ed.), Oscar Ratti and Adele Westbrook (trans.), New York: George Braziller, 1976.

Guy De Chauliac, *The Middle English Translation of Guy De Chauliac's Anatomy*, Bjorn Wallner (ed.), Lund, Sweden: Lund University, 1964.

———. *The Cyrurgie of Guy de Chauliac*, Margaret S. Ogden (ed.), London: Early English Text Society, 1971.

Logan Clendening (ed.), *Source Book of Medical History*, New York: Dover, 1942.

W. R. Dawson, *A Leechbook or Collection of Medical Recipes of the Fifteenth Century*, London: Macmillan, 1934.

Galen, *Galen: on Respiration and the Arteries*, David J. Furley and J. S. Wilkie (eds.), Princeton, NJ: Princeton University, 1984.

Marie Faye Getz (ed.), *Healing and Society in Medieval England: A Middle English Translation of the Pharmaceutical Writings of Gilbertus Anglicus*, Madison: University of Wisconsin, 1991.

Edward Grant (ed.), *A Source Book in Medieval Science*, Cambridge, MA: Harvard University, 1974.

John Harington (ed.), *The School of Salernum: Regimen Sanitatis Salerni*, Rome: Edizioni Saturnia, 1959.

Rosemary Horrox (ed. and trans.), *The Black Death*, Manchester: Manchester University, 1994.

Tony Hunt, *The Medieval Surgery*, Woodbridge: Boydell, 1992.

———. *Popular Medicine in Thirteenth-Century England*, Cambridge: D. S. Brewer, 1990.

Arderne John, *Treatises of Fistula in Ano*, D. Power (ed.), London: Early English Text Society, 1910.

Pearl Kibre (ed.), *Hippocrates Latinus: Repertorium of Hippocratic Writings in the Latin Middle Ages*, New York: Fordham University, 1985.

Margaret Sinclari Ogden (ed.), *The 'Liber de Diversis Medicinis,'* London: Early English Text Society, 1938.

Paracelsus (Aureolus Theophrastus Bombastus von Hohenheim), *Paracelsus: Selected Writings*, Jolande Jacobi (ed.), Princeton. NJ: Princeton University, 1979.

Carole Rawcliffe (ed.), *Source for the History of Medicine in Late Medieval England*, Kalamazoo. MI: Medieval Institute Publications, 1995.
Soranus of Ephesus, *Soranus' Gynecology*, Oswei Temkin (trans.), Baltimore: Johns Hopkins University, 1956.

History of Medicine

Darrel W. Amundsen, *Medicine, Society, and Faith in the Ancient and Medieval Worlds*, London: Johns Hopkins University, 1996.
M. L. Cameron, *Anglo-Saxon Medicine*, Cambridge: Cambridge University, 1993.
Luis Garcia-Ballester, Roger French, Jon Arrizabalaga, and Andrew Cunningham (eds.), *Practical Medicine from Salerno to the Black Death*, Cambridge: Cambridge University, 1994.
David C. Lindberg, *The Beginnings of Western Science*, Chicago: Chicago University, 1992.
Michael R. McVaugh, *Medicine before the Plague: Practitioners and Their Patients in the Crown of Aragon 1285–1345*, Cambridge: Cambridge University, 1993.
Timothy Miller, *The Birth of the Hospital in the Byzantine Empire*, Baltimore: Johns Hopkins University, 1997.
Katherine Park, *Doctors and Medicine in Early Renaissance Florence*, Princeton, NJ: Princeton University, 1985.
Carole Rawcliffe, *Medicine and Society in Later Medieval England*, Phoenix Mill, UK: Allan Sutton, 1997.
Nancy G. Siraisi, *Medieval and Early Renaissance Medicine*, Chicago: Chicago University, 1990.
Charles H. Talbot, *Medicine in Medieval England*, London: Oldbourne, 1967.
Oswei Temkin, *Galenism: Rise and Decline of a Medical Philosophy*, Ithaca, NY: Cornell University, 1973.
——. *Hippocrates in a World of Pagans and Christians*, London: Johns Hopkins University, 1991.

Leprosy

Saul Brody, *The Disease of the Soul: Leprosy in Medieval Literature*, Ithaca, NY: Cornell University, 1974.
Peter Richards, *The Medieval Leper*, New York: Barnes & Noble, 1977.
Charles Singer (ed. and trans.), "A Thirteenth Century Clinical Description on Leprosy," *Journal of the History of Medicine* 4, 1948, 237–9.

Bubonic Plague

Ann Margaret Campbell, *The Black Death and the Men of Learning*, New York: Columbia University, 1931.
Ann Carmichael, *Plague and the Poor in Renaissance Florence*, Cambridge: Cambridge University, 1986.
Michael W. Dols, *The Black Death in the Middle East*, Princeton, NJ: Princeton University, 1977.
Robert S. Gottfried, *The Black Death: Natural and Human Disaster in Medieval Europe*, New York: Macmillan, 1983.

Colin Platt, *King Death: The Black Death and Its Aftermath in Late-Medieval England*, Toronto: University of Toronto, 1997.
Hans Zinsser, *Rats, Lice and History: A Chronicle of Pestilence and Plagues*, New York: Black Dog, 1935.

Syphilis and Other Diseases

Jon Arrizabalaga, John Henderson, and Roger French, *The Great Pox: The French Disease in Renaissance Europe*, New Haven, CT: Yale University, 1997.
Marc Bloch, *The Royal Touch: Monarchy and Miracles in France and England*, J. E. Anderson (trans.), New York: Dorset, 1961.
Sheila Cambell, Bert Hall, and David Klausner (eds.), *Health, Disease, and Healing in Medieval Culture*, New York: St. Martin's, 1992.
Mirko D. Grmek, *Diseases in the Ancient Greek World*, Mireille Muellner and Leonard Muellner (trans.), Baltimore: Johns Hopkins University, 1989.
Claude Quetel, *History of Syphilis*, Judith Braddock and Brian Pike (trans.), Baltimore: Johns Hopkins University, 1990.
Sheldon Watts, *Epidemics and History: Disease, Power, and Imperialism*, New Haven, CT: Yale University, 1997.

Doctors and Surgeons

Theodore R. Beck, *The Cutting Edge: Early History of the Surgeons of London*, London: Lund Humphries, 1974.
Vern L. Bullough, *The Development of Medicine as a Profession*, New York: Hafner, 1966.
Edward J. Kealey, *Medieval Medicus: A Social History of Anglo-Norman Medicine*, Baltimore: Johns Hopkins University, 1981.
Piers D. Mitchell, *Medicine in the Crusades: Warfare, Wounds and the Medieval Surgeon*, Cambridge: Cambridge University, 2004.
Marie-Christine Pouchelle, *The Body and Surgery in the Middle Ages*, Rosemary Morris (trans.), New Brunswick, NJ: Rutgers University, 1990.

Sexuality and Medicine

Joan Cadden, *Meanings of Sex Difference in the Middle Ages: Medicine, Science, and Culture*, Cambridge, MA: Cambridge University, 1993.
Danielle Jacquart, and Claude Thomasset, *Sexuality and Medicine in the Middle Ages*, Matthew Adamson (trans.), Princeton: Princeton University, 1988.
John M. Riddle, *Contraception and Abortion from the Ancient World to the Renaissance*, Cambridge, MA: Harvard University, 1992.

NOTES

1. Charles Singer, *A Short History of Medicine*, New York: Oxford University, 1962, p. 31.
2. M. L. Cameron, *Anglo-Saxon Medicine*, Cambridge: Cambridge University, 1993, p. 3.
3. Peregrine Horden, "Disease, Dragons, and Saints: The Management of Epidemics in the Dark Ages," *Epidemics and Ideas: Essays on the Historical*

Perception of Pestilence, Terrence Ranger and Paul Slack (eds.), Cambridge: Cambridge University, 1992, pp. 45–76.

4. See Deborah Lupton, *Medicine as Culture: Illness, Disease, and the Body in Western Societies*, London: Sage, 1994, pp. 11–13.

5. Lupton, 98. See also Herzlich and Pierret, *Illness and Self in Society*, Baltimore: Johns Hopkins University, 1987, pp. 76–82.

6. Oswei Temkin, *Galenism: Rise and Decline of a Medical Philosophy*, Ithaca, NY: Cornell University, 1973, p. 15; and David C. Lindberg, *The Beginnings of Western Science*, Chicago: Chicago University, 1992, p. 188.

7. Temkin, *Galenism*, p. 19.

8. Temkin, *Galenism*, p. 19.

9. Temkin, *Galenism*, p. 32.

10. Temkin, *Galenism*, p. 61.

11. David Lyle Jeffrey (ed.), *The Dictionary of Biblical Tradition in English Literature*, Grand Rapids, MI: Wm. B. Eerdmans, 1992, p. 614.

12. Jeffrey, *Dictionary*, p. 614. See also Darrel W. Amundsen, *Medicine, Society, and Faith in the Ancient and Medieval Worlds*, London: Johns Hopkins University, 1996, pp. 133–4.

13. Amundsen, pp. 187–8.

14. Amundsen, p. 210.

15. Maxwell Luria and Richard L. Hoffman (eds.), *Middle English Lyrics*, New York: W. W. Norton, 1974, p. 112.

16. My thanks to Routledge and Taylor & Francis for permission to use portions of the first chapter of my *Pestilence in Medieval and Early Modern English Literature* (New York: Routledge, 2004).

IV
The Arts

17 Medieval Cuisine
Hog's Swill or Culinary Art?

Jean-François Kosta-Théfaine

(Translated from the French by Stephen J. Harris)[1]

Ideas concerning the Middle Ages are, unfortunately, longstanding, and it is very difficult to unencumber ourselves of their influence. There is one among them that has lasted a very long time and is held with relatively little justification: it concerns cuisine, considered for a long time as veritable hog's swill. We have as primary examples three opinions, written many years apart, but which together prove significant.

Emile Littré, reviewing an edition of a fourteenth-century treatise, wrote in 1837: "Our ancestors of the fourteenth century ate, as we have seen, little that we eat; but they ate other preparations. What would we think [of them]? It would be interesting for an intelligent cook to try to prepare one of these dishes, and to dine archaeologically, at the risk of a bad dinner."[2]

Henriette Parenté and Genvième de Ternant, in their work dedicated to the history of French cuisine published in 1981, observed: "Some have tried to make the recipes left by Taillevent and his contemporaries; the results were always deplorable. The historian Alfred Franklin wanted to prepare duck in red *dodine* and a hash[3] according to the directions of the head chef of Charles V. It was a true catastrophe."[4]

Finally, Maguelonne Toussaint-Sanat, much as her predecessors, painted in her book published in 1987 an image hardly flattering to medieval cuisine:

> During the celebrated banquet of the Pheasant in 1453, the Duke of Burgundy, Philip the Good, vowed over the pheasant to leave on crusade and there to provoke the Sultan into hand-to-hand combat. The pheasant did not press on anyone's stomach, and the solemn oath was quickly forgotten. It is often thus the case that great banquets, today as yesterday, serve gastronomy more than political ambition.[5]

Thus, during the century that elapsed between Emile Littré's remark in 1877 and Maguelonne Toussaint-Sanat's in 1987, the prejudice against medieval cuisine has not faded. Nevertheless, we can indicate a positive remark in a recent work, although it concerns the cuisine of Antiquity, more precisely a sauce of Apicius: "A recipe of Apicius, dated to the first century, is not obsolescent. It concerns a sauce . . . This sauce is good in all circumstances."[6]

On examining books of medieval cuisine more closely, it does not seem that this food, although remote from our current tastes, appears to be truly inedible.

The excessive use of spices in medieval cuisine is certainly that which contributed to its poor reputation. Indeed, a consultation of cookbooks from the Middle Ages reveals dishes often containing a considerable combination of spices and/or herbs. The main spices used are cumin, saffron, nutmeg, ginger, pepper (long and round), cinnamon, cinnamon flower, fruit of paradise or *maniguette*, cloves, etc.[7] It has often been said that they were used to mask the odor of putrefying meat! However, recent works concerning spices have demonstrated that nothing of the sort occurred. Their use, as Bruno Laurioux demonstrates, answers to precision only. They have in effect an "ostentatious function"[8] and correspond moreover to dietary criteria, being related to the theory of the four bodily humors: thus we are invited to see "ginger, a spice of relative equilibrium, neither too hot nor too dry."[9] Cookbooks do not advise anywhere or at any time the use of spices to mask either any odors or those of old meat. The only exception concerns wine, as mentioned in *Le Viandier* of Taillevent: the use of ginger allows for "preserving bottled wine where one smells the cask, the floral bouquet or the smell of rot."[10]

The other element which certainly contributed to making medieval cuisine seem something absolutely inedible lies in the fact that all the extant recipes lack precise measurements. Indeed, if the ingredients are given, one notes, the quantities are either merely approximate or completely nonexistent. In fact, reproducing a recipe under these conditions proves almost impossible. Moreover, the way in which the recipes are presented is brief and strange to see, since they consist in general of mixtures of chopped and ground spices and herbs which are afterwards added to liquids (wine or grape juice), filtered and eventually either incorporated into a meat broth or made into broth, or well folded into sauces. Indeed, thus presented, these recipes allow us to imagine that the dishes are truly inedible! However, one ought not to focus on this aspect of things but instead overlook the brevity of the editions of these recipes. It is important to underline at the outset that if the recipes insist as much as they do on the fact that one must grind the spices and mince the herbs, it is above all not so that they are reduced to powder but so that these two ingredients, especially the spices, are permitted to release all of their aroma. Thus, one recognizes that medieval cuisine was rich in flavors, which reveals a high level of refinement. How could one believe otherwise once it is known that a mixture of spices added to *hypocras* (a liquid made of wine, sugar, and cinnamon, and sometimes other spices) was passed through a strainer to eliminate all sediment? There is in this process a real finesse of execution worthy of the greatest chefs of our era. The vocabulary of the time, both limited and cursory, has also led modern readers to believe that the result was nothing but a vulgar mixture of ingredients whose taste consequently must have been a real disaster. Accordingly, we cannot lose sight of the fact that these cookbooks, or rather these culinary tracts we call cookbooks, were after all a kind of *aide-mémoire*, absent of precision, and each cook knew the quantities to use as well as the methods to execute—information which has not remained for posterity.

It is commonly believed that medieval cuisine was comprised only of inedible stews, whereas the cookbooks prove the opposite. First of all, it must be acknowledged that there was a great diversity of dishes on offer in medieval cuisine, and the cookbooks are proof enough. Thus, we can establish with some clarity that diversity was a quality which justifiably concerned them. As such, their cuisine was composed of soups, meats (including wild game, poultry, pork, mutton, goat, etc.), saltwater and freshwater fish, and desserts such as pies, flans, cheeses, fruits, and marzipan. Additionally, the *entremets* (sweet dish between cheese and dessert), which, from the beginning, constituted the *divertissements* (palate-cleansers) between each course, at the end of the fourteenth century amounted to a series of courses such as swan or peacock arranged in its own feathers, trout in jelly, gelatin of carp, or equally well-dressed ingredients.

There is also in this cuisine, which is certainly coarse compared to ours, a real art of creation. It is a matter of—let's not be afraid of the words—innovative cuisine. It is useful here to be reminded that *Le Viandier* of Taillevent truly innovated in suggesting balancing bitter wine (*vin aigre*) with *hypocras*, that is to say, a spiced wine with a sweet wine. This cuisine is the object of another type of innovation: an elaborate formation of dishes that compete with one another in their color and appearance and that are at the same time important and surprising. This is the case for "*blancmange*, divided in four colors"[11] of Master Chiquart, chef to Amadeus VIII at the court of Savoy, of which the colors are—and this is even more extraordinary since unthinkable for a dish—yellow, red, blue, and silver. The same dish is described in *Le Viandier* with, this time, different colors: red, blue, green, and yellow.[12] The *porées*, soups and sauces, could be yellow, green, chestnut, and indeed even black. The chromatic gamut of dishes constitutive of medieval cuisine is extraordinary and reveals a real sense of culinary creativity. In this respect it is important to remember the remarkable creation of Master Chiquart of an *entremets* shaped like a castle[13] containing a "fountain of love" where flows spiced wine and rose water; beneath this fountain one found cages full of doves and other birds, and on each side of the same fountain is enthroned "a peacock . . . skinned and dressed," baked animals adorning its plumes, and presented to the guests as if it were alive. This *entremets* of Master Chiquart, which also included many other elements, is remarkable for a number of reasons.[14] We ought not to leave out, moreover, the directions which concerned the recomposition of animals, for which the cookbooks offer advice, and reveal techniques for keeping the neck of an animal straight, as well as for repositioning the plumage on the skin. *Le Viandier* explains, concerning peacocks, that one is to proceed in the following manner:

> They are suitable to breathe into and inflate as with swans, and similarly to roast and gild them. And they must be served for the last course. And when they are dressed, it is suitable to have a long, thin spit of wood to hold and send through the tail feathers, where a small trellis is used to erect the plumes as if the pheasant itself were in display.[15]

We could cite many more examples of dishes that are both innovative and incredible, like "the two-faced tart" beneath cheese;[16] stuffed "eggs roasted on a spit";[17] "Pomeranian pies," which are marvelous pastries that reproduced a castle complete with crenels, towers, and banners;[18] or even "stag's tooth broth and brains," which is nothing other than a soup of stags' testicles![19]

Medieval cuisine, as we have seen, is relatively remote from the one we typically understand or read about, that is to say, the one composed of infamous stews—in short, hog's swill. It is true that it does not correspond to our criteria of taste, but it is important at the same time to remember its qualities. It is a varied cuisine that finds refinement in both taste and appearance. It is an innovative cuisine, which, in a certain way, need envy nothing about what we call *nouvelle cuisine*. It is, finally and contrary to modern ideas, an edible cuisine, as is shown by Odile Redon, Françoise Sabban, and Silvano Serventi in their book *La Gastronomie au Moyen Age: 150 recettes de France et d'Italie,*[20] as well as by Simone Morand in her little volume entitled *Cuisine du Temps Jadis: Moyen Age et Renaissance.*[21]

SUGGESTIONS FOR FURTHER READING

Primary Sources: Cookbooks (in French)

Chiquart's 'On Cookery'—A Fifteenth-Century Savoyard Culinary Treatise, T. Scully (ed. and trans.), New York, Berne, Frankfurt am Main: Peter Lang, 1986.

L. Douet-d'Arcq (ed.), "Un petit traité de cuisine écrit en français au commencement du XIVème siècle," *Bibliothèque de l'Ecole des Chartes*, vol. I, 5th ed., 1860, 209–27.

C. Lambert (ed.), *Le Recueil de Riom et la maniere de henter soutillement: Un livre de cuisine et un réceptaire sur les greffes du XVème siècle*, preface by J.-L. Flandrin, Montréal: CERES, 1987.

Le Mesnagier de Paris, G. E. Bereton and J. M. Ferrier (eds.), K. Ueltschi (trans.), Paris: Le Livre de Poche, 1994.

T. Scully (ed.), *The Viandier of the Taillevent: An Edition of all Extant Manuscripts*, Ottawa: University of Ottawa, 1988.

————. "*Du fait de cuisine* par maistre Chiquart, 1420," *Vallesia* 40, 1985, 101–231.

Taillevent, *Le Viandier, d'après l'édition de 1486*, preface by M. and Ph. Hyman, Pau: Éditions Manucius, 2001.

Le Viandier de Guillaume Tirel dit Taillevent, J. Pichon and G. Vicaire (eds.), Paris: Techener, 1892; S. Martinet (ed.), Genève: Slatkine, 1967.

Le Viandier de Taillevent: 14th Century Cookery, Based on the Vatican Library Manuscript, J. Prescott (trans.), Eugene, OR: Alfarhaugr, 1989.

The Vivendier: A Fifteenth-Century French Cookery Manuscript, T. Scully (ed. and trans.), Totnes, UK: Prospect, 1997.

Primary Sources: Cookbooks (in Other Languages)

Das bouch von gouter spize: Aus der Würzburg-Münchener Handschrift, H. Hajek (ed.), Berlin: Erich Schmidt, 1958.

The Forme of Cury, S. Pegge (ed.), London: J. Nichols, 1780.

B. Laurioux (ed.), "Le Registre de cuisine de Jean Bockenheim, cuisinier du pape Martin V," *Mélanges de l'ecole Française de Rome (Moyen Age, Temps Modernes)* 100, 1988, 709–60.

M. Mulon (ed.), "Deux traités inédits d'art culinaire," *Bulletin philologique et historique*, 1968 (1971), 369–45.

Secondary Sources: Studies in Medieval Cuisine and Related Topics (Articles)

K. Becker, "Kochkunst und Diätetik in der Dichtung Eustache Deschamps," *Zeitschrift für romanische Philologie* 111.3, 1995, 347–74.

J.-L. Flandrin, "Brouets, potages et bouillons," *Médiévales* 5, 1983, 5–14.

J.-F. Kosta-Théfaine, "De la littérature gastronomique et autres petits plaisirs littéraires et culinaires . . . ," *Lendemains*, 2001, 103–104, 213–5.

———— (ed.), "Des 'regles en françois' pour bien se tenir à table . . . ," in M. Colombo and Cl. Galderisi (eds.), *"Pour acquerir honneur et pris": Mélanges de moyen Français en hommage à Giuseppe Di Stefano*, Montréal: Editions CERES, 2004, 265–75.

————. "Le sel dans quelques poèmes d'Eustache Deschamps," in *De sel: Actes de la Journée d'Etudes 'Le Sel dans la littérature française' (Pau, 28 novembre 2003)*, Véronique Duché-Gavet et Jean-Gérard Lapacherie avec la collaboration de Frédérique Marty-Badiola (eds.), Biarritz: Atlantica, 2005, 29–48.

————. "De l'art des mots à l'art des mets: Les nourritures de la mer dans les poèmes d'Eustache Deschamps et dans la littérature culinaire française du Moyen Age," in *Les nourritures de la mer, de la criée à l'assiette: Actes du colloque organisée sur l'île de Tatihou du 2 au 4 octobre 2004*, Eric Barré et André Zysberg (eds.), Musée maritime de l'île de Tatihou et Caen: Universitaires de Caen, 2007 (forthcoming).

————. "Sucre et douceurs sucrées dans la littérature culinaire française du Moyen Age," in *Du Sucre: Actes de la Journée d'Etudes : 'Le sucre dans la littérature française' (Pau, 21 janvier 2005)*, Véronique Duchet-Gavet et Jean-Gérard Lapacherie avec la collaboration de Frédérique Marty-Badiola (eds.), Biarritz: Éditions Atlantica, 2007, 153–171.

————. "Du livre de cuisine à 'l'Art total': La littérature culinaire française du Moyen Age," in *Ecriture du repas: Fragments d'un discours gastronomique*, Karin Becker and Olivier Leplatre (eds.), Bern, Berlin, New York: Peter Lang, 2007, pp. 13–31.

B. Laurioux, "De l'usage des épices dans l'alimentation médiévale," *Médiévales* 5, 1983, 14–31.
———. "Spices in the Medieval Diet: A New Approach," *Food and Foodways* 1, 1985, 43–76.
———. "Cuisiner à l'Antique: Apicius au Moyen Age," *Médiévales* 26, 1994, 17–38.
M. Mulon, "Recettes médiévales," *Annales (Economies, Sociétés, Civilisations)* 19.4, 1964, 933–7.
Platine, "Les sauces 'légères' du Moyen Age," *L'Histoire* 35, 1981, 87–9.
L. Plouvier, "Taillevent, la première star de la gastronomie," *L'Histoire* 61, 1986, 93–4.
T. Scully, "Names of Medieval French Culinary Dishes," *Fifteenth-Century Studies* 10, 1984, 149–59.
———. " 'Aucune science de l'art de cuysinerie et de cuysine': Chiquart's *Du fait de cuisine*," *Food and Foodways* 2, 1987, 199–214.
———. "The Menus of the *Menagier de Paris*," *Le Moyen Français* 24–25, 1990, 215–42.

Secondary Sources: Studies in Medieval Cuisine and Related Topics (Monographs)

M.-J. Arn (ed.), *Medieval Food and Drink*, Binghamton, NY: SUNY, 1995.
J. Ayto, *The Glutton's Glossary: A Dictionary of Food and Drink Terms*, London and New York: Routledge, 1990.
Banquets et manières de table au Moyen Age, Aix-en-Provence: CUERMA, 1996.
I. Bitsch, T. Ehlert, and X. Ertzdorff with R. Schulz (eds.), *Essen und Trinken in Mittelalter und Neuzeit*, Sigmaringen, Germany: Jan Thorbecke, 1987.
M. Black, *The Medieval Cookbook*, London: Thames & Hudson, 1996.
R. Dale (ed.), *The Wordsworth Dictionary of Culinary and Menu Terms*, Ware, UK: Wordsworth, 2000.
F. Desportes, *Le Pain au Moyen Age*, Paris: Olivier Orban, 1987.
M. Ferrières, *Histoire des peurs alimentaires du Moyen Age à l'aube du XXème siècle*, Paris: Le Seuil, 2002.
J.-L. Flandrin and M. Montanari (eds.), *Histoire de l'alimentation*, Paris: Fayard, 1996.
———. (eds.), *Food: A Culinary History from Antiquity to the Present*, A. Sonnenfeld (ed.), C. Bostford et al. (trans.), New York: Columbia University, 1999.
B. A. Henisch, *Fast and Feast: Food in Medieval Society*, University Park, PA: Pennsylvania State University, 1976.
E. and F.-B. Huyghe, *Les Coureurs d'épices*, Paris: Petite Bibliothèque Payot, 2002.
B. Ketcham Wheaton, *Savoring the Past: The French Kitchen and Table from 1300 to 1789*, Philadelphia: University of Pennsylvania, 1983.
C. Lambert (ed.), *Du manuscrit à la table: Essais sur la cuisine au Moyen Age*, Montréal and Paris: Presses de l'université de Montréal & Champion, 1992.
B. Laurioux, *Manger au Moyen Age*, Paris: Hachette, 2002.
———. *Une histoire culinaire du Moyen Age*, Paris: Champion, 2005.
Manger et boire au Moyen Age. Actes du colloque de Nice, 15–17 octobre 1982, 2 vols., Paris: Les Belles Lettres, 1984.
M. Pelner Cosman, *Fabulous Feats: Medieval Cookery and Ceremony*, New York: G. Braziller, 1976.
J.-M. Pelt, *Les Epices*, Paris: Fayard, 2002.
T. Scully, *The Art of Cookery in the Middle Ages*, Woodbridge: Boydell, 1995.
J. Verdon, *Boire au Moyen Age*, Paris: Perrin, 2002.

M. Weiss Adamson (ed.), *Food in the Middle Ages*, New York and London: Garland, 1995.

———— (ed.), *Regional Cuisines of Medieval Europe: A Book of Essays*, New York: Routledge, 200s.

A. C. Wilson (ed.), *The Appetite and the Eye: Visuals Aspects of Food and Its Presentation within Their Historic Contexts (Papers from the Second Leeds Symposium on Food History and Traditions)*, Edinburgh: Edinburgh University, 1991.

Modern Adaptations of Medieval Recipes

S. Morand, *Cuisine du temps jadis: Moyen Age et Renaissance*, Rennes: Editions Ouest-France, 1996.

O. Redon, F. Sabban, and S. Serventi, *La Gastronomie au Moyen Age. 150 recettes de France et d'Italie*, Paris: Stock, 1991.

————. *The Medieval Kitchen: Recipes from France and Italy*, E. Schneider (trans.), Chicago: University of Chicago, 1998.

Studies on Medieval Cookbooks (Articles)

B. Laurioux, "Les premiers livres de cuisine," *L'Histoire* 85, 1986, 52–5.

————. "Entre savoir et pratiques: Le livre de cuisine à la fin du Moyen Age, *Médiévales* 14, 1988, 59–71.

————. "Un exemple de livre technique: Le livre de cuisine à la fin du Moyen Age," *Gazette du Livre Médiévale* 14, 1989, 12–6.

Studies on Medieval Cookbooks (Monographs)

B. Laurioux, *Le Règne Taillevent: Livres et pratiques culinaires à la fin du Moyen Age*, Paris: Publications de la Sorbonne, 1997.

————. *Les Livres de cuisine médiévaux*. Turnhout, Belgium: Brepols (Typologie des sources du Moyen Age occidental, 7), 1997.

Livres en bouche: Cinq siècles d'art culinaire français, du quatorzième au dix-huitième siècle, Paris: Bibliothèque Nationale de France et Hermann, 2001.

Web Sites

The Medieval / Renaissance Food Homepage, available at http://www.pbm.com/~lindahl/food.html.

Medieval Cookbook—An Annotated Bibliography, available at http://www.pbm.com/~lindahl/articles.food_bibliography.html.

Medieval Food, available at http://members.tripod.com/med_food.index.html.

Renaissance and Medieval Food and Drink, available at http://scils.rutgers.edu/~sroczyns.food.html.

NOTES

1. All infelicities of grammar, syntax, vocabulary, and translation are my own–SJH.
2. E. Littré, "Anonyme, auteur d'un Traité de cuisine," *Histoire Littéraire de la France* 27, 1877, 26–9, at 29.
3. A type of fricassee composed of a number of meats.
4. H. Parienté et G. de Ternant, *La fabuleuse histoire de la cuisine française*, Paris: O. D. I. L., 1981, p. 118.

5. M. Toussaint-Sanat, *Histoire naturelle et morale de la nourriture*, Paris: Bordas, 1994, p. 74.

6. G. Clément, *Eloge des vagabondes : Herbes, arbres et fleurs à la conquête du monde*, Paris: NiL, 2002, pp. 49–50.

7. Note that *Le Viandier* gives a list of spices used: "Espices qui appartiennent en cest present Viandier: premierement, gingembre, canelle, girofle, graine de paradis, poivre lonc, macis, espices en poudre, fleur de canelle, saffran, garingal, noys mugaites" (ms. B.N.); "Espices qu'il fault a ce present Viandier: gingenbre, canelle, giroffle, graine de paradis, poivre long, espic, poivre ront, fleur de canelle, saffren, noiz muguettes, feulles de lorier, garingal, mastic, lores, commin, succre, amandes, aulx, ongnons, ciboules, escaloignes. S'ensuit pour verdir: persil, salmonde, oseille, fueille de vigne ou bourjons, groseillier, blé vert en yvert" (ms. Vatican), in *Le Viandier*, op. cit., p. 34 and pp. 109–10; "Espices appartenantes a ce present Viandier: gingembre, canelle, girofle, graine de paradis, poyvre, mastic, garingal, noix muscade, safran, canelle, sucre, agnis et pouldre fine" (ed. of 1486), in *Le Viandier, d'après l'édition de 1486*, p. 153. Master Chiquart uses some of the same, and one also notes that the spices which he uses are almost identical: "Et puis prenne sa poudre de cynamomi, gingibre blanc, grayne de paradix, poyvre, noix de muscates, galinga, giroffle, macy et de toutes autres espices," in T. Scully (ed.), "*Du fait de cuisine* par maistre Chiquart, 1420," *Vallesia* 40, (1985), 139 (n° 4).

8. I borrow this phrase from B. Laurioux, "De l'usage des épices dans l'alimentation médiévale," *Médiévales* 5, 1983, 15–31, at 20.

9. Laurioux, "De l'usage," 20.

10. *Le Viandier de Guillaume Tirel dit Taillevent*, J. Pichon et G. Vicaire (eds.), Paris: Techener, 1892; new edition augmented and edited by S. Martinet, Genève: Slatkine Reprints, 1967, p. 111 (ms. Vatican).

11. T. Scully, "*Du fait de cuisine*," 144.

12. *Le Viandier de Guillaume Tirel dit Taillevent*, p. 122 (ms. Vatican).

13. Scully, "*Du fait de cuisine*," 145 ff.

14. D. Quéruel also gives other examples of ingredients in her article "Des entremets aux intermèdes dans les banquets bourguignons," in *Banquets et manières de tables au Moyen Age*, Aix-en-Provence, France: CUERMA, 1996), pp. 143–57.

15. *Le Viandier de Guillaume Tirel, dit Taillevent*, p. 130 (ms. Vatican).

16. *Le Viandier, d'après l'édition de 1486*, p. 101.

17. *Le Viandier 1486*, p. 81.

18. *Le Viandier de Guillaume Tirel dit Taillevent*, pp. 121–2 (ms. Vatican).

19. *Le Viandier de Taillevent*, pp. 118–9.

20. O. Redon, F. Sabban, and S. Serventi, *La Gastronomie au Moyen Age: 150 recettes de France et d'Italie*, Paris: Stock, 1991.

21. S. Morand, *Cuisine du temps jadis: Moyen Age et Renaissance*, Rennes, France: Editions Ouest-France, 1996.

18 What *Did* Medieval People Eat?

Christopher Roman

The stereotype of medieval eating habits includes such caricatures as the bedraggled peasant whose larder is stocked with only a little brownish-gray gruel and pieces of mealy bread. However, the people of the Middle Ages had a varied diet of meats, grains, vegetables, and fruits—varied according to their class, nationality, and region, as well as the time of year.[1] Not all people ate the same thing or could afford to, but the case of a life spent sipping cold porridge was rare. This essay will examine food as the center of an intersection: not only was the medieval diet varied, but food was connected to wealth and region (urban and rural). Medieval people ate seasonally, so the variety of food available was also connected to the success of the growing season and harvest.

Similar to our cookbooks, one source for medieval eating habits is the books of cookery that were owned by the upper and middle classes. These cookery books, like British Library Harley MS 279, have survived in a number of manuscript forms.[2] To look at the recipes contained in these manuscripts reveals a breadth and a scope to what some, particularly upper-class, people ate. What is noteworthy about these cookbooks is the lack of measurements. In modern-day cookbooks, the list of ingredients and the amounts are listed first. In cookery books, ingredients are introduced as the recipe moves along.

Regardless of class, medieval people frequently ate what is called pottage. These dishes, like cabbage and bean soups, were common enough to appear in cookbooks, as well as known to be eaten by the very poor. As Maggie Black writes, "[A] pottage might be thick (running) or almost thick enough to slice (stondyng). . . . The commonest pottages, however, were vegetable ones, made with red or green cabbage, lettuces, leeks, onions, and garlic."[3] A recipe for a "potage colde" appears in Harley 279 and is evidently a pottage for the upper classes because of its use of almond milk: "Take wyne, & drawe a gode thikke Milke of Almaundys with wyne, if thou mayste; then putte yt on a potte, caste ther-to Pouder Canelle & Gyngere & Saffroun; then lat it boyle, & do it on a clothe; & if thou wolt, late hym ben in dyuers colourys, that on white withowte Spyces. . . ."[4]

This cold pottage has a base of wine and almond milk. Almonds were considered a delicacy in the Middle Ages and were used as the base in the ubiquitous *blanc manger,* which is a creamy white dish made with chicken and rice. This pottage recipe also includes ginger and saffron. Although essentially a stew, this is a creamy and spicy dish.

Hen, for example, appears in many cookery manuscripts. Fowl was eaten by most everyone. The landed class would have had access to their own stocks, but even the lower class could raise chickens. Although hen is the most common of the domestic fowl, pheasants, ducks, geese, partridges, peacock, and swan were eaten, as well. This recipe for hen is a good example of the cook's uses of various techniques and spices. The recipe for hens in cumin sauce comes from a manuscript written in 1381 and reads: "Hennys in bruet schullyn be schalyd and sodyn with porke; & grynd pepper & comyn, bred and ale & temper it with the selue broth and boyle it, & colorwe it with safroun; salt it, & mes it forthe."[5]

This recipe, like modern recipes, directs the cook on how to cook the hen: first to "schaldyn" (boil) and then to "sodyn" (simmer); as well as in the use of spices, pepper, comyn (cumin), and salt; and presentation, "colorwe it with safroun." The influence of trade with the Middle East is evident in the use of cumin, which was an expensive spice cultivated there.

To complement the chicken and cumin, pork is also used in this recipe. Pig, called a "poor man's standby" for sheep (or "mouton") or cattle, was used in many medieval recipes. No part of the pig is wasted: "When slaughtered the flesh made good pickling pork or bacon. . . . The innards made blood puddings and other sausages, and the fat could be eaten on bread or used for cooking."[6] A recipe for a "caudel ferry departyd with a blamanger" calls for pork that is cut "small, & do it in a mortere."[7] This *blacmanger* uses ground pork instead of chicken (or fish); the dish is spiced with cloves and mace, as well as saffron.

Spices, clearly, were an important aspect of medieval cooking. Along with salt and cumin, recipes indicate that pepper, mustard, ginger, cinnamon, nutmeg, mace, cardamom, cloves, and chives were often used. Although by today's standards these recipes may seem overspiced, with its combination of cumin, mace, saffron, and salt, as well as others, however, there is no indication of the quantity of spice used in recipes. Sometimes a "pinch" of the spice would be used; as Constance Hieatt points out, if the recipe calls for a lot of spice it will usually say, "a great deal of."[8]

Saffron, as used in the recipes just discussed, is an example of the importance of spices in medieval cooking. Saffron is cultivated from the plant *Crocus sativas,* and is considered the world's most expensive spice, even today. Melitta Adamson writes that "on average a third of the dishes [from cookbooks] contain saffron. . . . Medieval medicine classified saffron as hot and dry and praised it for comforting the heart and liver and for aiding digestion."[9] It takes hundreds of flowers to produce a few strands of saffron. Saffron was brought across North Africa, along with Islam, into Spain. As

David Perry reports, "Medieval Spain quickly became the center of saffron production." Later, as the Middle Ages continued, both France and England began to produce saffron, where their climates were satisfactory. Provence and Essex, at various times, rivaled the Spanish production.[10]

Saffron was grown all over Europe, and many people could get small quantities in order to give their food a yellow-orange hue. Perry writes that during the holiday season, including "the Christmas celebrations of Provence, and St. Lucia's Day in Sweden,"[11] there were cakes and buns baked with saffron. Saffron was used for its exotic fragrance and its coloring. As Black writes, medieval food was "highly scented and coloured . . . saffron provided yellow, sandalwood red, parsley juice green, and turnsole purple."[12] Saffron is used for taste and aesthetics, but, of course, mostly by the upper classes.

The upper-class diet would have included meats that seem exotic even by today's standards. While hen was relatively common, swan was considered an expensive delicacy. Melitta Adamson notes, "[E]asily domesticated, and generally less tasty than most other fowl . . . the swan nevertheless fetched the highest price in the market."[13] In a cookery manuscript from the fifteenth century, a recipe for "swan rosted" reads: "Kutte a swan in the rove [roof] of the mouthe toward the brayne enlonge, and lete him blede, and kepe the bloode for chawdeyn; or ellese knytee a knot on his neck, And so lette his nekke brek; then skald him. Drawe him and rost him even as thou doest goce in all poyntes, and serue him forth with chawd-wyne."[14]

The recipe begins with the killing of the swan and ends with the serving of the roasted swan. This is a very complete recipe because it not only advises the cook or servant on the various method of killing a swan but also provides preparation tips—indicating how roasting swan is like roasting goose and recommending that it should be served with chawd-wyne. No part of the swan will be wasted. The swan's blood is the base of the sauce known as chawdeyn (or chad-wyne) and was made by putting the gizzards, liver, and heart in water and then straining the water and adding pepper, cinnamon, salt, and vinegar and letting it all boil together. From the variety of cooking methods, to the various spices and meats, the examples of recipes that have been discussed give the modern reader a sense of the variety of the medieval diet.

Cookery manuscripts are not the only texts representing what and how medieval people ate. The religious members of society had certain dietary requirements that can be seen in both the *Benedictine Rule* and Francis' *Third Order Rule*. The Benedictine Rule allowed the eating of fowl, but a chicken (hen) would cost two and a half pence; a swan, on the other hand, could cost anywhere from six to seven shillings.[15] Bread, fowl, fish, fruit, and fresh vegetables were all part of the monastic diet. The Benedictine Rule focuses on when a monk should eat. It is from these rules, however, that we get a sense of what the monks ate. Benedict writes that his monks should have "two cooked dishes"[16] because meat, presumably fowl, was allowed for those who were sick. If there were fruit or *fresh* vegetables avail-able, "let a third dish be added." The monks were also allowed to have a pound of bread a day. There were many kinds of bread in the Middle Ages. For example, pandemaine was of the highest quality and made from "flour sifted two or three times."[17] On the other hand, cheap breads made "of all grains" and horse bread made with "peas, beans and any other grain"[18] was common for the poorer classes.

Benedict calls for fresh vegetables and fruit. There is a premium placed on fresh ingredients in medieval eating, just as today. The vegetables and fruit that would be available to medieval consumers include the basics such as apples, pears, and strawberries. However, through trade, especially with the Middle East, the medieval diet also included citrus fruits such as lemons and limes, as well as oranges, figs, and dates. Fruits were often eaten as a dessert. Vegetables in the form of salads were not unheard of, either. From John Russell's *Boke of Nature,* there is this recipe for "salat": "Take parsel, sawge, garlic, chibollas, oynons, leek, borage, myntes, porrectes, fenel, and ton tressis, rew, rosemary, purslayne, lave, and waisshe hem clene. Pike hem, pluk hem small with thyn hond and myng hem wel with rawe oil. Lay on vinegar and salt and serve it forth."[19]

This recipe includes a number of greens, including parsley, fennel, mint, borage, and mint. Although in many recipes the fruits and vegetables are cooked to varying degrees, the myth of the medieval diet not including fresh fruits and vegetables is obviously false.

The Third Order Franciscans[20] also had dietary requirements and were expected to eat according to set guidelines found in the writings of St. Fran-cis. Francis felt that everyone in the Third Order should abstain from meat on Sundays, Tuesdays, and Thursdays, unless they were sick or had just been blood-let. On the other days, when they would not fast, they were allowed eggs and cheese. The milk of goats, sheep, and cows was commonly used throughout the Middle Ages. Black writes, "The milk and cream, butter and cheese made from [cow's milk], together with eggs, were called 'white meats.' "[21]

Dairy was an important foodstuff to many classes of people. As Adam-son points out, "Cheeses ranging from fresh and soft to well-aged and hard were popular across Europe."[22] Cheese itself had a social stigma and "was thought of as a coarse food suitable for people engaged in heavy labor."[23] In *Piers Plowman,* in order for the allegorical Hunger not to have an effect on the rural people, the country folk have to help work the fields and then feed him. Piers remarks that he does not have chickens, piglets, geese, bacon, or eggs—these are too expensive. However, he does have green cheeses (a sum-mer cheese also known as "spemyse"), curds, oaten cakes, parsley, onions, and kale. This is an example of what the rural poor had to eat during the late summer months; until harvest their diet was limited. Meanwhile, the other poor country people run to fetch pea-pods, beans, baked apples, spring onions, chervils, and cherries. Even as they are waiting for harvest, the country people do have a variety of vegetables and fruit. After harvest, they will hopefully have more food prosperity. When harvest does come, examples of what farmers would harvest include wheat, barley, rye, oats, millet, rice, beans, peas, chickpeas, garlic, onions, leeks, cabbage, lettuce, turnips, parsnips, carrots, beets, radishes, melons, cucumbers, asparagus, eggplant, and spinach.[24]

As was indicated in monastic diets, fish was a staple to many classes of people. In the "General Prologue" of the *Canterbury Tales*, Chaucer uses food to describe the Franklin. The Franklin, a middle-class pilgrim, never likes to be without fish or fowl in his house. He makes sure to always have partridges, breams (a freshwater fish), bread, wine, and ale. Chaucer remarks, "[I]t snewed in his house of meat and drinke" (A 345). Breams were just one of the many kinds of fish eaten in the Middle Ages and are indicative of the Franklin's class. Bream was plentiful in muddy and stagnant waters, and it was easy to raise bream in fish ponds (called "stews") on estates. Because of food restrictions, especially during Lent and on the eve of feast days (there were many feast days), fish was a substitute for other meats. If not eaten salted, dried, or pickled, fish such as salmon, herring, eel, trout, and perch were eaten fresh.

The availability of fresh fish depended on the season and a person's class, however. The Franklin's description also mentions that his pantry changes with the seasons. As Chaucer writes, "After the sundry sesons of the year,/So changed he his mete and his soper" (A 347–348). This indicates the cyclical nature of eating. One had to eat what was in season. As we have seen, for the lower classes, the summer seasons were the most difficult since it was not yet time to reap the harvest. Much of this discussion has focused on the upper-class and rural eating habits; however, the city also has its own variety of foodstuffs for sale.

Piers Plowman depicts city eating, specifically "fast" food and beverages. Langland writes this scene of London street-life:

> Cookis here knaves crieth 'hote pyes, hote!
> Goode gees gris; go we dyne, go we!'
> Tauerbers to hem tolde the same:
> 'Whit wyn of osay, wyn of gascoyne,
> Of the ryn of the rochel the rost to defie!' (104–108)

In this passage, Langland refers to street sellers, cooks, and tavern keepers, who are selling their hot pies, geese, and French wines from various locations (Gascony, the Rhine). The tavern owners even make it known that the wine they have to sell would go well with roasted meats. At the beginning of a meal, wine was often used to aid in digestion. There were many other kinds of beverages available to the medieval consumer as well. Ale, mead, and cider are such examples. The myth of constant beer drinking is also false; water was available to drink in many forms (rivers, rain water, melted snow) and was often used to dilute wine. Hippocras, a spiced wine, included "ginger, cinnamon, grains of paradise, pepper, galingale, nutmeg, cloves, mace, spikenard, and sugar."[25]

Along with "fast food" such as pies and hot geese, another medieval English poem, *London Lickpenny*,[26] indicates other fast-food offerings: "Then came there one, and cried 'Hot shepes feet!'" (85). Later on, other street vendors tempt the narrator with cod and mackerel, beef ribs, and "many a pie" (90). Walking down the street in medieval London, one would have heard cooks trying to sell hot pies (akin to pasties), geese, wine from France, sheep's feet, and other meats. According to the historian Martha Carlin there was a variety of hot, ready-to-eat food available to boat people, travelers, "rich knights," and the urban poor who probably did not have kitchens in their overcrowded living quarters.[27]

Carlin also quotes from John de Garland (ca. 1195–1272) as he writes about the "fast" food that he saw in Paris: waffles, light pastries, wafers, boiled and roasted beef, veal, mutton, pork, lamb, kid, pigeon, capon, goose, spiced pasties filled with chopped pork, chicken or eel, and tarts and flans filled with soft cheeses or eggs. This is similar to the hot food seen in medieval London. The Thames markets, a series of food stalls along the river, were an important place to get fast, hot food. However, notice the lack of fruits and vegetables in this city diet. The emphasis seemed to be on speed and proteins: eggs and meats, rather than on apples or kale.

Whether on a pilgrimage, in the country, or deep in the center of a metropolis, food in many varieties was available. A hot pasty, some baked apples, sheep's feet—the only thing stopping a hungry traveler from eating was availability and cost. The seasons were an important determinant in what one ate. If the harvest had not been good, chances were there would be no wheat, or little else, for the winter. However, the misconception of limited food or a lack of variety in the Middles Ages is dispelled by the cookery books and literature of the time. Though rich sauces or good bread were probably more available to the aristocracy or well-off merchants, it does not necessarily follow that the peasant or country person had a limited diet. If anything, the people with the most limited diet were probably the urban poor who lived without kitchens.

Medieval cookery has received a popular reception. Cookbooks such as Odile Redon's *The Medieval Kitchen*, Constant Hieatt, Brenda Hosington, and Sharon Butler's *Pleyn Delit*, or Maggie Black's *Medieval Cookery* are all based on medieval manuscripts and encourage readers to try the recipes of the medieval world in their own kitchens. While at the Medieval Congress in Leeds in 2001, my wife and I attended a medieval food tasting put on by Sally Grainger and Caroline Yeldman. My wife was surprised that there were so many kinds of things to eat on the medieval menu, and she noted that the food was not overspiced as she had assumed. Grainger and Yeldman prepared such things as Tarte de Brye (tart with Brie), Sawgey Farced (spicy pork balls), roasted mackerel, and hennys in bruet. Medieval recipes can still speak to the modern palate, as they did to ours that day.

SUGGESTIONS FOR FURTHER READING

Melitta Anderson, *Food in Medieval Times,* Westport: Greenwood, 2004.

Maggie Black, *Medieval Cookery: Recipes and History,* Swindon. UK: English Heritage, 2003.

Chiquart, *On Cookery,* Terence Scully (ed.), New York: Peter Lang, 1986.

Madeleine Pelner Cosman, *Fabulous Feasts: Medieval Cookery and Ceremony,* New York: George Braziller, 1976.

Curye on Inglysch, Constance B. Hieatt and Sharon Butler (eds.), London: EETS, 1985.

Food and Eating in Medieval Europe, Martha Carlin and Joel T. Rosenthal (eds.), London: Hambledon, 1998.

Food in the Middle Ages: A Book of Essays, Melitta Weiss Adamson (ed.), New York: Garland, 1995.

P. W. Hammond, *Food and Feast in Medieval England,* Gloucestershire, UK: Alan Sutton, 1995.

Bridget Ann Henisch, *Fast and Feast,* University Park, PA: Pennsylvania State University, 1978.

Constance B. Hieatt, Brenda Hosington, and Sharon Butler (eds.), *Pleyn Delit,* Toronto: University of Toronto, 1996.

Mary-Jo Arn, *Medieval Food and Drink,* Binghampton, NY: CMERS, 1995.

Stephen Mennell, *All Manners of Food: Eating and Taste in England and France from the Middle Ages to the Present,* 2nd ed., Chicago: University of Illinois, 1996.

Odile Redon, Francoise Sabban, and Silvano Servanti (eds.), *The Medieval Kitchen,* Chicago: University of Chicago, 1998.

Two Fifteenth Century Cookery Books, Thomas Austin (ed.), London: EETS, 1888.

NOTES

1. For the purposes of this essay, I am limiting my remarks and my sources to the later Middle Ages. For a discussion of feast and famine in the Middle Ages, see Christopher Dyer, "Did the Peasants Really Starve in Medieval England?" in Carlin and Rosenthal (eds.), *Food and Eating in Medieval Europe.* He argues that the threat of starvation for peasants passed in 1375, "which ushered in an era of cheap and plentiful food" (p. 70).
2. See *Curye on Inglysch,* Constance Hieatt (ed.); and *Two Fifteenth Century Cookery Books,* Thomas Austin (ed.), for examples of these manuscripts.
3. Maggie Black, *Medieval Cookery,* Swindon: English Heritage, 2003, p. 25.
4. *Two Fifteenth-Century Cookery Books,* p. 30.
5. *Curye on Inglysche,* p. 63.
6. Black, p. 16.
7. *Two Fifteenth Century Cookery Books,* p. 31.
8. Constance Hieatt, Brenda Hosington, and Sharon Butler (eds.), *Pleyn Delit,* Toronto: University of Toronto, 1996, p. xiv.
9. Melitta Weiss Adamson, *Food in Medieval Times,* Westport, CT: Greenwood, 2004.
10. David Perry, "Saffron in Early Modern Sweden," available at www.bell.lib.umn.edu/Products/saffron.html.
11. Perry, "Saffron."
12. Black, p. 33.
13. Adamson, p. 39.

168   *Christopher Roman*

14. *Two Fifteenth Century Cookery Books*, p. 78.
15. Larry D. Benson et al. (eds.), *The Riverside Chaucer*, 3rd ed., Boston: Houghton Mifflin, 1987, p. 807.
16. All quotes from the *Benedictine Rule* come from *Readings in Medieval History*, Patrick J. Geary (ed.), Peterborough, ON: Broadview, 2003.
17. Black, p. 9.
18. Black, p. 10.
19. Quoted in Black, p. 47.
20. The *Third Order Rule* comes from *Medieval Popular Religion*, John Shinners (ed.), Peterborough, ON: Broadview, 2007.
21. Black, p. 20.
22. Adamson, p. 46.
23. Adamson, p. 47.
24. For a complete description of the varieties of these foodstuffs, see Adamson, *Food in Medieval Times*, pp. 1–11.
25. Adamson, *Food in Medieval Times*, p. 50.
26. References to *London Lickpenny* come from *Medieval English Political Writing*, James M. Dean (ed.), Kalamazoo, MI: TEAMS, 1996.
27. Martha Carlin, "Fast Food and Urban Living Standards in Medieval England," in Carlin and Rosenthal (eds.), *Food and Eating in Medieval Europe*.

19 Medieval Drama

Carolyn Coulson-Grigsby

Probably the most pervasive misconception about medieval drama is the evolutionary assumption that the drama originated as an extension of Latin church services, that these liturgical dramas gradually grew in length and production size to the point that they had to move outside to the church steps, and that once outdoor production began, civic authorities naturally became involved as productions became more complex and involved the laity. Besides this long-debunked evolutionary theory, other misconceptions include the beliefs that the great urban "cycle" plays were the normal and ubiquitous form of drama, that all such biblical plays were alike in form and content and were performed on traveling wagons, and that medieval drama, especially the morality play, was merely a dramatized sermon (and therefore boring). On the contrary, recent scholarship *and* productions have revealed that some cycles were performed in a fixed platform area and did not move in procession, that there is distinct regional variety between plays that ostensibly treat the same subject, and that many of the medieval plays are funny, moving, and highly entertaining.

Any discussion of misconceptions about medieval drama must begin with a treatment of the evolutionary theory, which was most effectively promulgated by E. K. Chambers and Karl Young. When Karl Young compiled his magisterial two-volume collection, *The Drama of the Medieval Church*, published in 1933, he repeatedly organized his materials so that they demonstrated an evolution of form, moving from the simplest, shortest version of a particular dramatic interlude to the most complex, longest play that treated the same subject. In doing so, Young preferred to assume that forms always move from simple to complex, regardless of the fact that some very complex drama exists in very early manuscripts, while some of the simplest pieces exist in late manuscripts. He wiped dates aside with the assumption that simple, late plays were merely copies of early forms, and in some cases, Young slyly included an early, complex play with its counterparts from a hundred years later. For example, by all accounts, the Freising *Officium Stellae* is the most "ambitiously conceived and executed" form of the Christmas play of the three Magi's encounter with Herod the Great (Dronke 24). It is preserved in an eleventh-century manuscript, yet Young grouped the play with Magi plays from the twelfth century and cited it as a culmination. Rather, the Freising *Stellae* play demonstrates that some of the earliest church drama could feature complex characterization and form, which writers of later liturgical drama might ignore in preference to a simpler version.

Young did not spend much time on the vernacular plays performed outside of the church, but E. K. Chambers, in his *The Mediaeval Stage*, originally published in 1903, brought the evolutionary-anthropological model to the vernacular drama, especially to its relationship to the Latin church drama and to folk ceremonies. After presenting chapters on minstrelsy and folk drama, Chambers moves on to religious drama. Crucial to the misconception his work promulgated is his chapter on "The Secularization of the Plays," which begins:

> The *evolution* of the liturgical play described in the last two chapters may be fairly held to have been *complete* about the middle of the thirteenth century. The condition of *any further advance* was that the play should cease to be liturgic. The following hundred years are a transition period. During their course the newly-shaped drama underwent a process which, within the limits imposed by the fact that its subject-matter remained essentially religious, may be called *secularization*. (Chambers II 69; my italics)

Chambers follows this assertion with the statement to which too many general literature anthologies and introductory textbooks have clung: "Out of the hands of the clergy in their naves and choirs, [the drama] had passed to those of the laity in their market-places and guild-halls" (Chambers II 69).[1] The troubles with this statement are many. To begin, the vast cycle plays of the fourteenth and fifteenth centuries cannot be seen as unilaterally having fallen out of the hands of clerical writers. Second, although we know that some urban drama was performed in conjunction with guild organizations, we can no longer assume that what held true in York or Chester can be applied to other towns. Finally, in the late Middle Ages, church drama did not cease to exist. Rather, it continued as an extension of the Mass, which is inherently theatrical.

Both Young and Chambers are to be credited with the collection of vast amounts of manuscript materials. However, their shared mental framework, based on the evolutionary model so prevalent during the times in which they wrote, informed their books pervasively, and this evolutionary model left an indelible mark on the study of medieval drama, even after later scholars, notably O. B. Hardison, pointed out the flaws in Chambers' and Young's assumptions. While studies have pointed to sermons, the visual arts, and folk rituals as the roots of cycle plays, today's scholars seem to agree that the precise genesis of vernacular civic drama is, and will most likely remain, a mystery. In the comments that follow, I will focus on the drama of medieval

England, although the misconceptions I outline here are to a certain extent applicable to Continental drama as well.

A number of misconceptions about the medieval drama derive from one large one: that there are only two types of drama in the Middle Ages—cycle plays and morality plays—and that within each genre, there is little variation. This assumption is exacerbated by the repeated anthologizing of *Everyman* and the Towneley *Second Shepherds' Play*, to the frequent exclusion of any other examples of medieval drama. The *Second Shepherds' Play* is introduced as an example of the cycle pageant, and *Everyman* is introduced as an example of the morality play. A number of forms are ignored, such as the Saints' Play, pageants for royal entries, mummings and disguisings, interludes, late medieval liturgical drama, and other non-cycle religious plays, such as those in the Digby manuscript.

Further, the presentation to students of the *Second Shepherds' Play* and/or *Everyman* in isolation inherently, yet falsely, suggests that all the pageants are like the *Second Shepherds' Play* and all the moralities are like *Everyman*. However, neither play is representative of its genre. The so-called morality plays from England are so diverse in their styles that no one of them can really be used to represent the genre (and *Everyman* is generally believed to be a translation from the Dutch *Elckerlijc* and therefore not an English play at all), and the *Second Shepherd's Play* is singled out for its unique qualities more than for its representation of a typical cycle play.[2]

For many years, the collections of creation-to-doom biblical plays (sometimes referred to as Corpus Christi plays or, more archaically, as "mysteries") were considered to be analogous, and the four different English "cycles" were treated as interchangeable.[3] Students who were venturing beyond the ubiquitous *Second Shepherds' Play* would be assigned to read the "best" version of each different pageant, rather than an entire collection. Recent scholarship on medieval drama, however, has persistently queried old assumptions about the interchangeability of plays from different collections, and we now have critical discussions about the particular concerns, theology, and aesthetics of specific dramatists or cycles. For example, the Chester cycle, in contrast to the York cycle, which has many different authors, is acknowledged to be the work of one playwright and exhibits a unified theological message which stresses the trinity and Christ's divinity. Also, because of manuscript evidence, scholars of the Chester cycle can trace changes to the cycle over time. The N-Town collection from the region of East Anglia has been shown by scholars such as Gail McMurray Gibson to exhibit traits typical of that region's devotional traditions.

Perhaps the most pervasive branch of the misconception that all the cycles were alike is the assumption that all such drama was performed by guilds on pageant wagons that traveled around a city on the Feast of Corpus Christi. The York cycle in England was indeed performed by guilds on wagons that repeatedly performed their pageants at different stations throughout York on Corpus Christi Day. The manuscript containing the cycle identifies the guilds assigned to each pageant, and we know something about the York pageant wagons from documents like the 1433 Mercers' Guild inventory, which describes their wagon, props, and costumes. Other documentary records provide lists of the stations at which the play could be heard. For many years, scholars and students assumed that the staging conventions used at York were used for all cycles. More recent research and attention to the details of manuscript evidence (and lack of it) have revealed that these assumptions cannot be made. Records indicate that the Chester cycle's mode and date of performance changed over the years during which it was produced, and was, by the sixteenth century, performed processionally over three days at Whitsun, rather than on Corpus Christi Day. The N-Town plays, which are themselves an apparent composite of several separate cycles, seem to have been collected for a touring company, rather than for production by a particular city. The three main components of the collection (the Passion Play, the Proclamation Play, and the Mary Play) all seem to be designed for stationary performance in a "place-and-scaffold" setup. While it seems impossible to prove definitively how the N-Town plays were performed, scholars have come to a general consensus that rules out processional wagon staging.

Admittedly, people whose exposure to medieval drama consists of reading *Everyman* and nothing else are entitled to cling to the misconception that the medieval morality play is rather like a sermon and therefore, by some accounts, boring. However, should those same people either read or attend a performance of the fifteenth-century English morality play *Mankind*, they would be astonished to witness the still-effective bawdy and scatological humor of the Vices sharply contrasted with the Latin language and piety of the character of Mercy, not to mention the apparent audience interaction when the hat is passed to collect money before the devil Titivillus can make his entrance. Similarly, *The Castle of Perseverance*, generally considered the earliest English morality, features a devil with explosives coming out of his buttocks, not usually an apparatus featured in a sermon.

Anyone who has attended the recent modern productions of medieval plays has had the pleasure of discovering how entertaining they are. I direct the reader to the commentary that came out of the 1998 productions of the York cycle at the University of Toronto or in York itself. I participated in the Toronto production and was astounded to see children of three and four years of age still thoroughly engaged with the cycle during the Harrowing of Hell, many hours into the processional staging. Children are notoriously honest as audience members, and these ones were honestly enjoying themselves as much as the adults in the audience. While modern staging of medieval dramatic texts certainly predates 1980, the last twenty-five years have seen a wider acknowledgment of the scholarly value of performing medieval plays. Seeing an entire cycle performed adds to our appreciation for its unique content and staging qualities, and even the most traditional scholars have realized that we can learn much about the experience dramatic productions must have provided for a whole community, including the audience.

SUGGESTIONS FOR FURTHER READING

On the Evolutionary Theory and Its Undoing

E. K. Chambers, *The Mediaeval Stage*, 2 vols., London: Oxford University, 1903.
Lawrence M. Clopper, *Drama, Play, and Game: English Festive Culture in the Medieval and Early Modern Period*, Chicago: University of Chicago, 2001.
Hardin Craig, *English Religious Drama of the Middle Ages*, Oxford: Clarendon, 1955.
O. B. Hardison, Jr., *Christian Rite and Christian Drama in the Middle Ages*, Baltimore: Johns Hopkins University, 1965.
Karl Young, *The Drama of the Medieval Church*, 2 vols., Oxford: Clarendon, 1933.

Collections of Essays

John A. Alford (ed.), *From Page to Performance: Essays in Early English Drama*, East Lansing: Michigan State University, 1995.
Richard Beadle (ed.), *The Cambridge Companion to Medieval English Theatre*, Cambridge: Cambridge University, 1994. (This volume contains excellent bibliographic material divided into categories.)
Marianne Briscoe and John C. Coldewey (eds.), *Contexts for Early English Drama*, Bloomington and Indianapolis: Indiana University, 1989.
John D. Cox and David Scott Kastan (eds.), A New History of Early English Drama, New York: Columbia University, 1997.
Clifford Davidson et al. (eds.), *The Drama in the Middle Ages: Comparative and Critical Essays*, New York: AMS, 1982.

Cycle Plays, General

Stanley J. Kahrl, *Traditions of Medieval English Drama*, Pittsburgh: University of Pittsburgh, 1975.
V. A. Kolve, *The Play Called Corpus Christi*, Stanford, CA: Stanford University, 1966.
Alan H. Nelson, *The Medieval English Stage: Corpus Christi Pageants and Plays*, Chicago and London: University of Chicago, 1974.
Eleanor Prosser, *Drama and Religion in the English Mystery Plays: A Re-Evaluation*, Stanford, CA: Stanford University, 1961.
J. W. Robinson, *Studies in Fifteenth-Century Stagecraft*, Kalamazoo: Western Michigan University, Medieval Institute, 1991.
Martin Stevens, *Four Middle English Mystery Cycles: Textual, Contextual, and Critical Interpretations*, Princeton, NJ: Princeton University, 1987.
Rosemary Woolf, *The English Mystery Plays*, Berkeley and Los Angeles: University of California, 1972.

Art, Sermons, and Popular Religion

M. D. Anderson, *Drama and Imagery in English Medieval Churches*, Cambridge: Cambridge University, 1963.

Clifford Davidson, *Visualizing the Moral Life: Medieval Iconography and the Macro Morality Plays*, New York: AMS, 1989.

Gail McMurray Gibson, *The Theater of Devotion: East Anglian Drama and Society in the Late Middle Ages*, Chicago: University of Chicago, 1989.

G. R. Owst, *Literature and Pulpit in Medieval England*, 2d ed., rev., Oxford: Basil Blackwell, 1961.

Pamela Scheingorn, "On Using Medieval Art in the Study of Medieval Drama: An Introduction to Methodology," *Research Opportunities in Renaissance Drama* 22, 1979, 101–9.

Victor Scherb, *Staging Faith: East Anglian Drama in the Later Middle Ages*, Madison, WI: Fairleigh Dickinson University, 2001.

Meg Twycross, "Beyond the Picture Theory: Image and Activity in Medieval Drama," *Word and Image* 4, 1988, 589–617.

Studies of Individual Cycles

Kathleen Ashley, "Divine Power in Chester Cycle and Late Medieval Thought," *Journal of the History of Ideas* 39, 1978, 387–404.

Clifford Davidson, *From Creation to Doom: The York Cycle of Mystery Plays*, New York: AMS, 1984.

Warren Edminster, The Preaching Fox: Festive Subversion in the Plays of the Wakefield Master, London: Routledge, 2005.

John Gardner, *The Construction of the Wakefield Cycle*, Carbondale and Edwardsville: Southern Illinois University, 1974.

Kevin Harty (ed.), *The Chester Mystery Cycle: A Casebook*, New York and London: Garland Publishing, 1993.

Alexandra F. Johnston, "*The Word Made Flesh*: Augustinian Elements in the *York Cycle*," *The Centre and Its Compass: Studies in Medieval Literature in Honor of Professor John Leyerle*, Robert A. Taylor et al. (eds.), Kalamazoo, MI: Medieval Institute Publications, 1993, 225–246.

Pamela M. King, *The York Mystery Cycle and the Worship of the City*, Woodbridge, UK: Boydell and Brewer, 2006.

R. M. Lumiansky and David Mills, *The Chester Mystery Cycle: Essays and Documents*, Chapel Hill: University of North Carolina, 1983.

Barbara Palmer, "Recycling 'The Wakefield Cycle': The Records," *Research Opportunities in Renaissance Drama* 41, 2002, 88–130.

Martin Stevens, "Language as Theme in the Wakefield Plays," *Speculum* 52, 1977, 100–17.

Peter W. Travis, *Dramatic Design in the Chester Cycle*, Chicago: University of Chicago, 1982.

Morality Plays

David Bevington, *From Mankind to Marlowe: Growth of Structure in the Popular Drama of Tudor England*, Cambridge, MA: Harvard University, 1962.

W. A. Davenport, *Fifteenth-Century English Drama: The Early Moral Plays and Their Literary Relations*, Cambridge: D. S. Brewer, 1982.

Robert Potter, *The English Morality Play*, London: Routledge and Kegan Paul, 1975.

Staging

Philip Butterworth, *Magic on the Early English Stage*, Cambridge: Cambridge University, 2005.

Clifford Davidson, *Illustrations of the Stage and Acting in England to 1580*, Kalamazoo: Western Michigan University, Medieval Institute Publications, 1991.

Peter Meredith and John E. Tailby (eds.), *The Staging of Religious Drama in Europe in the Later Middle Ages: Texts and Documents in English Translation*, Kalamazoo, MI: Medieval Institute, 1983.

David Mills, *Staging the Chester Cycle*, Leeds, UK: University of Leeds, School of English, 1985.

Dunbar H. Ogden, *The Staging of Drama in the Medieval Church*, Newark, DE: University of Delaware, 2002.

Richard Southern, *The Medieval Theatre in the Round*, London: Faber, 1957, 2nd ed., 1975.

Documents and Records

Theresa Coletti, "Reading *REED*: History and the Records of Early English Drama," In *Literary Practice and Social Change in Britain 1380–1530*, Lee Patterson (ed.), Berkeley, Los Angeles, and Oxford: University of California, 1990, 248–84.

Alexandra F. Johnston, "What if No Texts Survived? External Evidence for Early English Drama," In *Contexts for Early English Drama*, M. Briscoe and J. C. Coldewey (eds.), Bloomington and Indianapolis: Indiana University, 1989, 1–9.

———. " 'All the World Was a Stage': Records of Early English Drama," In *The Theatre of Medieval Europe: New Research in Early Drama*, Eckehard Simon (ed.), Cambridge: Cambridge University, 1991, 117–29.

Records of Early English Drama series, Toronto: University of Toronto, 1978.

Play Editions and Anthologies

Donald C. Baker, John L. Murphy, and Louis B. Hall (eds.), *The Late Medieval Religious Plays of Bodleian Mss Digby 133 and E. Museo 160*, EETS o.s. 283, Oxford: Oxford University, 1982.

Richard Beadle and Pamela M. King (eds.), *York Mystery Plays*, Oxford: Clarendon, 1984.

David Bevington (ed.), *Medieval Drama*, Boston: Houghton Mifflin, 1975.

Peter Dronke (trans. and ed.), *Nine Medieval Latin Plays*. Cambridge: Cambridge University, 1994.

Mark Eccles, *The Macro Plays*, EETS o.s. 262, London: Oxford University, 1969.

Peter Happé, *English Mystery Plays: A Selection*, London: Penguin, 1975.

Pamela King and Clifford Davidson (eds.), *The Coventry Corpus Christi Plays*, Kalamazoo, MI: Medieval Institute, 2000.

R. M. Lumiansky and David Mills (eds.), *The Chester Mystery Cycle*, 2 vols., EETS s.s. 3, 9, Oxford: Oxford University, 1974.

Milla Cozart Riggio (ed.), *The Play of Wisdom: Its Texts and Contexts*, New York: AMS, 1998.

Stephen Spector (ed.), *The N-Town Play: Cotton MS Vespasian D.8*, 2 vols., EETS s.s. 11–12, Oxford: Oxford University, 1991.

Martin Stevens and A. C. Cawley (eds.), *The Towneley Plays*, 2 vols., EETS s.s. 13–14, Oxford: Oxford University, 1994.

NOTES

1. This generalization applies to general literature anthologies, especially anthologies of drama through the ages, not to anthologies of medieval drama. Anthologies of medieval literature are moving toward a more complex presentation of medieval drama. For example, in addition to *The Second Shepherds' Play* and *Everyman*, volume I of the *Broadview Anthology of British Literature* includes the liturgical *Quem Quaeritis* from the *Regularis Concordia*, the Noah's Flood pageant from Chester, the Towneley *Herodes Magnus*, the Anglo-Norman *Jeu D'Adam,*, and the morality play *Mankind*. The introductions to these works briefly summarize the failures of the evolutionary model of development. However, the ubiquitous *Norton Anthology of English Literature* only includes the York play of the Crucifixion in addition to the *Second Shepherds' Play* and *Everyman*.

2. Unlike many of the biblical pageants, the *Second Shepherds' Play* largely consists of an episode which is nonbiblical (the Mak episode), although very entertaining and incisive in its social commentary. The biblical material of the shepherds' visit to the infant Christ accounts for about 125 lines of the play's 769 lines.

3. My own use of the term "cycle" is problematic. Until recently, the collections of plays from York, Chester, "N-Town," and the Towneley family have been referred to as cycles of plays. Current scholarship allows for the term to be applied to the York and Chester plays, but it is misleading to use it to refer to the N-Town and Towneley manuscripts.

20 Shakespeare Did Not Write in Old English

Marijane Osborn

Those who claim that they've been reading Shakespeare in Old English betray their ignorance; they haven't. Similarly, it was a shock to hear the fictional, well-educated president of the United States on the TV program "West Wing" state baldly that *Beowulf* was in Middle English. That slip by a scriptwriter, one who was clearly *not* well-educated, broke the illusion of the drama. The anonymous *Beowulf* poet wrote in Old English, Chaucer wrote in Middle English, and Shakespeare wrote in Early Modern English. The following pairs of opening lines show the differences, which are huge:

> *Beowulf:*
> Hwæt! We Gardena in geardagum,
> þeodcyninga, þrym gefrunon!
> (Lo! We, of the Spear-Danes in days of yore,
> of the people-kings, heard glory!)

> Chaucer (*The Canterbury Tales*):
> Whan that Aprill with his shoures soote
> The droghte of March hath perced to the roote . . .
> (When April with its sweet showers
> Has pierced the drought of March to the root . . .)

> Shakespeare (*Richard III*):
> Now is the winter of our discontent
> Made glorious summer by this sun of York.

In the lines from *Beowulf* only two words in eight are familiar (*we* and *in*); in the sixteen words by Chaucer, possibly three are not, and that is just a matter of spelling (*shoures, soote, perced*); and the two lines from Shakespeare are perfectly clear to any reader of English who understands metaphor and recognizes a pun. Not all of Shakespeare is so "modern" as these two lines, but learning to read or hear his poetry is like learning to understand another dialect of English, whereas in order to read Old English one must study it like a foreign language. Old English even had five letters not in our modern alphabet, þ, ð, æ, 3, and Ƿ, named respectively thorn, eth, ash, yogh, and wynn. Thorn and eth are both pronounced like our combined consonants "th" (in either *thin* or *then*), ash is pronounced like the vowel in the word *ash*, wynn is pronounced "w," and yogh is sometimes pronounced like a hard "g" and sometimes like "y." Only thorn and ash appear in those two lines from *Beowulf*.

In addition to the sorts of changes that naturally occur over time, like sound changes and revised vocabulary, two major developments account for the "foreignness" of this early version of our own language. One is the Norman Conquest of 1066, when the conquerors coming from France to dominate England brought their French language along. As a result of that long-ago invasion, a great many of our words now are of French derivation. The other major development is structural; again, partly because of that conquest, our language has become far less inflected. Inflections are parts of a word that tell us how that word functions in a sentence, like the -s on "hers" (a genitive inflection) that indicates something belonging to her, or the -m on "him" or "whom" (an accusative or dative inflection) that indicates a direct or indirect object. In Modern English we know who is doing what to whom because of where the subject, verb, and object are located in the sentence: that is called "syntax." The normal syntax of modern English is, in fact, SVO (subject, verb, object), as in "John kissed Mary" or "he kissed her." Reversing this to "Mary kissed John" makes Mary the subject—the person doing the kissing—whereas in an inflected language, even if the subject and object were switched around in the sentence, the word endings would tell us who was kissing, or doing whatever it was, to whom: "her kissed he" would mean the same thing as "he kissed her," and would not be ungrammatical as it is in Modern English.

Whereas Modern English has some inflections, like those in the pronouns mentioned above, Old English is a *highly* inflected language. This means that instead of depending on word order as in Modern English, the language has many different word endings and some word-internal markers that offer help in understanding the grammar of a sentence. Function words also help. These words (such as *and, the, but, in,* etc.) serve as a sort of scaffolding for the language, propping it up, and they usually remain substantially the same when other elements of a language change.

The linguists Elizabeth Closs Traugott and Mary Louise Pratt use the first stanza of Lewis Carroll's poem "Jabberwocky" to distinguish *function* words—those that show how the grammar works—from *content* words—those that name or describe objects, concepts, etc. (88–9). Since Carroll originally wrote the stanza separately from the longer poem and titled it "A Stanza of Anglo-Saxon Poetry," its use is appropriate here:

'Twas *bryllyg*, and the *slythy tove*s
Did *gyre* and *gymble* in the *wabe*.
All *mimsy* were the *borogove*s
And the *mome rathe*s out*grabe*.

Even though the content words (italicized except for inflectional *yg*, *y*, and *s*) are all nonsense, the function words are in normal English, so we can understand these sentences in a rough way; that is, we can understand their grammar and interpret the text as "a description of an outdoor scene with creatures of various sorts frolicking or moving about" (Traugott and Pratt 88). Carroll has provided enough function words (*'twas, and, the, did, in, all,* and *were*) that we can follow what is said, and the parts of the content words not italicized, that is their inflectional endings, also help. The stanza is translated below into Anglo-Saxon (i.e., Old English) with the content elements italicized. (In their explanation, Traugott and Pratt italicized each content word entirely.) For ease of reading, "y" has mostly been standardized to "i," since "y" and "i" alternate in Old English; the "v" in "toves" becomes "f," because in Old English "f" between vowels is pronounced like "v"; and the combination "th" is represented by the single letter "þ" (thorn). The letter "æ" (ash) appears in the word "wæs." Except for these spelling changes, the content elements remain exactly the same:

> Wæs *brill*ig, ond þa *sliþ*igan *tof*as
> *Gyre*don ond *gymbl*on in tham *wab*e.
> Eall *mim*sige wæron *borogof*as,
> Ond *mome raþ*as ut*grab*e.

In the next set of examples, the content elements are suppressed, leaving only the function elements that tell us about the grammar: the function words and the inflectional parts of the content words. We recognize *ut* as the prefix "out," as in "out-ran" or "out-fought," which identifies Carroll's pseudo-English "out-grabe" as a verb:

> Wæs _____ig, and þa _____igan ___as
> _____don ond _____on in tham ___e.
> Eall _____ige wæron _____as,
> Ond ___e ___as ut___e.

> *Wæs* brill*ig, ond þa* sliþ*igan* tofas
> Gyre*don ond* gymbl*on in tham* wabe.
> *Eall* mim*sige* wæron *borogof*as,
> *Ond* mome raþas *ut*grabe.

This schematization tells us a number of things. We recognize *tofas* as a plural noun because of the final -*s*. *Sliþigan* describes those *tofas*. Since the -*ig* element becomes -*y* in Modern English, we see that *sliþigan* is an adjective modifying *tofas*; the -*an* after the *ig* marks the plural adjective needed to go with the plural noun. *Gyredon ond gymblon* are clearly verbs, in which the *d* in *gyredon* is a dental (a sound made by the tongue against the teeth) marking the past tense, like talk*ed* or shopp*ed*, and the -*on* after the *d* makes the verb plural, as it does also in *gymblon*. Where the *tofas* performed this action is *in tham wabe*, so from this we know that the -*m* on *tham* makes the article a dative; therefore the -*e* on *wabe* must make the noun a dative, since the article, like an adjective, must agree with its noun. (A dative declension is used in a prepositional phrase indicating location.) And so forth.

Of course, Carroll only pretends this stanza is Anglo-Saxon, using the *y*'s and the nonsense words to defamiliarize the language of the four lines, so we could have figured out most of this grammar on the basis of the function words and syntax. If the stanza were actually written in Old English, the order of the words might be so twisted around that those scaffolding elements alone would not be sufficient to unravel it. We would have to depend almost entirely on the inflections, so it would be crucial to have these well memorized. If Shakespeare decided to write in Old English while sticking to modern word order, some of his poetry would be easy enough to understand with just a little imagination: "Beon oððe ne beon, þat is seo frignung [question]." (The letter ð, like thorn, also signifies the -th-sound.) Easy enough so far, but can you imagine reading Hamlet's entire 34-line soliloquy in that form? Or would you like to read an Anglo-Saxon Juliet's moving balcony speech, where she says that it is Romeo's family, not he, who is her enemy, all the way through the seventeen lines after "Eala, Romeo, Romeo"?

Even if the problem of word order could be made to vanish so that you could manage the language with the help of a dictionary, those lines when translated into Old English would lack Shakespeare's music, because Old English had no iambic pentameter. Chaucer brought that five-beat verse line into English from Italian, and he made it so viable for poetry in our language that, after his work and Shakespeare's (and that of others), it has come to seem natural to us. Stressed syllables are capitalized and underlined:

> Chaucer: A <u>KNYGHT</u> there <u>WAS</u> and <u>THAT</u> a <u>WORTH</u>y <u>MAN</u>.
> Shakespeare: Now <u>CRACKS</u> a <u>NOB</u>le <u>HEART</u>. Good <u>NIGHT</u>, sweet PRINCE,
>
> And <u>FLIGHTS</u> of <u>ANG</u>els <u>TAKE</u> you <u>TO</u> your <u>REST</u>.
>
> Milton: Me<u>THOUGHT</u> I <u>SAW</u> my <u>LATE</u> e<u>SPOUS</u>ed <u>SAINT</u>.

Though the lines that precede and follow would soon correct you, you could even read the line from Chaucer, and any number of familiar lines of iambic pentameter, with only four stresses, thus: A *KNYGHT* there *WAS*, and that a *WORTH*y *MAN*, or, from Shakespeare's *Richard the Third*, *NOW* is the *WIN*ter of our *DIS*con*TENT*. Thus it becomes more like the standard Old English meter, that of *Beowulf*, for example. The meter of Old English poetry is a four-stress line with a varying number of syllables or none (instead of consistently one) between stressed syllables, and it is controlled by alliteration, not rhyme. Here, from the moor and hidden under mist-clouds, comes the cannibal monster Grendel, God's own enemy, to raid the Danish king's hall—and dine there. The stressed syllables are marked, as above, and you can hear the monster's heavy tread in the hard g-sounds of the second line:

> Ða com of more under mist-hleoþum
> Grendel gongan. Godes yrre bær! (*Beowulf*, lines 710–11)

No, Shakespeare did not write in Old English.

SUGGESTIONS FOR FURTHER READING

Some Dates

Calculating by major battles, each of the three main historical periods of the English language begins as follows: Old English in 449 (the invasion of the Angles, Saxons, and Jutes, according to the Venerable Bede); Middle English in 1066 (the Norman Conquest); Modern English in 1485 (the Battle of Bosworth Field). One can also divide the periods by centuries: Old English 500–1100, Middle English 1100–1500, and Modern English 1500–present.

Works Quoted or Mentioned

Bede, *A History of the English Church and Its People*, Leo Shirley-Price (trans.), Harmondsworth, UK: Penguin, 1988.

Beowulf and the Fight at Finnsburg, Fr. Klaeber (ed.), 3rd ed., Lexington, MA: D. C. Heath, 1950.

Lewis Carroll, "A Stanza of Anglo-Saxon Poetry," *The Book of Nonsense*, Roger Lancelyn Green (ed.), New York: Dutton, 1965, pp. 118–20.

Geoffrey Chaucer, *The Canterbury Tales Complete*, Larry D. Benson (ed.), Boston: Houghton Mifflin, 2000.

John Milton: Complete Poems and Major Prose, Merritt Y. Hughes (ed.), New York: Odyssey, 1957.

The Riverside Shakespeare, J. J. M. Tobin, Herschel Baker, and G. Blakemore Evans (eds.), 2nd ed., New York: Houghton Mifflin, 1997.

Elizabeth Closs Traugott and Mary Louise Pratt, *Linguistics for Students of Literature*, New York: Harcourt Brace, 1980.

Standard References

The Cambridge History of the English Language, Richard M. Hogg (ed.), 6 vols., Cambridge: Cambridge University, 1992.

Volume 1, *The Beginnings to 1066*, Richard M. Hogg (ed.).

Volume 2, *1066–1476*, Norman Blake (ed.).

Volume 3, *1476–1776*, Roger Lass (ed.).

Further Reading about Literature in Old English

Peter S. Baker (ed.), *The Beowulf Reader*, New York: Garland, 2000. (First published in 1995 as *Beowulf: Basic Readings*.) Contains thirteen of the essays that have most influenced our reading of *Beowulf* since the mid-1960s.

Allen J. Frantzen (ed.), *Speaking Two Languages: Traditional Disciplines and Contemporary Theory in Medieval Studies*, Albany: SUNY, 1991. This interesting collection of essays supplements the Greenfield-Calder history (following) with introductions to newer methods of reading the literature of the English Middle Ages; therefore it includes works in Middle English as well as in Old English.

Stanley B. Greenfield and Daniel G. Calder, *A New Critical History of Old English Literature*, New York: New York University, 1986. Old but unsurpassed, this one book takes the reader through all the major works in Old English literature both in poetry and in prose; it even contains a survey of the Anglo-Latin background. The title includes a pun, since the editor Greenfield was the field's most fervent advocate of the methodology of New Criticism.

Katherine O'Brien O'Keeffe (ed.), *Old English Shorter Poems: Basic Readings*, New York and London: Garland, 1994. Another collection of essays that have revised our way of reading significant Old English poetic texts exclusive of *Beowulf*.

Andy Orchard, *A Critical Companion to* Beowulf, Cambridge: D. S. Brewer, 2003. In my view this covers the many aspects of the poem and scholarship about it better than any book since R. W. Chambers, *Beowulf: An Introduction to the Study of the Poem*, last revised by C. L. Wrenn in 1959 (but still valuable for discussion of the analogues).

Further Reading about Shakespeare's English

Professor Ian Lancaster's bibliography of books about the language of Shakespeare, available at http://www.chass.utoronto.ca/~ian/2530bib.html, is an excellent resource. The three following titles are included in Lancaster's list.

Charles L. Barber, *Early Modern English*, London: Deutsch, 1976.

G. L. Brook, *The Language of Shakespeare*, London: Deutsch, 1976.

S. S. Hussey, *The Literary Language of Shakespeare*, 2nd ed., London: Longman, 1992.

21 An Austere Age Without Laughter

Michael W. George

A common misconception about the Middle Ages is that our medieval fore-fathers lacked a sense of humor. Such an attitude has arisen due perhaps to scholarly and classroom interest in more serious matters; medieval humor is neither studied nor taught nearly as much as more serious topics—religion, philosophy, warfare, high literature.[1] And "Scholars of medieval literature have long followed a tendency to separate comic from serious genres, so that comic elements in a 'serious' work are seen either as an aesthetic flaw incompatible with the work's overall purpose, or as a mere sugar coating covering the work's kernel of meaning" (Perfetti 1995: 38). Medieval people did, indeed, have a sense of humor. They told jokes, engaged in horseplay, and participated in a variety of recreational activities.[2] And scholarship is beginning to recognize comedy and laughter as meaningful.

While the vast majority of scholars focus on the serious side of the Mid-dle Ages, a number have ventured into the arena of humor and laughter. Johan Huizinga, for instance, sees laughter, wit, jest, joke, and the comic as related to the subject of his book—play.[3] Mikhail Bakhtin goes further. For Bakhtin, medieval and Renaissance society consisted of two ideologies.[4] The official ideology was completely serious. An unofficial, subversive ideology also existed, and this ideology contained within it subversive folk elements that, through their humor, ran contrary to official culture. In Bakhtin's view, medieval society was the battleground for these two competing ideologies. Though many scholars would caution using Bakhtin's ideas too readily, *Rabelais and His World* was a highly influential book, opening up entirely new avenues into cultural studies, avenues paved with humor.

To medieval thinkers, laughter was a complex subject, perhaps more complex than it is to most of us. It was considered to be a fundamental part of human nature, as the words of Notker Labeo, a monk of St. Gall who died in 1022, indicate: "Homo est animal rationale, mortale, risus capax" ("Man is a rational, moral animal, capable of laughter"; Kolve 1966: 127). But this principle only complicated the matter rather than simplifying it. The question remained: is laughter good or evil, and for whom is laughter appropriate? Whether or not clerics should jest occupied thinkers such as Walter of Châtillon (Curtius 1990: 422). Conduct books and religious rules commented on laughter. Conduct books like *Ratis Raving* and Pecock's *Reule of Crysten Religioun* stressed that laughter in moderation was acceptable (Kolve 1966: 127–8). In the end, the Middle Ages considered "its peril, its necessity, its potential usefulness" (Kolve 1966: 131) when thinking about laughter.

Regardless of scholastic thought about laughter, humorous stories were popular in the Middle Ages. The French *fabliaux* are, perhaps, the best-known medieval comic stories with at least 127 examples (Hines 1). Such stories are not, obviously, limited to the French language. We find comic tales along the lines of the *fabliaux* in the German *Schwänke*, the Italian *novelle* (including Boccaccio), the Middle Dutch *boerden*, in Welsh literature, and in England, most notably in *Dame Sirith* and Geoffrey Chaucer (ca.1343–1400), who seems to be particularly indebted to the French tradition.[5] Writers also wrote comic tales in Medieval Latin, as we find in the poetry of the Goliards and the parodic literature such as the *Coena Cypriani* (Cyprian's Supper) and parodic masses. Comic tales crossed national, social, and linguistic boundaries.[6] Exempla collections, which provided preachers with useful stories to use as illustrations in their sermons, often included humorous stories. Robert of Basevorn's *Ars predicandi* (The Art of Preaching, early fourteenth century) instructs that it is proper to use "opportune humor . . . when we add something jocular which will give pleasure when the listeners are bored, whether it will be about something which will provoke laughter, or some story or anecdote" (Murphy 1971: 212).[7]

By the late Middle Ages, humor seems to have found a home in most genres of writing. From the subtle witticisms in Geoffrey of Vinsauf's *Poetria nova* to the stage antics of vices in morality plays, we find writers attempting to evoke a chuckle from audiences. Even when dealing with the most serious and noble topics, medieval writers took the opportunity to propose humorous situations. Most of the cycle plays from England, for instance, have episodes dealing with Joseph's reaction to Mary's pregnancy. These episodes provide an almost farcical look at Joseph, who is convinced that he has become a cuckold. The York pageant on this subject depicts the old Joseph as one so upset that he comically considers escaping to the wilderness. Most of the interaction between Joseph and Mary in this pageant concerns Joseph's attempts to learn the name of the child's father.[8] Some humorous practices might seem exceptionally blasphemous to us. Festivals and texts that humorously mock orthodoxy arose in the Middle Ages. The Feast of Fools, for instance, was a parody of orthodox ceremonies (censing with sausages, for instance) and even had a parodic script associated with it. Parodies of the Mass arose, as well, replacing key terms and phrases from the Latin Mass with terms and phrases suitable to the subject. A variety of drinkers' masses exist, which use terms like *bacchus* in place of *deus*. Gamblers' masses also exist, as does a Mass for an ass, and Martha Bayless cites a variety of liturgical parodies in her *Parody in the Middle Ages*, indicating that no subject was too sacred to be immune from humor. These ceremonies and texts, unorthodox as they may seem, were evidently great fun for both participants and observers.[9]

This mixture of the serious with the comic is not unusual. The ideal story, according to both Chaucer and Gower, is one that mixes *sentence* and *solaas*, to use Chaucer's words (*CT* I.798), or earnest and game, as Gower asserts (*CA* 8.3108–9). What we find in these works, as well as in sermons, saint's lives, romances, lyrics, plays, rhetorical arts, and a host of other writings, is a mixture of serious and funny.[10] There seems not to have been a sharp distinction between serious and comic in the Middle Ages. Laughter was a part of recreation, and recreation was considered by many to be necessary for good health.[11]

It is important to note that no monolithic view on recreation (which included humor) existed in the Middle Ages. Glending Olson's work on the types of play indicates that attitudes differed greatly in the scholastic community. But even if one were to find that an overarching negative opinion about humor existed, such opinions were and are theoretical. The reality is that medieval people laughed and produced humorous texts.[12] Though the opinion of what Mikhail Bakhtin called "official culture" may have condemned such activities as the Feast of Fools, such activities continued to exist until well beyond the Middle Ages, indicating a real desire for laughter.

The place of laughter in human existence was, indeed, a topic of debate in the Middle Ages, as we find in Umberto Eco's *Name of the Rose*. Medieval people laughed, liked to laugh, and incorporated humorous material into their most sacred subjects. There are medieval equivalents to our *Southpark*, *Caddyshack*, and *Saturday Night Live*. To deny the existence and strong influence of humor and laughter in the Middle Ages is to deny medieval people an aspect of humanity that Aristotle claimed was unique to human beings: laughter.

SUGGESTIONS FOR FURTHER READING

Helen Adolf, "On Medieval Laughter," *Speculum* 22, 1947, 251–3.

Mikhail Bakhtin, *Rabelais and His World*, Hélène Iswolsky (trans.), Bloomington, IN: Indiana University, 1984.

Martha Bayless, *Parody in the Middle Ages: The Latin Tradition*, Ann Arbor, MI: University of Michigan, 1996.

Larry D. Benson and Theodore M. Andersson (eds. and trans.), *The Literary Context of Chaucer's Fabliaux: Texts and Translations*, Indianapolis, IN: Bobbs-Merrill, 1971.

Derek Brewer (ed.), *Medieval Comic Tales*, Suffolk, UK: Brewer, 1996.

Michael Camile, *Image on the Edge: The Margins of Medieval Art*, Cambridge, MA: Harvard University, 1992.

E. K. Chambers, *The Mediaeval Stage*, 2 vols. (bound as one), Mineola, NY: Dover, 1996.

Lawrence M. Clopper, *Drama, Play, and Game: English Festive Culture in the Medieval and Early Modern Period*, Chicago: University of Chicago, 2001.

E. R. Curtius, *European Literature and the Latin Middle Ages*, Willard R. Trask (trans.), Princeton, NJ: Princeton University, 1990.

Michael W. George, "Representation, Religion, and Sexuality in the York 'Joseph's Troubles' Pageant," in Susannah M. Chewning (ed.), *Intersections of Sexuality and the Divine in Medieval Literature: The Word Made Flesh*, London: Ashgate, 2005, pp. 9–17.

Johan Huizinga, *Homo Ludens: A Study of the Play-Element in Culture*, R. F. C. Hull (trans.), Boston: Beacon, 1967.

V. A. Kolve, *The Play Called Corpus Christi*, Stanford, CA: Stanford University, 1966.

James J. Murphy (trans.), *Three Medieval Rhetorical Arts*, Berkeley, CA: University of California, 1971.

Glending Olson, *Literature as Recreation in the Later Middle Ages*. Ithaca, NY: Cornell University, 1986.

———. "Plays as Play: A Medieval Ethical Theory of Performance and the Intellectual Context of the Tretise of Miraclis Pleyinge," *Viator* 26, 1995, 195–221.

Lisa R. Perfetti, "Taking Laughter Seriously: The Comic and Didactic Functions of Helmbrecht," in Thomas J. Farrell (ed.), *Bakhtin and Medieval Voices*, Gainesville, FL: University Press of Florida, 1995, pp. 38–60.

———. *Women and Laughter in Medieval Comic Literature*, Ann Arbor, MI: University of Michigan, 2003.

J. S. P. Tatlock, "Medieval Laughter," *Speculum* 21, 1946, 289–94.

NOTES

1. One need only look at some of the classic scholarship on the Middle Ages. E. R. Curtius's *European Literature in the Latin Middle Ages*, for instance, provides perhaps the most comprehensive coverage of medieval humor. Yet in a book of 653 pages he devotes a mere nineteen pages to "Earnest and Jest." Other scholars follow suit.
2. For ideas on recreation in the Middle Ages, see Glending Olson's *Literature as Recreation in the Later Middle Ages*.
3. See *Homo Ludens: A Study of the Play-Element in Culture*.
4. See *Rabelais and His World*. Bakhtin's views have been challenged in recent years. Critics like Wayne Booth, Peter Stallybrass and Allon White, Rietz-Rüdiger Moser, Heidy Greco-Kaufmann, and Aron Gurevich challenge Bakhtin's idea that humor forms a necessarily subversive element in culture. But regardless of the criticism, Bakhtin has left a deep impression on our thinking about laughter in the Middle Ages.
5. For some sources and analogues to Chaucer's fabliaux, see Benson and Anderson.
6. For an example of the breadth of comic literature, see Derek Brewer's *Medieval Comic Tales*. Brewer has also shown evidence of medieval ethnic jokes in a paper presented at the 31st International Congress on Medieval Studies in Kalamazoo, Michigan.
7. See the translation in *Three Medieval Rhetorical Arts*, James Murphy (ed.), Berkeley: University of California, 1971.
8. Each of the four extant English cycles contains an episode on Joseph's trouble about Mary's pregnancy. Chester incorporates it into the Annunciation and the Nativity, and Towneley includes it in the Annunciation. There is even a lyric devoted to the topic. All of these texts present Joseph as an old man, perhaps impotent (for he knows that he is physically incapable of impregnating Mary), who is upset over the recent turn of events.

9. Bakhtin discusses the Feast of Fools and related parodic materials briefly. For a full discussion of such festivals, see Chambers, especially Chapters XIII and XIV, which are devoted to the Feast of Fools, but also Chapters XI, XII, and XV.

10. See Curtius's short piece on "Jest and Earnest in Medieval Literature," pp. 417–35.

11. On justifications of recreation, see Glending Olson's *Literature as Recreation in the Later Middle Ages*, especially Chapters 2 and 3. Though Olson does not deal directly with laughter in his work, he does deal with texts that provoke laughter, especially in "Plays as Play," where he discusses attitudes on recreational forms such as drama, jests, jokes, storytelling, banter, and raillery, concluding that there was no set ethical view on the forms themselves.

12. These materials are not limited to written texts. Medieval art is filled with such imagery. See, for instance, Michael Camile's *Image on the Edge*.

22 King Arthur
The Once and Future Misconception

S. Elizabeth Passmore

Arthurian legend in general lends itself to misconceptions through its strong hold on the modern popular imagination, with the result that many lovers of fantasy create in their minds a view of the Middle Ages that never existed. No body of Arthurian legend holds more possibilities for imaginative re-creations, however, than the figure of King Arthur himself. Modern ideas about King Arthur come almost wholly from a vast collection of modern popular novels and films about the Arthurian legends.[1] T. H. White's *The Once and Future King*, a collection of four Arthurian books published under one binding in 1958, and inspired heavily by Sir Thomas Malory's fifteenth-century English *Le Morte Darthur* (ca.1470), supplies much of the basis for modern ideas about Arthur, even for those who have only come to it through the Disney movie, *The Sword in the Stone* (1963), or Warner Brothers' musical *Camelot* (1967).[2] Modern redactions of Arthur are anachronistic in many ways, broadly conceiving the king as living in an Anglo-Norman twelfth-century world of chivalric ideals, plate armor, and stone castles, far from the fifth-century surroundings of the original legend. Bluntly, if a historical Arthur ever existed, he would have lived in a world of large wooden halls, smoky with fires emanating from central fire pits, not in a world of ornate tapestries and turreted stone castles.

Every age, including our own, has created its own King Arthur, a figure so deeply compelling to the imagination that people have been retelling tales of King Arthur since at least the ninth century. The danger with coming to the Arthurian legends through popular modern reconstructions is that many modern lovers of Arthuriana go no further back into the Middle Ages than to Malory's late-fifteenth-century book, if they even venture that far. Malory's Arthur, however, represents the culmination of over five hundred years of Arthurian tale-telling told through the lens of the late medieval English political and social scene. Much of Malory's work is drawn from earlier tales of Arthur, dating from the twelfth to the fourteenth centuries, but filtered through his view of his own fifteenth-century world.[3] Arthurian enthusiasts need, above all, to understand that there is, in fact, no such thing as an accurate depiction of King Arthur.

One body of misconceptions about King Arthur centers on the question of whether a historical Arthur existed at all. In fact, if Arthur actually existed, he would have been a regional war leader of the fifth century, not a power-ful, unifying king of all England, Scotland, and Wales as he is depicted by later writers.[4] Had Arthur actually been a historically real figure, he would perhaps have had more in common with the Anglo-Saxon depiction of the warrior-hero Beowulf than with the later depictions of Arthur as a celebrated king holding court at an airy, crenellated castle, enjoying elaborate tourna-ments and jousting exercises performed by knights colorfully attired in shining armor, decorated with their heraldry.[5]

The latter vision of Arthur and his court is, in part, owed to Malory's fif-teenth-century depiction and in part to the imagination of Hollywood's set and costume designers. Since heraldry, crenellated castles, and tournaments were not invented until the eleventh and twelfth centuries, and the time period from which the "real" Arthur dates is the fifth to the sixth century in England, it is, in fact, easy to see the discrepancy. The image we have today of King Arthur muddies the question of historical veracity, as it is an entirely fabricated image formed from years of new conventions overlaid onto the original legend. The main thing to bear in mind when considering the modern conception of King Arthur is that, however tempting it is to imagine the environment of Arthur's England as representing medieval England in reality, this tendency is probably the biggest misconception of all, beginning with the idea that there is only one medieval England to imagine, that the country and people somehow remained static and unchanging from the fifth to the fifteenth centuries.

It is possible that an early Brittonic leader did exist soon after the departure of the Romans in the early 400s, at the time of invading Angles, Saxons, and Jutes. A great warrior, associated with Arthur, is alluded to briefly in several early Latin chronicles as a leader of the Britons (the Celtic natives of England) just at the end of the Roman period.[6] It is even possible that this leader was a "high king" over a number of lesser kings. "Riothamus" and "Vortigern" are two words used as names possibly associated with Arthur in the early Latin texts; they both, in fact, mean "high king."[7] Soon, however, the story of this great Brittonic leader was linked with numerous folkloric stories and tradi-tions, and the warrior leader was, over the centuries, transformed into that of a high medieval king living in a mythical world.[8] While the earliest writers mentioned little that connects Arthur to later legends, by the ninth century, it is clear that legends of Arthur were being passed through popular culture.[9] The transformed character eventually becomes surrounded in Arthurian tales by trappings of chivalry and feudalism that date initially from the twelfth-century environment of the first major works of Arthurian literature, including those by Geoffrey of Monmouth (*Historia regum Britanniae* [*History of the Kings of Britain*], ca.1138) and Chretien de Troyes (ca.1140–ca.1200), a twelfth-century French writer who authored a number of popular Arthurian romances which heavily influenced later tales of the legendary king.[10] The initial purpose of Geoffrey's book was purely political, to create and emphasize the idea that a great leader of the English predated the colonization of the country by Angles and Saxons.[11] Actually, even the later Arthurian tales were often written for political reasons, and a number of English kings, including Edward I (1272–1307) and Richard II (1377–99), drew on the wealth of Arthurian traditions to forge a strong identification between their own reigns and that of the legendary King Arthur.[12]

Certain people, places, and objects have long been associated with King Arthur. People such as Queen Guinevere, Sir Lancelot, and Merlin appear again and again in Arthurian legends. Places such as Tintagel, where Arthur is popularly supposed to have been conceived; Camelot, his great court; and Avalon, where he went finally to die or be healed, have all been located physically in one or another place in England, helping to one or another extent to further misconceptions about the hero.[13] Certain objects also are popularly connected with King Arthur, such as Excalibur, his sword; the Round Table, representing the fellowship of his knights; and the Holy Grail, the vessel supposedly used by Jesus at his Last Supper, which forms the final adventure of Arthur's knights. Each of these people, places, and objects could be discussed at length, but I will concentrate here on only two: the legendary association of the Round Table, and the location of Avalon, Arthur's final resting place. (I hope that you will be inspired to delve into the "Suggestions for Further Reading" to learn more about the others.)

Today, Arthurian enthusiasts from around the world flock to the Great Hall at Winchester Castle in England to see Arthur's Round Table. This Round Table in fact demonstrates the popularity of Arthurian legend in the late thirteenth century, for the wood has been dated through dendrochronology to 1275, during the reign of King Edward I.[14] The table, made of oak, 18 feet in diameter and weighing about a ton, was originally covered in fabric; it was repainted in 1522 during the reign of Henry VIII (complete with an image of the Tudor red and white rose). The earliest allusion to an Arthurian Round Table occurs in Wace's *Brut*, an Old Northern French translation of Geoffrey of Monmouth's *Historia,* written around 1160. Wace merely comments that Arthur had the table built in order to avoid fights among his knights about who was worthiest to sit closest to the king (ll. 9747–60). In Layamon's *Brut* (ca.1200), however, the story is expanded: after a fight broke out during one of Arthur's feasts, a Cornish carpenter offered to build Arthur a round table, capable of seating 1,600 knights, to end contentions among his knights about who had precedence in seating arrangements (ll. 11422–43). Other accounts of the creation of the Round Table exist, including that Merlin originally made the table or that Guinevere's father gave it to her when she married Arthur.[15]

Arthur's Round Table is, however, not only an object but also an idea representing the equality of Arthur's knights and an event, popular from the thirteenth century onward, that lasted several days and combined tournaments, feasts, and the acting out of scenes from popular Arthurian romances.[16] King Edward I, we know from the evidence of various chronicles, repeatedly held Arthurian-style banquets, "round tables," at which he took on the persona of King Arthur and named his knights for members of Arthur's Round Table. A (possibly apocryphal) story about one of these banquets, held in 1299, alleges that a squire dressed as an ugly hag played out a scene from Chretien de Troyes' Arthurian tale, *Perceval*. "She" entered the court on a horse and begged for the help of "King Arthur's" knights of the Round Table in dealing with ongoing problematic relations between the lords and the commons.[17] In the following century, one of the young King Richard II's feasts (in 1378) was also interrupted by a knight disguised as a lady.[18]

A famous Arthurian location, Avalon, the legendary home of Arthur's half sister, Morgan Le Fay, and the supposed final resting place of Arthur, is popularly assumed to refer to Glastonbury, England. The Pitkin Guide to Glastonbury Abbey, in fact, subtitles its book "The Island of Avalon," revealing how strongly tourism has influenced the modern conception of this area.[19] In Geoffrey of Monmouth's *Historia*, it is said that Arthur was carried off to the island of Avalon after being badly wounded in his final battle, and the myth that Arthur will someday return is also mentioned (§ 178). Wace later takes up the same story in his *Roman de Brut*, though he seems personally doubtful of the possibility of Arthur's future return (ll. 13275–98). Layamon expands on the story as he ends his own *Brut*, saying that Arthur declares he will be healed in Avalon by the fairy woman, Argante, and Layamon supports this declaration with Merlin's prophecy of Arthur's return (ll. 14277–87, ll. 14295–7). The idea that King Arthur and his Queen, Guinevere, are buried somewhere in Glastonbury Abbey actually dates from 1191, when, several years after suffering the near-total destruction of their abbey by fire, the monks of Glastonbury Abbey "discovered" a Celtic tomb on the grounds of their abbey, claiming that the burial site was that of King Arthur and his Queen, Guinevere.[20] This discovery served the abbey's immediate purpose of generating the interest (and financial help) of pilgrims desiring to see the site, turning the location into a popular tourist site, which continues to this day. Less than a hundred years later, in 1278, King Edward I and his queen, Eleanor, celebrated with the Glastonbury monks as they moved the grave to a new site in the choir (near the high altar) of the new abbey church, complete with an elaborate shrine that survived until the dissolution of the monastery in 1539 by Henry VIII (at which point the shrine was totally destroyed). Not until 1963, during an excavation of the area, was the site of this shrine rediscovered, and now a simple plaque identifies the "burial site" of this mythical couple.[21] An early Celtic belief, both Welsh and Brittonic, suggesting that Arthur will rise again when his country most needed him is clearly made defunct by this twelfth-century "discovery." King Edward I's presence at the later reburial served his political purposes as he attempted to conquer Wales, by ending the hope that King Arthur would return. At the same time, his popularity was enhanced by his careful association of himself and his reign with Arthur.

While we have been discussing predominantly English images of King Arthur, another misconception to redress is that Arthur was a purely English figure. In fact, though Arthur has served politically to represent the foundation of an English spirit, there are problems with this conception, since historical Arthur would have been a leader of the Celtic natives of England, not of the Anglo-Saxon peoples who eventually formed the foundation of England. Furthermore, there are, in fact, multiple Arthurs, one for each of many countries that translated Arthurian legends into their own vernacular (native) languages: the Welsh Arthur, the French Arthur, the German Arthur, the Old Norse Arthur, and the Spanish Arthur, to mention only a few.[22] The extent to which Arthur has captured the imagination of medieval (and modern) people is revealed by the number of international Arthurian tales dating from the medieval period and retold up to the present. King Arthur, whether based on history or not, has been transformed through literature into a truly "once and future" king.

SUGGESTIONS FOR FURTHER READING

Geoffrey Ashe, *The Discovery of King Arthur*, London: Guild, 1985.

W. R. J. Barron (ed.), *The Arthur of the English: The Arthurian Legend in Medieval English Life and Literature*, Cardiff: University of Wales, 1999.

N. J. Higham, *King Arthur: Myth-Making and History*, London and New York: Routledge, 2002.

Patricia Clare Ingham, *Sovereign Fantasies: Arthurian Romance and the Making of Britain*, Philadelphia: University of Pennsylvania, 2001.

Edward Donald Kennedy (ed.), *King Arthur: A Casebook*, New York: Garland, 1996.

Norris J. Lacy (ed.), *Medieval Arthurian Literature: A Guide to Recent Research*, New York: Garland, 1996.

Norris J. Lacy et al. (eds.), *The Arthurian Handbook*, 2nd ed., New York and London: Garland, 1997.

Jean Markale, *King of the Celts: Arthurian Legends and Celtic Tradition*, Christine Hauch (trans.), Rochester, VT: Inner Traditions, 1994.

Martin B. Shichtman and James P. Carley (eds.), *Culture and the King: The Social Implications of the Arthurian Legend; Essays in Honor of Valerie M. Lagorio*, Albany: SUNY, 1994.

Michelle R. Warren, *History on the Edge: Excalibur and the Borders of Britain, 1100–1300*, Minneapolis: University of Minnesota, 2000.

Richard White (ed.), *King Arthur in Legend and History*, New York: Routledge, 1998.

James J. Wilhelm (ed.), *The Romance of Arthur: An Anthology of Medieval Texts in Translation*, New York and London: Garland, 1994.

NOTES

1. Chris Brooks and Inga Bryden, "The Arthurian Legacy," *The Arthur of the English: The Arthurian Legend in Medieval English Life and Literature*, W. R. J. Barron (ed.), *Arthurian Literature in the Middle Ages* 2, Cardiff: University of Wales, 1999, p. 264.

2. T. H. White, *The Once and Future King*, New York: Berkeley, 1958; *Malory: Works*, Eugène Vinaver (ed.), 2nd ed., Oxford: Oxford University, 1977; *The Sword in the Stone*, dir. Wolfgang Reitherman, perf. Rickie Sorensen, Richard Reitherman, and Karl Swenson, Disney, 1963; *Camelot*, dir. Joshua Logan, perf. Richard Harris, Vanessa Redgrave, Laurence Naismith, Warner, 1967.

Camelot was originally performed on Broadway in a 1960 Lerner & Loewe musical with Richard Burton and Julie Andrews.

3. By far Malory's most popular source is the thirteenth-century French Vulgate Cycle, though he also uses the fourteenth-century English alliterative *Morte Arthure* and stanzaic *Mort Arthur*, as well as other sources. See P. J. C. Field, "Sir Thomas Malory's *Le Morte Darthur*" (Barron 224–46).

4. See Geoffrey Ashe, *The Discovery of King Arthur*, London: Guild, 1985, especially Chapter 3, pp. 40–55, and Norris J. Lacy and Geoffrey Ashe, *The Arthurian Handbook*, 2nd ed., New York: Garland, 1997, esp. Chapter 1, pp. 1–55.

5. Though, of course, the *Beowulf* poem survives only in a tenth-century manuscript, descriptions within it of weaponry and jewels are reinforced and validated by the 1938 archeological excavation of Sutton Hoo, the location in East Anglia, England, of a fifth-century burial site of an Anglo-Saxon war leader.

6. See *The Romance of Arthur: An Anthology of Medieval Texts in Translation*, James J. Wilhelm (ed.), New York: Garland, 1994, pp. 3–9.

7. For the connection between Riothamus or Vortigern and King Arthur, see Ashe, *Discovery*, pp. 96–100.

8. N. J. Higham, *King Arthur: Myth-Making and History*, London: Routledge, 2002, pp. 267–74.

9. The first work which hints at such a leader is that of Gildas, a monk who wrote around 547 AD a narrative called *De Excidio et conquestu Britanniae* (*On the Downfall and Conquest of Britain*). In this, Gildas mentions the leadership of a man named Ambrosius Aurelianus as well as a culminating battle at Mount Badon, later connected to King Arthur (Wilhelm 3–4). A later anonymous text, *Historia Brittonum* [*History of the Britons*], previously thought to have been composed by the Welsh monk Nennius, was written around 800 AD. This is the first work to actually mention Arthur's name, and it is clear from this record that the legend of Arthur had already taken firm root.

10. Geoffrey of Monmouth's *Historia regum Britannie* (*History of the Kings of Britain*) of 1138 lays the foundation for the future romances of King Arthur and his knights. The first vernacular, Old French, relation of the Arthurian story dates from about 1160: Wace's *Roman de Brut* mainly follows Geoffrey of Monmouth's *Historia* but expands on the Arthurian stories of the Round Table and of Avalon. Layamon's *Brut* (early 13th century) expands on Wace's Anglo-Norman *Brut* as he translates the "history" of Arthur into early Middle English. Chrétien de Troyes pulls the story of King Arthur from these so-called historical sources and transforms them into romance. See Judith Weiss (trans.), *Wace's* Roman de Brut: *A History of the British*, Exeter: University of Exeter, 1999, and W. R. J. Barron and S. C. Weinberg (trans. and eds.), *Layamon's Arthur: The Arthurian Section of Layamon's Brut*, Austin: University of Texas, 1989. One of the many translations available of Chrétien's romances is the Everyman edition: *Chrétien de Troyes: Arthurian Romances*, D. D. R. Owen (trans.), London: Dent, 1991.

11. Higham, *King Arthur*, pp. 1–9.

12. Patricia Clare Ingham, *Sovereign Fantasies: Arthurian Romance and the Making of Britain*, Philadelphia: University of Pennsylvania, 2001.

13. Tintagel is supposedly located on the coast of Cornwall, Camelot at Cadbury Castle, and Avalon in Glastonbury. The Pitkin Guides, available at virtually every tourist site in England, are invaluable sources of such information. They are published by Pitkin Unichrome, and a list of publications can be found at http://www.britguides.com. Also see John Darrah, *Paganism in Arthurian*

Romance, Woodbridge, UK: Boydell, 1994, especially pp. 215–50, and Lacy and Ashe, 290, 313–4, 351–2.

14. Juliet Vale, "Arthur in English Society," in Barron, *Arthur of the English*, p. 187.

15. From the thirteenth-century French Vulgate Cycle comes the idea that Merlin originally created the Round Table, and that it was given to Guinevere as a dowry gift by her father, Leodegrance. See Darrah, *Darrah*, p. 121.

16. Vale, "Arthur," pp. 185–96. It must be remembered, though, that Richard was only ten years old at the time and so may not have ordered the entertainment.

17. Michael Prestwich, *Edward I*, New Haven, CT: Yale University, 1997. Prestwich, however, finds this story to be unconvincing and suggests it is "best treated as evidence not of Edward's attitudes, but of the way in which foreigners viewed him" (p. 121). For the Arthurian romance to which this "interlude" referred, see *Chrétien de Troyes Perceval, or The Story of the Grail*, Ruth Harwood Cline (trans.), Athens, GA: University of Georgia, 1983. See also John Withrington, "*The Weddynge of Sir Gawen and Dame Ragnell* and *The Marriage of Sir Gawaine*," in Barron, *Layamon's Arthur*, p. 208, and Vale, "Arthur," 187–91, as well as R. S. Loomis, "Edward I, Arthurian Enthusiast," *Speculum* 28, 1953, 114–27.

18. Vale, "Arthur," 194.

19. C. A. Ralegh Radford and John McIlwain, *Glastonbury Abbey: The Isle of Avalon*, Andover, UK: Pitkin Unichrome, 1999.

20. See, for instance, Jean Markale, *King of the Celts: Arthurian Legend and Celtic Tradition*, Christine Hauch (trans.), Rochester, VT: Inner Traditions, 1994, pp. 73–80. The story is discussed in most works on the Arthurian legends.

21. Higham, *King Arthur*, pp. 230–3.

22. See the Arthurian Literature in the Middle Ages series, W. R. J. Barron (ed.), Cardiff: University of Wales. Also see Norris J. Lacy, *Medieval Arthurian Literature: A Guide to Recent Research*, New York: Garland, 1996.

V
Society

23 A "Peasants' Revolt"?

Paul Strohm

A general revolt—or, more accurately, an interrelated cluster of violent pro-
tests and disturbances—certainly did occur in England in 1381. Throughout
the spring of that year and into the month of July, numerous disturbances
occurred about the country. They ranged as far north as Yorkshire and as far
northwest as Cheshire, but with particular concentration during early and
mid-June in the southeast counties together with London itself. Only in the
last hundred or so years have these disturbances been, as it were, combined,
unified, and given a name that would have meant nothing to its participants:
"The Peasants' Revolt." "So what?" one might ask, but such designations,
especially when applied to charged political situations, are never conceptually or politically neutral. This one—suggesting to the modern ear a unified
action mounted by a coherent body of hayseeds and yokels—is extremely
misleading as to the nature of the event in question.

Certainly, the risings in Kent and Essex involved a significant proportion
of rural workers, and some of those were tillers of the simplest sort: serfs or
tenants (Latin *servi* or *nativi*) in traditionally sanctioned bondage to large
estates possessed by secular lords and large monasteries. Abolition of such
traditional restrictions was, indeed, a frequent demand of the tenants and
their sympathizers; but it was hardly a uniform or inevitable demand and
vied for prominence with other objects of protest, including unreasonable
taxes (the "spark" of the risings in Kent, Norfolk, and Essex), grievances
about city and town governance, and the undue influence of unpopular
nobility on the young king. In fact, humble rural workers never constituted
more than half the protesters and were usually in the minority. Swelling the
ranks of the protesters were significant numbers of relatively prosperous
rural entrepreneurs—reeves, millers, smiths, bakers, brewers, independent
agricultural contractors, small landholders, and more. In addition, depending on location, other classes of people were involved and were sometimes
in the majority. In towns and in regional cities like York, segments of the
citizenry or commonalty—that is, prosperous freemen, already involved
in town governance—seized the occasion to rise against rival factions or
against obnoxious ecclesiastical privileges. And in London, the majority
of the insurgents were (despite the contrary contentions of chroniclers and

parliamentary spokespersons) local rather than rural, consisting largely of disaffected urban workers or "journeymen" with no hope of attaining advancement in the guild system, as well as other inflamed urbanites with scores to settle. Against this mixed pattern, the simple write-off of the insurgents as a mob of angry peasants represents an abdication of serious analysis and an evasion of responsibility to weigh the causes and consequences of an occasion that, although politically premature, organizationally inchoate, and ultimately ineffective, represents its own kind of milestone in the unending struggle for social equity and justice.

STIGMATIZATION

Although somewhat condescending, the term "Peasants' Revolt" is only mildly condemnatory, if condemnatory at all,[1] compared with the kinds of language employed by its earliest chroniclers—all of whom were located among its vehement opponents and detractors.[2] The monastic chroniclers, on whose writings most of today's accounts of the rising still depend for their narrative thread and local imagery, occasionally describe the insurgents neutrally—as Latin *communes*, that is, "common people" or "members of the commons"—but more often employ terms freighted with class antipathy or outright derision. These are terms of *stigmatization*, terms that, by their very use, tend to direct sympathies against the people to whom they are applied. A whole range of such terminologies may be illustrated within the writings of master chronicler Thomas Walsingham and in the greatest of his chronicles, the *Historia Anglicana*. For Walsingham they are usually "rustics" or *rustici,* or "serfs" or *servi*. These unmodified terms are not, however, the worst at his disposal. When describing the rebels' occupation of the Tower of London (a stunning if temporary symbolic victory, which the rebels were unable to convert to a tactical one), he exclaims, "The rebels, who had formerly belonged to the most lowly condition of serf [*qui quondam fuerant vilissimae conditionis servi*] went in and out like lords; and swineherds [*subulci*] set themselves above soldiers although not knights but rustics [*rustici*]" (Dobson 172; Walsingham I.459). Here is the line Walsingham attributes to the now-vindictive king Richard, declaring the fate of the vanquished rebels—already lowly and about to go lower: "Rustics you were and rustics you are still [*Rustici quidem fuistis et estis*]; you will remain in bondage, not as before, but incomparably harsher [*incomparabiliter viliori*: note the Lat. *viliori*, which at once signals the harshness of their bondage and their own vile status]" (Dobson 311; Walsingham II.18). Walsingham finds other ways to refer, derisively, to the commotion surrounding the rising: the insurgents are madmen, members of an insane mob, raise terrible rackets, and the like. Most tellingly, he renders them altogether subhuman, consigning them to animal status: "Words could not be heard among their horrible shrieks but rather their throats sounded with the bleating of sheep, or, to be more accurate, with the devilish voices of peacocks" (Dobson 173; Walsingham I.460).

A similar representational strategy is pursued to an ultimate conclusion by contemporary writer John Gower, in whose *Vox Clamantis* (a work written entirely in hostile reaction to the events of 1381) the rebels are characterized as every kind of lowly and debased animal. He says that he had a dream in which "I saw innumerable terrifying monsters, various rascally bands of the common mob [*diuersas plebis sortes vulgaris*] wandering through the fields in countless throngs. And while my eyes gazed upon the crowds and I was greatly amazed at so much rowdiness, behold, the curse of God suddenly flashed upon them, and changing their shapes, it had made them into wild beasts. They who had been men of reason before had the look of unreasoning brutes" (Stockton, *Latin Works*: 54; *Vox* 27). As this transformation of troubling reality into stigmatizing literary metaphor completes itself, we encounter rebellious asses, oxen, bristling swine, mad dogs, cats and foxes, birds of prey and roosters with hellish shouts, and a plague of flies and frogs—all led by a "jackdaw," standing in for the mythical rebel leader Jack Straw. So, in a much softer rendition, do we get Chaucer's Nun's Priest conjoining animalism and noise in his observation, of a rout of barnyard animals, that "Certes, he jakke straw and his meynee/Ne made nevere shoutes half so shrille . . ." (*Nun's Priest's Tale*, ll. 3394–5).

ACTUAL SOCIAL COMPOSITION

Fortunately for our grasp of the situation, some contemporary descriptions are a bit less stigmatizing and more accurately descriptive—although only occasionally and incidentally so. These descriptions tend to be found in what historians call "documents of record": pieces of writing that have jobs to do, including jobs that require a fuller or more accurate rendering of the circumstances of an event or the composition of its participants. Such documents are hardly exempt from imaginative distortion but are typically reined in by their linkage to practical procedures, such as setting up commissions and tribunals, granting pardons, and the like. Early on, before the outcome of the rising was known, some "official" statements granted a good deal more social standing to the participants. Seeking to pacify the insurgents of St. Albans (who actually probably included a higher percentage of serfs and tenants than most such bodies), King Richard and his advisers go off the rails in another direction, flattering them as "burgesses and good people" (*burgeis et bones gentz*; Walsingham I.473) and, issuing a soon-to-be-rescinded letter of protection for the rebels, calling them "our lieges and commons" (*nos liges et communes*; Walsingham I.480).

A more inclusive, and perhaps more neutral, terminology is to be found in documents of a legal or prosecutorial nature, with a premium on full or accurate enumeration of persons under suspicion. Especially valuable in this regard, in my view, is the royal writ of 15 June 1381, issued in London immediately following the dispersal of the rebels in the city, setting up commissions of inquiry into the disturbance. In this document, with a particularity sponsored by its pragmatic purposes, the rebels are described as "an armed band [*milicia*] of our subjects, persons largely of middling and lesser status [*status mediocris et minoris*], such as workers [*laboratorum*], agricultural tenants [*operariorum*], servants [*seruientum*], and craftsmen [*artificum*], especially from the counties of Essex, Kent, Surrey, Sussex, and Middlesex" (Réville 235). To say that some of the rebels were of "middling status" does not sound especially flattering, but this term represents quite a concession, when compared with what the chroniclers had to say; especially when linked with "craftsmen," a category that could and did include not only journeymen and apprentices but also guildsmen and potentially substantial citizens of towns. (This is already, of course, an ominous document for participants in the now-suppressed rising; they are called an "armed band" for reasons of prosecution. Even in the fourteenth century, people would not have been hanged for participating in an unruly protest, or even for being members of a mob; but, once arms are taken up, an accusation of treason became available, together with all the sanctions the law could imagine.) Returning to the composition of this band: the absence of gentry should come as no particular surprise. As with such later movements as the sixteenth-century Pilgrimage of Grace, the insurgents seem to have sought to enlist a few, although without much success.[3] In summary, the fairest and most balanced characterization of the situation seems to me that of R. H. Hilton: "The rising was one of (or at least one recruited from) the whole people below the ranks of those who exercised lordship in the countryside and established authority in the towns" (p. 184).

Although the royal writ gives the most inclusive contemporary description I have seen, it still underplays the urban elements of the rising. These elements are acknowledged in its mention of craftsmen, whose ranks undoubtedly consisted mainly of town and city dwellers. They are also acknowledged in a typically backhanded way by the inclusion of Middlesex on the list of afflicted counties. Backhanded, because—unlike ancient times, when Middlesex would have included all of London, and modern times, when London includes all of Middlesex—fourteenth-century Middlesex would have included most of the areas immediately surrounding London but not the self-governing City of London itself. Covered up by the inclusion of Middlesex and the exclusion of London proper from the list is a fact that was not lost on contemporary observers: the events in London involved substantial numbers of the city's own inhabitants. Even the most biased of chroniclers sometimes allow themselves to acknowledge that the rising had considerable support within city walls. The gates were, after all, opened to rebels coming over from Southwark—a subject on which contemporary allegations flew and some of the city's own aldermen were falsely and rather fancifully charged. Much more relevantly, the city contained numbers of disenfranchised workers—wage laborers or journeymen who had no foot on the guild ladder, apprentices uncertain of their own advancement, and a host of other transients and aliens without hope of ultimate citizenship. The Westminster Chronicler comments on this element, when describing a certain paralysis that seemed to have overtaken the city's defenders: "It was, indeed, feared that if resistance were offered to the growing strength of the serfs [*servi*], the city's lower orders [*communes*] might champion their own class [literally, *fautores*: abettors or natural allies] and join the serfs in rising against the rest of the citizens and that in this way the entire city, divided against itself [*in seipsa divisa*], would be ruined." (*West Chron* 8–9) This specter of inner division and class-based turmoil haunted Londoners of the Middle Ages, and their usual response was one of denial. The idea of outside agitation was a convenient form of denial, and—just as in Jack Cade's rebellion in 1450 and in the Bastard of Fauconbrigge's supposed 1471 assault on the city—the insistence that a band of Kentish yokels was responsible for the unrest was a convenient explanatory avenue.[4]

WHAT SHOULD IT BE CALLED?

Not—for anyone seeking any fidelity to the actualities of 1381—"the *Peasants'* Revolt." Not only did persons we might call "peasants" comprise a likely minority of those involved in the broils of 1381; the word *peasant* itself did not even enter the English language (from French *paisant* or country-dweller) until the sixteenth century. Certainly, chronicle writers like Walsingham were reaching toward something like the "peasant" appellation when they spoke of *servi* and *nativi* and assigned rural origins to most of the insurgents. So, too, did later commentators look for alternative locutions that served the same purpose. For example, seventeenth-century royalist John Cleveland, in his tract *The Rustick Rampant, or Rurall Anarchy*, coined and employed a range of such similar terms as clownes (rustics), carles (peasants), and gnoffes (fellows of John the Carpenter in Chaucer's "Miller's Tale"), and he styles the event itself "the Rebellion of the Clownes" (p. 1). What we encounter in such descriptive experiments is less a matter of history and more a matter of rhetorical persuasion. *Nor*—for that matter— should we speak of the Peasants' *Revolt* either, since *revolt* suggests a degree of coordination and purpose that may hardly be assigned to what was effectively a disparate and widespread protest movement. As suggested by their "watchword" or slogan—"With Richard and the true commons"—these ardently concerned protestors had no intention of overthrowing the king or instituting a new form of government, only in reforming the old one. Which eighteenth- or nineteenth-century historian first used the doubly discredited phrase "Peasants' Revolt" I have been unable to determine. The earliest use I have seen is that of John Richard Green, in his *Short History of the English*

People (1874), in which he speaks of "the Peasant Revolt" as an established locution. In any event, it is established now, and unfortunately so.

Writings closer to the time pose a more satisfying and more adequately descriptive alternative, when they speak of unrest among the Latin *communes* or French *comunes* or English *commouns*. This term refers not to the parliamentary commons or the governing classes but to the "common people" of the realm, the majority of its nonaristocratic residents, whose sometimes-violent but undoubtedly earnest desire to petition for redress and to address the problems of the realm swept through England in 1381. This spontaneous and decentered and temporary movement—not really a rebellion at all—might perhaps best be called a "rising." The two parts of my recommended phrase are employed by the fifteenth century in the most populist of the extended chronicles, the *Great Chronicle of London*, which reports that, in the fourth year of Richard II's reign, "of the comons of Englond was a grete Risyng."

SUGGESTIONS FOR FURTHER READING

Primary Works

Geoffrey Chaucer, "Nun's Priest's Tale," *The Riverside Chaucer*, Larry D. Benson (ed.), Boston: Houghton-Mifflin, 1987.

John Cleveland, *The Rustick Rampant, or Rurall Anarchy*, London, 1658.

R. B. Dobson (ed. and trans.), *The Peasants' Revolt of 1381*, London: St Martin's, 1970.

John Gower, *Vox Clamantis*, in *Complete Works*, vol. 4: The Latin Works, G. C. Macaulay (ed.), Oxford: Clarendon Press, 1902.

———. *Vox Clamantis*, in *The Major Latin Works of John Gower*, Eric W. Stockton (trans.), Seattle: University of Washington, 1962.

Great Chronicle of London, A. H. Thomas and I. D. Thornley (eds.), Stroud, UK: Alan Sutton, 1983.

Thomas Walsingham, *Historia Anglicana*, H. T. Riley (ed.), Rolls series, no. 28: vols. 1 and 2, London, 1863.

Westminster Chronicle, 1381–1394, L. C. Hector and Barbara Harvey (ed. and trans.), Oxford: Clarendon Press, 1982.

Secondary Works

Susan Crane, "The Writing Lesson of 1381," *Chaucer's England: Literature in Historical Context*, Barbara Hanawalt (ed.), Minneapolis: Univ. of Minnesota Press, 1992.

Rodney Hilton, *Bond Men Made Free: Medieval Peasant Movements and the English Rising of 1381*, London: Temple Smith, 1973.

Steven Justice, *Writing and Rebellion: England in 1381*, Berkeley: University of California, 1994.

Andrew Prescott, *Judicial Records of the Rising of 1381*, dissertation, University of London, 1984.

André Réville, *Le Soulèvement des Travailleurs d' Angleterre en 1381*, Paris: Picard, 1898.

Paul Strohm, *Hochon's Arrow: The Social Imagination of Fourteenth-Century Texts*, Princeton: Princeton University, 1992.

NOTES

1. Sympathetic interest in the rising was taken by a number of left- and Marxist-influenced historians in the mid-twentieth century, analytically framed by study of medieval peasant movements; the subtitle of R. H. Hilton's splendid *Bond Men Made Free* is *Medieval Peasant Movements and the English Rising of 1381*.
2. No accounts of the rising favorable to the motives of its participants survive. A few scraps of insurgent rationale may be said to survive, like bugs in amber, in suspension within otherwise hostile contexts, because they are cited by derisive chroniclers. The best and most convenient analysis of these fragmentary evidences is that of Steven Justice, *Writing and Rebellion*. Other analysts have tried to read chronicle accounts "against the grain," seeking patterned or motivated rebel action within and behind the chroniclers' condemnations; see in this regard Paul Strohm, "A Revelle!" and Susan Crane, "The Writing Lesson of 1381." Even those chronicle accounts that *sound* sympathetic to modern ears (such as Froissart's re-creation of John Ball's sermon against social inequality) were presented by their original authors as self-evident exposure of the folly of the insurgents. (Dobson 371)
3. See, for example, Froissart's account of the attempted enlistment of Sir Robert Salle (Dobson 261–4).
4. In point of fact, as Andrew Prescott has argued (in an unpublished paper given at Harlaxton, summer 2004), very few rural insurgents would have had the time and resources to make the 70-some-mile trip from such places as Canterbury to Blackheath, London, in the three days (10 June–12 June) customarily allotted to them, let alone the two days (11 June–12 June) that Dobson supposes for them. Even riders on swift horses have been shown to make the three-day trip only with great difficulty, and few among this imagined rural throng would have been mounted for the journey.

24 The Medieval Sense of History

Richard H. Godden

The most common misperception about the medieval sense of the past is simply that there was not one. In lacking a historical consciousness, the argument goes, people in the Middle Ages were unable or unwilling to approach the past in its own terms but instead could only see it through the lens of a specifically Christian present. Benedict Anderson, in his *Imagined Communities*, states the fundamental tenets of this position: "Figuring the Virgin Mary with 'Semitic' features or 'first-century' costumes in the restoring spirit of the modern museum was unimaginable because the mediaeval Christian mind had no conception of history as an endless chain of cause and effect or of radical separations between past and present."[1] Far from being presented in "first-century" garb, Mary would often look particularly contemporary. So, the historical period of Christ's life (or any period) cannot be depicted as it actually was but only in terms of the present because of the monolithic nature of "the mediaeval Christian mind," which ceaselessly related all things to its indivisibly dogmatic worldview. Anderson, then, opposes the medieval view of history to that of the modern, which privileges "cause and effect" and "radical separations between past and present." Such an opposition is stunning in its simplicity! This sort of arbitrary demarcation between medieval and modern (or early modern) often produces a monolithic view of the medieval period. However, the period of time from the fall of the Roman Empire until Petrarch and the Renaissance was not dark and unenlightened, and it was definitely not organized under one totalizing, homogenous rule.

In this essay, I set out some of the varying confrontations with history and time that are found in the later Middle Ages. However, there are as many approaches to time and history in this period as there are people experiencing them. So my sketch of medieval views of history will focus on one or two aspects, namely, the view of time as a fall from eternity and history as series of disasters and disruptions. The final portion of this essay will take a brief look at a fourteenth-century English poem, *Saint Erkenwald*, which illustrates a sophisticated view of the past.

Any consideration of the Christian view of time usefully begins with the apostle Paul. In the first letter to the Corinthians, he writes, "This therefore

I say, brethren; the time is short" (1 Cor. 7.29).[2] For Paul, time is finite, and the Resurrection of the Messiah announces its coming end.[3] This belief informs how Paul preaches to his followers: "Let every man abide in the same calling in which he was called" (1 Cor. 7.20). Whether that calling be marriage, circumcision, freedom, or slavery, all should stay in the state that they are currently in because "time is short." The finitude of Man is set against the eternity of God and Christ, for God will be "all in all" (1 Cor. 15.28). These positions on time and eternity contribute to the predominant approaches to history from the early medieval period up through the later Middle Ages.

After Paul, however, the centuries rolled on and time did not end, but the *certainty* that time would end did not abate. Time would end because time was finite. In *The City of God*, Saint Augustine argues that time is inextricable from the world.[4] Time began with creation and would end with creation. Time, therefore, is a fall from eternity, the wholeness that is God. God exists in an omnitemporal present, from which man is separated in his mortality. Augustine emphasizes these points when he orders the history of the world into six ages, with each age corresponding to one of the days of Creation.[5] Augustine's six ages are as follows: the first age, from Adam to the Flood; the second age, from the Flood to Abraham; the third age, from Abraham to David; the fourth age from David to the Exile in Babylon; the fifth age until the coming of Christ; the sixth age from Christ until Judgment. In this scheme, we are *still* in the sixth age, an age whose duration and division Augustine argues cannot be reckoned. And since God rested on the seventh day, so too would we rest in the seventh age. The end of the sixth age is the end of human time. Later writers like Bede would relate the Six Ages of the World to the Six Ages of Man, from infancy to old age.[6] The Seventh Age of Man would be death.

Augustine writes *The City of God* in response to the pagan charge that Christianity is the reason that Rome has suffered so much in the last few centuries. Augustine refutes this argument through a critique of pagan thought in comparison with scripture, but he also decides that the argument could be addressed through the lens of history. Busily working on Book XI at the time, he delegates this task and asks Paulus Orosius to write a history, from Creation to the present time, in order to show that evil existed in the pagan world before the coming of Christianity.[7] *The Seven Books of History against the Pagans* became one of the most important early universal histories, and much of Orosius's work was preserved during the medieval period not only in manuscript but as a source for writers like Isidore of Seville.

Orosius's history amply demonstrates that history is fracture and confusion—that destruction and sin existed in the world since the beginning. But what of history after Christ? David Lawton addresses this question in his analysis of the Orosian features of the late thirteenth-century *mappamundi*, the Hereford Map:

The point at which Orosius reaches Christ's birth and enthusiastic self-enrolment in Augustan empire marks an intellectual crisis in the sequence of Orosius's text through Book VII. First, he faces the obvious: the Christian world is not without its share of disasters. Augustinian logic responds at once, by agreeing: there are still disasters because there are still pagans.[8]

In Augustine's framework, perfection cannot be achieved on Earth before time's end. Orosius's description of Christ's birth presents a brief exception to this, for Christ chose to be born during the *Pax Romana*, and that for a time, all the world was united under the peace of empire.[9] But such a peace cannot come again. There will continue to be division among men while there are still pagans and Jews left to be converted, and there will continue to be Jews and pagans while there is still division. The continuous presence of confusion, both external in terms of Jews and pagans, and internal in terms of doctrinal disagreements and heresy, opens a space for the medieval Christian to develop multiple temporalities and historical schemata in order to make sense of the fallenness and fracture of human time.

These multiple temporalities and schemata are seen in the varying approaches to writing history in the period. Richard W. Southern organizes them into three general types, which he terms "classical, early scientific, and prophetic":

> The aim of the classical imitators was to exemplify virtues and vices for moral instruction, and to extract from the confusion of the past a clear picture of the destinies of peoples. The aim of the scientific students of universal history was to exhibit the divine plan for mankind throughout history, and to demonstrate the congruity between the facts of history revealed in the Bible and the facts provided by secular sources. As for the prophetic historians, their aim was first to identify the historical landmarks referred to in prophetic utterances, then to discover the point at which history had arrived, and finally to predict the future from the still unfulfilled portions of prophecy.[10]

The first type of history is often more literary and dramatic and is concerned with one group of people, like Geoffrey of Monmouth's *History of the Kings of Britain*. Universal history is generally sparser in detail and narrative and encompasses the world from creation to the present day. Important to both of these, however, is the prevalent notion of *translatio imperii*, or the "translation of empire."[11] According to this theory, *imperium* (authority) moves westward as civilizations rise and fall. For example, from the ashes of ruined Troy comes the great Roman Empire as Aeneas rescued the relics and destiny of his homeland from destruction. *Translatio imperii* bears a debt to the Book of Daniel and its interpretations and traces a westward movement from Babylon to Persia to Greece to Rome and so on. Thus, there is only one major, world-dominating empire in the world at a single time. Modern history still has this impulse of westward expansion, and *translatio imperii* can be seen as a somewhat distant grandsire of Manifest Destiny.

In the hands of a writer like Hugh of Saint-Victor, *translatio imperii* becomes a series of signposts on the way to the end of time. Linking the march of time to the movement of empire across space, Hugh writes:

> It seems to have been arranged by divine providence, so that those things which happened at the beginning of time should happen in the East, as at the beginning of the world; and that then as time moved on towards the end, the climax of events should pass to the West, from which we might conclude that the end of time is approaching, since the course of events has now reached the end of the world. (*De arca Noe morali* iv. 9)[12]

For Orosius, Rome would be the final empire, but later writers continued to follow the movement of *imperium*. Time's failure to end required new reckonings of history. M. D. Chenu notes that "Otto of Freising found a way to perpetuate the theme of Orosius, based on the description of the succession of empires in Daniel. He showed authority passing providentially from Rome to Byzantium to the Franks to the Lombards and finally to the Germans, along the same route taken by civilization."[13] Following another route of civilization, most European countries at one point or another traced their lineage to Aeneas or one his companions. Geoffrey of Monmouth's *History of the Kings of Britain* follows a Virgilian model and depicts Britain being founded by a descendant of Aeneas, Brutus, for which the island was named. Rather than authority "passing providentially" from Rome to another country, these histories present a country equal to Rome, not just its successor.

The Nine Worthies are another example of new historical schemata that are used to make sense of the continued march of time. The Nine Worthies consist of three sets of three, one each for the pagans (Hector, Alexander, and Julius Caesar), the Jews (Joshua, David, and Judas Maccabaeus), and Christians (Arthur, Charlemagne, and Godfrey of Bouillon). The selection of these historical luminaries originates with a fourteenth-century French romance of Alexander called *Vouex de Paon* ("The Vowing of the Peacock"). The Nine Worthies later make appearances in English poems, like *The Parliament of the Three Ages* and the alliterative *Morte Arthure*. This schema updates the approach to history inherited from Augustine and Orosius but also presents some important differences. Linked to the familiar patterns of rise and fall—made palpable in the two English poems and their pairing of the Nine Worthies with either Old Age or Fortune's wheel—is a note of Christian heroism and triumph. This runs subtly counter to the conception of history that Augustine gives to the Middle Ages. The three Christian Worthies, Arthur, Charlemagne, and Godfrey de Bouillon, are varieties of conquerors and paragons, and in the case of Godfrey, an example of the heroic energies of Christendom to recapture the Holy Land. Rather than existing in the sixth age, whose duration cannot be reckoned, Christian Europe occupies a time when the glories of the ancient world can be rivaled and surpassed.

More overt challenges to an Augustinian view of history can be found in the types of history that Southern categorizes as prophetic. In the twelfth century, the apocalyptic writer Joachim of Fiore organized the history of the world into three ages: the first being the Age of the Father, which corresponded to the time from Creation up to the advent of Christ; the second, the Age of the Son, from the advent to (around) the current time; and the third, the Age of the Holy Spirit, an impending age that would see the perfection of the Kingdom of God on Earth.[14] Joachim's eschatological vision not only introduces yet another schema for understanding history but also argues that perfection can be achieved *in* time, not because of time's ending. This is a radically different view of time and history from that put forth by Augustine and Orosius. However, it is important to note that I am not proposing a causal link between updated schemata such as the Nine Worthies and the apocalyptic writing of Joachim and others like Hildegard of Bingen. Rather, the proliferation of new conceptions of time and history reflect the need to constantly update these views because of the continued existence of the world.

The problems posed both by time's finitude and its continued unfolding gave rise to multiple possible temporalities, or ways of experiencing time in the Middle Ages.[15] The subjective experience of time is dependent upon a large array of factors, including but not limited to questions of empire, national histories, religion, methods of timekeeping, and space.[16] The Middle English *Saint Erkenwald*, for example, dramatizes the ways that differing temporalities confront each other. The setting of the poem is London of Anglo-Saxon England, shortly after Augustine of Canterbury began the conversion process. The poem begins with the conversion of pagan temples to Christian churches: they "chaungit cheuely hor nomes and chargit hom better" (18).[17] Now, "Þat ere was of Appolyn is now of Saynt Petre" (19) and so on.[18] The transformations are made on little more than similarity in sound most of the time, like Mahoun into Saint Margaret. The central action of the poem involves an archaeological discovery, that of a tomb with a well-preserved corpse. Erkenwald, a bishop, is called upon to see this wondrous discovery and to quell the disquieted citizenry who are disturbed by their inability to locate the identity of the corpse. The corpse miraculously speaks, and Erkenwald interrogates him, discovering that the man was a judge in ancient pagan Britain. At the end, Erkenwald sheds some tears over his interlocutor and the judge is baptized and goes to heaven (this act echoes Pope Gregory and the Emperor Trajan). Thus, Erkenwald rescues the pagan British past that the judge metonymically represents.

The history of England is one of disruptions, with the Britons being displaced by the Anglo-Saxons, who sustained invasions from the Danes and then the Normans. Through baptism, Erkenwald is able to reach back in time to a pregrace period of history and lead the pagan to salvation. The past loses some of its threatening nature as it is domesticated and merges seamlessly into the affirming picture of history that medieval England would like to maintain. For example, the pagan judge lived in "Newe Troye," and at the tournament at Smithfield in 1390, London was referred to as "la neufe troy." Another example of this is that the cultural appropriation of turning pagan temples into Christian churches was "New Werke hit hatte" (38),[19] which is also the same name for a project of rebuilding the abbey of this poem in the thirteenth century. So not only does the net of universal history try to swallow the troublesome past in this poem, but there are also several echoes and connections between the various times involved in the poem—it should be noted that there are three: the time of the poet (contemporary England), the time of Erkenwald (the Anglo-Saxon past), and the time of the pagan judge (the pagan British past). The three times are linked together by the poet in an effort to produce a narrative of continuity. Just as the tournament at Smithfield rehearses the past in order to strengthen the present, the baptism of a long-dead pagan rehearses Christ's Harrowing of Hell as a way to save the pagan past. These echoes and connections recognize the ruptures of history at the same time that they seek to smooth them over.

And yet, the cultural appropriation at work in this poem is by no means unproblematic. The pagan judge, who metonymically figures the past, remains unnamed. This is important because the Londoners in the poem try in vain to locate in their historical records any mention of such a splendid tomb being buried at that site. Nor does the tomb itself help anyone, as the writing contained upon it is illegible, not from the writing wearing away, but because it is not a language that anyone can read. This poem points to the failure of the historical record, and despite the affirming act of baptism performed by Bishop Erkenwald, the past may still be largely unreadable. In the end, though, the poem ultimately recognizes the difference of the past, how truly separate from us it is.

The idea of history in the Middle Ages is not a simple one. There are multiple schemata and approaches for reckoning time and history, ranging from the Six Ages of the World to the continued development of *translatio imperii*. My refutation of Anderson's portrayal of the medieval period lies not in arguing that medieval thinkers had a historical consciousness akin to what we moderns supposedly possess (though many writers did). Instead, my central point is to underscore that there is no one medieval sense of history. If medieval historians do not share with modern ones the sensibility of the "restoring spirit" of the museum, they do share the propensity for multiple understandings of history, for the sense of human time as division and fracture. Beginning with Paul, and threaded through Augustine and Orosius, was the idea that time was short and that time is a fall from eternity. In an age shaped by intellectual movements like postmodernism, phenomenology, and anthropology, and with historical ruptures on a staggering scale, the modern view of time tends to seem more and more like the medieval.

SUGGESTIONS FOR FURTHER READING

Giorgio Agamben, *The Time that Remains: A Commentary on the Letter to the Romans*, Patricia Dailey (trans.), Stanford, CA: Stanford University, 2005.

Christopher Baswell, *Virgil in Medieval England: Figuring the* Aeneid *from the Twelfth Century to Chaucer*, New York: Cambridge University, 1995.

Morton W. Bloomfield, "Chaucer's Sense of History," *Essays and Explorations: Studies in Ideas, Language, and Literature*, Cambridge, MA: Harvard University, 1970.

———. *Piers Plowman as a Fourteenth-Century Apocalypse*, New Brunswick, NJ: Rutgers University, 1962.

Ernst Breisach, *Historiography: Ancient, Medieval & Modern*, 2nd ed, Chicago: University of Chicago, 1994.

J. A. Burrow, *The Ages of Man: A Study in Medieval Writing and Thought*, New York: Oxford University, 1988.

Marie-Dominique Chenu, *Nature, Man and Society in the Twelfth Century: Essays on New Theological Perspectives in the Latin West*, Jerome Taylor and Lester K. Little (trans.), Toronto: University of Toronto, 1997.

Janet Coleman, *Ancient and Medieval Memories: Studies in the Reconstruction of the Past*, New York: Cambridge University, 1992.

Patricia Ingham, *Sovereign Fantasies: Arthurian Romance and the Making of Britain*, Philadelphia: University of Pennsylvania, 2001.

David Lawton, "1453 and the Stream of Time," *Journal of Medieval and Early Modern Studies* 37.3, 2007, 469–491.

Jacques Le Goff, *Time, Work, and Culture in the Middle Ages*, Arthur Goldhammer (trans.), Chicago: University of Chicago, 1982.

Medieval Concepts of the Past: Ritual Memory, Historiography, Gerd Althoff, Johannes Fried, and Patrick J. Geary (eds.), New York: Cambridge University, 2002.

Ruth Nissé, " 'A Coroun Ful Riche': The Rule of History in *St. Erkenwald*," *ELH* 65, 1998, 277–95.

Monika Otter, *Inventiones: Fiction and Referentiality in Twelfth-Century English Historical Writing*, Chapel Hill: University of North Carolina, 1996.

———. " 'New Werke': *St. Erkenwald*, St. Albans, and the Medieval Sense of the Past," *Journal of Medieval and Early Modern Studies* 24.3, 1994, 387–414.

Lee Patterson, *Chaucer and the Subject of History*, Madison, WI: University of Wisconsin, 1991

———. *Negotiating the Past: The Historical Understanding of Medieval Literature*, Madison, WI: University of Wisconsin, 1987.

———. "On the Margin: Postmodernism, Ironic History, and Medieval Studies," *Speculum* 65.1, 1990, 87–108.

The Postcolonial Middle Ages, Jeffrey Jerome Cohen (ed.), New York: St. Martin's, 2000.

James Simpson, *1350–1547: Reform and Cultural Revolution*, Oxford: Oxford University, 2002.

Gabrielle M. Spiegel, *The Past as Text: The Theory and Practice of Medieval Historiography*, Berkeley: University of California, 1997.

———. *Romancing the Past: The Rise of Vernacular Prose Historiography in Thirteenth-Century France*, Berkeley: University of California, 1993.

R. W. Southern, *History and Historians: Selected Papers of R. W. Southern*, R. J. Bartlett (ed.), Malden, MA: Blackwell, 2004.

Brian Stock, *The Implications of Literacy: Written Languages and Models of Interpretation in the Eleventh and Twelfth Centuries*, Princeton, NJ: Princeton University, 1983.

———. *Listening for the Text: On the Uses of the Past*, Baltimore, MD: John Hopkins University, 1990.

Time in the Medieval World, Chris Humphrey and W. M. Ormrod (eds.), Rochester, NY: Boydell, 2001.

The Uses of the Past in the Early Middle Ages, Yitzhak Hen and Matthew Innes (eds.), New York: Cambridge University, 2000.

Michelle R. Warren, *History on the Edge: Excalibur and the Borders of Britain, 1100–1300*, Minneapolis: University of Minnesota, 2000.

NOTES

1. Benedict Anderson, *Imagined Communities: Reflections on the Origin and Spread of Nationalism*, New York: Verso, 1983, p. 23.
2. All citations of the Bible will be taken from the Douay-Rheims translation of the Latin Vulgate.
3. For an extended study on St. Paul's conception of time, see Giorgio Agamben, *The Time that Remains: A Commentary on the Letter to the Romans*, Patricia Dailey (trans.), Stanford, CA: Stanford University, 2005.
4. Augustine, *City of God: Against the Pagans*, Henry Bettenson (trans.), New York: Penguin, 1984, Book XI, Chapters 4–8.
5. Augustine, Book XXII, Chapter 30.
6. See J. A. Burrow, *The Ages of Man: A Study in Medieval Writing and Thought*, New York: Oxford University, 1988. As Burrow points out, six ages was not the only number to be used for figuring the stages of a man's life. He continues to discuss three, four, and seven ages of both the world and of man.
7. Paulus Orosius, *The Seven Books of History Against the Pagans: The Apology of Paulus Orosius*, Irving Woodward Raymond (trans.), New York: Columbia University, 1936.
8. David A. Lawton, "The Surveying Subject," *New Medieval Literatures* 4, 2001, 9–37. See also Orosius, pp. 322–323.
9. Orosius, p. 322.
10. R. W. Southern, *History and Historians: Selected Papers of R. W. Southern*, R. J. Bartlett (ed.), Malden, MA: Blackwell, 2004, p. 66. The first three papers collected in this volume are dedicated, one each, to the three types of history that Southern outlines.
11. For some discussion of this, see Marie-Dominique Chenu, *Nature, Man and Society in the Twelfth Century: Essays on New Theological Perspectives in the Latin West*, Jerome Taylor and Lester K. Little (trans.), Toronto: University of Toronto, 1997, p. 187.
12. For the Latin text, see J.-P. Migne (ed.), *Patrologiae Latina*, CLXXVI, p. 667. For an English translation, see Hugh of Saint-Victor, *Selected Spiritual Writings*, trans. by a religious of the Community of St. Mary the Virgin, New York: 1962, p. 147.
13. Chenu, 187.
14. For some discussion of Joachim of Fiore, see Southern's chapter on prophetic history. Also, see Morton Bloomfield, *Piers Plowman as a Fourteenth-Century Apocalypse*, New Brunswick, NJ: Rutgers University, 1962; and Kathryn Kerby-Fulton, *Books Under Suspicion: Censorship and Tolerance of Revela-*

212 Richard H. Godden

tory Writing in Late Medieval England, Notre Dame, IN: University of Notre Dame, 2006. Kerby-Fulton discusses the effect of revelatory writing on vernacular literature in late medieval England, and on pp. 45–50, writes of the difference between the Augustinian view and those of Joachim of Fiore and Hildegard of Bingen.

15. A major area of study that this essay has not addressed is the various methods for measuring time in the medieval period. One method for measuring time was the Liturgy of the Hours. Liturgical time (for example, the hours of Terce, Sext, and None) inserts history as recurrence into linear time. Another method is the twenty-four-hour clock, which was being introduced during this period. The effects that timekeeping had on the view of both time and history in the Middle Ages is a large topic for further work.

16. My understanding of temporalities is particularly indebted to Paul Ricoeur, *Time and Narrative*, 3 vols., Kathleen McLaughlin and David Pellauer (trans.), Chicago: University of Chicago, 1984–1988. For a searching exploration of the play of multiple temporalities in medieval literature, see David Lawton, "1453 and the Stream of Time," *Journal of Medieval and Early Modern Studies* 37.3, 2007, 469–491. Lawton explores the conflicting temporalities that surround places and people, specifically in this case the place of Byzantium and Constantinople in the medieval and modern imaginations.

17. *Saint Erkenwald, Alliterative Poetry of the Later Middle Ages: An Anthology*, Thorlac Turville-Petre (ed.), Washington, DC: The Catholic University of America, 1989. The line roughly translates to "changed especially their names and dedicated them better."

18. "That which was of Apollo is now of Saint Peter."

19. "The New Work it was called."

25 The Medieval Peasant

Dinah Hazell

> Hark! the note,
> The natural music of the mountain reed—
> For here the patriarchal days are not
> A pastoral fable—pipes in the liberal air,
> Mixed with the sweet bells of the sauntering herd;
> My soul would drink these echoes.

—George Gordon, Lord Byron, *Manfred* (II.47–52)

The Romantic nineteenth-century depiction of the simple peasant, envied for a bucolic existence far from modern society, still clings to our perception. From a distance, the feudal model suggests that medieval peasants lived in a snug, secure world, protected by their lord in return for services. However, that image is no more characteristic than one of hopeless exploitation and powerlessness. While both extremes existed, the medieval peasant participated in a world of complex economic forces and social relations.

A discussion of medieval peasantry, the conditions of which varied with time period, place, and other factors, must have a directed focus in a chapter of this brevity. Rather than attempt a broad view of European peasantry in all eras, this study will concentrate on manorial village peasantry in England during the late Middle Ages. But in general the purpose is to dispel misconceptions about peasants and to give a more realistic and familiar appreciation of their life.

The most basic misconception is the image of the peasantry as a faceless, homogeneous group. Variations and ranges of condition and experience existed in many elements of peasant life, even within the same village. Socioeconomic status ranged from poor to prosperous, personal status from servile to free, and landholding status (which conferred possession but not ownership of the lord's property) from landless to customary tenant to freeholder, with ranges in between. At the lowest level were those with no land. Excluding the indigent, most landless peasants were the *famuli*, who worked as servants for the manorial lord, or those who worked for wealthy peasants. Next were customary tenants, who held land from the lord by "custom," usually passed down through family generations, and those who held land relatively freely; benefits and encumbrances varied with each type of holding. Combinations were possible, such as both free and customary tenancies held by one peasant.

Economic success was determined by the size and/or type of landholding, which could range from small plots to many acres, and was dependent on labor and monetary resources to maximize returns from holdings, as well as the type and weight of manorial obligations and debts. At the lowest strata, those with insufficient land were generally forced to hire out as workers to supplement their livelihood. At the upper levels, prosperity was a matter of abundance rather than variety, since the staples of peasant life were fixed. It was rare for wealthy peasants to move upwardly out of that social group, although their ambition applied pressure on the social hierarchy, and legislative attempts such as sumptuary laws governing dress were designed to keep them in their place.

Regardless of their landholding status, all tenurial members of a village community had obligations to the manorial lord, including rent and/or labor service depending on the conditions attached to their holding. The villein (unfree tenant, also known as serf and naïf) was subject to the lord's control in many areas of life, including geographic mobility, marriage, and the use of manorial property and resources. Violations were subject to fees and fines in monetary and/or material form. Control was based on economics; to ensure profit from the cultivatable manorial land (the "demesne"), the lord collected labor, produce, and/or cash in lieu of service, and income from leases, tenant rents, tolls, fines, and fees. Although there was some barter, the economy was largely money-based, and cash or credit was needed to purchase livestock, tools, equipment, household and personal goods, and other items that the peasant could not manufacture or supply. Additionally, there were church tithes (a tenth of agricultural produce), state taxes and levies, ceremonial expenses, and charitable contributions. Peasant income to meet these obligations could be derived from wage labor on the demesne and for wealthy peasants; villagers might also work in industry, trade or crafts, and sell surplus produce.

Our discussion of the peasantry so far has focused on economics, since the agricultural system they supported was the base upon which the feudal economy rested. But ideas about their daily life are also subject to some misconceptions: for instance, the vision of all peasants living in rickety hovels. Quality and size of housing varied with time period, location, and economic status, ranging from small, cramped cottages to larger structures. Often there was one building that housed both family and livestock, usually in separate sections, but in many areas peasant households included areas and/or outbuildings for livestock, farming equipment, and domestic activities in addition to living quarters. Construction methods varied, but based on archeological digs and findings, buildings could be quite sturdy; some late medieval peasant structures still stand. However, buildings frequently decayed, often due to lack of maintenance. Peasant families were nuclear rather than extended, usually with parents and children occupying and supporting the household. Most peasant properties included a garden of herbs and vegetables for family consumption and, if large enough, surplus sale. Possessions such as livestock, household items, and other "movables" (personal possessions) are documented in surviving wills and manorial court and account records, which enliven our image of peasant life.

England was primarily agrarian, with cities sprinkled across a countryside of manors and their villages, isolated homesteads and hamlets, agricultural and industrial areas, forests, and inland and seacoast ports. A typical village was dominated by the manor house; villagers' homes and gardens lined the streets, and there was a church, a mill (owned by the lord), sometimes an oven, possibly an alehouse, and a village green, surrounded by arable fields, pasturage, meadows, and perhaps wooded, waste, and marsh lands.

We should not envision medieval peasants as toiling endlessly in the fields. It is true that labor was intensive, particularly during peak seasons, on the peasants' own land, in the common fields, and on the demesne property. But there was time for churchgoing, social events, village games, and leisure activities. Village life was not necessarily insulated, as peddlers, itinerant clergy, mobile craftsmen and laborers, and other wayfarers passed through, and there was opportunity for social interaction, as well as commodities exchange, at markets and fairs. Peasants also plied trades and crafts, some in addition to working smallholdings, and some as specialists, such as carpenters, dyers, bakers, butchers, fullers, and masons. Ale brewing was ubiquitous, since the beverage was indispensable to the peasant diet. Peasant fare consisted mainly of fruits and vegetables, which the nobility considered unhealthy and fit only for the lower classes, grains, and dairy products, with less abundance of meat, which was the focus of the aristocratic diet. Quantity and quality, rather than type of food, varied with economic status within the peasantry and depended on weather conditions, famine, livestock disease, and other factors that impacted grain crops and other foodstuffs. During adverse times everyone suffered both hunger and economic setback.

Peasant life included the use of communal manorial resources designated by the lord, such as the open field, pasturage, and woodland, and reciprocal sharing of labor, equipment, and food. Although the peasantry participated in a cooperative community, as in any complex social group there were alliances, disputes, elitism, and complicated political relations within the peasantry and with manorial administration, in which some villagers (usually the more prosperous) participated as representatives, thus causing divided interests and loyalties. While the lord had a great deal of control over his tenants, it was not absolute or unassailable, and peasants were not completely voiceless. They participated in the government of their village, serving as jurors, witnesses, litigants, and pledges in manorial court and in creating the village bylaws that regulated communal life. But their power was limited, and demands on and treatment of the peasantry by lords and both manorial and royal officials are often characterized by medieval social critics and modern historians as exploitative and oppressive. Though peasants protested through refusal to perform services and other obligations and attempted to appeal their rights, their greatest strength came from coalesced resistance, of which the Rising of 1381, also known (if not entirely accurately) as the Peasants' Revolt, is a dramatic example.

Following a period of overpopulation and land scarcity in the thirteenth century, the mid-fourteenth century brought changes in response to the Plague, many of which were adverse for the landlord and positive for the peasant. Decreased population led to plentiful land so that many were able to increase their landholdings, which they could work or even rent out. The labor shortage led to higher wages and a mobile workforce; legislative attempts to curb this movement generally failed. Landlords' increased need for cash caused by rising labor costs and falling agricultural prices and land values led to an increase in the leasing out of lands and the receipt of cash in lieu of services, which allowed some peasants to obtain freedom. Despite these improvements, there was unrest, culminating in revolt. The Rising was sparked by the third in a series of poll taxes to raise funds for the continuing (and failing) war with France. The anatomy of peasant resistance movements is extremely complex and cannot be discussed here. However, many historians agree that while issues raised during the Rising involved the desire for freedom from seigneurial control and obligations, resentment over being blocked from taking advantage of the opportunities provided by the economic upswing was as strong an impetus as escape from exploitation. Often perceived as a rebellion of the poor peasantry, the Rising participants also included, perhaps primarily, those in the middling ranks. The rebels were joined in several areas by city workers who took the opportunity to address their own grievances.

While the standard of living for the lower classes generally rose, conditions did not improve for all. Then as now, resources were needed to increase economic status. Those unable to work and earn higher wages or those without land, access to land, or manual and material resources to work the land were not able to take advantage of opportunities. Poverty, ever-present in the medieval world, continued for many. In law and literature, there is evidence of the "false" beggar who feigned poverty in order to escape work, but there were many "true" beggars: the indigent, the "working poor," and those unable because of age, physical infirmity, poor health, or insufficient resources to provide for themselves and their families adequately or rise above bare subsistence level.

As we try to adjust our image of the medieval peasantry, it is worth brief consideration of how they were viewed by their contemporaries. Most peasants were not literate, so the information we have about them is usually from the viewpoint of other classes. Lively portraits are occasionally found in literature, particularly in works by Chaucer and Langland, which help illuminate attitudes but do not speak for a large part of the populace. The function of the peasantry, who occupied the lowest rung on the three-estate model that conceptually but not operatively undergirded medieval society, was to support the other two estates, the nobility and the clergy, with their labor. Attitudes towards the lower classes often vacillated between disdain and suspicion, and tolerance and idealization. This was much the same as the medieval attitude towards the poverty-stricken, with the exception that peasant behavior might be derided but endured since they were essential to the medieval economy. Not so with the poor, who did not contribute to material life, so that charitable attitudes and actions towards them were found in other than economic bases. Naturally, the peasantry may have had a quite different view of themselves, and perhaps medieval contemporaries removed from daily rural life had as many misconceptions about the peasantry as do moderns.

SUGGESTIONS FOR FURTHER READING

H. S. Bennett, *Life on the English Manor: A Study of Peasant Conditions 1150–1400*, Cambridge: Cambridge University, 1948.

Edwin Brezette DeWindt (ed. and trans.), *A Slice of Life: Selected Documents of Medieval English Peasant Experience*, Kalamazoo, MI: Medieval Institute, 1996.

Christopher Dyer, "English Diet in the Later Middle Ages," *Social Relations and Ideas: Essays in Honour of R. H. Hilton*, T. H. Aston, P. R. Coss, Christopher Dyer, and Joan Thirsk (eds.), Cambridge: Cambridge University, 1983, pp. 191–216.

———. *Everyday Life in Medieval England*, London: Hambledon & London, 2000.

———. *Standards of Living in the Later Middle Ages: Social Change in England c. 1200–1520*, Cambridge University, 1989.

Paul Freedman, *Images of the Medieval Peasant*, Stanford, CA: Stanford University, 1999.

Barbara A. Hanawalt, *The Ties That Bound: Peasant Families in Medieval England*, New York: Oxford University, 1986.

Rodney Hilton, *Bond Men Made Free: Medieval Peasant Movements and the English Rising of 1381*, London: Routledge, 1973.

———. *The English Peasantry in the Later Middle Ages*, Oxford: Clarendon, 1975.

May McKisack, *The Fourteenth Century 1307–1399*, Oxford: Clarendon, 1959.

Michel Mollat, *The Poor in the Middle Ages: An Essay in Social History*, Arthur Goldhammer (trans.), New Haven, CT: Yale University, 1986.

M. M. Postan, *The Medieval Economy and Society: An Economic History of Britain 1100–1500*, Berkeley: University of California, 1972.

J. Ambrose Raftis, *Tenure and Mobility: Studies in the Social History of the Medieval English Village*, Toronto: Pontifical Institute of Medieval Studies, 1964.

Werner Rösener, *The Peasantry of Europe*, Thomas M. Barker (trans.), Oxford: Blackwell, 1994.

———. *Peasants in the Middle Ages*, Alexander Stützer (trans.), Urbana: University of Illinois, 1992.

J. Z. Titow, *English Rural Society 1200–1350*, London: George Allen and Unwin, 1969.

26 Witches and the Myth of the Medieval *Burning Times*[1]

Anita Obermeier

Witches as black-clad, broomstick-riding, ugly old hags dominate Western representations in movies, stories, and especially at Halloween. Popular misconceptions hold that systematic, massive European witch hunts, trials, and executions happened during the Middle Ages. Although medieval thinkers contributed intellectual and legal ideas that helped develop the concept of witchcraft, the large-scale witch hunts belong to the early-modern period, comprising both the Protestant Reformation and the humanist Renaissance. The sheer volume of scholarly work on the witch phenomenon in postmedieval periods attests to that. Numerous scholarly opinions abound as to the reasons for the witch hunts that developed sporadically from 1430 on and reached their apex between 1560 and 1650. This chapter addresses the mistaken attribution of the early-modern witch hunts to the Middle Ages, while simultaneously chronicling the development of the image of the witch from antiquity to the seventeenth century.

First, some definitions might be helpful. Magic is most often associated with witchcraft, and it is a concept with dichotomous subdivisions: popular magic versus intellectual magic, natural magic versus demonic magic.[2] A basic definition of magic is "all efforts to manipulate or compel supernatural forces without reference to a God or Gods or to matters of ultimate meaning" (Stark 2003: 8). Mechanical sorcery is the lowest form of magic, relying on spells and charms. Sorcery comprises most of popular magic. Witchcraft grew out of sorcery but was considered distinct from it during the time of the European witch hunts. The root of the word *sorcery* is the French *sors*, meaning spell. Anthropologists have defined sorcery as "harmful magic" executed by a professional sorcerer. This definition differs from that of a witch, usually a woman, who is "believed to be inherently evil, born with the power to commit evil against others, and filled with anger and envy" (Guiley 1999: 212–3, 314). The term *witch* derives from the Old English *wicca* and the Middle English *witche*, meaning to work sorcery, to bewitch. The idea of magic is not fixed in the Middle Ages but rather developed from 500–1500 with major changes in the conversion period, the twelfth-century Renaissance, as well as the late-fourteenth-century and early-fifteenth-century cusp (Jolly 2001: 13).

Earlier, in Greek and Roman times, both good and bad magic was imputed to witches, but Roman law only prosecuted damage to property or people. By the early third century, Roman critics of Christianity combined admonitions against sorcery with fear of "unnatural religious practices" and blamed Christians for deviating from Roman religious customs, denying Roman gods, and congregating at night to practice perverted sexual acts and cannibalism (Kors and Peters 2001: 42). Ironically, many later Christian writers use similar rhetoric to discredit and indict heretics and witches. The patristic writer most influential on later medieval thought, Augustine, treated demonology in several of his works. He argued that pagan deities were "demons in disguise," considered pagan religions "superstitious abominations," believed that "demons and humans entered agreements [pacts]," and distinguished between "demonic magic" and "legitimate miracles" (Kors and Peters 2001: 43).

By the fifth century, ancient myths and legal customs, spreading Christianity, and Germanic paganism formed a new amalgam. The most persistent classical myths entering the early Middle Ages were those of the "night-flying, bloodsucking *striga*" and *lamia*, based on the Greek goddesses Hecate and Diana, that later blended with Nordic Valkyries (Russell 1972: 56, 79). *Lamiae* and *strigae* were differentiated from sorcerers (*maleficus* or *herbarius*), who were not linked with evil spirits. Throughout the early medieval conversion period, when Christian monotheism was establishing itself against existing magical pagan rituals, sorcerers were considered unwitting dupes of the devil and their practices "demonic illusion" (Jolly 2001: 16–8). For instance, during Charlemagne's reign (ca. 800), false accusations of witchcraft were punishable, and in 1080, Pope Gregory VII admonished King Harold of Denmark not to impute natural calamities to innocent women (Russell 1972: 148). At that time, the church was not as interested in witchcraft as in heresy, condemning belief in night-flying creatures as superstitious and heretical in the tenth-century *Canon episcopi (Canon of the Bishop*; Kors and Peters 2001: 176). In contrast, the late fifteenth-century *Malleus maleficarum (The Hammer of Witches)* insists that disbelief in witches equals heresy (Kramer and Sprenger 1971: 1). In the eleventh century, when sorcery was a secular crime, ecclesiastical punishment for sorcery and heresy was preceded by numerous reprimands; nonetheless, the first official burning for heresy happened in 1022 in Orleans, another one in Monforte in 1028 (Russell 1972: 71). Little burning happened in the eleventh and twelfth centuries, but in the thirteenth century, burning as punishment for "sorcerers and relapsed heretics" became standard; from the fifteenth century on, witches were burned upon "first conviction rather than upon relapse" (Russell 1972: 149–51).[3]

Two main theories try to explain the increasing interest in witchcraft in the Middle Ages: Jeffrey Burton Russell's "reformist heresy" and Alan C. Kors's and Edward Peters's notion that scholastic writers codified the understanding and description of the witch through their treatises. Russell views witchcraft as emanating from folklore and frames his notion in the larger contexts of various medieval groups' wishes to reform the church, often leading to dissent and repression as well as an increased fear of heretics. Cathars, Waldensians, and other heretical groups were frequently accused of being in league with the Devil. Stories about witches increased in the thirteenth century because "witchcraft, increasingly separated from simple magic and sorcery, began to be more and more closely bound to heresy, a process that would culminate in the fifteenth century" (Russell 1972: 99–100). Russell claims that the dualism of the Cathar heresy, in people's imagination, turned Satan from an abstract into a powerful figure that is literally haunting people's bodies and minds (1972: 101).

Kors and Peters demonstrate that the eleventh and twelfth centuries experienced a flurry of legal and theological writings expounding clerical and lay attitudes toward magic and sorcery. Before 1300, even ecclesiastical lawyers "lacked systematic categories of diabolism and occult powers" (Kors and Peters 2001: 59). Magical practices had been considered pagan, episodic, individual, and private attempts at personal gain. The most famous scholastic writer on demonology, Thomas Aquinas (1225–74), helped synthesize these "isolated cases of sorcery, 'witchcraft,' and possession" into a systematic theory of how Satan and his minions, later including witches, attack humanity (Kors and Peters 2001: 112). According to Aquinas, who championed Aristotle's denial of the existence of natural magic, "magic must be either divine or demonic" (Guiley 1999: 367). Aquinas also contested the validity of the Canon episcopi, instead asserting that "witches copulated with demons, flew through the air, shape-shifted, raised storms and performed other maleficia," evil acts, through a pact with the Devil that violates God's supreme power and "constitutes apostasy from the true faith" (Guiley 1999: 367; Kors and Peters 2001: 89, 112).

Since Church teaching was by this time shifting magic and sorcery away from paganism and toward heresy, canon law and papal authority became involved. In 1230, the "office of inquisitor of heretical depravity" was founded. When in 1258 Pope Alexander IV was petitioned to include sorcery in the list of offenses the Inquisition could investigate, he repudiated the request but permitted prosecution of sorcerers and witches in cases in which there was strong evidence of heresy (Trevor-Roper 1969: 30). Law schools and inquisitors' handbooks made this connection between sorcery and heresy so systematically and effectively that, by the middle of the fourteenth century, diabolical sorcery—no longer just an illusion—had become an accepted fact among ecclesiastical elites and fixed in canon law.

Michael D. Bailey nuances these theories with his argument that common and clerical concepts of sorcery were conflated and produced the later concept of witchcraft. In the early fourteenth century, Pope John XXII condemned all forms of necromancy practiced by the male Latinate elite with paraphernalia such as "rings, mirrors, and phials" (Bailey 2001: 966–7, 984). A century later, the prevalent usage of "common spells, charms, blessings, potions, powders, and talismans" had morphed into the conviction, as demonstrated by Pope Eugenius IV's statement, that illiterate people of both sexes "could perform terrible demonic sorcery 'by a single word, touch, or sign'" (Bailey 2001: 965, 984). This belief conjures up "an organized demonic sect of sorcery, witchcraft, and necromancy" that needs to be declared criminal and heretical and stamped out (Jolly 2001: 22). Although the fourteenth-century Dominicans Bernard Gui,[4] Nicholas Eymeric, and Johannes Nider and their learned treatises did not invent the concept of witchcraft, they propelled this conflation of common and elite magic, paving the road for fears such as Pope Eugenius IV's. Therefore, it is difficult to disagree with the enlightening comment by the early seventeenth-century inquisitor Salazar: "'There were neither witches nor bewitched until they were talked and written about'" (qtd. in Levack 2006: 178). Thus, the unfelicitous conflation of common and elite forms of magic and sorcery eventually melded with heresy to lay the groundwork for a full-blown image of witchcraft later.

From 1300 to 1330, the first secular court cases focused on political sorcerers, initially in France and later in England, mostly alleging treasonous plots against royalty or prominent officials. This element of treason also characterized the most famous political sorcery trials of the Order of Knights Templar, which was a concerted effort by Philip IV, Edward II, and Clement V to rid themselves of a politically influential and wealthy group (Behringer 2004: 57; Russell 1972: 195). Renunciation of Christianity, Devil worship, and sodomy were the gravest charges laid upon the Templars; the structure of their trials was later used in the witch persecutions (Stark 2003: 235; Russell 1972: 195, 198). The years 1330 to 1375 featured sorcery cases without diabolism charges, while the period of 1375 to 1435 saw an increase both in trials and in diabolism charges, especially in southeastern France, southwestern Germany, northwestern Italy, central and western Switzerland—the original and traditional Cathar and Waldensian strongholds (Levack 2006: 42, 90, 205).[5] Rodney Stark, extrapolating from Richard Kieckhofer's data on sorcery trials between 1300 and 1499, argues that only 935 people had stood trial, the majority of them from 1450 to 1499 (2003: 240–4). Nevertheless, by 1500, medieval ideas about diabolical sorcery and heresy had coalesced into the witchcraft concept that served as a model for the persecutions of the sixteenth and seventeenth centuries.

What exactly was this view of the witch that prevailed for the next two centuries? From 1500 on, witches were considered agents of the Devil, who commit *maleficia* against other humans as well as animals. They made pacts with the Devil and congregated in covens, kept familiars, and flew to witches' sabbats on brooms or beasts to meet their master. Once there, they engaged in gross banquets, naked dancing, cannibalistic infanticide, ritual intercourse with the Devil, and, above all, Devil worship (Levack 2006: 41).[6] The famous mark of the Devil was an addition by early sixteenth-century Protestant hunters and inquisitors of witches (Levack 2006: 52).[7] Many witches were accused by political rivals, economic competitors, neighbors, and even family because people feared they could cause these evils: illness, impotence, frigidity, sterility, death, severe weather changes, crop failures, livestock problems, and demonic possessions.

Scholars disagree on the reasons for the late-fifteenth-century outbreak of sorcery and witch trials. Some claim that the many misfortunes that beset Europe from 1300 to 1500, such as famines, plagues, economic woes, repeated wars, and papal schism, cannot be directly connected to these early witch-hunt outbreaks, as they are not contained to the geographic areas with the heaviest persecutions. Still others pinpoint the church's anxiety surrounding the growing need for ecclesiastical and devotional reform as well as the fear of a collaborative countersociety ruled by the Devil out to destroy Christian society through diabolical sorcerers and assemblies of witches. Stark denies validity to the following eight often touted reasons for the European witch hunts: witches were indeed real, mental illness, sexism, social change, group solidarity, greed, fanatical clergy, and mass psychosis (2004: 208–25). Instead, he argues, three other factors in collusion resulted in the witch hunts between 1500 and 1750: continued practice of magic, weak governance, and religious conflict (Stark 2004: 244–55).

Although witchcraft became a secular, rather than an ecclesiastical, crime again in the sixteenth and seventeenth centuries, and the persecutions increased in severity under secular control, their uneven geographical distribution in the Germanophone borderlands along the Rhine River valley nevertheless suggests a continued connection between witch-hunting and religious conflict. While witch hunting cannot be blamed on the Reformation per se, it cannot be denied that, because of heightened religious sensibilities, both the Reformation and Counter-Reformation intensified witch persecutions and their dissemination. For instance, the *Malleus maleficarum* was sanctioned by the papacy, and both Calvin and Luther endorsed witch trials. Interestingly, Protestant witch hunters did not acquire their own distinct demonology but espoused the existing late-medieval view with minor alterations. Elaine Breslaw posits that "in Lutheran Germany the witch-hunt became a way of disposing of political opposition and consolidating the powers of the new local authorities. The Catholics may have created the modern stereotype of the witch, but the Protestants made more zealous use of it" (Breslaw 2000: 8). Furthermore, Protestants were more intent on purging society of immoral behavior, gave more prominence to the Devil in their theology, and attacked both "low" magic in the form of charms and spells and Catholic "ecclesiastical" magic in the form of holy water and making the sign of the cross (Levack 2006: 118).

The Reformation alone, however, was not the culprit. After the limited witch hunts of the late fifteenth century, the early sixteenth century experienced a lull in prosecutions, attributed to the initial shock of the Reformation and the political demands of warfare (Levack 2006: 206–7). Changes in the secular legal system helped gear up for the individual trials and small hunts between 1550 and 1570. Secular courts had adopted the church's inquisitorial structure, and torture was allowed after 1480 in witchcraft trials (Harris 1974: 213). The large witch hunts peaked from 1580 to 1650, well into the humanist Renaissance; those peak witch-hunting years roughly correspond to the worst hundred-year period (1550–1650) Europe had ever seen: it endured inflation, transition to commercial agriculture, famines, depression in trade, revolts, civil and religious wars, national revolutions, and plague outbreaks.[8] Additional factors fostered intense persecutions. After 1570, old treatises, such as the *Malleus*, were reprinted and witch hunting resumed. The printing press, unfortunately, facilitated the spreading of witch-hunting propaganda, including the biblical injunction found in Exodus 22.18, which Reformers translated as "Thou shalt not suffer a witch to live," even though the Hebrew word does not have that connotation.[9]

Briefly examining the situation in individual European countries throws a surprising light on certain modern misconceptions about witch hunts. In Spain, Portugal, and Italy, where the Inquisition held sway over most witch trials, the numbers were rather low. The Spanish Inquisition, for instance, hesitated to define magic and sorcery as diabolical and gave more credence to the stories of the accused than to stock answers and expectations from witch-hunting manuals. Between 1540 and 1700, the Spanish Inquisition tried 44,701 people for various heretical offenses, as well as bigamy, blasphemy, sexual transgressions, superstition, and witchcraft; out of those, only 826 people (or 1.8%) were executed (Stark 2003: 256–9). In fact, the Spanish Inquisition in the early seventeenth century boasted the most indulgent measures, where out of 1,900 persons tried, only 11 were executed (Levack 2006: 95). In contrast, in unchecked local witch persecutions by secular authorities, satanic explanations were hyped and led to almost half of the executions in Spain (Stark 2003: 260). Portugal mirrored Spain in this aspect and had almost no witch trials. The Italian Inquisition was even more lenient. Over the two-hundred-year period of 1540–1740 in Rome, 97 died. Many Italian witch trials ended in not-guilty verdicts, a fact that may have been influenced by Italy's geographic distance from the religious wars (Stark 2003: 261–2).

In Scandinavia, 1,500 to 1,800 people were executed, although things are not evenly distributed across the individual countries. In Sweden, a country with intense magical and sorcerer activity, the arrival of satanism coincides with the influx of Protestant clergy educated in Germany; the worst Swedish witch hunts are imputed to the power vacuum of the 1660 and early 1670s, as they were in the Finnish province (Stark 2003: 268–70, 273). In Denmark, as in its dependencies Iceland and Norway, militant Lutheran theologians controlled the persecutions, but because the courts disallowed torture and hearsay, the hunts petered out (Stark 2003: 270–2). Similarly, England neither permitted torture nor incorporated the inquisitional structure and thus had fewer witchcraft trials than Spain and Italy (Russell 1972: 229; Levack 2006: 78–9).[10] In both England and Scotland, Reformation circumstances prompted persecutions.

Finally, the examples of France and Germany illustrate the importance of centralized government. France was chronically plagued by the kind of religious strife that could easily lead to witch hunting. In central France, *Parlement*, the high court of Paris, insisted on "reasonable standards of evidence and procedure" as well as reconciliation with the church, not execution; Parlement also had to review the verdicts of lower courts, and in the case of witch trials, it overturned 75 percent of them (Stark 2003: 262–3).[11] Monter claims that altogether until 1650, the kingdom of France legally sentenced to death at most 500 people (2002: 14). While witch hunts were both a rural and urban phenomenon, the type of court played a major role in execution rates: the more centralized the court, the greater an accused witch's chance of survival. This holds true in France, where in some French border regions with less direct control as many as 90 percent of the accused were killed (Levack 2006: 23). It is assumed that local courts were fiercer because of judges' personal knowledge of and possible vendettas against the accused. This assumption might explain the harshness of witch persecutions in France and Germany's decentralized court system in the borderlands.

Even though published figures differ, the most accepted numbers between 1500 and 1700 seem to be 90,000 witch trials overall with 45,000 executions, or an execution rate of about 50 per cent; William Monter cautions that Levack's numbers should be downgraded even further (Levack 2006: 24; Monter 2002: 13).[12] The truly astonishing fact is that the bulk of witch trials happened in the Germanophone borderlands, clustering in western Germany, Switzerland, and eastern France along the Rhine; to put it in William Monter's words: "Three of every four witches executed in Europe between 1560 and 1660 spoke some dialect of German, while six of every seven lived—and died—within the boundaries of the pre-1648 Holy Roman Empire, a region holding about 20 per cent of Europe's population" (2002: 16). Before 1560, there was no notable witch persecution in the loosely organized empire that contained 300 hundred different entities. Between 1520 and 1560, witch hunts originated in Switzerland and the Low Countries (Monter 2002: 19–20). After 1560, Germany's superhunts at the height of persecutions (1586–1639) can be charged to the three Rhineland archbishop-electors of Trier, Mainz, and Cologne, three Counter-Reformation prelates reigning in areas of "notoriously loose government control" (Monter 2002: 16–7, 22).[13] Although these hunts were sponsored by Catholic bishops, religion is not the primary causal factor, as the largest secular Catholic state in Germany, the duchy of Bavaria, effectively withstood the panics being incited in other German territories and had very low trial numbers (Monter 2002: 29–31).

Most witch trials showed a certain similar anatomy: first, a single arrest led to laddering and accusations of other persons, often on the next higher social tier; second, 80 percent of the involved were older rustic women; third, most hunts started from below; fourth, accusations did not always lead to arrests, and arrests did not always lead to death sentences; fifth, the accused could question their accusers' motives; sixth, if a more centralized authority was involved, first verdicts would often be overturned (Monter 2002: 7). Still, even if things ended badly, most witches were not burned alive. Burning at the stake replaced trial by fire and was initially advocated by Augustine to prevent bodily resurrection (Russell 1972: 149–50; Stark 2003: 204). In France, Germany, Switzerland, and Scotland, they were first strangled and then their corpses burned. In some German or Scandinavian towns, the condemned were drowned or executed by sword and then burned at the stake; English and North American witches were hanged (Levack 2006: 94).[14]

Gender has been a vexing factor in the witch persecutions. Prevalent medieval and early modern clerical misogyny emphasized women's higher propensity for weakness, corruptibility, and therefore higher susceptibility to witchcraft. This gender bias culminated in the *Malleus maleficarum*, whose Latin title coded a witch as female, a prescriptive rather than a descriptive bias (Broedel 2004: 167).[15] Statistics of witch persecutions correspond to this codification. Between 1300 and 1399, 50 percent of defendants were female, 32 percent male; between 1400 and 1499, 66 percent were female, and 24 percent male (Stark 2003: 243).[16] After 1500, 75 percent of the executed were female, except in Normandy, Russia, Estonia, and Iceland, where more men than women were indicted (Levack 2006: 141).[17] Village healers and midwives were often suspected due to their professions,[18] but not all of the women were old hags, as popular opinion as well as Halloween customs and costumes still purport. Lyndal Roper claims that concerns of fertility, sterility, childbirth, and infant mortality were at the root of the witch phenomenon, with many blamed women providing prenatal, birthing, and postpartum care to their accusers (2004: 127–59). Furthermore, women probably appeared more suspicious because they generally outlived men and may have survived the plague better (Russell 1972: 202).

It is difficult to miss the sexual element in the witch persecution in the image of the sexually insatiable witch who has repeated intercourse with the Devil, so prevalent in the witch theorists' manuals; therefore, unmarried or widowed older women who were outspoken about sex might have inspired the "depiction of the old, sexually voracious hag [exacerbating] a deep male fear of the sexually experienced, sexually independent woman" (Levack 2006: 152). A great number of the accused female witches were from the lower economic stratum, probably cantankerous and quarrelsome beggar women and "village scolds," possibly senile or mentally ill, and often accused of "non-attendance at church, Sabbath-breaking, cursing, fornication, prostitution, abortion, and even adultery" (Levack 2006: 160–1).

When the major outbreaks had come to an end, they had come late to some eastern areas and had been surprisingly light in Austria, Hungary, Ireland, New England, Poland, and Transylvania.[19] From 1675 to 1750, witch-hunting slowed to a few individual trials and finally ceased. Scholarly opinions on the reasons for this decline are also varied. All along, contemporary writers had spoken out against the witch hunts—for instance, Johan Weyer in 1563 (*De Praestigiis deamonum*), Reginald Scot in 1584 (*The Discoverie of Witchcraft*), and Friedrich Spee in 1631 (*Cautio criminalis*)—but were not heeded.[20] Brian Levack sums up the main arguments as follows: changes in the legal system, as courts became more regulated, judges more cautious, procedures changed, torture became restricted or prohibited, and new standards for evidence were introduced; modifications of philosophy and worldview in the form of skepticism towards authority, the introduction of mechanical philosophy, and the belief that supernatural occurrences can be explained by natural causes; a waning of religious enthusiasm, an increase in biblical scholarship and the sovereignty of God, who can trump the Devil; and lastly, social factors, such as decriminalization, as witchcraft laws were abolished and courts stopped prosecuting witches for lack of legal proof (2006: 253–81). R. W. Thurston suggests that a revised image of women contributed as well (2001: 158–60). Although the witch hunts ceased, both the sixteenth-century witch stereotype and the erroneous belief in the Middle Ages as the witch "burning times" remain strong in modern times and lore.

SUGGESTIONS FOR FURTHER READING

Primary Sources

Hobbins, D., trans. (2005). *The Trial of Joan of Arc*, Cambridge, MA: Harvard University Press.

Kramer, H., and Sprenger, J. (1971). *The Malleus Maleficarum*. Trans. M. Summers, New York: Dover Publications.

Mckay, C. K. (forthcoming). *Malleus Maleficarum*, Cambridge, UK: Cambridge University Press.

Secondary Sources

Bailey, M. D. (2001). "From Sorcery to Witchcraft: Clerical Conceptions of Magic in the Later Middle Ages," *Speculum*, 76, 960–90.

Barstow, A. L. (1994). *Witchcraze: A New History of the European Witch Hunts*, San Francisco: Pandora/HarperCollins.

Behringer, W. (2004). *Witches and Witch-Hunts: A Global History*, Cambridge, UK: Polity Press.

———. (2005). "How Waldensians Became Witches: Heretics and Their Journey to the Other World," in G. Klaniczay and E. Pocs (eds.), *Communicating with the Spirits: Demons, Spirits, Witches*, Budapest: Central European University Press.

Breslaw, E. G. (2000). "Introduction," in E. G. Breslaw (ed.), *Witches of the Atlantic World: A Historical Reader and Primary Sourcebook*, New York: New York University Press.

Broedel, H. P. (2004). *The Malleus Maleficarum and the Construction of Witchcraft: Theology and Popular Belief*, Manchester, UK: Manchester University Press.

Clark, S. (2002). "Witchcraft and Magic in Early Modern Culture," in B. Ankarloo and S. Clark (eds.), *Witchcraft and Magic in Europe: The Period of the Witch Trials*, Philadelphia: University of Pennsylvania Press.

Durschmied, E. (2005). *Whores of the Devil: Witch-Hunts and Witch-Trials*, Phoenix Mill, UK: Sutton Publishing.

Guiley, R. E. (1989; 2nd ed., 1999). *The Encyclopedia of Witches and Witchcraft*, New York: Facts on File, Inc.

Harris, M. (1974). *Cows, Pigs, Wars and Witches: The Riddles of Culture*, New York: Random House.

Henningsen, G. (1980). *The Witches' Advocate: Basque Witchcraft and the Spanish Inquisition (1609–1614)*, Reno, NV: University of Nevada Press.

Hoyt, C. A. (1981; 2nd ed., 1989). *Witchcraft*, Carbondale: Southern Illinois University Press.

Jolly, K. (2001). "Medieval Magic: Definitions, Beliefs, Practices," in B. Ankarloo and S. Clark (eds.), *Witchcraft and Magic in Europe: The Middle Ages*, Philadelphia: University of Pennsylvania Press.

Kieckhefer, R. (1976). *European Witch Trials: Their Foundations in Popular and Learned Culture, 1300–1500*, Berkeley: University of California Press.

—— (1989). *Magic in the Middle Ages*, Cambridge, UK: Cambridge University Press.

Klaits, J. (1985). *Servants of Satan: The Age of the Witch Hunts*, Bloomington: Indiana University Press.

Kors, A. C., & Peters, E. (eds.) (1972; 2nd ed., 2001). *Witchcraft in Europe, 1100–1700: A Documentary History*, Philadelphia: University of Pennsylvania Press.

Levack, B. P. (1987; 3rd ed., 2006). *The Witch-Hunt in Early Modern Europe*, London: Longman.

Meltzer, M. (1999). *Witches and Witch-Hunts: A History of Persecution*, New York: Blue Sky Press.

Monter, W. E. (2002). "Witch Trials in Continental Europe 1560–1660," in B. Ankarloo and S. Clark (eds.), *Witchcraft and Magic in Europe: The Period of the Witch Trials*, Philadelphia: University of Pennsylvania Press.

Roper, L. (2004). *Witch Craze: Terror and Fantasy in Baroque Germany*, New Haven, CT: Yale University Press.

Russell, J. B. (1972). *Witchcraft in the Middle Ages*, Ithaca, NY: Cornell University Press.

Shlain, L. (1998). *The Alphabet Versus the Goddess: The Conflict between Word and Image*, New York: Viking.

Stark, R. (2003). *For the Glory of God: How Monotheism Led to Reformations, Science, Witch-Hunts, and the End of Slavery*, Princeton, NJ: Princeton University Press.

Stephens, W. (2002). *Demon Lovers: Witchcraft, Sex, and the Crisis of Belief*, Chicago: University of Chicago Press.

Thurston, R. W. (2001). *Witch, Wicce, Mother Goose: The Rise and Fall of the Witch Hunts in Europe and North America*, Harlow, UK: Longman.

Trevor-Roper, H. (1969). "Religion, the Reformation, and Social Change," in W. E. Monter (ed.), *European Witchcraft*, New York: John Wiley.

Willis, D. (1995). *Malevolent Nurture: Witch-Hunting and Maternal Power in Early Modern England*, Ithaca, NY: Cornell University Press.

NOTES

1. *Burning Times* is a term "used by contemporary Witches and Pagans to refer to the period in Western history of intense witch hunting and executions," from the mid-fifteenth to the mid-eighteenth centuries (Guiley 1999: 39).
2. For detailed definitions of these ideas, see Stuart Clark (2002: 97–169).
3. For instance, the trial records of Joan of Arc (1431) show that the judges were trying to implicate Joan as a witch first, even insisting she possessed and used a mandrake, a plant that had started to be associated with witchcraft. Eventually,

Joan was burned as a relapsed heretic, when she dressed herself again in man's clothing and reaffirmed her voices (Hobbins 2005: 127, 196–203).

4. Between 1321 and 1324, Bernard Gui compiled the first inquisitorial manual in his *Practica inquisitionis heretice pravitatis* and tried over a thousand heretics but no sorcerer; this attests to the relative lack of interest in sorcery at that time (Bailey 2001: 968).

5. Russell shows that between 1427 and 1486, the hundred witch trials conducted were still more concerned with sorcery than witchcraft. Also, Scandinavia, southern Italy, and Spain had few Cathars or witches (1972: 244, 126).

6. The witches' sabbat increased in importance at the height of persecutions, around 1580–1590, while one hundred years earlier in the time of the *Malleus* is was hardly known (Monter 2002: 8–9). Wolfgang Behringer continues the debate about the reality of witchcraft by arguing that in specific areas the witches' sabbat may have been rooted in Waldensian spiritual practices (2005).

7. It was believed that all witches had a mark signaling their allegiance to the Devil. This mark was considered the ultimate sign of a witch. People's natural blemishes were often taken for the Devil's mark (Levack 2006: 52). Furthermore, black masses did not exist in the Middle Ages (Breslaw 2000: 1).

8. A factor only recently examined that could be responsible for some of the calamities above is the so-called Little Ice Age that gradually started around 1400 and peaked between 1560 and 1580; because "witchcraft was traditionally associated with weather-making," it was no great leap to blame the climate changes of the Little Ice Age on "poor old women" (Behringer 2004: 87–88).

9. Leonard Shlain posits a connection between the severity of the witch hunts in Germany and the fastest rising literacy rate in Europe being located there (1998: 372).

10. The English had no interest in the *Malleus*; there was no English edition of the *Malleus* and no translation until 1928 (Stark 2003: 274).

11. Here are some illustrative numbers about local self-governments in contrast to appellate courts: "At the opposite extreme from French parlements, which generally rejected village testimony, stood the 550 villages and eleven small towns which today comprise Germany's Saarland. During the half-century after 1580, these virtually autonomous rustics executed 450 per cent more witches than the Parlement of Paris, in a corner of the Empire divided among four principal overlords, two Protestant and two Catholic" (Monter 2002: 9).

12. The grossly exaggerated number of nine million women burned as witches has been perpetuated in scholarly literature despite the fact that Matilda Joslyn Gage, in her 1893 book *Woman, Church and State*, came up with this figure without any historical research or evidence (Stark 2003: 202, 398, n. 7).

13. For further statistics on other prelates, rulers, and areas, see Monter (2002: 16–31).

14. In England, "burning was reserved for wives killing their husbands or servants their masters" (Breslaw 2000: 6).

15. For a more rehabilitating take on the *Malleus*, see Walter Stephens (2002: 32–57).

16. The remaining percentage refers to trials in which defendants of both sexes were accused.

17. Broedel cites an interesting comparison: "In Lucerne, where witches were tried by the secular authorities, over 90 percent of those accused of witchcraft between 1398 and 1551 were women. Judges in this region had a quite rudi-

mentary knowledge of contemporary demonology, and focused principally upon the concerns of the witnesses themselves, especially *maleficium*. In Lausanne, on the other hand, witchcraft prosecution was controlled by the episcopal inquisition, for whom heresy and demonolatry were major concerns, and only 38 percent of those prosecuted were women" (2004: 169–70).

18. Also see Barstow for further explanations on singling out healers and midwives (1994: 109–27).

19. For statistics on Eastern Europe witch hunts, see Levack (2006: 230–7) and Monter (2002: 49–51).

20. An example of civil disobedience can be seen in this incident: "A recently discovered royal pardon issued by King Charles VII of France in 1460 illustrates the case of a local man in southwestern France who killed a 'witch-finder' who had accused the man's female relatives of sorcery and witchcraft" (Kors and Peters 2001: 152).

27 The Medieval Child

An Unknown Phenomenon?

Sophie Oosterwijk

It seems inconceivable that, in a period when the most popular image was that of the Madonna and Child, there was little or no understanding of—or affection for—children in everyday life, yet such is the popular misconception about medieval childhood. One factor that has contributed to this idea is infant and child mortality during the Middle Ages. Of course, mortality rates may well have differed greatly among the different classes of society as well as per period and geographical location, which makes it hazardous to generalize. Nevertheless, there is no doubt that medieval child mortality rates were extremely high compared to those in modern Western society. This has led to a general belief that medieval parents could not bring themselves to become emotionally attached to offspring so likely to die. In turn, it is argued that medieval adults failed to understand or to recognize the nature of childhood, and thus the medieval child was regarded, portrayed, and treated as a miniature adult.

The notion of medieval indifference towards children certainly did not originate with the late French historian Philippe Ariès and his 1960 book *L'enfant et la vie familiale sous l'Ancien Régime*, but it was his theory of childhood as a concept not "discovered" until much later that stirred up a heated debate on the nature of childhood in the past.[1] While most scholars nowadays feel that Ariès's ideas have already received sufficient criticism, some have proposed even more controversial and bleak pictures of child life in the past. Thus, according to one psychohistorian, "The history of childhood is a nightmare from which we have only recently begun to awaken."[2]

One example of the supposedly indifferent attitude of medieval parents towards their children is the chronicle description of Edward I's reaction while on crusade at hearing the news of the deaths of first his son John and then of his father, king Henry III of England.[3] According to the chronicler, Edward grieved far more for his sixty-five-year-old father than for his five-year-old son, and, when asked to explain the reason, he replied that the loss of a child is easier to bear as one may have many more children but that the loss of a father is irremediable. This has often been taken as the typical medieval response to the death of a child; indeed, Edward himself was due to experience such losses all too often, for only six of the (possibly) sixteen children he had by his first wife Eleanor of Castile reached adulthood.[4]

However, what has often been overlooked is the fact that Edward's reaction, instead of being typical, was in fact seen as unusual even if proper and devout; the episode illustrates surprise at his behaviour both on the part of Charles of Anjou, who asked Edward to explain it, and on the part of the chronicler, who considered it significant enough to record. Although it may have been exemplary of Edward to mourn so much more for the death of his aged father (which actually made him the new king) than for his own little son, it seems at the same time to have been considered far from normal. In comparison, Edward's own parents Henry III and Eleanor of Provence are recorded as being overcome with grief at the death of their three-year-old daughter Katherine in 1257, despite the fact that she had not been a healthy child.[5] Over two centuries later, in 1484, Richard III and his wife Anne Neville are likewise described as nearly mad with grief at the death of their only child Edward, Prince of Wales.[6]

The popular misconception about medieval indifference towards children may be partly based on the apparent absence of children from medieval art; at first sight, there seem to be very few images of medieval children other than the almost ubiquitous Christ child. However, upon closer inspection one finds that medieval artists actually showed a predilection for depicting the births of all kinds of biblical and historical figures, from Samuel and St John the Baptist to Julius Caesar and Tristram, to name but a few. Admittedly, these scenes were often chosen because of the miraculous circumstances surrounding the birth or because of the children's subsequent exploits as adults. Nonetheless, other depictions clearly play a more important role as emblems of childhood: for example, the Virgin Mary, whose birth and early childhood are frequently presented in art and literature.

Nor should we dismiss many of these artistic and literary representations as merely depictions of "miniature adults." Although the children are shown larger than life in art, we must remember that realism in a modern sense was not the medieval artist's objective; even so, contemporary audiences could not have failed to understand the message. Similarly, the precocious maturity displayed by these exceptional children in literature and drama was actually quite different from the behaviour expected of children in real life; the 'puer senex' and his female equivalent were popular *topoi* exactly because they were so obviously unnatural. Thus, in the Middle English N-Town play of the Presentation of Mary, when the three-year-old Virgin is not only able to walk up the fifteen steps of the Temple unaided but also talk with exceptional maturity, her astonished father Joachim exclaims: 'Ye answere and [as if] ye were twenty yere olde!'[7]

There is certainly other evidence of interest in children in the Middle Ages. The hugely popular theme of the Ages of Man, in all its variations, included at least one stage dedicated to childhood with its specific characteristics.[8]

Children were known to be weak and dependent but also innocent and playful. In the more extensive versions of the Ages of Man, infants are usually shown as swaddled babies, and toddlers may try out their first steps in a child walker, while older children play with toys or carry schoolbooks. Numerous toys from Antiquity and the Middle Ages have come down to us, both as actual objects preserved through the ages or discovered by archaeologists and as depictions in art or mentioned in documents: toys made of leather, wood, clay, and metal, but also of precious or more perishable materials.[9] Some are still familiar to us today in some form or other, such as rattles, dolls, balls, kites, spinning-tops, hobbyhorses, and whirligigs. Like their modern counterparts, medieval children also enjoyed imitating adult life in their games, and their toys could comprise miniature objects such as toy boats and carts or cups and jugs. It may only have been royal children who were pampered with sophisticated toy castles, swords, and armour, but play was characteristic of all children, whatever their class or means. Gerald of Wales (1146–1226) relates in his autobiography how he as a small boy built churches and monasteries out of sand and dirt while his elder brothers preferred the more traditional, if worldly, sandcastles or palaces; convinced thereby that Gerald was destined for the church, his father decided to give him a proper education and called him his "little bishop."[10] All in all, there are too many examples in medieval art and literature that show an understanding of childhood for it to be possible for us to adhere to the misconception that the medieval child as such did not exist.

High child-mortality rates do not seem to have prevented parents from being fond of their children, however likely they were to lose at least some of them to diseases or accidents. Miracle reports and other types of documents attest to the lengths to which parents were prepared to go to obtain healing, rescue, or salvation for their children, as well as to their grief when their efforts proved futile.[11] The popularity of the theme of the Massacre of the Holy Innocents and its vivid depiction in medieval art and drama also suggest that medieval people viewed child death with anything but indifference.[12] Nor can a supposed lack of tomb effigies for medieval children be used as evidence of parental indifference, as Ariès claimed; although costly burials and monuments were affordable only to the wealthy few, some royal and aristocratic parents seem to have spared no expense in the funerals of their deceased children, who might subsequently be commemorated by costly monuments.[13] However, it must be remembered that such monuments were as much displays of family status as of affection. Countless other bereft parents opted for less tangible means of commemoration, such as masses for their dead children's souls.

So did medieval parents love and understand their children? Obviously, it would be wrong to believe that things then were just the same as they are now in the West. Life was much harsher and children were expected to play a role in working life from an early age, to the best of their abilities, albeit probably under better conditions than those of the industrial child-labour system in the nineteenth century. Survival would have seemed very uncertain for adults and children alike; childbirth could prove fatal for both mothers and babies while infancy itself was quite a hazardous phase with particularly high mortality rates due to infection and disease. Childcare was also different: the practice of swaddling infants is particularly likely to strike horror in modern minds, and depictions of swaddled cocoons have no doubt added to the negative image of medieval childhood. It is all too easy to forget that this custom, which dates back to antiquity and is still practised in parts of the world today, was genuinely thought to benefit newborn babies, whose soft and pliable limbs might otherwise grow crooked. The Kings Lynn mystic Margery Kempe (born ca.1373), herself a mother of some twelve children, was obviously aware that tight swaddling could actually harm infants. While meditating on her role as the Christ child's wet nurse, she actually promised her charge: "Lord, I schal fare fayr with yow; I schal not byndyn yow soor. I pray yow beth not dysplesyd with me."[14]

Nevertheless, some basic facts cannot be ignored. Medieval reality may have been a far cry from our own twentieth-century idea of childhood as a joyous and carefree phase of life—in itself rather a modern Western idealization—but the medieval popularity of the Virgin and Child could only have worked if people recognized its fundamental truth: the bond of affection between mother and child. We must not forget that the lullabies from Mary to her son in Middle English literature are echoes of real-life cradle songs, just as the popular representation in art of the *virgo lactans* was based on the earliest and most natural way of feeding an infant.[15] Child mortality rates may have been high, but that did not stop parents from caring for their children to the best of their abilities and mourning their loss deeply. The medieval image of the child is best understood with an understanding eye. The Middle Ages may have been different, but perhaps not quite so alien, after all.

SUGGESTIONS FOR FURTHER READING

Danièle Alexandre-Bidon and Monique Closson, *L'Enfant à l'ombre des cathédrales*, Lyon: Presses Universitaires de Lyon, 1985.

Philippe Ariès, *L'Enfant et la vie familiale sous l'Ancien Régime*, Paris: Plon, 1960; translated by Robert Baldick as *Centuries of Childhood*, New York: Vintage, 1962.

Klaus Arnold, *Kind und Gesellschaft in Mittelalter und Renaissance: Beiträge und Texte zur Geschichte der Kindheit*, Sammlung Zebra (Bücher für die Ausbildung und Weiterbildung der Erzieher), Reihe B, Band 2, Paderborn, Germany: Schöningh, 1980.

John Boswell, *The Kindness of Strangers: The Abandonment of Children in Western Europe from Late Antiquity to the Renaissance*, New York: Pantheon, 1988.

Sally Crawford, *Childhood in Anglo-Saxon England*, Stroud, UK: Sutton, 1999.

Lloyd deMause, *The History of Childhood: The Evolution of Parent-Child Relationships as a Factor in History*, London: Souvenir, 1980.

Ronald C. Finucane, *The Rescue of the Innocents: Endangered Children in Medieval Miracles*, Basingstoke, UK: Macmillan, 1997.

Barbara Hanawalt, *Growing Up in Medieval London: The Experience of Childhood in History*, New York: Oxford, 1993.

Sylvie Laurent, *Naître au Moyen Âge: de la conception à la naissance: la grossesse et l'Accouchement (XIIe–XVe siècle)*, Paris: Léopard d'Or, 1989.

Didier Lett, *L'Enfant des Miracles: Enfance et Société au Moyen Âge (XIIe–XIIIe siècle)*, Paris: Aubier, 1997.

Cornelia Löhmer, *Die Welt der Kinder im fünfzehnten Jahrhundert*, Weinheim: Deutscher Studien, 1989.

Sophie Oosterwijk, *"Litel Enfaunt that Were but Late Borne": The Image of the Infant in Medieval Culture in North-Western Europe*, Turnhout, Belgium: Brepols, 2007 (forthcoming).

Nicholas Orme, *Medieval Children*, New Haven, CT: Yale University, 2001.

Pierre Riché and Danièle Alexandre-Bidon, *L'Enfance au Moyen Age*, Paris: Seuil, 1994.

Shulamith Shahar, *Childhood in the Middle Ages*, London: Routledge, 1990.

Annemarieke Willemsen, *Kinder Delijt: Middeleeuws Speelgoed in de Nederlanden*, Nijmeegse Kunsthistorische Studies 6, Nijmegen, 1998.

NOTES

1. Already in 1907, Elizabeth Godfrey noted in her book *English Children in the Olden Time* that "because children are so rarely and so briefly mentioned in old chronicles, some have fancied they must have been looked on with indifference." For two perceptive discussions of the work of Ariès, see Anthony Burton, "Looking Forward from Ariès? Pictorial and Material Evidence for the History of Childhood and Family Life," *Continuity and Change*, 4.2, 1989, 203–29, and Adrian Wilson, "The Infancy of the History of Childhood: An Appraisal of Philippe Ariès," *History and Theory*, 19, 1980, 132–53. Even as late as 1994, the exhibition "L'Enfance au Moyen Age" at the Bibliothèque Nationale in Paris was very much a reaction against the ideas of Ariès and his followers.

2. Opening sentence of Lloyd deMause, *Evolution of Childhood*, p. 1, chapter 1 in Lloyd deMause (ed.), *The History of Childhood: The Evolution of Parent-Child Relationships as a Factor in History* (1974) London: Souvenir, 1980. More articles by deMause and other authors can be found in the *Journal of Psychohistory* (previously named the *History of Childhood Quarterly*).

3. William Rishanger, *Chronica et Annales, Regnantibus Henrico Tertio et Edwardo Primo*, Henry Thomas Riley (ed.), Rolls Series 28, London, 1865, 2.78; although the chronicler names the son as Henry, it was actually John who died in 1271 a few months prior to his grandfather Henry III. The episode is quoted as a typical reaction in John Page-Phillips, *Children on Brasses*, London Allen and Unwin, 1970, p. 10.

4. See, for example, John Carmi Parsons, "The Year of Eleanor of Castile's Birth and Her Children by Edward I," *Mediaeval Studies*, 46, 1984, 245–65, and the discussion in his later study *Eleanor of Castile: Queen and Society in Thirteenth-Century England*, Basingstoke, UK: Macmillan, 1994.

5. Henry Richards Luard (ed.), *Matthaei Parisiensis, Monachi Sancti Albani, Chronica Majora*, vol. 2, A.D. 1067 to A.D. 1216, Rolls Series 57 (1872), 1964, v. 632, 643; Matthew Paris describes Katherine as "muta et inutilis," which is usually translated as "deaf and dumb." A more recent explanation is that Katherine may have suffered from a degenerative disease: see Margaret Howell, "The Children of Henry III and Eleanor of Provence," in Peter R.

Coss and Simon D. Lloyd (eds.), *Thirteenth Century England*, vol. 4, proceedings of the Newcastle upon Tyne Conference 1991,Woodbridge, UK: Boydell, 1992, pp. 63–4, and esp. n. 48.

6. Nicholas Pronay and John Cox (eds.), *The Crowland Chronicle Continuations, 1459–1486*, Gloucester: Richard III and Yorkist History Trust, 1986, p. 171.

7. Stephen Spector (ed.), *The N-Town Play: Cotton MS Vespasian D.8*, 2 vols., EETS, s.s. 11 and 12, Oxford: Oxford University, 1991, play 9, l. 43. Mary's age is emphasised throughout the play in stage directions and in the words of Joachim (l. 22) and the High Priest or Episcopus (l. 162, 164–5).

8. For the Ages of Man, see Elizabeth Sears, *The Ages of Man: Medieval Interpretations of the Life Cycle*, Princeton University, 1986; J. A. Burrow, *The Ages of Man: A Study in Medieval Writing and Thought*, Oxford: Clarendon 1988; Michael Goodich, *From Birth to Old Age: The Medieval Life Cycle in Medieval Thought, 1250–1350*, Lanham/London: University Press of America, 1989; Deborah Youngs, *The Life-Cycle in Medieval Europe, c.1300–c.1500*, Manchester Medieval Studies, Manchester, 2006.

9. For medieval toys, see Annemarieke Willemsen, *Kinder Delijt: Middeleeuws Speelgoed in de Nederlanden*, Nijmeegse Kunsthistorische Studies 6, Nijmegen, 1998; also Nicholas Orme, *Medieval Children*, New Haven, CT: Yale University, 2001, chapter 5.

10. Gerald of Wales, or Giraldus Cambrensis, relates this story in his autobiography *De Rebus a se Gestis*; see J. S. Brewer (ed.), *Giraldi Cambrensis Opera*, London, 1861, 1.21. To his regret, Gerald was never to become a bishop.

11. Apart from Barbara Hanawalt's work on medieval coroners' inquests in particular, there is a wealth of interesting material in Ronald C Finucane, *Miracles and Pilgrims: Popular Beliefs in Medieval England*, Guildford: Dent, 1977, and his subsequent book *The Rescue of the Innocents: Endangered Children in Medieval Miracles*, London: Macmillan, 1997; also Elizabeth C. Gordon, "Accidents among Medieval Children as Seen from the Miracles of Six English Saints and Martyrs," *Medical History*, 35, 1991, 145–63.

12. See Sophie Oosterwijk, " 'Long Lullynge Haue I Lorn!': The Massacre of the Innocents in Word and Image," *Medieval English Theatre*, 25, 2003, 3–53.

13. Examples of medieval child effigies are the Limoges slabs of Jean and Blanche of France, infant children of St Louis, formerly at Royaumont and now preserved at Saint-Denis, and the alabaster figures of Edward III's children William of Hatfield at York Minster and Blanche of the Tower and William of Windsor at Westminster Abbey. However, the notions that tombs are signs of affection and that tomb effigies should faithfully portray the deceased are in themselves popular misconceptions. See Sophie Oosterwijk, " 'A Swithe Feire Graue': The Appearance of Children on Medieval Tomb Monuments," in R. Eales and S. Tyas (eds.), *Family and Dynasty in the Middle Ages*, Harlaxton Medieval Studies 9 (1997 Harlaxton Symposium Proceedings), Donington, 2003, pp. 172–92.

14. Barry Windeatt (ed.), *The Book of Margery Kempe* (2000), Cambridge: D. S. Brewer, 2006, chapter 6, ll. 588–9.

15. Of course, many upper-class women are known to have handed their babies over to wet nurses, especially in Italy where there was a huge demand for dependable *balie*, but the church clearly advocated the ideal of mothers suckling their own children. See, for example, Beth A. Williamson, "The Virgin *Lactans* as Second Eve: Image of the *Salvatrix*," *Studies in Iconography*, 19, 1998, 105–38.

28 Were Women Able to Read and Write in the Middle Ages?

Helen Conrad-O'Briain

It is often assumed that the laity in the European Middle Ages was over-whelmingly illiterate and that women, whether lay or religious, were more likely to be illiterate than their male counterparts.[1] Before the rise of state-sponsored, universal primary education in nineteenth-century Europe, North America, and Japan, relatively high levels of illiteracy were likely in the largely agrarian world society.[2] The assumption of higher levels of illiteracy among women, sometimes encouraged by a scholarly misogyny that until recently often ignored or denied female authorship in a period when authorship is one of the few firm indications of literacy, is not, however, borne out by the evidence.

Few things are more difficult to quantify or qualify than literacy. Even in modern society, with its ubiquitous surveys and documentation, it is almost impossible to produce truly accurate figures on the ability to read or, almost more importantly, to establish the level and nature of literacy across a population. One can distinguish, as Parkes did, between a "pragmatic" and a "cultured" literacy in every society and age, but both are broad definitions, made broader by the importance of Latin in the European Middle Ages: "'Pragmatic literacy' may extend from the capacity to recognize, if not sign, one's own name, to the ability to write a formal document in Latin . . . 'cultural literacy' . . . from reading free prose in the vernacular to composing Latin in the classical tradition."[3]

Until the seventeenth century at the earliest, there is not sufficient material for even the most tentative quantitative analysis of either male or female literacy of any sort. Turning to other kinds of information—the composition or translation of texts, manuscript production and ownership, and anecdotal evidence from written sources—a picture emerges that does not conform to the popular view. Women were not overwhelmingly illiterate compared to their male counterparts, or, at many times and places, lay-women were more likely to be literate, and literate to a higher standard, than their fathers, husbands, and brothers. As trade and industry revived, and literacy as well as numeracy became necessary, women of the mercantile and gentry class became literate, particularly in the vernacular, for the same reasons, and often to the same level, that their menfolk did. That they lagged behind them proportionately is possible, even probable, but not necessary. In the ninth century, Eberhard of Friuli left books (including law texts) to his daughters as well as his sons.[4] In the thirteenth century, Beatrijs of Nazareth, a merchant's daughter, had been taught both Latin and calligraphy before entering the convent in her early teens.[5] At the end of the period, in that most literate of trades, printing, there is good evidence for daughters, wives, and widows working beside their menfolk or carrying on their business.

Roman literacy has probably been consistently overestimated.[6] Even allowing for the imperial bureaucracy and the social importance of a rhetorical education, most of the empire's inhabitants were unlikely to have had even basic literacy, let alone the highly developed skills associated with the composition of rhetorical Latin and the ability to read Vergil with appreciation.[7] But while the numbers of fully literate men and women were small, most came from the ruling classes and had a disproportionate effect on the development of Western European culture. Upper-class Roman women were given essentially the same education as their brothers until the time when the sons of ambitious parents would be sent from the grammarian to the rhetorician to begin the training necessary for a public career. There were women celebrated in antiquity as disciples of philosophers, but rhetoricians apparently did not admit female pupils.[8] A course of study with a good grammarian, however, would have produced a high level of literacy and a sound knowledge of composition.[9]

Jerome's circle of learned ladies, the Christian product of that classical tradition, became a model for women's education and literary culture in the early Middle Ages. Deeply religious and intellectually sophisticated, their stance of humility joined with their intellectual persistence is repeated again and again in the coming centuries. Jerome's famous disdain for the *mulierculis* did not extend to them. They were more than his audience; they were his critics. His most extended discussion of education was directed towards the education of a young girl to be the ideal ascetic scholar as earlier Quintilian's was towards training boys to be ideal orators.[10] In the courts of the successor kingdoms, although there might be deep suspicion concerning "Roman education" for young princes, princely women were educated as Roman women of the senatorial classes and regularly praised for their grasp of Latin literary culture—including the intensely practical political skill of rhetoric. Even if this was flattery, the choice of flattery is telling, as is Amalsuitha's determined, if futile, attempt to educate her son in the Roman manner. Amalsuitha understood, as her fellow tribesmen did not, the power implicit in that education. It was not an ornament but a tool.[11] This fashion for learned ladies joined to the example of the circle of Jerome lies behind the culture of the great Merovingian double houses, behind Radegunde, Bertilla, and even the English slave girl become queen, Balthild, as well as Anglo-Saxon nuns both in Britain and on the Continent, and the later intellectual interests and achievements of the Carolingian and Ottonian convents.[12] Thanks to the heroic efforts of the Anglo-Saxon church in the conversion of the Germans on the Continent, we know that it was not remarkable that convents could rely on female grammarians[13] or that men would approach women's houses for the production of high-status manuscripts. Throughout the period, the evidence for laywomen's literary education is greater than that of men. Noble laymen, possibly still affected by Germanic fears for warriors who had experienced the schoolmaster's strap, depended upon their women for primary education and the encouragement of learning. Even at times and places when our evidence shrinks to little less than a whisper, in one of the darkest periods of English intellectual history, a woman encouraged literary culture as Alfred's mother offered her sons a book of poetry to the one who could first learn it.

It must be noted that as the monastic schools lost their intellectual functions to the cathedral schools and then to the universities, the education of women may have suffered, since it was only in a monastic setting that women could have "safely" been educated. Heloise's fate only fed the anxieties of a male-dominated church. It may be an invidious comparison, but whereas the most gifted woman writer of the late tenth century, Hrosvitha, wrote in Latin, her counterpart in the late twelfth, Marie de France, wrote in the vernacular.

Woman authors multiplied from the twelfth century onward with a series of gifted mystical writers in Latin and the vernacular. With Christine de Pisan at the gates of the Renaissance and its "new" learning, came new problems as well as opportunities for women's literacy and education.

SUGGESTIONS FOR FURTHER READING

Alan K. Bowman, *Life and Letters on the Roman Frontier*, London, 1998.

Alison I. Beach, *Women as Scribes*, Cambridge, 2004.

Cassiodorus, *Variae*, S. J. B. Barnish (trans.), *Translated Texts for Historians*, 12, Liverpool University, 1992.

Dhuoda, *A Handbook for William: A Carolingian Woman's Counsel for Her Son*, Carol Neel (trans.), Washington, DC, 1991.

Peter Dronke, *Medieval Latin and the Rise of the European Love Lyric*, 2nd ed., 2 vols., Oxford, 1968.

———. *Women Writers of the Middle Ages*, Cambridge, 1984.

Christine Fell, "Some Implications of the Boniface Correspondence," in *New Readings on Women in Old English Literature*, Helen Damico and Alexandra Hennessey Olsen (eds.), Bloomington, IN: Indiana University, 1990, pp. 29–43.

Joan M. Ferrante, *To the Glory of Her Sex: Women's Roles in the Composition of Medieval Texts*, Bloomington, IN, 1997.

William V. Harris, *Ancient Literacy*, Cambridge, MA, 1991.

Emily A. Hemelrijk, *Matrona Docta: Educated Women in the Roman Elite from Cornelia to Julia Domna*, London, 2004.

Wilhelm Levison, *England and the Continent in the Eighth Century*, Oxford University, 1946.

H. I. A. Marrou, *A History of Education in Antiquity*, George Lamb (trans.), New York, 1964.

Rosamund McKittrick (ed.), *The Uses of Literacy in Early Mediaeval Europe*, Cambridge University, 1991.
———. *The Carolingians and the Written Word*, Cambridge University, 1989.
M. B. Parkes, "The Literacy of the Laity," in *Literature and Western Civilization: The Medieval World*, D. Daiches and A. Thorlby (eds.), London, 1973.
E. K. Rand, *Founders of the Middle Ages*, New York, 1957.
Jane Stevenson, *Women Latin Poets*, Oxford, 2005.
C. H. Talbot (trans and ed.), *The Anglo-Saxon Missionaries in Germany*, New York, 1954.
Suzanne Fonay Wemple, *Women in Frankish Society: Marriage and the Cloister 500–900*, Philadelphia, 1981.
Virginia Woolf, *A Room of One's Own*, New York: Harcourt Brace, 1991.
C. P. Wormald, "The Uses of Literacy in Anglo-Saxon England and Its Neighbours," *Transactions of the Royal Historical Society*, 5th ser. 27, 1977, pp. 95–114.

NOTES

1. An assumption that is apparently shared by Virginia Woolf in her influential essay "A Room of One's Own"; Woolf's apparent ignorance of women writers before the seventeenth century probably represents the interests and prejudices of her milieu as much as those of the academic community.
2. In the early sixteenth century, Thomas More estimated that somewhat less than half the population could read. See Richard Altick, *The English Common Reader* (1957), University of Chicago, 1983; excerpted in David Finkelstein and Alister McCleery, *The Book History Reader*, London: Routledge, 2002, pp. 340–9, at p. 340.
3. M. B. Parkes, "The Literacy of the Laity," *Literature and Western Civilization: The Medieval World*, D. Daiches and A. Thorlby (eds.), London, 1973, p. 555.
4. Rosamund McKittrick, *The Carolingians and the Written Word*, Cambridge University, 1989, pp. 246–7.
5. Jana K. Schulman (ed.), *The Rise of the Medieval World 500–1300*, Westport, CT, 2002, pp. 53–4.
6. William V. Harris, *Ancient Literacy*, Cambridge, MA, 1991.
7. Note, however, the social spread and relatively high level of practical literacy preserved in the Vindolanda tablets: Alan K. Bowman, *Life and Letters on the Roman Frontier*, London, 1998, esp. pp. 82–99.
8. H. I. Marrou, *A History of Education in Antiquity*, George Lamb (trans.), New York, 1964, pp. 282–3.
9. Based on the questions that are treated in the surviving Vergilian commentaries.
10. E. K. Rand, *Founders of the Middle Ages*, New York, 1957, pp. 102–34, esp. pp. 117–8, 130–1.
11. Cassiodorus, *Variae*, S. J. B. Barnish (trans.), *Translated Texts for Historians*, 12, Liverpool University, 1992, pp. 74, 145–50.
12. Suzanne Fonay Wemple, *Women in Frankish Society: Marriage and the Cloister 500–900*, Philadelphia, 1981, pp. 175–88.
13. Rudolph of Fulda, "The Life of St. Leoba," in *The Anglo-Saxon Missionaries in Germany*, C. H. Talbot (trans.), New York, 1954, pp. 207, 211, 215.

29 Teaching Chaucer in Middle English

C. David Benson

How often will Chaucer be read and taught in the future and in what form? Although Geoffrey Chaucer is acknowledged to be one of the three or four greatest poets in our language, there is real danger that his works are falling out of the general literary curriculum. We are turning out English BAs, MAs, and PhDs who have not read a single work in Old or Middle English. For many educated people, English literature now begins no earlier than Shakespeare—and then often skips directly to Jane Austen. This is too bad because there are many who would love Chaucer's poetry, if only that had the opportunity to get to know it. Although the fictional pilgrimage of the *Canterbury Tales* is supposed to have taken place more than 600 years ago, its tales still have the capacity to excite, amuse, challenge, and delight first-time readers.

The first thing I want to say is that Chaucer should be read only in his original Middle English. New students will be baffled at first by his language, but they soon get used to it, the way one becomes quickly accustomed to a person's strongly accented English, however hard to understand at the beginning. If there is only a short time available for Chaucer, then teach only brief selections from his works. The *Canterbury Tales* is well designed for this because it has tales of all different kinds at all different lengths. It is better that students know a little of the real thing than more of a mere imitation. That does not mean that translations cannot be used at all. I often encourage my students to consult one when they begin reading Chaucer. It makes some feel more comfortable to have a trot beside them, but my secret purpose is that comparing the original Chaucer with the modern rendering is the quickest way I know to reveal his literary achievement. As Robert Frost said, poetry is what gets lost in translation. Although modern English versions of Chaucer may not seem all that different from the original (most of the vocabulary is the same, which is why it is not as hard as it first looks), there is one fundamental difference: Chaucer writes great poetry and the modern translators do not, at least until Seamus Heaney decides to tackle his works.

Let me offer a more or less random example from the *Clerk's Tale*. In this passage, an unnamed representative of the people urges their ruler Walter to marry and beget an heir by warning him of the uncertainty of life. Robert Lumiansky, who made what is perhaps the best prose translation of the *Canterbury Tales*, gives this version of the passage:

> And think, lord, in your wisdom, how rapidly our time passes in various ways. For though we sleep or wake or travel or ride, the time always flees; it will wait for no man. And though you are still in the flower of your young manhood, age creeps on steadily, as quiet as a stone, and death menaces every age and strikes in every rank, for no one escapes. As surely as we know that we shall die, so we are uncertain of the day when death shall fall on us. (Lumiansky 201)

As translation this is perfectly acceptable, but the result is flat, hardly much like real speech, and not very engaging.

Verse translations are no better, and sometimes worse, largely because of the demands of the rhyme, as in Nevill Coghill's version of the first part of the passage:

> Invoke
> Your wisdom, ponder carefully and see
> How variously days pass: the seasons flee
> Away in sleeping, waking, roaming, riding.
> Time passes on and there is no abiding. (Coghill 347)

Compare these two translations with Chaucer's original:

> And thenketh, lord, among youre thoughtes wyse
> How that oure dayes passe in sondry wyse,
> For thogh we slepe, or wake, or rome, or ryde,
> Ay fleeth the tyme; it nyl no man abyde.
>
> And thogh youre grene youthe floure as yit,
> In crepeth age alwey, as stille as stoon,
> And deeth manaceth every age, and smyt
> In ech estaat, for ther escapeth noon;
> And al so certein as we knowe echoon
> That we shul deye, as uncerteyn we alle
> Been of that day whan deeth shal on us falle. (*Riverside* IV.116–26)

These lines have a restrained beauty and spiritual resonance without ever losing the sound of a genuine human voice. They are as elegant as they are simple and direct.

Chaucer's comedy is also much more effective in the original language. I must admit that when I teach the *Canterbury Tales*, I often start out with the

Miller's Tale because I assume that its bawdiness (though it contains little real sex) and knockabout farce will grab the students' attention. In contrast, I have found that the *General Prologue* is the hardest thing to teach at the beginning of a course because of all the technical language associated with the different professions.

A wonderful scene from the *Miller's Tale* occurs near the end when the student Nicholas is frolicking the bed with the carpenter's wife, Alisoun. The parish clerk, who hopes to make time with Alisoun himself, arrives outside her window, but while she promises him a kiss, what she actually offers his lips in the dark is her rump. When Nicholas later tries to repeat the trick of Alisoun's mooning of Absolon, however, the parish clerk is now prepared and burns Nicholas's rear with a red-hot piece of metal from a plow. Meanwhile, almost forgotten by the reader, Alisoun's cuckolded husband, the carpenter John, has been sleeping in the rafters of his barn, having been tricked by the adulterous couple to expect a new Noah's flood. Here are Chaucer's lines just after Nicholas has been scorched by the clerk.

> Of gooth the skyn an hande-brede aboute,
> The hoote kultour brende so his toute,
> And for the smert he wende for to dye.
> As he were wood, for wo he gan to crye,
> "Help! Water! Water! Help, for Goddes herte!"
> This carpenter out of his slomber sterte,
> And herde oon crien "water!" as he were wood,
> And thoughte, "Allas, now comth Nowelis flood!"
> He sit hym up withouten wordes mo,
> And with his ax he smoot the corde atwo,
> And doun gooth al; he foond neither to selle,
> Ne breed ne ale, til he can to the celle
> Upon the floor, and ther aswowne he lay. (*Riverside* I.3811–23).

With Nicholas's anguished cry of "water," Chaucer brilliantly brings together the two parts of his simple plot: the flood trick and what is delicately called by folklorists the "misdirected kiss."

Here is Lumiansky's translation of the passage:

> The skin came off a hand's-breadth across, the hot colter had so scorched his buttocks, and Nicholas thought he would die of the pain. Like a mad man, he began to shout, "Help, water! Water, help, for God's sake!" The carpenter started out of his sleep and heard someone madly shouting, "Water!" He thought, "Alas, here comes Nowell's flood!" He sat up at once and cut the cords in two with his ax. Down went everything, without a stop on the way, until it hit the floor, and there the carpenter lay unconscious" (Lumiansky 73).

Not bad, but "hand's-breadth across" is hardly modern English, "buttocks" is nowhere near as good as the expressive dialect word "toute," and Lumiansky doesn't even attempt to render Chaucer's joke that the carpenter fell so quickly that he had no time to sell bread or ale on the way down. The wit of Chaucer's rhyming couplets is completely missing in Lumiansky's prose, of course, but when another translator tries to rhyme, the result is even lamer: "Off flew the skin, a good hand-breadth of fat, lay bare the iron so scorches him where he set."

Chaucer's poetry is so much better when it is taught in its original language, and that language is not that difficult. In fact, Chaucer is probably not much harder for modern students to read than Hawthorne or Melville—and much funnier. Although Chaucer lived two hundred years earlier than Shakespeare, his direct, often physical, comedy is much more accessible to the average reader today than, for example, the complex verbal humor of a Falstaff. The *Miller's Tale* has the ability to make students laugh out loud even when they are reading Middle English for the first time. No previous preparation or knowledge of another language helps much with Middle English, so all students start at approximately the same level. They get much of the excitement and pride of learning a foreign language with a small fraction of the effort. And students know a lot more about Middle English than they think they do (Chaucer's language looks stranger that it really is), but they need a teacher to become confident with it. Few are going to pick up Chaucer and start reading him alone. Those of us who teacher Chaucer have the privilege of being able to introduce students to one of the greatest and most entertaining writers ever.

As they start reading Chaucer's poetry, students will be delighted by two of his "failures." First, they will soon realize that, whatever their own problems with spelling, they are nothing compared to the poet's or to those of most other Middle English writers and scribes, who were capable of using two different spellings for the same word in a single line. As Ben Jonson is supposed to have later said, "It's a dull man who can spell a word only one way." The other thing that amuses students is realizing that Chaucer would have flunked freshman English. He changes tenses, his pronoun references are unsteady, and he is careless about subject/verb agreement, as in these lines describing the Reeve in the *General Prologue*: "His lordes sheep, his neet, his dayerye, / His swyn, his hors, his stoor, and his pultrye / *Was* hoolly in this Reves governynge" (*Riverside* I.598–99). He also uses double, even triple negatives: of the Friar he says ironically, "Ther nas no man nowher so vertuous" (*Riverside* I.251).

In order to get the full flavor of Chaucer's poetry, it must be read out loud. I think this may be what stops many people from teaching his works. They are unsure of their ability to pronounce his language and want to avoid looking foolish. But such fears can and should be overcome. It's nice to be accurate in pronunciation but not if seeking perfection prevents one from reading at all. In fact, scholars do not agree among themselves on all

244 C. David Benson

the rules of pronouncing Chaucer, so why should anyone else be fussy? A few simple rules are enough to get students going. The two most important are (1) vowels should be given their Continental values (for example, "i" is like our "e"), and (2) everything should be sounded (the initial "g" in "gnaw" and the "l" in "folk"). Because of this second rule, some familiar words become wonderfully exotic in Middle English, for instance, "knight." Although some scholars say the "k' was no longer pronounced in Chaucer's day, I will never believe it—it would take away half the fun of the word "knight"; the other half is the juicy sound of "gh." If some students go on to the finer points of Middle English pronunciation (recognizing, for instance, that certain "o's" as in "love" are actually sounded as "u's"), that is all the better, but the main thing is to find a fairly accurate, fairly consistent way of reading that lets the poetry be heard. Recordings of others reading Chaucer aloud, which are widely available, can help because Middle English is more of an English dialect than a foreign language, and many students will quickly be able to imitate the sounds they hear. On the Internet, the Chaucer metapage[1] contains links to many relevant sites, including the excellent pronunciation lessons (as well as much else) available on Larry Benson's Harvard page.[2] The embarrassment that students feel when first reading Chaucer aloud can actually be a benefit. These inevitable mistakes often produce mutual entertainment if not taken too seriously. If students are asked to read in turn a couple lines each, especially from a comic tale, they will be giggling at themselves and at the tale in no time.

Memorization is crucial to get a firm grip on Chaucer's verse. When my father-in-law was seventy-five he was proud that he could still recite the first eighteen lines of the *General Prologue*, which he had learned fifty years before in college. In fact, once when he was in a hospital's intensive care unit and the doctors were trying to assess his mental condition, he began to recite Chaucer's lines to prove that he still had all his faculties. Unfortunately the doctors were not as well educated and he was, and hearing these strange words, they were convinced he had indeed gone off his rocker. In all other circumstances, however, how could one hear those first eighteen lines and not want to hear more?

> Whan that Aprill with his shoures soote
> The droghte of March hath perced to the roote,
> And bathed every veyne in swich licour
> Of which vertu engendred is the flour;
> Whan Zephirus eek with his sweete breeth
> Inspired hath in every holt and heeth
> The tendre croppes, and the yonge sonne
> Hath in the Ram his half cours yronne,
> And smale foweles maken melodye,
> That slepen al the nyght with open ye
> (So Priketh hem Nature in hir corages),

Thanne longen folk to goon on pilgrimages,
And palmeres for to seken straunge strondes,
To ferne halwes, kowthe in sondry londes;
And specially from every shires ende
Of Engelond to Caunterbury they wende,
The hooly blisful martir for to seke,
That hem hath holpen whan that they were seeke. (*Riverside* I.1–18)

Modern English verse has trouble duplicating Middle English's mixture of strength and sweetness that is so well exploited here. As a poet friend of mine said about the line, "And palmeres for to seken straunge strondes"— "O Chaucer, with all those beautiful vowels."

Reading Chaucer aloud is not only fun, but it also reveals much that is hidden in silent reading. Chaucer was part of an oral verse tradition and probably read his poems publicly. Speech is central to his literary achievement: he is a master of dialogue, as we can see in the witty interchanges in the tales of the Miller and Shipman, as well as in more formal speeches in the tales of the Knight and the Clerk. The magnificent *Prologue* to the *Wife of Bath's Tale* is one long soliloquy in the Wife's distinctive and powerful voice, and Chaucer uses fragments of the pilgrims' own voices in the *General Prologue*, as is especially evident in the portraits of the Monk and Friar.

Chaucer exploits the sound of his lines in other ways. In the *Merchant's Tale*, for instance, the knight January's young wife May receives a love letter from the squire Damian. Given that January is such a nasty old lecher, the reader is probably disposed to be sympathetic with May's desire for a lover, but not after the way Chaucer describes her response to Damian's letter. He describes her going into what used to be called the "littlest room" to read the missive (not the most romantic setting), and when she has finished, he says: "She rente it al to cloutes atte laste,/ And in the pryvee softely it caste" (*Riverside* IV.1954). The most brilliant stroke of these lines, which only becomes fully apparent when they are read aloud, is the appearance of the usually lovely word "softely," which, in this context, has the paradoxical effect of damning May's sordid affair.

Reading aloud is also necessary to get the full effect of Chaucerian comedy. Near the end of the *Nun's Priest's Tale*, there is a wonderful Mack Sennett chase in which the widow, her daughter, and every kind of farm animals (including bees) madly chase the fox, which has snatched away their rooster Chauntecleer. As with so much else in this mock epic, the chase is built up by extravagant rhetoric only to result in crashing anticlimax (the pursuers race dramatically before our eyes and out of the picture without being mentioned again), but the description itself is a wonderful piece of spoken verse:

This sely wydwe and eek hir doghtres two
Herden thise hennes crie and maken wo,
And out at dores stirten they anon,

And syen the fox toward the grove gon,
And bar upon his bak the cok away,
And cryden, "Out! Harrow and weylaway!
Ha, ha! The fox!" and after hym they ran.
And eek with staves many another man.
Ran Colle oure dogge, and Talbot and Gerland,
And Malkyn, with a dystaf in hir hand:
Ran cow and calf, and eek the verray hogges,
So fered for the berkyng of the dogges
And shoutyng of the men and wommen eeke
They ronne so hem thoughte hir herte breeke.
They yolleden as feednes doon in helle;
The dokes cryden as men wolde hem quelle;
The gees for feere flowen over the trees;
Out of the hyve cam the swarm of bees.
So hydous was the noyse—a, benedicitee!—
Certes, he Jakke Straw and his meynee
Ne made nevere shoutes half so shrille
Whan they wolden any Flemyng kille,
As thilke day was maad upon the fox.
Of bras they brighten bemes, and of box,
Of horn, of boon, in whiche they blewe and powped,
And therwithal they skriked and they howped.
It semed as that hevene sholde falle. (*Riverside* VII.3375–3401)

To be sure that my students actually know Chaucer in Middle English, I give them weekly quizzes, asking them to translate and identify short passages. If teachers did nothing more than make students read closely the tales assigned (regardless of their critical understanding), we would be doing a great deal. One of the problems with education these days is that many students are such poor readers of modern English. They will often glance at a text, notice a word or two that looks familiar, and decide what the story is about without comprehending it in detail. Because Chaucer writes in an unfamiliar dialect, he cannot be read so casually. Some words will be completely new and others will have new meanings. The very difficulty that students have with Middle English can be a benefit in forcing them to read with special care.

Whether one is reading Chaucer for the first or the fifteenth time, there is nothing more important than reading the text carefully with attention to the connotations of Chaucer's words. For example, in the *Miller's Tale* the young amorous student Nicholas is repeatedly referred to as "hende." Glossaries will tell you that this means "gracious" or "courteous," and so it does. But, as others have noted (see, especially, Beichner), that is not all. "Hende" is a word common in popular English romance (those energetic poems that made up so much of native literature before Chaucer) and was commonly used to praise the hero. "Hende" appeared so often that it became a general, nonspecific words of romance commendation, meaning nothing more than, say, "nice." Chaucer's calling Nicholas "hende," then, is another example of chivalric terms being comically applied to an academic. But there is still more, for "hende" is the ancestor of our word "handy," which of course means both "skillful" ("good with one's hands") and "nearby" ("at hand"). In the plot of the *Miller's Tale*, Nicholas literally fulfills both meanings: he shows he is "hende" (good with his hands) in his initial wooing (or rather mauling) of Alisoun, which is courtly in form but not in fact, and he is also "hende" (at hand), when he is at the right (or wrong) place to receive the hot colter and get his "toute" burned at the end of the tale.

Understanding Middle English is necessary to recognize the full extent of Chaucer's achievement. Even translations can make clear the variety of genres in the *Canterbury Tales:* for instance, the sharp contrast between comic fabliau and religious tale, as when the cold, calculating *Shipman's Tale*, in which a wife sells her sexual favors to both a family friend and her own husband, is followed by the warm, sentimental *Prioress's Tale*, in which a little boy unjustly killed is saved by his devotion to the Virgin Mary. But only careful reading of the original Middle English allows us to appreciate more subtle stylistic differences between tales of the very same genre, the high-spirited *Miller's Tale* compared to the dark, bitter *Reeve's Tale*, for example, or even differences within a single tale, as in the mixture of beauty and disgust in the *Merchant's Tale* or the Pardoner's ranting, demagogic sermon on the three sins in contrast to his calm, haunting *exemplum* of the three revelers, which may be the simplest and most powerful piece of spiritual narrative that Chaucer ever wrote.

Chaucer is fun to declaim aloud, and he can help students learn how to read a literary text closely, but the main reason why we ought to continue and expand to teach him in his original language is because of his excellence as a poet. He occupies a special place in English literature, being both medieval and modern: both a conduit into a distant time and an accessible contemporary. As a medieval poet (indeed, the father of English poetry, as he was often called in the Renaissance and after), he can give students a sense of the past that so many now lack; at the same time, his comic, multilayered, open poetry often seems amazingly modern, or postmodern, strikingly like the ideas of recent literary theory.

In a sense, Chaucer's poetry is so old that it is new. Although his work has important philosophical differences with modern literary theory, both are united against the realistic assumptions that dominated literature in the eighteenth and nineteenth centuries. For instance, Chaucer shares with much postmodern theory an irrepressible playfulness and insistence on the multiplicity of meaning. He is undoubtedly the least solemn of the major English poets, a quality that brought down upon him Matthew Arnold's famous judgment that he lacked "high seriousness" (101). We should not scorn Arnold; although he seems not to have actually read all that much

Chaucer, he is absolutely right: Chaucer often does lack high seriousness, as in his representation of himself as an ignorant fool throughout the *Canterbury Tales*, or when he blithely violates the proprieties of fiction by allowing an allegorical character in one story, Justinus in the *Merchant's Tale*, to refer to a pilgrim who has just spoken—the Wife of Bath—as if he (Justinus) had been present on the pilgrimage to hear her tale.

Multiplicity of meaning also links Chaucer and modern theory. Nothing offended Roland Barthes more than the claim that a text has one clear, literal meaning: in the words of one commentator, "he supports whatever is plural or discontinuous" (Sturrock 53). The father of deconstruction, Jacques Derrida, questioned not only unity of meaning but also binary oppositions like written/spoken and man/woman so natural to traditional thought and central even to structuralism. Derrida goes beyond complexity and ambiguity to argue for an endless production of meaning that can never be completely controlled. The *Canterbury Tales* seems to anticipate this modern desire for promiscuous plurality. We are not even sure of the sequence in which the tales ought to be read because manuscripts and scholarly ingenuity have given us a number of different tale-telling sequences, none of which is truly reliable.

The varying order of the tales in various manuscripts may be the result of Chaucer's early death, but it also reflects something essential about the work as a whole. In contrast to the careful hierarchies and logical order of many medieval narratives, the variety of tellers and genres in the *Canterbury Tales* is protean and without clear pattern. For example, the opening *Knight's Tale*, a philosophical romance about ancient heroes, could not be more of a contrast to the following tale of the Miller, a bawdy comedy of contemporary life in Oxford (there is also a conflict in class between the two pilgrims). But in addition, the *Knight's Tale* has associations with other romances in the *Tales* (especially the very different one told by the Knight's son), as well as with those tales also set in pagan times and with the long religious as opposed to knightly romance told by the Man of Law, which it may have displaced as the first tale in the collection. In the *General Prologue*, Chaucer apologizes for not presenting the pilgrims in their proper hierarchical "degree" (*Riverside* I.744), and, before the *Miller's Tale*, his narrator says that anyone who might be offended by such a churl's tale should "turne over the leef" and choose another (*Riverside* I.3177), thus inviting every reader to create his own individual anthology from the collection. The result is something very much like the plurality of meaning urged by modern theorists. Not just many meanings, but potentially infinite, even contradictory, meanings.

Among the most dramatic claims of literary theory, articulated by range of critics from very different schools, are arguments for the death of the author and a corresponding birth of the reader. Barthes and Michel Foucault especially urge us to ignore authorial intent, which is only accidentally the source of meaning, and look instead at texts themselves. Although this dismissal of the author was meant to irritate traditionalists (and often has), it will not really upset Chaucerians, who are familiar with their poet's consistent effort to minimize his own importance in his work and erase himself. In the early works, he presents himself as dull little man whose material comes entirely from outside sources like dreams, and in his two greatest works, he claims to be only an unimaginative, word-for-word recorder of others: of a certain Lollius in *Troilus and Criseyde* and of the pilgrim-tellers on the *Canterbury Tales*. We might say that if Chaucer does not exactly demonstrate the death of the author, he does present us with his slyly comic attempts at suicide.

In place of the author, modern theorists privilege the reader. Barthes extols "writerly" texts, which demand the participation of readers, over merely "readerly" ones, which are to be received passively, and many in the last generation have examined the role of the reader and the poetics of reception. The idea that readers rewrite a text each time they engage with it seemed shocking not too long ago to many, for it seemed to attack the dignity of authors and their difference from interpreters. It would not, however, have shocked W. H. Auden, who declared in his elegy for Yeats that the words of this dead man "are modified in the guts of the living" (53), and it would not have shocked Chaucer. Indeed, Chaucer *demands* that the reader rewrite the text. Before the *Miller's Tale*, as we have seen, he invites readers to make their own personal selections, and throughout the *Canterbury Tales* leaves to us to decide how to respond to these various narratives. Chaucer offers us no authoritative interpretation, either in his own person or in that of another character. When the pilgrim Chaucer appears to tell a tale, the tale of Sir Thopas, it is such a splendidly wretched performance that the Host stops it, dismissing it as no more than "rym dogerel" (*Riverside* VII.925). England's greatest poet is then reduced to telling a long prose translation, the *Melibee*. Yet the Host, despite his pretensions, is no sure authority either: although he often offers his opinion of individual tales, he is invariably misguided in his views (as in not recognizing the brilliance of the spoof in *Sir Thopas*), though often in provocative ways. We, the readers, are left to understand the tales as we will and are required to become something like Chaucer's collaborator.

Of course the similarities I have suggested between Chaucer and recent theorists collapse if pushed too far; they are suggestive rather than definitive. Although they may be unknowing allies of a sort, there remain two crucial differences between the practices of postmodern thought and Chaucer: first, he knows what he is doing, and, second, he is a Christian. Whereas theorists take delight in exposing the indeterminacy and multiplicity of texts that they believed are unacknowledged by their authors, Chaucer himself calls attention to such instability. Moreover, Chaucer represents the philosophical position most dreaded by Barthes and others: he is an essentialist. He believes in something. Far different from the deconstructionist, Chaucer's playfulness seem to derive directly from his faith. He recognizes an ultimate truth and it sets him free.

For even if Chaucer still speaks to us today, he is not a modern man and we should not try to make him one. There are limits to his variety and flexibility. In the swinging sixties, a popular word, along with "groovy," "meaningful," "fab," and "far out," was "relevant." To be meaningful, not to say groovy, a book or idea was supposed to be relevant, though it was not always clear relevant to what. Yet one of the most important reasons for reading older literature is precisely because it is not directly relevant to our time but instead offers a fundamentally different view of the world, such as chivalric values of the Knight and Squire and the pervasiveness of religion in everyday life. The current critical terms for this cultural difference are alternity and otherness. The alternity or otherness of a medieval work can be as exciting and revolutionary as the latest literary theory. In the modern world it becomes harder and harder to find truly independent cultures—coke and blue jeans are everywhere—and therefore the otherness of the medieval world is especially valuable. In many ways, Chaucer is more foreign to us than any current Third World culture. But because he is such an appealing poet, Chaucer offers an easy road back to the past, a sense of which our students so desperately need.

Because the otherness of Chaucer is one of his most important qualities, we must be careful not to apply modern ideas of psychology too crudely to his characters and thus reduce Griselda in the *Clerk's Tale* only to a neurotic masochist or the Prioress only to a frustrated bigot. We must attempt to read Chaucer in the context of his own complex culture, resisting the temptation to settle for easy irony or simple morality. Understanding the *Canterbury Tales* demands learning and judgment and, hardest of all, resisting the assumption that Chaucer must finally agree with the enlightened thought of the present day. This ideological appropriation of Chaucer is the ultimate arrogance, the presumption that we are bestowing an honor on Chaucer by claiming him as one of us.

Of course this does not mean that Chaucer cannot sometimes speak to modern concerns even when he is being most medieval. For instance, Chaucer's religious tales are beginning to be interpreted as more complex than recently thought, especially in their portrayals of their women heroines. It would be anachronistic to call Chaucer a feminist in the modern sense of the term, but his religious tales do call into question secular political power, usually exercised by men, as opposed to the spiritual power of women. It might be said that males in such tales are seen as good only when, like Alla in the *Man of Law's Tale* or Valerian in the *Second Nun's Tale*, they renounce their male privilege and imitate their wives in humbly following the Lord.

The *Parson's Tale* may offer an insight into Chaucer's unique mixture of medieval and modern. This long penitential tract, which is found at the end of most Canterbury manuscripts, explains the sacrament of penance and then analyzes in detail the seven deadly sins and their remedies. Some critics have questioned whether the *Parson's Tale* really belongs with the *Canterbury Tales* and wondered if it might have been included by the scribes only after the poet's death. Other moralistic critics, in contrast, take the *Parson's Tale* to be the thematic center of the tales—the straightforward doctrine that is only implied in the previous tales. I suggest a third approach. The *Parson's Tale* is the only Canterbury Tale that does not provide an actual narrative. Instead, it is a work that demands that the readers make up their own stories or rather discover their own stories. As a penitential manual, the *Parson's Tale*'s accounts of the various sins is to be used by an individual reader to examine his or her life and conscience and then tell in confession what is discovered there. The result is not fiction at all but rather readers' personal narratives of their moral states in order to bring about their salvation. If this good result is achieved, it is only partially due to the Parson or Chaucer; the *Parson's Tale* is the ultimate "writerly" text, to use Barthes's term, for readers employ its materials to find the story written in their own souls. The *Parson's Tale* is a text that can produce an infinite number of other texts, as many texts as there are readers.

The *Parson's Tale* suggests that the lessons of the *Canterbury Tales* are neither exclusively medieval nor modern. On the one hand, Chaucer does not set out to indoctrinate his audience with conventional Christian lessons, as some have suggested; instead, he wants to give us the experience of real moral thought. He does not tell us what to think so much as he shows us how to think. Chaucer's controlled openness of meaning is announced at the end of Chaucer's most brilliant tale, the mock-heroic *Nun's Priest's Tale*. After the wonderful account of the adventures of that overeducated rooster Chaunticleer and his temporary snatching away by Daun Russell, the fox, Chaucer concludes:

> But ye that holden this tale a folye,
> As of a fox, or of a cok and hen,
> Taketh the moralite, goode men.
> For Seint Paul seith that al that writen is,
> To oure doctrine it is ywrite, ywis;
> Taketh the fruyt, and lat the chaf be stille.
> Now, goode God, if that it be thy wille,
> As seith my lord, so make us alle goode men,
> And brynge us to his heighe blisse! Amen. (*Riverside* VII.3438–46)

I suggest that these lines tell us exactly how Chaucer expected all his poetry to be read and taught. His job as a poet is not to instruct, but to entertain, so that we might be instructed by ourselves. He will excite our interest and involve us in his stories, but whatever we finally learn must come from our own efforts—and the grace of God. Medieval historians from the time of Bede take the same position when they advise their readers to imitate the good in the events to be narrated and to avoid the bad. Of course in these histories, as in the *Canterbury Tales,* it remains for the reader to determine for himself what is, in fact, good and bad. On this same principle, Chaucer is able to include ribald tales such as the Miller's and Reeve's in the *Canterbury Tales*. He does so not because he is advocating the nasty behavior of these stories but because he trusts his readers to separate good from bad, in the way that is most useful for each reader. He believes we can learn from folly without being converted by it.

An undergraduate student of mine once made a telling comparison between Dante and Chaucer. Most of Dante's characters, he pointed out, are fixed for all time, they have received their punishment or their reward (or their promise of reward), and so we can make final judgments about them. Pablo and Francesca are in the circle of the lustful and Ugolino and Ruggerio in the circle of the treacherous. Chaucer is different: the characters in the *Canterbury Tales* are not fixed or clearly judged, he said, but still on the road to unknown destinations. Although Chaucer is a man of his time, a medieval Christian poet, it is the open-endedness of the *Tales* within this tradition that is Chaucer's great achievement and why it is so important that he be read and taught in the years to come.

CITATIONS

All citations from Chaucer are from *The Riverside Chaucer*, Larry D. Benson et al. (eds.), 3rd ed., Boston: Houghton Mifflin, 1987.

Matthew Arnold, "From the 'Study of Poetry,'" *Geoffrey Chaucer: A Critical Anthology*, J. A. Burrow (ed.), Harmondsworth, UK: Penguin, 1969, pp. 96–101.

W. H. Auden, "In Memory of W. B. Yeats," *Selected Poetry of W. H. Auden*, 2nd ed., New York: Vintage, 1971, pp. 52–4.

Roland Barthes, *S/Z*, Richard Miller (trans.), New York: Hill and Wang, 1974.

Paul E. Beichner, "Characterization in *The Miller's Tale*," in Richard J. Schoeck and Jerome Taylor (eds.), *Chaucer Criticism: The Canterbury Tales*, Notre Dame, IN: University of Notre Dame, 1960, pp. 117–29.

Nevill Coghill (trans.), *Chaucer: The Canterbury Tales*, Baltimore: Penguin Books, 1952.

R. M. Lumiansky (trans.), *The Canterbury Tales of Geoffrey Chaucer* (1948), New York: Washington Square, 1972.

John Sturrock, "Roland Barthes," in John Sturrock (ed.), *Structuralism and Since*, Oxford: Oxford University, 1979, pp. 52–80.

SUGGESTIONS FOR FURTHER READING

C. David Benson, *Chaucer's Drama of Style: Poetic Variety and Contrast in the* Canterbury Tales, Chapel Hill: University of North Carolina, 1986.

Betsy Bowden, *Chaucer Aloud: The Varieties of Textual Interpretation*, Philadelphia: University of Pennsylvania, 1987. [On reading Chaucer aloud]

Helen Cooper, *Oxford Guides to Chaucer: The Canterbury Tales*, 2nd ed., Oxford: Oxford University, 1996. [Surveys of criticism on all tales, with sections on style]

Charles Muscatine, *Chaucer and the French Tradition: A Study in Style and Meaning*, Berkeley, University of California, 1957. [The classic study of Chaucerian stylistics]

Derek Pearsall, *The Canterbury Tales* (1985), London: Routledge, 1993. [Excellent close readings of individual tales]

NOTES

1. Available at http://www.unc.edu/depts/chaucer/.
2. Available at http://www.courses.fas.harvard.edu/~chaucer/.

30 The Medieval Chastity Belt Unbuckled

Linda Migl Keyser

For many, the image of the adventurous, medieval knight bravely riding off on quest or crusade simultaneously evokes an image of the devoted lady-wife watching from the ramparts, safely buckled up in her chastity belt. Modern historians, however, dispute the popular misconception that the chastity belt or girdle, a device designed to prevent women from engaging in sexual intercourse, is a medieval invention. In fact, in 1996, the British Museum in London removed a purportedly medieval chastity belt from exhibition where it had been on view since 1846. A spokesman for the museum noted, "The majority of existing examples [of chastity belts] were made in the nineteenth century as curiosities for the prurient or jokes for the tasteless."[1] One by one, many extant belts have been reappraised, branded fakes, and retired from display; two belts, for instance, have been relabeled as medieval dog collars.

The symbolic representation of chastity does exist in western Europe in the Middle Ages, as it does in many cultures. In fact, the cincture or girdle medieval clerics wore over their robes signified the vow of chastity they took upon entering religious orders.[2] The identification of actual chastity belts with the medieval period, however, remains a controversial subject, resting primarily on the early twentieth-century scholarship of physician-anthropologist Eric John Dingwall. In *The Girdle of Chastity*, Dingwall argues that belts devised to prevent women from engaging in sexual relations existed in Europe as early as the twelfth century, though he bases his conclusions solely on the image of a belt in Marie de France's lay *Guigemar*.[3] Specifically, Guigemar's love ties a knot in his shirt; the knight, in turn, secures a "ceinture" or belt around the bare flesh of his lady's hips. The couple give each other leave to love any person who can undo the knot in the shirt or the buckle of the belt without cutting or tearing the items, both secure in the knowledge that this is impossible for anyone but themselves (ll. 543–76).[4] Dingwall contends that the belt in this scene is "suggestive of a girdle of chastity" and, further, argues that this literary reference confirms the theory that chastity belts were introduced into Europe during the time of the Crusades.[5]

Reading Guigemar's belt as a girdle of chastity, however, introduces serious inconsistencies into Marie's narrative design that must be addressed. For example, the lady's jealous old husband attempts to ensure his wife's conjugal fidelity by locking her, first, in a secure enclosure guarded by an impotent old priest and, later, in a marble tower (ll. 209–58 and 655–9). The husband's extensive efforts to sexually "lock up" his wife make it virtually incongruous that he would not avail himself of a device designed to do just that. Marie's lay, in fact, highlights the ultimate futility of securing sexual loyalty without having first secured the consenting heart of the true lover. Subsequent events in the poem reveal that rather than precluding sexual relations, the lovers' "knots" serve both as symbols of their mutual vows of fidelity and as a means of identification when they are reunited after months of separation. The lady unknots the knight's shirt; but Guigemar "couldn't bring himself to believe firmly it was she" until "he put his hands on her hips, / and found the belt" (ll. 814 and 820–1).[6]

Dingwall's argument, that Marie's belt in *Guigemar* provides evidence for the use of chastity belts in medieval society, also suffers from the fact that no other medieval writers refer to such devices, including the prolific and often sexually explicit Chaucer. It is worth noting that in *The Girdle of Chastity*, Dingwall does mention an equivocal reference in the early fourteenth century by French poet Guillaume de Machaut. In Machaut's *Le Livre dou Voir Dit*, a noblewoman about to be separated from her lover gives him a small golden key to assure him of her future faithfulness. She informs him that it is "la clef de mon tresor . . . cest monneur cest ma richesse" ("the key to my treasure . . . it's my honor, my riches," ll. 4244, 4248).[7] As in *Guigemar*, the lover responds by giving his lady a token of his own fidelity, a ring from his finger. From the gift of the key, Dingwall and some critics extrapolate a veiled allusion to an actual girdle of chastity that protects the lady's "richesse." The allegorical nature of the poem's discourse, however, forces Dingwall to acknowledge that many critics refute a literal interpretation of Machaut's language; he guardedly admits, "the evidence is not wholly conclusive in either direction."[8]

In fact, the earliest conclusive evidence documenting that some form of chastity belt existed in Europe appears in Conrad Kyeser of Eichstätt's encyclopedia of warfare and military equipment, *Bellifortis* (ca. 1405). Held in the library of Göttingen University, the fifteenth-century manuscript contains an illustration of a metal belt capable of preventing sexual relations. The caption accompanying the picture reads: "Est florentinarum hoc bracile dominarum ferreum et durum ab antea sic reseratum" ("This is the girdle of Florentine ladies, iron and hard, that is closed from the front.").[9] It is suggested that the women of Florence wore this device to protect themselves from being raped by the soldiers of invading armies. Rather than men forcing the belts onto women's bodies, women wore the belts to prevent their bodies from being forced by men.

While the image of Kyeser's metal belt confirms the arrival of chastity devices in Western society, it also raises significant questions about their function and use. Generally, the technical design of a chastity belt or girdle, past or present, "consists of a jointed metal part that passes between the legs and hooks both to the back and to the front of a padded hip band. The jointed metal plates are furnished with openings, one over the urethra and one over the anus, which allow urination and evacuation but are not large enough to allow the insertion of a finger."[10]

Additional research is still required, however, to determine how widely accepted chastity belts were by members of society at any given time, as well as what risks they posed to the hygiene and health of the women who wore them. Were the belts primarily a means of ensuring sexual fidelity imposed by men on women, a form of erotica, a torture device, an abusive sexual implement, or a self-chosen protective shield? While visiting Austria in 1889, researcher A. M. Pachinger reports recovering one of the oldest surviving belts from a female skeleton probably interred early in the seventeenth century.[11] The young woman was buried while wearing a metal belt that passed between her thighs. The rest of her story is unknown.

The increasingly numerous and detailed references to chastity belts in the literature of the early-modern period offer some degree of insight into their social role. In the sixteenth century, for instance, François Rabelais writes of the ribald and rascally Panurge in *Pantagruel*. Fearful of being cuckolded if he marries, Panurge swears that he will buckle up his would-be wife "à la Bergamasque" whenever he leaves home, an allusion to the legendary association of the belts with the northern Italian city of Bergamo.[12] His companion, the philosopher Trouillogan, responds to the outburst by admonishing Panurge to mend his speech. Also, in the erotic and sexually scandalous history of *Les Dames Galantes* (*Lives of Fair and Gallant Ladies*), Pierre de Bourdeille, Abbé de Brantôme (1556–1614), delivers a discourse on cuckoldry, which includes the story of how chastity belts first arrived in France.[13] According to the abbot, a jeweler imports a dozen belts to Saint-Germain in the mid-sixteenth century and sells them at the fair to several jealous husbands. One wife has a duplicate key made by the town locksmith, who later becomes the first to benefit from her renewed freedom. Brantôme describes how the honorable gentlemen of the court force the vendor to destroy his remaining belts and threaten him with death if he brings them to the fair again.

While the texts themselves may speak more to the literary invention than the historical accuracy of Rabelais and Brantôme, their scenarios do exhibit some of the elements common to stories about chastity belts: an extremely jealous and often wealthy husband, a wife forced to wear the belt, and a rival lover.[14] Thematically, tales about the belts emphasize the husband's responsibility for bringing upon himself what he fears most—the horns of the cuckold. His actions directly motivate the wife's desire for release and revenge, usually effected by a new lover. The stories also frequently include a reference to Italy, the traditional birthplace of the belts. One enduring legend, in fact, credits their invention to Francesco II of Carrara, *signore* of Padua (1388–1405). Carrara's association with the chastity belt stems from a specimen once on display in the armory museum at Venice's Ducal

Palace. Included among the various torture devices attributed to his reign, the Carrara girdle, however, receives no mention in the memoirs of the museum's visitors until the eighteenth century, raising questions regarding the belt's authenticity. Despite the legend's modern adherents, even Dingwall asserts that the Carrara legend "does not seem to have any good evidence to support it."[15] Attempting to argue for an earlier date of origin, Dingwall himself posits that when knights returned to Italy from the Crusades, they brought with them the *idea* of the chastity belt, a result of their exposure to the practice of female infibulation by Eastern cultures. He contends that the excessive jealousy of Italian men combined with Italian society's notorious sexual license provided the appropriate environment for the creation and use of the belts.[16] In any case, similar to other tales of chastity girdles, the episodes in both *Pantagruel* and *Les Dames Galantes* appear to support the theory that the belts were never widely accepted ,and their use was associated with inappropriate and deviant social behavior.[17]

Ultimately, however, the modern notion of medieval crusaders locking up their wives in girdles of chastity lacks foundation and reliable historical evidence. The pervasive silence of medieval writers about these devices in medical texts, theological treatises, and fictional literature speaks volumes. The girdles themselves are noticeably absent from the critical work of medieval historians and from discussions of medieval sexual behavior. Some scholars have suggested that the belts were the urban legends of later centuries, the invention of Renaissance satirists and the props of burlesque writers.[18] Individuals seeking erotic experimentation or, unfortunately, practicing abuse transformed the idea into a physical reality. As noted above, the authenticity of the few extant belts attributed to the Middle Ages suffers severely when reexamined and scrutinized by museum curators and historians. Both the British Museum and England's Royal Armouries have retired "medieval" belts. Fraudulent artifacts dating from the early-modern period, the era more appropriately associated with the belts, have also been identified. For example, a richly made belt once on display at the Cluny Museum in Paris, supposedly given to Catherine de Medici by Henry II, king of France (1547–59), has been exposed as a nineteenth-century fake.

In fact, most of the belts that have found their way into museums and antique stores have, upon inspection, been identified as deliberate fakes, gags, or antimasturbatory devices manufactured in the 1800s and early 1900s.[19] Nineteenth- and twentieth-century inventors, for example, responded to the widespread belief that sexual activity, especially masturbation, could lead to insanity. Promoted by such respected medical theorists as S. A. D. Tissot, Edward Bliss Foote, Sylvester Graham, and John Harvey Kellogg, the theory that sex and insanity went hand in hand led to a boom in the development of beltlike antimasturbatory devices for both males and females, mostly purchased by parents fearing for the health of their teenaged children.[20] In addition, fascinated with the romantic image of an exotic, erotic past, Victorian writers and artists reshaped, reinvented, and revised the medieval period. Popular culture's appetite for a dangerous Gothic past encouraged the unscrupulous to fabricate memorabilia and curiosities like chastity belts, making future research into the belts perhaps more appropriately a study of medievalism. In the twenty-first century, the potential for sexual titillation offered by chastity belts continues to support their exploitation in movies, books, and cartoons as well as their manufacture and use. If, however, you are hoping to find a brutish knight shopping for a fashionable chastity belt on sale at his local medieval village fair, I fear you are bound to be disappointed.

SUGGESTIONS FOR FURTHER READING

Primary Sources

Pierre de Bourdeille Brantôme, *Les Dames Galantes*, ed. Pascal Pia, Paris: Gallimard, 1981.
———. *Lives of Fair and Gallant Ladies*, trans. A. R. Allinson, intro. Georg Harsdörfer, New York: Liveright, 1933.
Guillaume de Machaut, *Le Livre dou voir dit (The Book of the True Poem)*, Daniel Leech-Wilkinson (ed.), R. Barton Palmer (trans.), New York: Garland, 1998.
Conrad Kyeser, *Bellifortis*, Götz Quarg (ed.), 2 vols, Düsseldorf: VDI-Verlag, 1967.
Marie de France, *Guigemar*, in *Les Lais de Marie de France*, Jean Rychner (ed.), Paris: H. Champion, 1973.
———. *Guigemar*, in *The Lais of Marie de France*, Robert Hanning and Joan Ferrante (trans.), Durham, NC: Labyrinth, 1978.
François Rabelais, *Le Tiers livre*, M. A. Screech (ed.), Geneva: Droz, 1964.
———. *The Complete Works of François Rabelais*, Donald M. Frame (trans.), Berkeley: University of California, 1991.

Secondary Sources

James A. Brundage, *Law, Sex, and Christian Society in Medieval Europe*, Chicago: University of Chicago, 1987.
Vern L. Bullough, "Technology for the Prevention of 'Les Maladies Produites par la Masturbation,'" *Technology and Culture* 28, 1987, 828–32.
Vern Bullough and Bonnie Bullough (eds.), "Chastity Girdles," in *Human Sexuality: An Encyclopedia*, New York: Garland, 1994.
Vern Bullough and James A. Brundage (eds.), *Handbook of Medieval Sexuality*, New York: Garland, 1996.
Joan Cadden, *Meanings of Sex Difference in the Middle Ages: Medicine, Science, and Culture*, Cambridge: Cambridge University, 1993.
Albrecht Classen, *The Medieval Chastity Belt: A Myth-Making Process*, New York: Palgrave, 2007.
Eric John Dingwall, *The Girdle of Chastity: A Fascinating History of Chastity Belts* (1931), New York: Clarion, 1959.
David O. Frantz, *"Festum Voluptatis": A Study of Renaissance Erotica*, Columbus, OH: Ohio State University, 1989.
John Harlow, "Damsels Not Distressed by Medieval Chastity Belt," *Sunday Times* (London), 23 June 1996, News 1.

Clive Hart and Kay Gilliland Stevenson, *Heaven and the Flesh: Imagery of Desire from the Renaissance to the Rococo*, Cambridge: Cambridge University, 1995.
Danielle Jacquart and Claude Thomasset, *Sexuality and Medicine in the Middle Ages*, Matthew Adamson (trans.), Cambridge: Polity, 1988.
Kathleen Coyne Kelly, *Performing Virginity and Testing Chastity in the Middle Ages*, Routledge Research in Medieval Studies, vol. 2, London: Routledge, 2000.
Kathleen Coyne Kelly and Marina Leslie (eds.), *Menacing Virgins: Representing Virginity in the Middle Ages and Renaissance*, Newark: University of Delaware, 1999.
John M. Riddle, *Contraception and Abortion from the Ancient World to the Renaissance*, Cambridge: Harvard University, 1992.

NOTES

1. John Harlow, "Damsels Not Distressed by Medieval Chastity Belt," *Sunday Times* (London), 23 June 1996, News 1.
2. The *Catholic Encyclopedia* (s.v. "cincture") notes that when a modern-day priest puts on the belt or girdle, the prayer he recites begins "Gird me, O Lord, with the girdle of purity," suggesting that "this vestment should be regarded as typical of priestly chastity." Significantly, belts may also represent characteristics diametrically opposite those of chastity. From antiquity, the "girdle of Venus," for instance, symbolized sexual desire and prowess rather than sexual abstinence. Ironically, modern vendors of sexual paraphernalia use the term as a synonym for chastity devices. For discussions of the cultural forces that shape representations of chastity and virginity in the Middle Ages, especially with regard to women, see Kathleen Coyne Kelly and Marina Leslie (eds.), *Menacing Virgins: Representing Virginity in the Middle Ages and Renaissance*, Newark: University of Delaware, 1999, and Kathleen Coyne Kelly, *Performing Virginity and Testing Chastity in the Middle Ages*, Routledge Research in Medieval Studies, vol. 2, London: Routledge, 2000.
3. Eric John Dingwall, *The Girdle of Chastity: A Fascinating History of Chastity Belts* (1931), New York: Clarion, 1959, pp. 15 and 18.
4. Marie de France, *Les Lais de Marie de France*, Jean Rychner (ed.), Paris: H. Champion, 1973.
5. Dingwall, *Girdle of Chastity*, pp. 15 and 18.
6. Modern English translation taken from *The Lais of Marie de France*, Robert Hanning and Joan Ferrante (trans.), Durham, NC: Labyrinth, 1978. Nancy Bradley Warren discusses Marie's use of objects and possessions both as a system of identification and as a means of characterization in the lays *Fresne*, *Bisclavret*, *Lanval*, *Laüstic*, and *Chaitivel*; see "Objects, Possession and Identity in the *Lais* of Marie de France," *RLA* 6, 1994, 189–92.
7. Guillaume de Machaut, *Le Livre dou voir dit (The Book of the True Poem)*, Daniel Leech-Wilkinson (ed.), R. Barton Palmer (trans.), New York: Garland, 1998. Also note that keys figuratively implied sexual activity; for example, to turn the key or to lock was a popular euphemism for sexual intercourse; see David O. Frantz, *"Festum voluptatis": A Study of Renaissance Erotica*, Columbus, OH: Ohio State University, 1989, pp. 9–42.
8. Dingwall, *Girdle of Chastity*, p. 18.
9. See the facsimile edition of Conrad Kyeser's *Bellifortis*, Götz Quarg (ed.), 2 vols., Düsseldorf: VDI-Verlag, 1967, p. 1.130r (editor's German translation, p. 2.95: "Dies ist ein Schurz florentinischer Damen, Eisern und hart, von innen her sei er aufschließbar"). While facsimiles of the manuscript may be somewhat difficult to locate, the image from *Bellifortis* has been reprinted in several secondary sources, such as Dingwall, *The Girdle of Chastity*, p. 49, plate II.

10. Vern L. Bullough and Bonnie Bullough (eds.), "Chastity Girdles," in *Human Sexuality: An Encyclopedia*, New York: Garland, 1994, p. 107. Dingwall identifies seven variations on this design; see *Girdle of Chastity*, pp. 160–2. Images of chastity belts, both antique and modern, can be found on numerous Internet web sites. Researchers should be forewarned, however, that most are not academic sites, and they often contain information that is garbled, inaccurate, sexually exploitive, and pornographic.

11. Dingwall, *Girdle of Chastity*, pp. 84–9. Any trace of Pachinger's belt has been lost.

12. François Rabelais, *Le Tiers livre*, M. A. Screech (ed.), Geneva: Droz, 1964, p. 251. For a modern English translation, see *The Complete Works of François Rabelais*, Donald M. Frame (trans.), Berkeley: University of California, 1991, p. 366.

13. Pierre de Bourdeille, seigneur de Brantôme, *Les Dames Galantes*, Pascal Pia (ed.), Paris: Gallimard, 1981, pp. 136–7. For a modern English translation, see *Lives of Fair and Gallant Ladies*, A. R. Allinson (trans.), New York: Liveright, 1933, pp. 88–9.

14. Georg Harsdörfer states that as a historian, "Brantôme's accuracy is in no way to be relied upon [. . . he is] more a chronicler and a writer of memoirs," "Introduction," in Allinson, *Fair and Gallant Ladies*, p. xv. For comprehensive studies of erotica in the Renaissance, see Frantz, *"Festum voluptatis,"* and Clive Hart and Kay Gilliland Stevenson, *Heaven and the Flesh: Imagery of Desire from the Renaissance to the Rococo*, Cambridge: Cambridge University, 1995.

15. Dingwall, *Girdle of Chastity*, p. 43. Dating from the seventeenth century, memoirs of visitors to the armory museum record various extraordinary items on display, including an iron collar. Dingwall suggests that the belt may have been acquired at the same time as the other instruments of torture and was associated with Carrara because of the stories about his barbarous acts and the "hatred of the Venetians for him."

16. Dingwall, *Girdle of Chastity*, pp. 18–19 and 25–32. Dingwall also states, however, that the chastity belt's first appearance in "ordinary use" among Italians was not until "the Renaissance or perhaps somewhat later," p. 129.

17. For example, dating from the eighteenth century, legal cases involving women forced to wear chastity belts or chastitylike devices treat their situations as evidence of criminal abuse. See Dingwall, *Girdle of Chastity*, pp. 92–123.

18. See Harlow, "Damsels Not Distressed." Historians have also suggested that, in a few cases, the belts may have provided protection for female prisoners against libidinous guards. For in-depth studies on sexuality in the Middle Ages, see Vern L. Bullough and James A. Brundage (eds.), *Handbook of Medieval Sexuality*, New York: Garland, 1996; James A. Brundage, *Law, Sex, and Christian Society in Medieval Europe*, Chicago: University of Chicago, 1987; Joan Cadden, *Meanings of Sex Difference in the Middle Ages: Medicine, Science, and Culture*, Cambridge: Cambridge University, 1993; Danielle Jacquart and Claude Thomasset, *Sexuality and Medicine in the Middle Ages*, Matthew Adamson (trans.), Cambridge: Polity, 1988; and John M. Riddle, *Contraception and Abortion from the Ancient World to the Renaissance*, Cambridge: Harvard University, 1992.

19. Writing in the early twentieth century, Dingwall himself states, "no specimens of undoubtedly early date have been discovered. Few, if any, go back to a time anterior to the sixteenth century, and many of those on exhibition are, in my opinion at least, not to be considered genuine," *Girdle of Chastity*, p. 33. He also notes that from his survey of belts on display, "no good evidence" exists of their actually having been worn by women; see pp. 71–84. Generally

speaking, small, private museums tending to display more sensational items, such as instruments of torture, offer more resistance to questioning the authenticity of the belts they exhibit.

20. In the nineteenth and early twentieth century, the technology for antimasturbatory devices ranged from special gloves, surgical devices, appliances that inflicted electric shocks, castration, and clitoridectomies to burning irons applied to the thighs of young girls. Male "chastity belts" consisted of sheaths lined with metal teeth that would pierce the penis if it became erect. Eventually, members of the medical community discarded the theory that sex led to insanity and began a "full-scale assault" on the notion in the 1920s and 30s. Unfortunately, it took at least another generation before the fallacy of these ideas was exposed to the general public. See Vern L. Bullough, "Technology for the Prevention of 'Les Maladies Produites par la Masturbation,' " *Technology and Culture* 28, 1987, 828–32.

Bibliography

Acta et decreta sacrosancta oecumenici concili Vaticani in quatuor prioribus sessionibus, Rome: P. Lazzarini, 1872.

Banquets et manières de table au Moyen Âge, Aix-en-Provence: CUERMA, 1996.

CETEDOC *Library of Christian Latin Texts*, Turnhout, Belgium: Brepols, 1991.

Chronica minor auctore minorita Erphordiensi, O. Holder-Egger (ed.), *MGH Scriptores* 24, 1879, pp. 172–213.

Corpus Christianorum Series Latina (= CCSL), Turnhout, Belgium: Brepols, 1954.

Gesta Romanorum: or Entertaining Moral Stories, C. Swan and W. Hooper (trans. and eds), London: Constable, 1959.

Glossa ordinaria, in *Patrologiae Cursus Completus: Series Latina*, vol. 113, J. P. Migne (ed.), Paris, 1844-64.

John Milton: Complete Poems and Major Prose, Merritt Y. Hughes (ed.), New York: Odyssey, 1957.

Livres en bouche: Cinq siècles d'art culinaire français, du quatorzième au dix-huitième siècle, Paris: Bibliothèque Nationale de France et Hermann, 2001.

Manger et boire au Moyen Âge: Actes du colloque de Nice, 15–17 octobre 1982, 2 vols., Paris: Les Belles Lettres, 1984.

New Catholic Encyclopedia, 15 vols., 2nd ed., Detroit: Gale, 2003.

Patrologia cursus completus . . . series Graeca (= PG), 81 vols., Jean-Paul Migne (ed.), Paris: Migne, 1856–1867.

Patrologia cursus completus . . . series Latina (= PL), 221 vols., Jean-Paul Migne (ed.), Paris: Migne, 1844–1902.

Records of Early English Drama series, Toronto: University of Toronto, 1978.

Recueil des historiens des Gaules et de la France, 13 vols., Paris, 1738–1786.

Rerum Britannicorum medii aevi scriptores (Rolls Series), 253 vols., London, 1858–96.

The Küng Dialogue: A Documentation on the Efforts of the Congregation for the Doctrine of the Faith and of the Conference of German Bishops to Achieve an Appropriate Clarification of the Controversial Views of Dr. Hans Küng (Tübingen), Washington DC: U.S. Catholic Conference, 1980.

The New Cambridge Medieval History, 8 vols., Cambridge: Cambridge University, 1995–2005.

Peter Abelard, *A Dialogue of a Philosopher with a Jew and a Christian*, Pierre Payer (trans.), Toronto: Pontifical Institute of Medieval Studies, 1979.

Adam of Usk, *Chronicon Adae de Usk 1377–1404*, Edward Maunde Thompson (ed. and trans.), London: J. Murray, 1876.

Melitta Weiss Adamson (ed.), *Food in the Middle Ages: A Book of Essays*, New York, Garland, 1995.

————, (ed.), *Regional Cuisines of Medieval Europe: A Book of Essays*, New York: Routledge, 2002.

Helen Adolf, "On Medieval Laughter," *Speculum*, 22, 1947, 251–3.

David Aers, "A Whisper in the Ear of Early Modernists; or, Reflections of Literary Critics Writing the 'History of the Subject,'" *Culture and History, 1350–1600: Essays on English Communities, Identities, and Writings*, David Aers (ed.), London: Harvester Wheatsheaf, 1992, pp. 177–202.

Giorgio Agamben, *The Time that Remains: A Commentary on the Letter to the Romans*, Patricia Dailey (trans.), Stanford: Stanford University Press, 2005.

Danièle Alexandre-Bidon and Monique Closson, *L'enfant à l'ombre des cathédrales*, Lyon: Presses Universitaires de Lyon, 1985.

John A. Alford (ed.), *From Page to Performance: Essays in Early English Drama*, East Lansing: Michigan State University, 1995.

Dante Alighieri, *La Vita Nuova*, Barbara Reynolds (trans.), New York: Penguin, 1969.

P. Alphandéry and A. Dupront, *La Chrétienté et l'idée de croisade*, 2 vols., Paris: A. Michel, 1954–9.

Gerd Althoff, Johannes Fried, Patrick J. Geary (eds.), *Medieval Concepts of the Past: Ritual Memory, Historiography*, New York: Cambridge University, 2002.

Ambrose, *Hexameron, Paradise, and Cain and Abel*, John J. Savage (trans.) New York: Fathers of the Church, 1961.

Darrel W. Amundsen, *Medicine, Society, and Faith in the Ancient and Medieval Worlds*, London: Johns Hopkins University, 1996.

Emilie Amt and S. J. Allen (eds.), *The Crusades: A Reader*, Peterborough, ON: Broadview, 2003.

M. D. Anderson, *Drama and Imagery in English Medieval Churches*, Cambridge: Cambridge University, 1963.

Melitta Anderson, *Food in Medieval Times*, Westport, CT: Greenwood, 2004.

Arnold Angenendt, *Geschichte der Religiosität im Mittelalter*, Darmstadt, Germany: Wissenschaftliche Buchgesellschaft, 1997.

Thomas Aquinas, *Summa Contra Gentiles*, Vernon J. Bourke (trans.) Notre Dame University, 1989.

————, *Summa Theologica*, Fathers of the English Dominican Province (trans.) London, 1922.

John Arderne, *Treatises of Fistula in Ano*, D. Power (ed.), London: EETS, 1910.

Philippe Ariès, *L'enfant et la vie familiale sous l'Ancien Régime*, Paris: Plon, 1960; translated as *Centuries of Childhood*, New York: Vintage, 1962.

M.-J. Arn (ed.), *Medieval Food and Drink*, Binghamton, NY: SUNY, 1995.

John H. Arnold, *Belief and Unbelief in Medieval Europe*, London: Hodder Arnold, 2005.

Klaus Arnold, *Kind und Gesellschaft in Mittelalter und Renaissance: Beiträge und Texte zur Geschichte der Kindheit*, Weiterbildung der Erzieher), Paderborn, Germany: Schöningh, 1980.

Matthew Arnold, "From the 'Study of Poetry,'" *Geoffrey Chaucer: A Critical Anthology*, J. A. Burrow (ed.), Harmondsworth, UK: Penguin, 1969, pp. 96–101.

Jon Arrizabalaga, John Henderson, and Roger French, *The Great Pox: The French Disease in Renaissance Europe*, New Haven: Yale University, 1997.

Geoffrey Ashe, *The Discovery of King Arthur*, London: Guild, 1985.

Kathleen Ashley, "Divine Power in Chester Cycle and Late Medieval Thought," *Journal of the History of Ideas* 39, 1978, 387–404.

Clarissa Atkinson, *The Oldest Vocation: Christian Motherhood in the Middle Ages*, Ithaca: Cornell University, 1991.

W. H. Auden, "In Memory of W. B. Yeats," *Selected Poetry of W. H. Auden*, 2nd ed., New York: Vintage, 1971, pp. 52–4.

———, Augustine, *Confessions*, R. S. Pine-Coffin (trans.) Harmondsworth: Penguin, 1961.

Augustine, *City of God*, Henry Bettenson (trans.) Harmondsworth: Penguin, 1984.

Augustine, *On Christian Doctrine*, D.W. Robertson (trans.) New York: Liberal Arts, 1958.

Augustine, *Soliloquies: Augustine's Inner Dialogue*, John E. Rotelle (ed.) and Kim Paffenroth (trans.), Brooklyn, NY: New City, 2000.

Thomas Austin (ed.), *Two Fifteenth Century Cookery Books,* London: EETS, 1888.

J. Ayto, *The Glutton's Glossary: A Dictionary of Food and Drink Terms*, London: Routledge, 1990.

Michael Bailey, *Magic and Superstition in Europe: A Concise History from Antiquity to the Present*, Lanham, MD: Rowman & Littlefield, 2007.

———, "From Sorcery to Witchcraft: Clerical Conceptions of Magic in the Later Middle Ages," *Speculum* 76, 2001, 960–90.

Donald C. Baker, John L. Murphy, and Louis B. Hall (eds.), *The Late Medieval Religious Plays of Bodleian Mss Digby 133 and E. Museo 160*, EETS o.s. 283, Oxford: Oxford University, 1982.

Peter S. Baker (ed.), *The Beowulf Reader*, New York: Garland, 2000.

Mikhail Bakhtin, *Rabelais and His World*, Hélène Iswolsky (trans.), Bloomington, IN: Indiana University, 1984.

John W. Baldwin, *The Scholastic Culture of the Middle Ages, 1000-1300* (1971) Prospect Heights: Waveland, 1997.

Marshall W. Baldwin, *The Medieval Church* (The Development of Western Civilization), Ithaca, NY: Cornell University, 1953.

Geoffrey Barraclough, *The Medieval Papacy* (History of European Civilization Library), New York: Harcourt Brace and World, 1968.

W. R. J. Barron (ed.), *The Arthur of the English: The Arthurian Legend in Medieval English Life and Literature*, Cardiff: University of Wales, 1999.

A. L. Barstow, *Witchcraze: A New History of the European Witch Hunts*, San Francisco: Pandora/HarperCollins, 1994.

Roland Barthes, *S/Z*, Richard Miller (trans.), New York: Hill and Wang, 1974.

Christopher Baswell, *Virgil in Medieval England: Figuring the* Aeneid *from the Twelfth Century to Chaucer*, New York: Cambridge University, 1995.

J. Baycroft, "An Emerging Ecumenical Consensus on Papal Primacy?" *Journal of Ecumenical Studies* 35, 1998, 36–69.

Martha Bayless, *Parody in the Middle Ages: The Latin Tradition*, Ann Arbor, MI: University of Michigan, 1996.

Alison I. Beach, *Women as Scribes: Book Production and Monastic Reform in Twelfth-Century Bavaria*, Cambridge Studies in Palaeography and Codicology, Cambridge: Cambridge University, 2004.

Richard Beadle and Pamela M. King (eds.), *York Mystery Plays: A Selection in Modern Spelling*, Oxford: Oxford University, 1984.

Richard Beadle (ed.), *The Cambridge Companion to Medieval English Theatre*, Cambridge: Cambridge University, 1994.

Theodore R. Beck, *The Cutting Edge: Early History of the Surgeons of London*, London: Lund Humphries, 1974.

K. Becker, "Kochkunst und Diätetik in der Dichtung Eustache Deschamps," *Zeitschrift für Romanische Philologie* 111.3, 1995, 347–74.

Bede, *A History of the English Church and Its People*, Leo Shirley-Price (trans.), Harmondsworth, UK: Penguin, 1988.

W. Behringer, *Witches and Witch-Hunts: A Global History*, Cambridge, UK: Polity, 2004.

———, "How Waldensians Became Witches: Heretics and Their Journey to the Other World," in G. Klaniczay and E. Pocs (eds.), *Communicating with the Spirits: Demons, Spirits, Witches*, Budapest: Central European University, 2005.

Paul E. Beichner, "Characterization in *The Miller's Tale*," in Richard J. Schoeck and Jerome Taylor (eds.), *Chaucer Criticism: The Canterbury Tales*, Notre Dame, IN: University of Notre Dame, 1960, pp. 117–29.

Robert Bellarmine, *Disputationes de controversiis christianae fidei*, (1586) Ingolstadt, Germany: Adami Sartorii, 1599.

H. S. Bennett, *Life on the English Manor: A Study of Peasant Conditions 1150–1400*, Cambridge: Cambridge University, 1948.

C. David Benson, *Chaucer's Drama of Style: Poetic Variety and Contrast in the Canterbury Tales*, Chapel Hill: University of North Carolina, 1986.

Larry D. Benson et al. (eds.), *The Riverside Chaucer*, 3rd ed., Boston: Houghton Mifflin, 1987.

Larry D. Benson and Theodore M. Andersson (eds. and trans.), *The Literary Context of Chaucer's Fabliaux: Texts and Translations*, Indianapolis, IN: Bobbs-Merrill, 1971.

J. Benzinger, *Invectiva in Romam: Romkritik im Mittelalter vom 9. bis zum 12. Jahrhundert*, Lübeck, Germany: Matthiesen, 1968.

G. E. Bereton and J. M. Ferrier (eds.) and K. Ueltschi (trans.), *Le mesnagier de Paris*, Paris: Le Livre de Poche, 1994.

Francis S. Betten, "Knowledge of the Sphericity of the Earth During the Earlier Middle Ages," *Catholic Historical Review* 3, 1923, 74–90.

David Bevington (ed.), *Medieval Drama*, Boston: Houghton Mifflin, 1975.

———, *From Mankind to Marlowe: Growth of Structure in the Popular Drama of Tudor England*, Cambridge: Harvard University, 1962.

I. Bitsch, T. Ehlert, and X. Ertzdorff with R. Schulz (eds.), *Essen und Trinken in Mittelalter und Neuzeit*, Sigmaringen, Germany: Jan Thorbecke, 1987.

A. Black, "What was Conciliarism? Conciliar Theory in Historical Perspective," in B. Tierney and P. Linehan (eds.), *Authority and Power: Studies in Medieval Law and Government Presented to Walter Ullmann on his Seventieth Birthday*, Cambridge: Cambridge University, 1980, pp. 213–35.

———, *Political Thought in Europe 1250–1450*, Cambridge: Cambridge University, 1992.

M. Black, *The Medieval Cookbook*, London: Thames & Hudson, 1996.

———, *Medieval Cookery: Recipes and History*, Swindon, UK: English Heritage, 2003.

John Blair, *The Church in Anglo-Saxon Society*, Oxford: Oxford University, 2005.

David R. Blanks and Michael Frassetto, *Western Views of Islam in Medieval and Early Modern Europe: Perception of Other*, New York: Palgrave Macmillan, 1999.

Marc Bloch, *The Royal Touch: Monarchy and Miracles in France and England*, J. E. Anderson (trans.), New York: Dorset, 1961.

David Blondel, *Familier esclaircissement de la question, si une femme a esté assise au siège papal de Rome ...*, Amsterdam: I. Blaev, 1647.

Morton W. Bloomfield, "Chaucer's Sense of History," *Essays and Explorations: Studies in Ideas, Language, and Literature*, Cambridge: Harvard University, 1970.

———, *Piers Plowman as a Fourteenth-Century Apocalypse*, New Brunswick, NJ: Rutgers University, 1962.

Giovanni Boccaccio, *Concerning Famous Women*, Guido A. Guarino (trans.), London: G. Allen & Unwin, 1964.

Boethius, *The Consolation of Philosophy*, Richard Green (trans.), New York: Macmillan, 1962.

Wilifrid Bonser, *The Medical Background of the Anglo-Saxons*, London: The Wellcome Historical Medical Library, 1963.

Daniel Boorstin, *The Discoverers*, New York: Random House, 1983.

George Borodin, *The Book of Johanna*, London: Staples, 1947.

John Boswell, *The Kindness of Strangers: The Abandonment of Children in Western Europe from Late Antiquity to the Renaissance*, New York: Pantheon, 1988.

Pierre de Bourdeille Brantôme, *Les Dames Galantes*, Pascal Pia (ed.), Paris: Gallimard, 1981.

———, *Lives of Fair and Gallant Ladies*, A. R. Allinson (trans.), New York: Liveright, 1933.

Alain Boureau, "Joan," in *The Papacy: An Encyclopedia*, Philippe Levillain (gen. ed.), New York: Routledge, 2002, 2:829–30.

———, *The Myth of Pope Joan*, Lydia Cochrane (trans.), Chicago: University of Chicago, 2001.

Betsy Bowden, *Chaucer Aloud: The Varieties of Textual Interpretation*, Philadelphia: University of Pennsylvania, 1987.

Alan K. Bowman, *Life and Letters on the Roman Frontier*, London: British Museum, 1998.

Jim Bradley, *The Routledge Companion to Medieval Warfare*, London: Routledge, 2004.

Ernst Breisach, *Historiography: Ancient, Medieval & Modern*, 2nd ed, Chicago: University of Chicago, 1994.

E. G. Breslaw, "Introduction," in E. G. Breslaw (ed.), *Witches of the Atlantic World: A Historical Reader and Primary Sourcebook*, New York: New York University, 2000.

Derek Brewer (ed.), *Medieval Comic Tales*, Suffolk: Brewer, 1996.

Marianne Briscoe and John C. Coldewey (ed.), *Contexts for Early English Drama*, Bloomington: Indiana University, 1989.

Saul Brody, *The Disease of the Soul: Leprosy in Medieval Literature*, Ithaca: Cornell University, 1974.

H. P. Broedel, *The Malleus Maleficarum and the Construction of Witchcraft: Theology and Popular Belief*, Manchester, UK: Manchester University, 2004.

Rosalind B. Brooke and Christopher N. L. Brooke, *Popular Religion in the Middle Ages: Western Europe, 1000–1300*, London: Thames and Hudson, 1984.

A. R. Brown, "The Tyranny of a Construct: Feudalism and Historians of Medieval Europe," *American Historical Review* 79, 1974, pp. 1063–88.

James A. Brundage, *Law, Sex, and Christian Society in Medieval Europe*, Chicago: University of Chicago, 1987.

———, *Medieval Canon Law and the Crusader*, Madison: University of Wisconsin, 1966.

———, *The Crusades: Motives and Achievements*, Lexington, MA: Heath, 1964.

———, (ed.), *The Crusades: A Documentary Survey*, Milwaukee: Marquette University, 1962.

Marcus Bull, *Knightly Piety and the Lay Response to the First Crusade*, Oxford: Clarendon, 1993.

William Bullein, *A Dialogue against the Feuer Pestilence*, Mark W. Bullen and A. H. Auden (eds.), London: Early English Text Society, 1888.

Vern L. Bullough, "Technology for the Prevention of 'Les Maladies Produites par la Masturbation,'" *Technology and Culture* 28 1987, 828–32.

———, *The Development of Medicine as a Profession*, New York: Hafner, 1966.

Vern L. Bullough and Bonnie Bullough (eds.), "Chastity Girdles," in *Human Sexuality: An Encyclopedia*, New York: Garland, 1994.

Vern L. Bullough and James A. Brundage (eds.), *Handbook of Medieval Sexuality*, New York: Garland, 1996.

Johann Burchard, *Johannis Burchardi argentinensis capelle pontificie sacrorum rituum magistri diarum*, Louis Thusane (ed.), Paris: E. Leroux, 1883.

J. H. Burns (ed.), *The Cambridge History of Medieval Political Thought c. 350–c. 1450*, Cambridge: Cambridge University, 1988.

J. A. Burrow, *The Ages of Man: A Study in Medieval Writing and Thought*, New York: Oxford University, 1988.

Ibn Butlan, *The Medieval Health Handbook Tacuinum Sanitatis*, Luisa Cogliati Arano (ed.), Oscar Ratti and Adele Westbrook (trans.), New York: George Braziller, 1976.

Philip Butterworth, *Magic on the Early English Stage*, Cambridge: Cambridge University, 2005.

Joan Cadden, *Meanings of Sex Difference in the Middle Ages: Medicine, Science, and Culture*, Cambridge: Cambridge University, 1993.

Sheila Cambell, Bert Hall, and David Klausner (eds.), *Health, Disease, and Healing in Medieval Culture*, New York: St. Martin's, 1992.

M. L. Cameron, *Anglo-Saxon Medicine*, Cambridge: Cambridge University, 1993.

——, "Anglo-Saxon Medicine and Magic," in *Anglo-Saxon England* 17, 1988, 191–215.

Michael Camille, *Image on the Edge: The Margins of Medieval Art*, Cambridge, MA: Harvard University, 1992.

Ann Margaret Campbell, *The Black Death and the Men of Learning*, New York: Columbia University, 1931.

Sheila Campbell, Bert Hall, and David Klausner (eds.), *Health, Disease and Healing in Medieval Culture*, New York: St. Martin's, 1992.

J. Canning, *A History of Medieval Political Thought 300–1450*, Cambridge: Cambridge University, 1996.

Martha Carlin and Joel T. Rosenthal (eds.), *Food and Eating in Medieval Europe*, London: Hambledon, 1998.

R. W. Carlyle and A. J. Carlyle, *History of Mediaeval Political Theory in the West*, 6 vols., London: W. Blackwood, 1903–36.

Ann Carmichael, *Plague and the Poor in Renaissance Florence*, Cambridge: Cambridge University, 1986.

Lewis Carroll, "A Stanza of Anglo-Saxon Poetry," *The Book of Nonsense*, Roger Lancelyn Green (ed.), New York: Dutton, 1965, pp. 118–20.

Phillip Cary, *Augustine's Invention of the Inner Self: The Legacy of a Christian Platonist*, Oxford: Oxford University, 2000.

Cassiodorus, *An Introduction to Divine and Human Readings*, Leslie Webber Jones (trans.) New York: Octagon, 1966.

Cassiodorus, *Variae*, S. J. B. Barnish (trans.), Translated Texts for Historians 12, Liverpool: Liverpool University, 1992.

William Caxton, *Mirror of the World* (1490), Oliver H. Prior (ed.), EETS, Oxford: Oxford University, 1966.

E. K. Chambers, *The Mediaeval Stage*, 2 vols., London: Oxford University, 1903.

R. W. Chambers, *Beowulf: An Introduction to the Study of the Poem*, 2nd ed., Cambridge: Cambridge University, 1932.

Geoffrey Chaucer, *The Canterbury Tales Complete*, Larry D. Benson (ed.), Boston: Houghton Mifflin, 2000.

Robert Chazan, *Medieval Stereotypes and Modern Antisemitism*, Berkeley: University of California, 1997.

Marie-Dominique Chenu, *Nature, Man and Society in the Twelfth Century: Essays on New Theological Perspectives in the Latin West*, Jerome Taylor and Lester K. Little (trans.), Toronto: University of Toronto, 1997.

P. Chirico, "Infallibility: Rapprochement between Küng and the Official Church?" *Theological Studies*, 42, 1981, 529–60.

Chrétien de Troyes, *The Knight with the Lion, or, Yvain*, Willian W. Kilber (ed. and trans.), New York: Garland, 1985.

Eric Christiansen, *The Northern Crusades*, London: Penguin, 1997.

M. T. Clanchy, *Abelard: A Medieval Life*, Oxford: Blackwell, 1997.

S. Clark, "Witchcraft and Magic in Early Modern Culture," in B. Ankarloo and S. Clark (eds.), *Witchcraft and Magic in Europe: The Period of The Witch Trials*, Philadelphia: University of Pennsylvania, 2002.

Logan Clendening (ed.), *Source Book of Medical History*, New York: Dover, 1942.

John Cleveland, *The Rustick Rampant, or Rurall Anarchy*, London, 1658.

Lawrence M. Clopper, *Drama, Play, and Game: English Festive Culture in the Medieval and Early Modern Period*, Chicago: University of Chicago, 2001.

Oswald Cockayne, *Leechdoms, Wortcunning and Starcraft of Early England* (1864), London: Kraus Reprint, 1965.

Nevill Coghill (trans.), *Chaucer: The Canterbury Tales*, Baltimore: Penguin, 1952.

Jeffrey Jerome Cohen (ed.), *The Postcolonial Middle Ages*, New York: St. Martin's, 2000.

Jeremy Cohen, *Living Letters of the Law: Ideas of the Jew in Medieval Christianity*, Berkeley: University of California, 1999.

Norman Cohn, *The Pursuit of the Millennium*, Oxford: Oxford University, 1970.

Penny J. Cole, *The Preaching of the Crusades to the Holy Land, 1095–1270*, Cambridge: Harvard University, 1991.

Janet Coleman, *Ancient and Medieval Memories: Studies in the Reconstruction of the Past*, New York: Cambridge University, 1992.

Theresa Coletti, "Reading *REED*: History and the Records of Early English Drama," in *Literary Practice and Social Change in Britain 1380–1530*, Lee Patterson (ed.), Berkeley: University of California, 1990, 248–84.

Bertram Colgrave and R. A. B. Mynors (eds.), *Bede's Ecclesiastical History of the English People*, Oxford: Clarendon, 1969.

M. Collins, *The Fisherman's Net: The Influence of the Papacy on History*, rev. ed., Mahwah, NJ: HiddenSpring, 2005.

P. Collins, *Upon This Rock: The Popes in Their Changing Role*, New York: Crossroad, 2000.

Y. M.-J. Congar, *L'écclesiologie au Moyen Âge de Saint Grégoire le Grand à la désunion entre Byzance et Rome*, Paris: Éditions de Cerf, 1968.

Giles Constable, *The Reformation of the Twelfth Century*, Cambridge: Cambridge University, 1996.

Helen Cooper, *Oxford Guides to Chaucer: The Canterbury Tales*, 2nd ed., Oxford: Oxford University, 1996.

Madeleine Pelner Cosman, *Fabulous Feats: Medieval Cookery and Ceremony*, New York: G. Braziller, 1976.

J. F. Costanzo, *The Historical Credibility of Hans Küng: An Inquiry and Commentary*, North Quincy, MA: Christopher Publishing, 1979.

Michael Costen, *The Cathars and the Albigensian Crusade*, Manchester, UK, 1997.

R. F. Costigan, *The Consensus of the Church and Papal Infallibility: A Study of the Background of Vatican I*, Washington, DC: Catholic University, 2006.

H. E. J. Cowdrey, "The Peace and Truce of God in the Eleventh Century," in *Past and Present*, 46, 1970.

John D. Cox and David Scott Kastan (eds.), *A New History of Early English Drama*, New York: Columbia University, 1997.

Hardin Craig, *English Religious Drama of the Middle Ages*, Oxford: Clarendon, 1955.

Susan Crane, "The Writing Lesson of 1381," *Chaucer's England: Literature in Historical Context*, Barbara Hanawalt (ed.), Minneapolis: Univ. of Minnesota, 1992.

Sally Crawford, *Childhood in Anglo-Saxon England*, Stroud, UK: Sutton, 1999.

Donna Woolford Cross, *Pope Joan: A Novel*, New York: Crown, 1996.

A. Cunningham (ed.), *The Bishop in the Church: Patristic Texts on the Role of the Episkopos*, Wilmington, DE: Michael Glazier, 1985.

Walter Clyde Curry, *Chaucer and the Medieval Sciences*, New York: Barnes and Noble, 1960.

E. R. Curtius, *European Literature and the Latin Middle Ages*, Willard R. Trask (trans.), Princeton: Princeton University, 1990.

R. Dale (ed.), *The Wordsworth Dictionary of Culinary and Menu Terms*, Ware, UK: Wordsworth, 2000.

Norman Daniel, *Islam and the West: The Making of an Image*, Oxford: Oneworld, 1993.

M. A. D'Aronco and M. L. Cameron, *The Old English Illustrated Pharmacopoeia*, Copenhagen: Rosenkilde and Bagger, 1998.

L.J. Daston, and K. Park, *Wonders and the Order of Nature*, 1150-1750, New York: Zone Books, 1998.

W. A. Davenport, *Fifteenth-Century English Drama: The Early Moral Plays and Their Literary Relations*, Cambridge: D. S. Brewer, 1982.

Clifford Davidson, *Illustrations of the Stage and Acting in England to 1580*, Kalamazoo, MI: Medieval Institute Publications, 1991.

———, *Visualizing the Moral Life: Medieval Iconography and the Macro Morality Plays*, New York: AMS, 1989.

———, *From Creation to Doom: The York Cycle of Mystery Plays*, New York: AMS, 1984.

Clifford Davidson et al. (eds.), *The Drama in the Middle Ages: Comparative and Critical Essays*, New York: AMS, 1982.

Elizabeth Gould Davis, *The First Sex*, New York: Putnam, 1971.

W. R. Dawson, *A Leechbook or Collection of Medical Recipes of the Fifteenth Century*, London: Macmillan, 1934.

Guy De Chauliac, *The Cyrurgie of Guy de Chauliac*, Margaret S. Ogden (ed.), London: EETS, 1971.

Geoffrey de Courlon, *Chronique de l'abbaye de Sainte-Pierre-le-Vif de Sens*, G. Juillot (ed.), Sens: C. Duchemin, 1876.

———, *The Middle English Translation of Guy De Chauliac's Anatomy*, Bjorn Wallner (ed.), Lund, UK: Lund University, 1964.

Lloyd deMause, *The History of Childhood: The Evolution of Parent-Child Relationships as a Factor in History* (1974), London: Souvenir, 1980.

F. Desportes, *Le Pain au Moyen Age*, Paris: Olivier Orban, 1987.

Kelly DeVries, *A Cumulative Bibliography of Medieval Military History and Technology*, Leiden, Netherlands: Brill, 2005.

———, *Infantry Warfare in the Early Fourteenth Century*, Woodbridge, UK: Boydell, 1996.

Edwin Brezette DeWindt (ed. and trans.), *A Slice of Life: Selected Documents of Medieval English Peasant Experience*, Kalamazoo, MI: Medieval Institute, 1996.

Isaac D'Israeli, "Quodlibets, or Scholastic Disquisitions," in Curiosities of Literature and The Literary Character Illustrated, with *Curiosities of American Literature by Rufus W. Griswold*, New York, 1875.

Dhuoda, *A Handbook for William: A Carolingian Woman's Counsel for Her Son*, Carol Neel (trans.), Washington, DC: Catholic University of America, 1991.

Gary Dickson, "Stephen of Cloyes, Philip Augustus, and the Children's Crusade of 1212," in *Journeys Toward God: Pilgrimage and Crusade*, ed. B. N. Sargent-Baur, Kalamazoo, MI: Medieval Institute, 1992, pp. 83–105.

———, "The Flagellants and the Crusades," *Journal of Medieval History* 15, 1989, 227–67.

———, "The Advent of the *Pastores* (1251)," *Revue Belge de Philologie et d'Histoire* 66.2, 1988, 249–67.

Eric John Dingwall, *The Girdle of Chastity: A Fascinating History of Chastity Belts* (1931), New York: Clarion, 1959.

G. Dix, *Jurisdiction in the Early Church: Episcopal and Papal*, London: Church Literature Association, 1975.

R. B. Dobson (ed. and trans.), *The Peasants' Revolt of 1381*, London: St Martin's, 1970.

Mary Dockray-Miller, *Motherhood and Mothering in Anglo-Saxon England*, New York: St. Martin's, 2000.

Johann Joseph Ignaz von Döllinger, *Die Papst-Fabeln des Mittelalters*, Stuttgart: J. G. Cotta, 1890.

———, *Fables Respecting the Popes of the Middle Ages*, Alfred Plummer (trans.), London: Rivingtons, 1871.

Michael W. Dols, *The Black Death in the Middle East*, Princeton: Princeton University, 1977.

Cesare D'Onofrio, *La Papessa Giovanna*, Rome: Romana società editrice, Studi e testi per la storia della d: Roma 2 città, 1979.

L. Douet-d'Arcq (ed.) "Un Petit Traité de Cuisine Écrit en Français au Commencement du XIVème Siècle," *Bibliothèque de l'Ecole des Chartes* 1, 1860, 209–27.

David C. Douglas (ed.), *English Historical Documents*, 10 vols., London: Routledge, 1996.

Peter Dronke (trans. and ed.), *Nine Medieval Latin Plays*, Cambridge: Cambridge University, 1994.

———, *Women Writers of the Middle Ages*, Cambridge, 1984.

———, *Medieval Latin and the Rise of the European Love Lyric*, 2nd ed., 2 vols., Oxford, 1968.

E. Duffy, *Saints and Sinners: A History of the Popes*, 2nd ed., New Haven: Yale University, 2002.

A. Dulles and P. Granfield (eds.), *The Church: A Bibliography*, Wilmington, DE: Michael Glazier, 1985.

Renée Dunan, *Pope Joan*, H. Graeme (trans.), London: Hutchinson, 1930.

Oliver Dunn and James E. Kelley, Jr. (eds. and trans.), *The Diario of Christopher Columbus's First Voyage to America 1492–1493, Abstracted by Fray Bartolome de las Casas*, Norman, OK: University of Oklahoma, 1989.

Will Durant, *The Age of Faith*, New York: Simon & Schuster, 1950.

E. Durschmied, *Whores of the Devil: Witch-Hunts and Witch-Trials*, Phoenix Mill, UK: Sutton, 2005.

F. Dvornik, *Byzantium and the Roman Primacy*, rev. ed., New York: Fordham University, 1979.

Christopher Dyer, *Everyday Life in Medieval England*, London: Hambledon & London, 2000.

———, *Standards of Living in the Later Middle Ages: Social Change in England c. 1200–1520*, Cambridge: Cambridge University, 1989.

———, "English Diet in the Later Middle Ages," *Social Relations and Ideas: Essays in Honour of R. H. Hilton*, T. H. Aston, P. R. Coss, Christopher Dyer, and Joan Thirsk (eds.), Cambridge: Cambridge University, 1983, pp. 191–216.

Mark Eccles, *The Macro Plays*, EETS o.s. 262, London: Oxford University, 1969.

Warren Edminster, *The Preaching Fox: Festive Subversion in the Plays of the Wakefield Master*, London: Routledge, 2005.

Evelyn Edson, *Mapping Time and Space: How Medieval Mapmakers Viewed Their World*, British Library Studies in Map History 1, London: British Library, 1997.

David Eggenberger, *An Encyclopedia of Battles: Accounts of Over 1,560 Battles from 1479 BC to the Present*, New York: Dover, 1967.

Gustav Ehrismann, *Geschichte der deutschen Literatur bis zum Ausgang des Mittelalters*, 4 vols., München: Beck, 1932.

Einhard and Notker the Stammerer, *Two Lives of Charlemagne*, Lewis Thorpe (trans.), New York: Penguin, 1969.

R. B. Ekelund et al., *Sacred Trust: The Medieval Church as an Economic Firm*, Oxford: Oxford University, 1996.

Erasmus, *Praise of Folly*, B. Radice (trans.) (1971) Harmondsworth: Penguin, 1993.

Karl Erdmann, *The Origin of the Idea of the Crusade*, Marshall W. Baldwin and Walter Goffart (trans.), Princeton: Princeton University, 1977.

W. R. Farmer and R. Kereszty, *Peter and Paul in the Church of Rome: The Ecumenical Potential of a Forgotten Perspective*, New York: Paulist, 1990.

C. Fasolt, "Voluntarism and Conciliarism in the Work of Francis Oakley," *History of Political Thought* 22, 2001, 41–52.

Christine Fell, "Some Implications of the Boniface Correspondence," in *New Readings on Women in Old English Literature*, Helen Damico and Alexandra Hennessey Olsen (eds.), Bloomington, IN: Indiana University, 1990, pp. 29–43.

Joan M. Ferrante, *To the Glory of Her Sex: Women's Roles in the Composition of Medieval Texts*, Bloomington IN: Indiana University, 1997.

M. Ferrières, *Histoire des peurs alimentaires du Moyen Âge à l'aube du XXème Siècle*, Paris: Le Seuil, 2002.

Ronald C. Finucane, *The Rescue of the Innocents: Endangered Children in Medieval Miracles*, Basingstoke, UK: Macmillan, 1997.

J.-L. Flandrin, "Brouets, Potages et Bouillons," *Médiévales* 5, 1983, 5–14.

J.-L. Flandrin and M. Montanari, *Food: A Culinary History from Antiquity to the Present*, A. Sonnenfeld (ed.), C. Bostford et al. (trans.), New York: Columbia University, 1999.

——, (eds.), *Histoire de l'alimentation*, Paris: Fayard, 1996.

A. Flannery (ed.), *Vatican II, Vol. 1: The Conciliar and Post-Conciliar Documents*, rev. ed., Northport, NY: Costello, 1996.

W. Fleischmann-Bisten (ed.), *Papstamt—Pro und Con: geschichtliche Entwicklungen und ökumenische Perspektiven*, Göttingen, Germany: Vandenhoeck & Ruprecht, 2001.

Richard Fletcher, *The Cross and the Crescent: Christianity and Islam from Muhammad to the Reformation*, New York: Viking, 2003.

Robin Lane Fox, *The Unauthorized Version: Truth and Fiction in the Bible*, London: Viking Penguin, 1991.

John France, "Patronage and the Appeal of the First Crusade," in *The First Crusade: Origins and Impact*, Jonathan Phillips (ed.), Manchester: Manchester University, 1997, pp. 5–20.

David O. Frantz, *"Festum Voluptatis": A Study of Renaissance Erotica*, Columbus, OH: Ohio State University, 1989.

Allen J. Frantzen (ed.), *Speaking Two Languages: Traditional Disciplines and Contemporary Theory in Medieval Studies*, Albany, NY: SUNY, 1991.

Paul Freedman, *Images of the Medieval Peasant*, Stanford: Stanford University, 1999.

Amos Funkenstein, *Theology and the Scientific Imagination from the Middle Ages to the Seventeenth Century*, Princeton University, 1986.

Francesco Gabrieli (ed. and trans.), *Arab Historians of the Crusades*, E. J. Costello (trans.), New York, 1969.

Galen, *Galen: On Respiration and the Arteries*, David J. Furley and J. S. Wilkie (eds.), Princeton: Princeton University, 1984.

F. L. Ganshof, *The Carolingians and the Frankish Monarchy*, Janet Sondheimer (trans.), London: Longman, 1971.

———, *Feudalism*, Philip Grierson (trans.), New York: Harper, 1961.

Luis Garcia-Ballester, Roger French, Jon Arrizabalaga, and Andrew Cunningham (eds.), *Practical Medicine from Salerno to the Black Death*, Cambridge: Cambridge University, 1994.

John Gardner, *The Construction of the Wakefield Cycle*, Carbondale: Southern Illinois University, 1974.

Michael W. George, "Representation, Religion, and Sexuality in the York 'Joseph's Troubles' Pageant," in Susannah M. Chewning (ed.), *Intersections of Sexuality and the Divine in Medieval Literature: The Word Made Flesh*, London: Ashgate, 2005, pp. 9–17.

Faye Getz, *Medicine in the English Middle Ages*, Princeton: Princeton University, 1998.

———, (ed.), *Healing and Society in Medieval England: A Middle English Translation of the Pharmaceutical Writings of Gilbertus Anglicus*, Madison: University of Wisconsin, 1991.

Gail McMurray Gibson, *The Theater of Devotion: East Anglian Drama and Society in the Late Middle Ages*, Chicago: University of Chicago, 1989.

Sean Gilsdorf (trans.), *Queenship and Sanctity: The Lives of Mathilda and the Epitaph of Adelheid*, Washington, DC: Catholic University of America, 2004.

E. Gilson, *Reason and Revelation in the Middle Ages*, New York: Scribner, 1938.

Michael Goodich, *Other Middle Ages: Witnesses at the Margins of Medieval Society*, Philadelphia: University of Pennsylvania, 1998.

Robert S. Gottfried, *The Black Death: Natural and Human Disaster in Medieval Europe*, New York: Macmillan, 1983.

John Gower, *Vox Clamantis*, in *The Major Latin Works of John Gower*, Eric W. Stockton (trans.), Seattle: University of Washington, 1962.

S. J. Grabowski, *The Church: An Introduction to the Theology of St. Augustine*, St. Louis: Herder, 1957.

Edward Grant, *The Foundations of Modern Science in the Middle Ages: Their Religious, Institutional, and Intellectual Contexts*, Cambridge History of Science, Cambridge: Cambridge University, 1996.

———, *Planets, Stars, and Orbs: The Medieval Cosmos, 1200–1687*, Cambridge: Cambridge University, 1994.

———, (ed.), *A Source Book in Medieval Science*, Cambridge: Harvard University, 1974.

J. H. G. Grattan and Charles Singer, *Anglo-Saxon Magic and Medicine*, London: Oxford University, 1952.

Monica Green, *The Trotula: A Medieval Compendium of Women's Medicine*, Philadelphia: University of Pennsylvania, 2001.

Stanley B. Greenfield and Daniel G. Calder, *A New Critical History of Old English Literature*, New York: New York University, 1986.

Mirko D. Grmek, *Diseases in the Ancient Greek World*, Mireille Muellner and Leonard Muellner (trans.), Baltimore: Johns Hopkins University, 1989.

Guibert of Nogent, *A Monk's Confession: The Memoirs of Guibert of Nogent*, Paul J. Archambault (trans.), University Park, PA: Pennsylvania State University, 1996.

R. E. Guiley, *The Encyclopedia of Witches and Witchcraft*, 2nd ed. (1989), New York: Facts on File, 1999.

Aaron Gurevitch, *The Origins of European Individualism*, Oxford: Blackwell, 1995.

T. P. Halton (ed.), *The Church*, Wilmington, DE: Michael Glazier, 1985.

Bernard Hamilton, *Religion in the Medieval West*, London: Edward Arnold, 1986.

P. W. Hammond, *Food and Feast in Medieval England*, Gloucestershire, UK: Alan Sutton, 1995.

Barbara Hanawalt, *Growing Up in Medieval London: The Experience of Childhood in History*, Oxford: Oxford University, 1993.

———, *The Ties That Bound: Peasant Families in Medieval England*, New York: Oxford University, 1986.

Victor David Hanson, *Carnage and Culture: Landmark Battles in the Rise of Western Power*, New York: Doubleday, 2001.

Peter Happé, *English Mystery Plays: A Selection*, London: Penguin, 1975.

Antonina Harbus, *The Life of the Mind in Old English Poetry*, Amsterdam: Rodopi, 2002.

O. B. Hardison, Jr., *Christian Rite and Christian Drama in the Middle Ages*, Baltimore: Johns Hopkins University, 1965.

John Harington (ed.), *The School of Salernum: regimen sanitatis Salerni*, Rome: Edizioni Saturnia, 1959.

John Harlow, "Damsels Not Distressed by Medieval Chastity Belt," *Sunday Times* (London), 23 June 1996, News 1.

M. Harris, *Cows, Pigs, Wars and Witches: The Riddles of Culture*, New York: Random House, 1974.

William V. Harris, *Ancient Literacy*, Cambridge: Harvard University, 1991.

Clive Hart and Kay Gilliland Stevenson, *Heaven and the Flesh: Imagery of Desire from the Renaissance to the Rococo*, Cambridge: Cambridge University, 1995.

Kevin Harty (ed.), *The Chester Mystery Cycle: A Casebook*, New York: Garland Publishing, 1993.

A. Hasler, *How the Pope Became Infallible: Pius IX and the Politics of Persuasion*, P. Heinegg (trans.), New York: Doubleday, 1981.

Thomas Head and Richard Landes (eds.), *The Peace of God: Social Violence and Religious Response in France around the Year 1000*, Ithaca/London: Cornell University, 1992.

L. C. Hector and Barbara Harvey (ed. and trans.), *Westminster Chronicle, 1381–1394*, Oxford: Clarendon, 1982.

Emily A. Hemelrijk, *Matrona Docta: Educated Women in the Roman Elite from Cornelia to Julia Domna*, London, 2004.

Yitzhak Hen and Matthew Innes (eds.), *The Uses of the Past in the Early Middle Ages*, New York: Cambridge University, 2000.

B. A. Henisch, *Fast and Feast: Food in Medieval Society*, University Park, PA: Pennsylvania State University, 1976.

W. Henn, *The Honor of My Brothers: A Short History of the Relation between the Pope and the Bishops*, New York: Crossroad, 2000.

J. Hennesey, *The First Council of the Vatican: The American Experience*, New York: Herder & Herder, 1963.

G. Henningsen, *The Witches' Advocate: Basque Witchcraft and the Spanish Inquisition (1609–1614)*, Reno, NV: University of Nevada, 1980.

L. Hertling, *Communio: Church and Papacy in Early Christianity*, J. Wicks (trans.), Chicago: Loyola University, 1972.

Constance B. Hieatt and Sharon Butler (eds.), *Curye on Inglysch*, London: EETS, 1985.

Constance B. Hieatt, Brenda Hosington, and Sharon Butler (eds.), *Pleyn Delit*, Toronto: University of Toronto, 1996.

N. J. Higham, *King Arthur: Myth-Making and History*, London and New York: Routledge, 2002.

Carole Hillenbrand (ed.), *Crusades: Islamic Perspectives*, Edinburgh: Edinburgh University, 1999.

Rodney Hilton, *The English Peasantry in the Later Middle Ages*, Oxford: Clarendon, 1975.

———, *Bond Men Made Free: Medieval Peasant Movements and the English Rising of 1381*, London: Temple Smith, 1973.

D. Hobbins (trans.), *The Trial of Joan of Arc*, Cambridge: Harvard University, 2005.

Richard M. Hogg (ed.), *The Cambridge History of the English Language*, 6 vols., Cambridge: Cambridge University, 1992.

Bart Holland (ed.), *Prospecting for Drugs in Ancient and Medieval European Texts: A Scientific Approach*, Amsterdam: Harwood Academic, 1996.

Stephanie Hollis, *Anglo-Saxon Women and the Church*, Woodbridge, UK: Boydell, 1992.

Peregrine Horden and Emilie Savage-Smith (eds.), "Social History of Medicine: The Year 1000, Medical Practice at the End of the First Millennium," *The Journal of the Society for the Social History of Medicine* 13.2, 2000.

Simon Hornblower and Antony Spawforth (eds.) *Oxford Classical Dictionary*, 3rd ed. Oxford University, 1996.

Rosemary Horrox (ed. and trans.), *The Black Death*, Manchester, UK: Manchester University, 1994.

U. Horst, *Unfehlbarkeit und Geschichte: Studien zur Unfehlbarkeitsdiskussion von Melchior Cano bis zum I vatikanischen Konzil*, Mainz, Germany: Matthias Grünewald, 1982.

Norman Housley, *Contesting the Crusades*, Oxford: Blackwell, 2006.

———, (ed.), *Documents on the Later Crusades, 1274–1580*, London: Macmillan, 1996.

———, *The Later Crusades from Lyon to Alcazar, 1274–1580*, Oxford: Oxford University, 1992.

———, *The Italian Crusades*, Oxford: Oxford University, 1982.

A. Houtepen, "Modernity and the Crisis of Spirituality in the Nineteenth Century: The Case of Papal Infallibility," in J. Frishman, W. Otten, and G. Rouwhorst (eds.), *Religious Identity and the Problem of Historical Foundation: The Foundational Character of Authoritative Sources in the History of Christianity and Judaism*, Leiden, Netherlands: Brill, 2004, pp. 95–113.

C. A. Hoyt, *Witchcraft*, 2nd ed. (1981), Carbondale: Southern Illinois University, 1989.

Johan Huizinga, *The Autumn of the Middle Ages*, Rodney J. Payton and Ulrich Mammitzsch (trans.), Chicago: University of Chicago, 1996.

———, *Homo Ludens: A Study of the Play-Element in Culture*, R. F. C. Hull (trans.), Boston: Beacon, 1967.

Chris Humphrey and W. M. Ormrod (eds.), *Time in the Medieval World*, Rochester, NY: Boydell, 2001.

Tony Hunt, *The Medieval Surgery*, Woodbridge, UK: Boydell, 1992.

———, *Popular Medicine in Thirteenth-Century England*, Cambridge: D. S. Brewer, 1990.

E. and F.-B. Huyghe, *Les coureurs d'épices*, Paris: Petite Bibliothèque Payot, 2002.

Richard Ince, *When Joan Was Pope*, London: Partridge, 1931.

Patricia Ingham, *Sovereign Fantasies: Arthurian Romance and the Making of Britain*, Philadelphia: University of Pennsylvania, 2001.

M. Innes, *State and Society in the Early Middle Ages: The Middle Rhine Valley 400–1000*, Cambridge: Cambridge University, 2000.

Dominique Iogna-Prat, *Order and Exclusion: Cluny and Christendom Face Heresy, Judaism, and Islam (1000–1150)*, Graham Robert Edwards (trans.), Ithaca: Cornell University, 2002.

T. M. Izbicki, "Papalist Reaction to the Council of Constance: Juan de Torquemada to the Present," *Church History* 55, 1986, 7–20.

——, "Infallibility and the Erring Pope: Guido Terreni and Johannes de Turrecremata," in K. Pennington and R. Somerville (eds.), *Law, Church, and Society: Essays in Honor of Stephen Kuttner*, Philadelphia: University of Pennsylvania, 1977, pp. 97–111.

E. F. Jacob, *The Fifteenth Century, 1399–1485*, Oxford: Oxford University, 1961.

Danielle Jacquart, and Claude Thomasset, *Sexuality and Medicine in the Middle Ages*, Matthew Adamson (trans.), Princeton: Princeton University, 1988.

David Lyle Jeffrey (ed.), *A Dictionary of Biblical Tradition in English Literature*, Grand Rapids, MI: Eerdman's, 1992.

Jocelin of Brakelond, *Chronicle of the Abbey of Bury St Edmunds*, Diana Greenway and Jane Sayers (trans.), Oxford: Oxford University, 1989.

Johannes of Viktring, *Liber certarum historiarum*, Fedorum Schneider (ed.), *MGH Scriptores* 36, 1909.

Alexandra F. Johnston, "*The Word Made Flesh*: Augustinian Elements in the *York Cycle*," in *The Centre and its Compass: Studies in Medieval Literature in Honor of Professor John Leyerle*, Robert A. Taylor et al. (eds.), Kalamazoo, MI: Medieval Institute, 1993, pp. 225–246.

——, " 'All the World Was a Stage': Records of Early English Drama," in *The Theatre of Medieval Europe: New Research in Early Drama*, Eckehard Simon (ed.), Cambridge: Cambridge University, 1991, pp. 117–29.

——, "What if No Texts Survived? External Evidence for Early English Drama," in *Contexts for Early English Drama*, (eds.) M. Briscoe and J. C. Coldewey (eds.), Bloomington: Indiana University, 1989, pp. 1–9.

Karen L. Jolly, "Medieval Magic: Definitions, Beliefs, Practices," in B. Ankarloo and S. Clark (eds.), *Witchcraft and Magic in Europe: The Middle Ages*, Philadelphia: University of Pennsylvania, 2001.

——, *Popular Religion in Late Saxon England: Elf Charms in Context*, Chapel Hill, NC: University of North Carolina, 1996.

Charles W. Jones, "The Flat Earth," *Thought* 9, 1934, 296–307.

Steven Justice, *Writing and Rebellion: England in 1381*, Berkeley: University of California, 1994.

Stanley J. Kahrl, *Traditions of Medieval English Drama*, Pittsburgh: University of Pittsburgh, 1975.

E. H. Kantorowicz, *The King's Two Bodies: A Study in Mediaeval Political Theology*, Princeton: Princeton University, 1957.

W. Kasper (ed.), *The Petrine Ministry: Catholics and Orthodox in Dialogue*, New York: Newman, 2006.

Edward J. Kealey, *Medieval Medicus: A Social History of Anglo-Norman Medicine*, Baltimore: Johns Hopkins University, 1981.

John Keegan, *A History of Warfare*, New York: Alfred A. Knopf, 1993.

——, *The Face of Battle*, New York: Dorset, 1976.

Maurice Keen (ed.), *Medieval Warfare: A History*, New York: Oxford University, 1999.

Gundolf Keil, *Fachprosa-Studien: Beiträge zur mittelalterliche Wissenschafts und Geistesgeschichte*, Berlin: E. Schmidt, 1982.

Gundolf Keil and Paul Schnitzer (eds.), *Das lorscher Arzneibuch und die frühmittelalterlice Medizin*, Lorsch, Germany: Laurissa, 1991.

Kathleen Coyne Kelly, *Performing Virginity and Testing Chastity in the Middle Ages*, Routledge Research in Medieval Studies, vol., 2, London: Routledge, 2000.

Kathleen Coyne Kelly and Marina Leslie (eds.), *Menacing Virgins: Representing Virginity in the Middle Ages and Renaissance*, Newark: University of Delaware, 1999.

E. W. Kemp, *Canonization and Authority in the Western Church*, Oxford: Oxford University, 1948.

Margery Kempe, *The Book of Margery Kempe*, Barry Windeatt (trans.), New York: Penguin, 1985.

Edward Donald Kennedy (ed.), *King Arthur: A Casebook*, New York: Garland, 1996.

W. P. Ker, *The Dark Ages*, New York: Scribner's, 1904.

Kathryn Kerby-Fulton, *Books Under Suspicion: Censorship and Tolerance of Revelatory Writing in Late Medieval England*, Notre Dame, IN: University of Notre Dame, 2006.

F. Kern, *Kingship and Law in the Middle Ages* (1939), Oxford, 1968.

Simon Keynes and Michael Lapidge (trans.), *Alfred the Great: Asser's Life of King Alfred and other Contemporary Sources*, New York: Penguin, 1983.

Pearl Kibre (ed.), *Hippocrates Latinus: Repertorium of Hippocratic Writings in the Latin Middle Ages*, New York: Fordham University, 1985.

Richard Kieckhefer, *Magic in the Middle Ages*, Cambridge: Cambridge University, 1989.

——, *European Witch Trials: Their Foundations in Popular And Learned Culture, 1300–1500*, Berkeley: University of California, 1976.

Beverly Mayne Kienzle, *Cistercians, Heresy, and Crusade in Occitania, 1145–1229*, Rochester, NY: York Medieval, 2001.

Pamela M. King, *The York Mystery Cycle and the Worship of the City*, Woodbridge, UK: Boydell and Brewer, 2006.

Pamela King and Clifford Davidson (eds.), *The Coventry Corpus Christi Plays*, Kalamazoo, MI: Medieval Institute, 2000.

Fr. Klaeber (ed.), *Beowulf and the Fight at Finnsburg*, 3rd ed., Lexington, MA: D. C. Heath, 1950.

J. Klaits, *Servants of Satan: The Age of the Witch Hunts*, Bloomington: Indiana University, 1985.

David Knowles, *The Evolution of Medieval Thought*, New York: Vintage Books, 1962.

V. A. Kolve, *The Play Called Corpus Christi*, Stanford: Stanford University, 1966.

A. C. Kors and E. Peters (eds.), *Witchcraft in Europe, 1100–1700: A Documentary History*, 2nd ed. (1972), Philadelphia: University of Pennsylvania, 2001.

J.-F. Kosta-Théfaine, "De l'art des mots à l'art des mets: les nourritures de la mer dans les poèmes d'Eustache Deschamps et dans la littérature culinaire française du Moyen âge," in *Les nourritures de la mer, de la criée à l'assiette: actes du colloque organisée sur l'Île de Tatihou du 2 au 4 Octobre 2004*, Eric Barré et André Zysberg (eds.), Musée Maritime de l'Île de Tatihou et Caen, France: Universitaires de Caen, (forthcoming).

——, "Le sel dans quelques poèmes d'Eustache Deschamps," in *De sel: actes de la Journée d'Études 'Le sel dans la littérature française' (Pau, 28 Novembre 2003)*, Véronique Duché-Gavet and Jean-Gérard Lapacherie with the collaboration of Frédérique Marty-Badiola (eds.), Biarritz, France: Atlantica, 2005, 29–48.

——, (ed.), "Des 'regles en françois' pour bien se tenir à table . . . ," in M. Colombo and Cl. Galderisi (eds.), *"Pour acquerir honneur et pris": mélanges de Moyen Français en hommage à Giuseppe Di Stefano*, Montréal: Editions CERES, 2004, pp. 265–75.

——, "De la littérature gastronomique et autres petits plaisirs littéraires et culinaires . . . ," *Lendemains* 103–4, 2001, 213–5.

——, "Sucre et douceurs sucrées dans la littérature culinaire française du Moyen Âge," in *Du sucre: actes de la Journée d'Études 'Plus aloës quam mellis habet:*

Le sucre dans la littérature française' (Pau, 21 Janvier 2005) Véronique Duchet-Gavet and Jean-Gérard Lapacherie (eds.), Biarritz, France: Éditions Atlantica, 2007, pp. 153–171.

——, "Du livre de cuisine à 'l'art total': la littérature culinaire française du Moyen Âge," in *Ecriture du repas: fragments d'un discours gastronomique*, Karin Becker and Olivier Leplatre (eds.), Berlin: Peter Lang, 2007, pp. 13–32.

H. Kramer and J. Sprenger, *The Malleus Maleficarum*, M. Summers (trans.), New York: Dover, 1971.

George Philip Krapp and Elliott van Kirk Dobbie (eds.), *The Anglo-Saxon Poetic Records*, 6 vols., New York: Columbia University, 1931–1942.

H. Küng, *Infallible? An Inquiry*, E. Quinn (trans.), New York: Doubleday, 1971.

Conrad Kyeser, *Bellifortis*, Götz Quarg (ed.), 2 vols., Düsseldorf: VDI, 1967.

Norris J. Lacy (ed.), *Medieval Arthurian Literature: A Guide to Recent Research*, New York: Garland, 1996.

Norris J. Lacy et al. (eds.), *The Arthurian Handbook*, 2nd ed., New York and London: Garland, 1997.

Gerhardt B. Ladner, *The Idea of Reform; Its Impact on Christian Thought and Action in the Age of the Fathers*, Cambridge: Harvard University, 1959.

W. J. La Due, *The Chair of Saint Peter: A History of the Papacy*, Maryknoll, NY: Orbis, 1999.

M. L. W. Laistner, *Thoughts and Letters in Western Europe, AD 500–900*, Ithaca: Cornell University, 1957.

C. Lambert (ed.), *Du manuscrit à la table: essais sur la cuisine au Moyen Âge*, Montréal and Paris: Presses de l'Université de Montréal & Champion, 1992.

——, (ed.), *le recueil de riom et la maniere de henter soutillement: un livre de cuisine et un réceptaire sur les greffes du XVème siècle*, Montréal: CERES, 1987.

William Langland, *Piers the Ploughman*, J. F. Goodridge (ed.), New York: Penguin, 1966.

Gavin Langmuir, *History, Religion, and Antisemitism*, Berkeley: University of California, 1990.

Sylvie Laurent, *Naître au Moyen Âge: de la conception à la naissance: la grossesse et l'accouchement (XIIe–XVe Siècle)*, Paris: Léopard d'Or, 1989.

B. Laurioux, *Une Histoire Culinaire du Moyen Age*, Paris: Champion, 2005.

——, *Manger au Moyen Age*, Paris: Hachette, 2002.

——, *Le règne Taillevent: livres et pratiques culinaires à la fin du Moyen Âge*, Paris: Sorbonne, 1997.

——, *Les livres de cuisine médiévaux*. Turnhout, Belgium: Brepols, 1997.

——, "Cuisiner à l'Antique: Apicius au Moyen Âge," *Médiévales* 26, 1994, 17–38.

——, "Un exemple de livre technique: le livre de cuisine à la fin du Moyen Âge," *Gazette du Livre Médiéval* 14, 1989, 12–6.

——, (ed.), "Le registre de cuisine de Jean Bockenheim, cuisinier du Pape Martin V," *Mélanges de l'école française de Rome (Moyen Âge, Temps modernes)* 100, 1988, 709–60.

——, "Entre savoir et pratiques: le livre de cuisine à la fin du Moyen Âge, *Médiévales* 14, 1988, 59–71.

——, "Les Premiers Livres de Cuisine," *L'Histoire* 85, 1986, 52–5.

——, "Spices in the Medieval Diet: A New Approach," *Food and Foodways* 1, 1985, 43–76.

——, "De l'usage des épices dans l'alimentation médiévale," *Médiévales* 5, 1983, 14–31.

John C. Laursen and Cary J. Nederman (eds.), *Beyond the Persecuting Society: Religious Toleration before the Enlightenment*, Philadelphia: University of Pennsylvania, 1998.

David Lawton, "1453 and the Stream of Time," *Journal of Medieval and Early Modern Studies* 37.3, 2007, 469–491.
———, "The Surveying Subject," *New Medieval Literatures* 4, 2001, 9–37.
Henry Charles Lea, *A History of Auricular Confession and Indulgences in the Latin Church*, 3 vols., Philadelphia: Lea Bros., 1896.
Clare A. Lees and Gillian R. Overing, *Double Agents: Women and Clerical Culture in Anglo-Saxon England*, Philadelphia: University of Pennsylvania, 2001.
Jacques Le Goff, *Time, Work, and Culture in the Middle Ages*, Arthur Goldhammer (trans.), Chicago: University of Chicago, 1982.
Jacques Le Goff et al. (eds.), *Dictionnaire raisonné de l'occident médiévale*, Paris: Fayard, 1999.
Robert E. Lerner, *The Feast of Saint Abraham: Medieval Millenarians and the Jews*, Philadelphia: University of Pennsylvania Press, 2001.
Didier Lett, *L'enfant des miracles: enfance et société au Moyen Âge (XIIe–XIIIe Siècle)*, Paris: Aubier, 1997.
B. P. Levack, *The Witch-Hunt in Early Modern Europe*, 3rd ed. (1987), London: Longman, 2006.
Wilhelm Levison, *England and the Continent in the Eighth Century*, Oxford: Oxford University, 1946.
Bernard Lewis, *Islam and the West*, New York: Oxford University, 1993.
C. S. Lewis, *The Allegory of Love: A Study in Medieval Tradition*, London: Oxford University, 1938.
———, The Discarded Image: An Introduction to Medieval and Renaissance Literature (1964) Cambridge: Canto, 1994.
E. Lewis, *Medieval Political Ideas*, 2 vols. (1954), New York: Knopf, 1974.
K. Leyser, *Rule and Conflict in an Early Medieval Society: Ottonian Saxony*, London: E. Arnold, 1979.
Carl Lindahl, John McNamara, and John Lindow (eds.), *Medieval Folklore: A Guide to Myths, Legends, Tales, Beliefs, and Customs*, Oxford: Oxford University, 2002.
David C. Lindberg, *The Beginnings of Western Science*, Chicago: Chicago University, 1992.
David Lindberg and Ronald Numbers, *God and Nature: Historical Essays on the Encounter Between Christianity and Science*, Berkeley: University of California, 1986.
Simon Lloyd, *English Society and the Crusade, 1216–1307*, Oxford: Clarendon, 1988.
Cornelia Löhmer, *Die Welt der Kinder im fünfzehnten Jahrhundert*, Weinheim, Germany: Deutscher Studien, 1989.
R. M. Lumiansky (trans.), *The Canterbury Tales of Geoffrey Chaucer* (1948), New York: Washington Square, 1972.
R. M. Lumiansky and David Mills, *The Chester Mystery Cycle: Essays and Documents*, Chapel Hill: University of North Carolina, 1983.
———, (eds.), *The Chester Mystery Cycle*, 2 vols., EETS s.s. 3, 9, Oxford: Oxford University, 1974.
Walter E. Lunt (ed.), *Papal Revenues in the Middle Ages*, 2 vols., New York, 1934
———, *Financial Relations of the Papacy with England to 1327*, Cambridge: Harvard University, 1939.
David Luscombe, *The School of Peter Abelard: the Influence of Abelard's Thought in the Early Scholastic Period*, Cambridge University, 1969.
Guillaume de Machaut, *Le livre dou voir dit (The Book of the True Poem)*, Daniel Leech-Wilkinson (ed.), R. Barton Palmer (trans.), New York: Garland, 1998.
Loren MacKinney, *Early Medieval Medicine*, Baltimore: Johns Hopkins, 1937.

Thomas F. Madden, *The New Concise History of the Crusades*, Lanham, MD: Rowman & Littlefield, 2005.

Christoph Maier, *Crusade Propaganda and Ideology: Model Sermons for the Preaching of the Cross*, Cambridge: Cambridge University, 2000.

———, *Preaching the Crusades: Mendicant Friars and the Cross in the Thirteenth Century*, Cambridge: Cambridge University, 1994.

Jean de Mailly, *Chronica universalis Mettensis*, G. Waitz (ed.), *MGH Scriptores* 24, 1879, pp. 172–213.

A. P. Manahan, *Consent, Coercion and Limit: The Medieval Origins of Parliamentary Democracy*, Kingston, ON: McGill-Queen's University, 1987.

Marie de France, *Guigemar*, in *Les Lais de Marie de France*, Jean Rychner (ed.), Paris: H. Champion, 1973.

———, *Guigemar*, in *The Lais of Marie de France*, Robert Hanning and Joan Ferrante (trans.), Durham, NC: Labyrinth, 1978.

Jean Markale, *King of the Celts: Arthurian Legends and Celtic Tradition*, Christine Hauch (trans.), Rochester, VT: Inner Traditions, 1994.

H. I. A. Marrou, *A History of Education in Antiquity*, George Lamb (trans.), New York: New American Library, 1964.

Dale B. Martin, *Inventing Superstition: From the Hippocratics to the Christians*, Cambridge: Harvard University, 2004.

Hans Eberhard Mayer, *The Crusades*, John Gillingham (trans.), Oxford: Oxford University, 1972.

R. P. McBrien, *Catholicism: Study Edition*, San Francisco: HarperCollins, 1981.

———, (ed.) *The HarperCollins Encyclopedia of Catholicism*, San Francisco: HarperCollins, 1995.

R. McClory, *Power and the Papacy: The People and Politics behind the Doctrine of Infallibility*, Ligouri, MO: Triumph, 1997.

Bernard McGinn, John Meyendorff, and Jean Leclercq (eds.), *Christian Spirituality*, New York: Crossroad, 1996–97.

C. K. Mckay, *Malleus Maleficarum*, Cambridge: Cambridge University (forthcoming).

May McKisack, *The Fourteenth Century, 1307–1399*, Oxford: Oxford University, 1959.

Rosamund McKittrick, *The Carolingians and the Written Word*, Cambridge: Cambridge University, 1989.

———, (ed.), *The Uses of Literacy in Early Mediaeval Europe*, Cambridge: Cambridge University, 1991.

M. R. McVaugh, *Medicine Before the Plague: Practitioners and Their Patients in the Crown of Aragon, 1285–1345*, Cambridge: Cambridge University, 1993.

M. Meltzer, *Witches and Witch-Hunts: A History of Persecution*, New York: Blue Sky, 1999.

Stephen Mennell, *All Manners of Food: Eating and Taste in England and France from the Middle Ages to the Present*, 2nd ed., Chicago: University of Illinois, 1996.

María Rose Menocal, *The Arabic Role in Medieval Literary History: A Forgotten Heritage*, Philadelphia: University of Pennsylvania, 2003.

Peter Meredith and John E. Tailby (eds.), *The Staging of Religious Drama in Europe in the Later Middle Ages: Texts and Documents in English Translation*, Kalamazoo: Medieval Institute, 1983.

L. Meulenberg, "Une question toujours ouverte: Grégoire VII et l'infaillibilité du Pape," in H. Mordek (ed.), *Aus Kirche und Reich: Studien zur Theologie, Politik, und Recht im Mittelalter*, Sigmaringen, Germany: J. Thorbecke, 1983, pp. 159–71.

J. M. Miller, *The Shepherd and the Rock: Origins, Development and Mission of the Papacy*, Huntington, IN: Our Sunday Visitor, 1995.

Robert P. Miller, "Chaucer's Pardoner, The Scriptural Eunuch, and the Pardoner's Tale," *Speculum* 30, 1955, 180–9.

Timothy Miller, *The Birth of the Hospital in the Byzantine Empire*, Baltimore: Johns Hopkins University, 1997.

David Mills, *Staging the Chester Cycle*, Leeds: University of Leeds, 1985.

Piers D. Mitchell, *Medicine in the Crusades: Warfare, Wounds and the Medieval Surgeon*, Cambridge: Cambridge University, 2004.

Guillaume Mollat, *The Popes at Avignon 1305–1378*, Janet Love (trans.), London: Nelson, 1963.

Michel Mollat, *The Poor in the Middle Ages: An Essay in Social History*, Arthur Goldhammer (trans.), New Haven: Yale University, 1986.

W. E. Monter, "Witch Trials in Continental Europe 1560–1660," in B. Ankarloo and S. Clark (eds.), *Witchcraft and Magic in Europe: The Period of the Witch Trials*, Philadelphia: University of Pennsylvania, 2002.

R. I. Moore, *The Formation of a Persecuting Society: Power and Deviance in Western Europe, 950–1250*, Oxford: Basil Blackwell, 1987.

S. Morand, *Cuisine du temps jadis: Moyen Age et Renaissance*, Rennes, France: Editions Ouest-France, 1996.

Colin Morris, *The Discovery of the Individual, 1050–1200*, New York: Harper & Row, 1972.

Joan Morris, *Pope John VIII, an English Woman, Alias Pope Joan*, London: Vrai, 1985.

K. F. Morrison, *Tradition and Authority in the Western Church, 300–1140*, Princeton: Princeton University, 1969.

M. Mulon, "Recettes médiévales," *Annales (Economies, Sociétés, Civilisations)* 19.4, 1964, 933–7.

———, (ed.), "Deux traités inédits d'art culinaire," *Bulletin philologique et historique*, 1968 (1971), 369–45.

James J. Murphy (trans.), *Three Medieval Rhetorical Arts*, Berkeley: University of California, 1971.

Charles Muscatine, *Chaucer and the French Tradition: A Study in Style and Meaning*, Berkeley: University of California, 1957.

C. J. Nederman, "Conciliarism and Constitutionalism: Jean Gerson and Medieval Political Thought," *History of European Ideas* 12, 1990, 189–209.

Alan H. Nelson, *The Medieval English Stage: Corpus Christi Pageants and Plays*, Chicago: University of Chicago, 1974.

Janet Nelson, "Kingship and Empire in the Carolingian World," in *Carolingian Culture*, R. McKitterick (ed.), Cambridge: Cambridge University, 1993, pp. 52–87.

———, "Kingship, Law and Liturgy in the Political Thought of Hincmar of Rheims," in *Politics and Ritual in Early Medieval Europe*, J. Nelson (ed.), London: Ronceverte, 1986, pp. 133–71.

Venetia Newall, *The Encyclopedia of Witchcraft and Magic*, New York: Dial, 1974.

Jay Newman, *Foundations of Religious Tolerance*, Toronto: University of Toronto, 1982.

A. Nichols, *Rome and the Eastern Churches: A Study in Schism*, Edinburgh: T & T Clark, 1992.

Ruth Nissé, "'A Coroun Ful Riche': The Rule of History in *St. Erkenwald*," *ELH* 65, 1998, 277–95.

T. F. X. Noble, "Morbidity and Vitality in the History of the Early Medieval Papacy," *Catholic Historical Review* 81, 1995, 505–40.

F. Oakley, *The Conciliarist Tradition: Constitutionalism in the Catholic Church, 1300–1870*, Oxford: Oxford University, 2003.

————, "Verius est licet difficilius: Tierney's *Foundations of the Conciliar Theory after Forty Years*," in G. Christianson and T. M. Izbicki (eds.), *Nicholas of Cusa on Christ and the Church: Essays in Memory of Chandler McCuskey Brooks for the American Cusanus Society*, Leiden, Netherlands: Brill, 1996, pp. 15–34.

————, *The Western Church in the Later Middle Ages*, Ithaca: Cornell University, 1979.

————, *Council over Pope? Towards a Provisional Ecclesiology*, New York: Herder & Herder, 1969.

M. O'Gara, *Triumph in Defeat: Infallibility, Vatican I, and the French Minority Bishops*, Washington, DC: Catholic University, 1988.

Dunbar H. Ogden, *The Staging of Drama in the Medieval Church*, Newark, DE: University of Delaware, 2002.

Margaret Sinclair Ogden (ed.), *The 'Liber de diversis medicinis,'* London: Early English Text Society, 1938.

Katherine O'Brien O'Keeffe (ed.), *Old English Shorter Poems: Basic Readings*, New York: Garland, 1994.

Samir Okasha, *Philosophy of Science: A Very Short Introduction*, Oxford University, 2002.

Glending Olson, "Plays as Play: A Medieval Ethical Theory of Performance and the Intellectual Context of the Tretise of Miraclis Pleyinge," *Viator* 26, 1995, 195–221.

————, *Literature as Recreation in the Later Middle Ages*, Ithaca: Cornell University, 1986.

Sophie Oosterwijk, *"Litel Enfaunt that Were but Late Borne": The Image of the Infant in Medieval Culture in North-Western Europe*, Turnhout, Belgium: Brepols, 2007 (forthcoming).

Iona Opie and Moira Tatem (eds.), *A Dictionary of Superstitions*, Oxford: Oxford University, 1989.

Andy Orchard, *A Critical Companion to* Beowulf, Cambridge: D. S. Brewer, 2003.

Nicholas Orme, *Medieval Children*, New Haven: Yale University, 2001.

Paulus Orosius, *The Seven Books of History Against the Pagans: The Apology of Paulus Orosius*, Irving Woodward Raymond (trans.), New York: Columbia University, 1936.

Monika Otter, *Inventiones: Fiction and Referentiality in Twelfth-Century English Historical Writing*, Chapel Hill: University of North Carolina, 1996.

————, "'New Werke': *St. Erkenwald*, St. Albans, and the Medieval Sense of the Past," *Journal of Medieval and Early Modern Studies* 24.3, 1994, 387–414.

G. R. Owst, *Literature and Pulpit in Medieval England*, 2d rev. ed., Oxford: Basil Blackwell, 1961.

S. Ozment, *The Age of Reform, 1250–1550: An Intellectual and Religious History of Late Medieval and Reformation Europe*, New Haven: Yale University, 1980.

J. R. Page, *What will Dr. Newman Do? John Henry Newman and Papal Infallibility 1865–75*, Collegeville, MN: Liturgical Press, 1994.

Barbara Palmer, "Recycling 'The Wakefield Cycle': The Records," *Research Opportunities in Renaissance Drama* 41, 2002, 88–130.

Onofrio Panvinio, Revision of Platina, *Vitae Pontificum,*Venice, 1563.

Paracelsus [Aureolus Theophrastus Bombastus von Hohenheim], *Paracelsus: Selected Writings*, Jolande Jacobi (ed.), Princeton: Princeton University, 1979.

Rosemary and Darroll Pardoe, *The Female Pope*, Wellingborough, Northamptonshire, UK: Aquarian, 1988.

Katherine Park, *Doctors and Medicine in Early Renaissance Florence*, Princeton: Princeton University, 1985.

Geoffrey Parker (ed.), *Cambridge Illustrated History of Warfare*, Cambridge: Cambridge University, 1995.

M. B. Parkes, "The Literacy of the Laity" in *Literature and Western Civilization: The Medieval World*, D. Daiches and A. Thorlby (eds.), London: Aldus, 1973.

Lee Patterson, *Chaucer and the Subject of History*, Madison, WI: University of Wisconsin, 1991.

———, "On the Margin: Postmodernism, Ironic History, and Medieval Studies," *Speculum* 65.1, 1990, 87–108.

———, *Negotiating the Past: The Historical Understanding of Medieval Literature*, Madison: University of Wisconsin, 1987.

Joseph F. Payne, "English Medicine in the Anglo-Saxon Times," *The Fitz-Patrick Lectures for 1903*, London: Clarendon, 1904.

Derek Pearsall, *The Canterbury Tales* (1985), London: Routledge, 1993.

S. Pegge (ed.), *The Forme of Cury*, London: J. Nichols, 1780.

J.-M. Pelt, *Les epices*, Paris: Fayard, 2002.

K. Pennington, *Popes and Bishops: The Papal Monarchy in the Twelfth and Thirteenth Centuries*, Philadelphia: University of Pennsylvania, 1984.

Lisa R. Perfetti, *Women and Laughter in Medieval Comic Literature*, Ann Arbor: University of Michigan, 2003.

———, "Taking Laughter Seriously: The Comic and Didactic Functions of Helmbrecht," in *Bakhtin and Medieval Voices*, Thomas J. Farrell (ed.), Gainesville: University Press of Florida, 1995, pp. 38–60.

Henri Perrodo-Le Moyne, *Un Pape Nommè Jeanne*, Angiers, France: Coopèrative Angevine, 1972.

R. Pesch, *Die biblischen Grundlagen des Primat*, Freiburg, Germany: Herder, 2001.

Edward Peters (ed.): University of Pennsylvania, *The First Crusade: The Chronicle of Fulcher of Chartres and Other Source Materials*, 2nd rev. ed., Philadelphia, 1998.

———, *Inquisition*, Berkeley: University of California, 1989.

———, (ed.), *Christian Society and the Crusades, 1198–1229*, Philadelphia: University of Pennsylvania, 1971.

Francesco Petrarch, *Petrarch's Secretum*, Davy A. Carozza and H. James Shey (ed. and trans.), New York: Peter Lang, 1989.

Platina [Bartolomeo Sacchi of Piàdena], *Platynae historici liber de vita Christi ac omnium pontificum*, Giacinto Gaida (ed.), Città di Castello, *Rerum Italicarum Scriptores* 3.1, 1933.

Platine, "Les sauces 'légères' du Moyen Âge," *L'Histoire* 35, 1981, 87–9.

Colin Platt, *King Death: The Black Death and Its Aftermath in Late-Medieval England*, Toronto: University of Toronto, 1997.

Pliny the Elder, *Natural History*, H. Rackham, W.H.S. Jones and D.E. Eichholz (trans. and eds.), 10 vols, London: Heinemann, 1979.

L. Plouvier, "Taillevent, la première star de la gastronomie," *L'Histoire* 61, 1986, 93–4.

Alfred Plummer (trans.), *Fables Respecting the Popes of the Middle Ages*, London: Rivingtons, 1871.

Léon Poliakov, *The History of Anti-Semitism: From the Time of Christ to the Court Jews*, Richard Howard (trans.), London: Elk, 1965.

Martinus Polonus [Martin of Troppau], *Chronicon pontificum et imperatorum*, L. Weiland (ed.), MGH *Scriptores* 22, 1872, pp. 377–475.

A. L. Poole, *Domesday Book to Magna Carta, 1087–1216*, 2nd ed., Oxford: Oxford University, 1955.

Alexander Pope, *Memoirs of the Extraordinary Life, Works, and Discoveries of Martinus Scriblerus*, Dublin, 1741.

Bernhard Poschmann, *Penance and the Anointing of the Sick*, T. Courtney (trans. and rev.), New York: Herder and Herder, 1964.

M. M. Postan, *The Medieval Economy and Society: An Economic History of Britain 1100–1500*, Berkeley: University of California, 1972.

Robert Potter, *The English Morality Play*, London: Routledge and Kegan Paul, 1975.

Marie-Christine Pouchelle, *The Body and Surgery in the Middle Ages*, Rosemary Morris (trans.), New Brunswick, NJ: Rutgers University, 1990.

Maurice Powicke, *The Thirteenth Century, 1216–1307*, 2nd ed., Oxford: Oxford University, 1962.

Andrew Prescott, *Judicial Records of the Rising of 1381*, dissertation, University of London, 1984.

Eleanor Prosser, *Drama and Religion in the English Mystery Plays: A Re-Evaluation*, Stanford: Stanford University, 1961.

J. F. Puglisi (ed.), *Petrine Ministry and the Unity of the Church*, Collegeville, MN: Liturgical Press, 1999.

Claude Quetel, *History of Syphilis*, Judith Braddock and Brian Pike (trans.), Baltimore: Johns Hopkins University, 1990.

François Rabelais, *The Complete Works of François Rabelais*, Donald M. Frame (trans.), Berkeley: University of California, 1991.

———, *Le tiers livre*, M. A. Screech (ed.), Geneva: Droz, 1964.

Charles M. Radding, *A World Made by Men: Cognition and Society, 400–1200*, Chapel Hill: University of North Carolina, 1985.

J. Ambrose Raftis, *Tenure and Mobility: Studies in the Social History of the Medieval English Village*, Toronto: Pontifical Institute of Medieval Studies, 1964.

K. Rahner et al. (eds.), *Sacramentum Mundi: An Encyclopedia of Theology*, New York: Herder & Herder, 1968.

Jill Raitt (ed.), *Christian Spirituality: High Middle Ages and Reformation*, New York: Crossroad, 1987.

E. K. Rand, *Founders of the Middle Ages*, New York: Dover, 1957.

Carole Rawcliffe, *Medicine and Society in Later Medieval England*, Phoenix Mill, UK: Allan Sutton, 1997.

———, (ed.), *Sources for the History of Medicine in Late Medieval England*, Kalamazoo, MI: Medieval Institute, 1995.

S. K. Ray, *Upon This Rock: St. Peter and the Primacy of Rome in Scripture and the Early Church*, San Francisco: Ignatius, 1999.

O. F. Redon, F. Sabban, and S. Serventi, *The Medieval Kitchen: Recipes from France and Italy*, E. Schneider (trans.), Chicago: University of Chicago, 1998.

———, *La gastronomie au Moyen Âge: 150 recettes de France et d'Italie*, Paris: Stock, 1991.

André Réville, *Le soulèvement des travailleurs d' Angleterre en 1381*, Paris: Picard, 1898.

Susan Reynolds, *Fiefs and Vassals: The Medieval Evidence Reinterpreted*, Oxford: Oxford University, 1994.

Emmanouël D. Rhoidès, *Pope Joan, the Female Pope: A Historical Study*, Charles H. Collette (trans.), London: Redway, 1886.

Jean Richard, *The Crusades, c.1071–c.1291*, Jean Birrell (trans.) Cambridge: Cambridge University, 1999.

Peter Richards, *The Medieval Leper*, New York: Barnes & Noble, 1977.

Pierre Riché, *Education and Culture in the Barbarian West: From the Sixth through the Eighth Century*, John J. Contreni (trans.), Columbia, SC: University of South Carolina, 1978.

Pierre Riché and Danièle Alexandre-Bidon, *L'enfance au Moyen Age*, Paris: Seuil, 1994.

Paul Ricoeur, *Time and Narrative*, 3 vols., Kathleen McLaughlin and David Pellauer (trans.), Chicago: University of Chicago, 1984–1988.

John Riddle, *Contraception and Abortion from the Ancient World to the Renaissance*, Cambridge: Harvard University, 1992.

———, "Theory and Practice in Medieval Medicine," *Viator* 5, 1974, 157–84.

Susan Ridyard, *The Royal Saints of Anglo-Saxon England*, Cambridge: Cambridge University, 1988.

Milla Cozart Riggio (ed.), *The Play of Wisdom: Its Texts and Contexts*, New York: AMS, 1998.

Jonathan Riley-Smith, *The Crusades: A History*, 2nd rev. ed., New Haven, CT: Yale University, 2005.

———, *The First Crusaders, 1095–1131*, Cambridge: Cambridge University, 1997.

———, *The Oxford Illustrated History of the Crusades*, Oxford: Oxford University, 1995.

———, *What Were the Crusades?* London: Macmillan, 1977.

Jonathan and Louise Riley-Smith (eds.), *The Crusades: Idea and Reality, 1095–1274*, London: E. Arnold, 1974.

Mariangela Rinaldi and Mariangela Vicini, *Buon Appetito, Your Holiness* (1998), Adam Victor (trans.), New York: Macmillan, 2000.

D. W. Robertson, Jr., *A Preface to Chaucer: Studies in Medieval Perspectives*, Princeton: Princeton University, 1962.

J. W. Robinson, *Studies in Fifteenth-Century Stagecraft*, Kalamazoo: Medieval Institute, 1991.

Jerry Root, *"Space to Speke": The Confessional Subject in Medieval Literature*, New York: Peter Lang, 1997.

L. Roper, *Witch Craze: Terror and Fantasy in Baroque Germany*, New Haven: Yale University, 2004.

Werner Rösener, *The Peasantry of Europe*, Thomas M. Barker (trans.), Oxford: Blackwell, 1994.

———, *Peasants in the Middle Ages*, Alexander Stützer (trans.), Urbana: University of Illinois, 1992.

J.B. Russell, *Inventing the Flat Earth: Columbus and Modern Historians*, New York: Praeger, 1991.

———, *Witchcraft in the Middle Ages*, Ithaca: Cornell University, 1972.

C. Ryan (ed.), *The Religious Roles of the Papacy: Ideals and Realities, 1150–1300*, Toronto: Pontifical Institute of Medieval Studies, 1989.

K. Schatz, *Papal Primacy: From Its Origins to the Present*, Collegeville, MN: Liturgical Press, 1996.

———, *Vaticanum I, 1869–70, Vol. III: Unfehlbarkeitsdiskussion und Rezeption*, Paderborn, Germany: Schöningh, 1992.

Pamela Scheingorn, "On Using Medieval Art in the Study of Medieval Drama: An Introduction to Methodology," *Research Opportunities in Renaissance Drama* 22, 1979, 101–9.

Victor Scherb, *Staging Faith: East Anglian Drama in the Later Middle Ages*, Madison, WI: Fairleigh Dickinson University, 2001.

Martin B. Shichtman and James P. Carley (eds.), *Culture and the King: The Social Implications of the Arthurian Legend; Essays in Honor of Valerie M. Lagorio*, Albany, NY: SUNY, 1994.

Margaret Schleissner, *Manuscript Sources of Medieval Medicine*, New York: Garland, 1995.

T. Scully (ed. and trans.), *The Vivendier: A Fifteenth-Century French Cookery Manuscript*, Totnes, UK: Prospect, 1997.

———, *The Art of Cookery in the Middle Ages*, Woodbridge, UK: Boydell, 1995.

———, "The Menus of the *Menagier de Paris*," *Le Moyen Français* 24–25, 1990, 215–42.

———, (ed.), *The Viandier of the Taillevent: An Edition of All Extant Manuscripts*, Ottawa: University of Ottawa, 1988.

———, " 'Aucune science de l'art de cuysinerie et de cuysine': Chiquart's *Du Fait de Cuisine*," *Food and Foodways* 2, 1987, 199–214.

———, (ed. and trans.), *Chiquart's 'On Cookery'—A Fifteenth-Century Savoyard Culinary Treatise*, New York: Peter Lang, 1986.

———, "*Du fait de cuisine* par Maistre Chiquart, 1420," *Vallesia* 40, 1985, 101–231.

———, "Names of Medieval French Culinary Dishes," *Fifteenth-Century Studies* 10, 1984, 149–59.

Jerome Seigel, *The Idea of the Self: Thought and Experience in Western Europe Since the Seventeenth Century*, Cambridge: Cambridge University, 2005.

Elkanah Settle, *The Female Prelate: Being the History of the Life and Death of Pope Joan*, London: W. Cademan, 1680.

Shulamith Shahar, *Childhood in the Middle Ages*, London: Routledge, 1990.

Richard Sharpe, *A Handlist of the Latin Writers of Great Britain and Ireland before 1550*, Turnhout, Belgium: Brepols, 2001.

L. Shlain, *The Alphabet Versus the Goddess: The Conflict between Word and Image*, New York: Viking, 1998.

Elizabeth Siberry, *Criticism of Crusading*, Oxford: Clarendon, 1985.

James Simpson, *1350–1547: Reform and Cultural Revolution*, Oxford: Oxford University, 2002.

Charles Singer (ed. and trans.), "A Thirteenth-Century Clinical Description of Leprosy," *Journal of the History of Medicine* 4, 1948, 237–9.

Nancy Siraisi, *Medieval and Early Renaissance Medicine*, Chicago: University of Chicago, 1990.

Beryl Smalley, *The Study of the Bible in the Middle Ages*, Notre Dame, IN: University of Notre Dame, 1964.

Soranus of Ephesus, *Soranus' Gynecology*, Oswei Temkin (trans.), Baltimore: Johns Hopkins University, 1956.

R. W. Southern, *History and Historians: Selected Papers of R. W. Southern*, R. J. Bartlett (ed.), Malden, MA: Blackwell, 2004.

———, *Western Society and the Church in the Middle Ages*, Harmondsworth, UK: Penguin, 1970.

———, *Western Views of Islam in the Middle Ages*, Cambridge: Harvard University, 1962.

———, *The Making of the Middle Ages*, New Haven: Yale University, 1953.

Richard Southern, *The Medieval Theatre in the Round*, (1957) London: Faber, 1975.

Friederich Spanheim, *Disquisitio historica de papa foemina inter Leonem IV et Benedictum III*, Leiden, Netherlands, 1691.

Stephen Spector (ed.), *The N-Town Play: Cotton MS Vespasian D.8*, 2 vols., EETS s.s. 11–12, Oxford: Oxford University, 1991.

Gabrielle M. Spiegel, *Romancing the Past: The Rise of Vernacular Prose Historiography in Thirteenth-Century France*, Berkeley: University of California, 1993.

Peter Stanford, *The Legend of Pope Joan*, New York: Henry Holt, 1998.

Jerry Stannard, *Herbs and Herbalism in the Middle Ages and Renaissance*, London: Ashgate Variorum, 1999.

———, *Pristina Medicamenta: Ancient and Medieval Medical Botany*, London: Ashgate Variorum, 1999.

R. Stark, *For the Glory of God: How Monotheism Led to Reformations, Science, Witch-Hunts, and the End of Slavery*, Princeton: Princeton University, 2003.

Gordon Stein (ed.), *The Encyclopedia of the Paranormal*, Amherst, NY: Prometheus, 1996.

Frank Stenton, *Anglo-Saxon England*, Oxford: Oxford University, 1943.

W. Stephens, *Demon Lovers: Witchcraft, Sex, and the Crisis of Belief*, Chicago: University of Chicago, 2002.

Martin Stevens, *Four Middle English Mystery Cycles: Textual, Contextual, and Critical Interpretations*, Princeton: Princeton University, 1987.

——, "Language as Theme in the Wakefield Plays," *Speculum* 52, 1977, 100–17.

Martin Stevens and A. C. Cawley (eds.), *The Towneley Plays*, 2 vols., EETS s.s. 13–14, Oxford: Oxford University, 1994.

Jane Stevenson, *Women Latin Poets, Language Gender and Authority from Antiquity to the Eighteenth Century*, Oxford, 2005.

Eugène Müntz, "La légende de la Papesse Jeanne dans l'illustration des livres, du XVe au XIXe siècle," *La Bibliofilia*, 1900, 325–39.

Brian Stock, *Augustine the Reader: Meditation, Self-knowledge, and the Ethics of Interpretation*, Cambridge: Harvard University, 1996.

——, *Listening for the Text: On the Uses of the Past*, Baltimore, MD: Johns Hopkins University, 1990.

——, *The Implications of Literacy: Written Languages and Models of Interpretation in the Eleventh and Twelfth Centuries*, Princeton: Princeton University, 1983.

J. R. Strayer (ed.), *Dictionary of the Middle Ages*, 13 vols., New York: Scribner, 1982–2004.

——, *On the Medieval Origins of the Modern State*, Princeton: Princeton University, 1970.

Paul Strohm, *Hochon's Arrow: The Social Imagination of Fourteenth-Century Texts*, Princeton: Princeton University, 1992.

S.G.B. Stubbs and E.W. Bligh, *Sixty Years if Health and Physik*, London: Sampson, Low, 1931.

John Sturrock, "Roland Barthes," in John Sturrock (ed.), *Structuralism and Since*, Oxford: Oxford University, 1979, pp. 52–80.

F. A. Sullivan, "The Meaning of Conciliar Dogmas," in D. Kendall and S. T. Davis (eds.), *The Convergence of Theology: A Festschrift Honoring Gerard O'Collins, S.J.*, New York: Paulist, 2001, pp. 73–86.

Jonathan Sumption, *Pilgrimage: An Image of Medieval Religion*, London, 1975, reprinted as *The Age of Pilgrimage: The Medieval Journey to God*, Mahwah NJ: Hidden Spring, 2005.

——, *The Albigensian Crusade*, London: Faber, 1978.

Taillevent, *Le viandier, d'après l'édition de 1486*, Pau, France: Éditions Manucius, 2001.

——, *Le viandier de Taillevent: 14th Century Cookery, Based on the Vatican Library Manuscript*, J. Prescott (trans.), Eugene, OR: Alfarhaugr, 1989.

——, *Le viandier de Guillaume Tirel dit Taillevent*, J. Pichon and G. Vicaire (eds.), Paris: Techener, 1892; S. Martinet (ed.), Genève: Slatkine, 1967.

C. H. Talbot (ed. and trans.), *The Life of Christina of Markyate: A Twelfth Century Recluse*, Toronto: University of Toronto, 1998.

——, *Medicine in Medieval England*, London: Oldbourne, 1967.

——, (trans. and ed.), *The Anglo-Saxon Missionaries in Germany*, New York: Sheed and Ward, 1954.

J. S. P. Tatlock, "Medieval Laughter," *Speculum* 21, 1946, 289–94.

Charles Taylor, *Sources of the Self: The Making of Modern Identity*, Cambridge: Harvard University, 1989.

Oswei Temkin, *Hippocrates in a World of Pagans and Christians*, London: Johns Hopkins University, 1991.

——, *Galenism: Rise and Decline of a Medical Philosophy*, Ithaca: Cornell University, 1973.

A. H. Thomas and I. D. Thornley (eds.), *Great Chronicle of London*, Stroud, UK: Alan Sutton, 1983.

Lynn Thorndike (ed. and trans.), *The Sphere of Sacrobosco and Its Commentators*, Chicago: University of Chicago, 1949.

Palmer A. Throop, *Criticism of the Crusade: A Study of Public Opinion and Crusade Propaganda*, Amsterdam: Swets & Zeitlinger, 1940.

James Thrower, *Western Atheism: A Short History*, Amherst, NY: Prometheus Books, 2000.

Herbert Thurston, *Pope Joan*, London: Catholic Truth Society, 1917.

R. W. Thurston, *Witch, Wicce, Mother Goose: The Rise and Fall of the Witch Hunts in Europe and North America*, Harlow, UK: Longman, 2001.

B. Tierney, *The Crisis of Church and State, 1050–1300*, Englewood Cliffs, NJ: Prentice Hall, 1980.

———, *Origins of Papal Infallibility, 1150–1350: A Study on the Concepts of Infallibility, Sovereignty, and Tradition in the Middle Ages*, Leiden, Netherlands: Brill, 1972.

———, *Foundations of the Conciliar Theory: The Contribution of the Medieval Canonists from Gratian to the Great Schism*, Cambridge: Cambridge University, 1955.

J. Z. Titow, *English Rural Society 1200–1350*, London: George Allen and Unwin, 1969.

J. J. M. Tobin, Herschel Baker, and G. Blakemore Evans (eds.), *The Riverside Shakespeare*, 2nd ed., New York: Houghton Mifflin, 1997.

John Victor Tolan, *Saracens: Islam in the Medieval European Imagination*, New York: Columbia University, 2002.

Edward Topsell, *The historie of foure-footed beastes*, London, 1607.

Joshua Trachtenberg, *The Devil and the Jews: The Medieval Conception of the Jew and Its Relation to Modern Anti-Semitism*, Philadelphia: Jewish Publication Society, 1983.

Elizabeth Closs Traugott and Mary Louise Pratt, *Linguistics for Students of Literature*, New York: Harcourt Brace, 1980.

Peter W. Travis, *Dramatic Design in the Chester Cycle*, Chicago: University of Chicago, 1982.

H. Trevor-Roper, "Religion, the Reformation, and Social Change," in W. E. Monter (ed.), *European Witchcraft*, New York: John Wiley, 1969.

Sharon Turner, *The History of the Anglo-Saxons: Comprising the History of England from the Earliest Period to the Norman Conquest*, (1799-1805) 3 vols. London: Longman, Hurst, Rees, Orme, and Brown, 1823.

Meg Twycross, "Beyond the Picture Theory: Image and Activity in Medieval Drama," *Word and Image* 4, 1988, 589–617.

Christopher Tyerman, *Fighting for Christendom: Holy War and the Crusades*, Oxford: Oxford University, 2004.

———, *The Invention of the Crusades*, Toronto: Macmillan, 1998.

———, *England and the Crusades, 1095–1588*, Chicago: University of Chicago, 1988.

W. Ullmann, *A Short History of the Papacy in the Middle Ages*, 2nd ed., London: Routledge, 2003.

Robert de Uzès, *Le livre des visions*, Jeanne Bignami Odier (ed.), *Archivum fratrum praedicatorum* 25, 1955, 258–320.

———, *The Individual and Society in the Middle Ages*, London: Methuen, 1967.

———, *The Relevance of Medieval Ecclesiastical History: An Inaugural Lecture*, Cambridge: Cambridge University, 1966.

———, *Principles of Government and Politics in the Middle Ages* (1961), London: Methuen, 1974.

Anne Van Arsdall, *Medieval Herbal Remedies: The Old English Herbarium and Anglo-Saxon Medicine*, New York: Routledge, 2002.

E. M. Van de Helder, *Pope Joan in Legend and Drama: a Case Study in German Medieval Drama*, Armidale, N. S. W.: University of New England, 1988.

J. Verdon, *Boire au Moyen Age*, Paris: Perrin, 2002.

Linda E. Voigts, "Anglo-Saxon Plant Remedies and the Anglo-Saxons," *Isis* 70, 1979, 250–68.

Linda E. Voigts and M. R. McVaugh, *A Latin Technical Phlebotomy and Its Middle English Translation*, Philadelphia: American Philosophical Society, 1984.

Jacopo de Voraigne, *Iacopo da Varagine e la sua Cronaca di Genova dalle Origini al MCCXCVII*, Giovanni Monleone (ed.), Rome: Tipografia del Senato, 1941.

Stuart A. Vyse, *Believing in Magic: The Psychology of Superstition*, New York: Oxford University, 1997.

Walter L. Wakefield, *Heresy, Crusade and Inquisition in Southern France, 1100–1250*, Berkeley: University of California, 1974.

Thomas Walsingham, *Historia Anglicana*, H. T. Riley (ed.), Rolls series, no. 28, vols. 1 and 2, London, 1863.

Michelle R. Warren, *History on the Edge: Excalibur and the Borders of Britain, 1100–1300*, Minneapolis: University of Minnesota, 2000.

Sheldon Watts, *Epidemics and History: Disease, Power, and Imperialism*, New Haven: Yale University, 1997.

Diane Webb, *Pilgrims and Pilgrimage in the Medieval West*, London: J. B. Tauris, 1999.

John Edwin Wells (ed.), *A Manual of the Writings in Middle English, 1050–1500*, 10 vols., New Haven: Connecticut Academy of Arts and Sciences, 1919–1951.

Suzanne Fonay Wemple, *Women in Frankish Society: Marriage and the Cloister 500–900*, Philadelphia: University of Philadelphia, 1981.

B. Ketcham Wheaton, *Savoring the Past: The French Kitchen and Table from 1300 to 1789*, Philadelphia: University of Pennsylvania, 1983.

Carolinne White (ed. and trans.), *Early Christian Lives*, New York: Penguin, 1998.

Richard White (ed.), *King Arthur in Legend and History*, New York: Routledge, 1998.

T. H. White, *The Once and Future King*, (1939) New York: G. P. Putnam's Sons, 1987.

James J. Wilhelm (ed.), *The Romance of Arthur: An Anthology of Medieval Texts in Translation*, New York and London: Garland, 1994.

Annemarieke Willemsen, *Kinder delijt: middeleeuws speelgoed in de Nederlanden*, Nijmeegse Kunsthistorische Studies 6, Nijmegen, 1998.

D. Willis, *Malevolent Nurture: Witch-Hunting and Maternal Power in Early Modern England*, Ithaca: Cornell University, 1995.

A. C. Wilson (ed.), *The Appetite and the Eye: Visuals Aspects of Food and Its Presentation within Their Historic Contexts (Papers from the Second Leeds Symposium on Food History and Traditions)*, Edinburgh: Edinburgh University, 1991.

Terence Wise, *Medieval Warfare*, New York: Hastings House, 1976.

Rudolf Wittkower, "Marvels of the East: a Study in the History of Monsters," *Journal of the Warburg and Courtauld Institutes* 5, 1942, 159–97.

Clement Wood, *The Woman Who Was Pope: A Biography of Pope Joan , 853–855 A.D.*, New York: Faro, 1931.

Rosemary Woolf, *The English Mystery Plays*, Berkeley: University of California, 1972.

Virginia Woolf, *A Room of One's Own*, New York: Harcourt Brace, 1991.

C. P. Wormald, "The Uses of Literacy in Anglo-Saxon England and Its Neighbours," *Transactions of the Royal Historical Society* 27, 1977, 95–114.

Barbara Yorke, *Nunneries and the Anglos-Saxon Royal Houses*, London: Continuum, 2003.

Karl Young, *The Drama of the Medieval Church*, 2 vols., Oxford: Clarendon, 1933.

Henry Yule (ed.) *Cathay and the Way Thither, Being a Collection of Medieval Notices of China*, vol. 2, *Odoric of Pordenone*, London: Hakluyt Society, 1913.

Dan Zahavi, *Subjectivity and Selfhood: Investigating the First-Person Perspective*, Cambridge, MA: MIT, 2006.

——, (ed.), *Hidden Resources*, Charlottesville, NC: Imprint Academic, 2004.

Michel Zink, *The Invention of Literary Subjectivity*, David Sices (trans.), Baltimore: Johns Hopkins University, 1999.

Hans Zinsser, *Rats, Lice and History: A Chronicle of Pestilence and Plagues*, New York: Black Dog, 1935.

Contributors

C. David Benson is Professor of Medieval English Literature at the University of Connecticut.

Elaine M. Beretz is a research associate at the Center for Visual Culture at Bryn Mawr College.

Jessalynn Bird an independent scholar based in Naperville, Illinois.

Louise M. Bishop is Associate Professor of Literature at the Clark Honors College, University of Oregon.

Helen Conrad-O'Briain is Research Associate and departmental librarian in the School of English, Trinity College, Dublin.

Carolyn Coulson-Grigsby is Assistant Professor of Theatre and Humanities at Centenary College in New Jersey.

Peter Dendle is Associate Professor of English at Pennsylvania State University, Mont Alto.

Vincent DiMarco is Professor of English (Emeritus) at the University of Massachusetts, Amherst.

Mary Dockray-Miller is Associate Professor of English at Lesley University.

Michael D. C. Drout is the William C. H. and Elsie D. Prentice Associate Professor of English and Millicent C. McIntosh Fellow at Wheaton College, MA.

Liam Ethan Felsen is Assistant Professor of English, Indiana University Southeast.

Michael Frassetto is an independent scholar in Medford, NJ.

Ronald J. Ganze is Visiting Assistant Professor of English at The University of South Dakota.

Michael W. George is Assistant Professor of English at Millikin University.

Richard H. Godden is currently ABD in medieval literature at Washington University, St. Louis.

Bryon L. Grigsby is Provost and Chief Operating Officer of Centenary College in New Jersey.

Stephen J. Harris is Associate Professor of English at the University of Massachusetts, Amherst.

Dinah Hazell is an independent scholar and coeditor of the electronic Medieval Forum.

Linda Migl Keyser is Assistant Professor at Georgetown University School of Medicine and adjunct faculty at the University of Maryland, College Park.

Jean-François Kosta-Théfaine is a research associate at Centre d'Etudes des Textes Médiévaux–Université de Rennes 2, France.

Anita Obermeier is Associate Professor of English and Director of the Feminist Research Institute at the University of New Mexico.

Sophie Oosterwijk is Lecturer in History of Art and Acting Director of the Centre for the Study of the Country House at the University of Leicester.

Marijane Osborn is Professor in the Department of English at the University of California–Davis.

S. Elizabeth Passmore is Assistant Professor of English at the University of Southern Indiana.

James G. Patterson is Associate Professor of History at Centenary College, New Jersey.

Richard Raiswell is Assistant Professor of History at the University of Prince Edward Island.

Christopher Roman is Assistant Professor at Kent State University Tuscarawas.

Paul Strohm is Professor of English at Columbia University.

Anne Van Arsdall is a Fellow of the Institute for Medieval Studies at the University of New Mexico.

Frans van Liere is Associate Professor of History at Calvin College.

Index